Images of
Schools

Images of Schools

Structures and Roles in Organizational Behavior

Editors
Samuel B. Bacharach
Bryan Mundell

CORWIN PRESS, INC.
A Sage Publications Company
Thousand Oaks, California

For information, address:

Corwin Press, Inc.
A Sage Publications Company
2455 Teller Road
Thousand Oaks, California 91320

SAGE Publications Ltd.
6 Bonhill Street
London EC2A 4PU
United Kingdom

SAGE Publications India Pvt. Ltd.
M-32 Market
Greater Kailash I
New Delhi 110 048 India

Printed in the United States of America

Library of Congress Cataloging-in-Publication Data

Images of schools: Structures and roles in organizational behavior/
edited by Samuel B. Bacharach, Bryan Mundell.
    p. cm.
    Includes bibliographical references and index.
    ISBN 0-8039-6250-9 (cloth: alk. paper).—ISBN 0-8039-6251-7
(pbk.: alk. paper)
    1. School management and organization—United States. 2. School
personnel management—United States. 3. Organizational behavior—
United States. I. Bacharach, Samuel B. II. Mundell, Bryan.
LB2805.I42 1995
371'.00973—dc20   95-2533

This book is printed on acid-free paper.

95 96 97 98 99 10 9 8 7 6 5 4 3 2 1

Corwin Press Production Editor: Gillian Dickens

Contents

Preface

This book brings together analytical perspectives from organizational theory and applies them to examinations of schools. Indeed, each of the authors has both a specific interest in organizational theory and a detailed knowledge of school organizations. This book is predicated on the assumption that good analysis will lead to good practice. In this age of reform, quick fixes, and hopeful promises, it is often forgotten that a key to any successful organizational change is to empower practitioners with analytical vocabularies and theories that will help them to bring order to their environment. The contribution of the academic theorist is no more and no less than this. Therefore, this book is put together not with the intent of giving practitioners new experiences but rather to help them to recast their experiences in a way that enables them to use the analytical tools herein to develop more effective strategies and tactics of organization. To achieve this goal, we have asked the contributors to this book to apply the language of organizational theory to their analyses of schools.

Organizational theories may be viewed as different answers to the questions of why and how individual behavior is organized in formal groups. The current debate over how to reform education (specifically the debate about school restructuring) is inevitably a debate about the strategy of organizing. Whether one is speaking about creating systems with more accountability versus more autonomy, more empowerment versus more centralization, or more standardization versus more flexibility, one is inevitably concerned with the conflict between strategies of organizing.

Organizational theory suggests that there are two primary mechanisms that may be used in organizing behavior—the organization as a whole and specific roles in the organization. This book is therefore divided into two parts. In Part I, images of school organizations are presented as modes of organizing behavior. By concentrating in Part I on the images of schools as organizations, we are trying to understand how organizational theorists who use different images to describe schools tend to organize behavior in schools differently. For example, although these images obviously are not necessarily mutually exclusive, behavior organized on the basis of a political image of schools may be subtly different than behavior organized on the basis of a cultural image of schools.

Each of the four chapters in Part I presents a different answer to the question of what must be organized in schools. In Chapter 1, Rowan suggests that the primary problem of organization is finding the best compromise between mechanistic and organic structures, each of which has unique advantages and disadvantages. In Chapter 2, Kerchner and Caufman argue that schools must organize around the decision-making processes. In Chapter 3, Rait suggests that schools must organize to become learning organizations. Finally, in Chapter 4, Deal claims that schools need to pay more attention to organizing their culture so as to make them more meaningful.

In Part II, images of roles in schools are presented as modes of organizing behavior. We examine how roles (specifically those of teachers and administrators) can be viewed as mechanisms for organizing behavior. Viewing the role of teachers differently obviously will result in different ways of organizing their behavior. Similarly, viewing the administrative role as incorporating one type of leadership instead of another type of leadership may result in a different mode of organizing administrative behavior.

The first three chapters in Part II are concerned with organizing the role of the teacher. In Chapter 5, Hart starts our focus on the role of the teacher by arguing that what needs to be reorganized is the actual work of the teacher. In contrast, Mitchell argues in Chapter 6 that for teachers to perform effectively, schools must be organized around clear goals and the provision of adequate resources. In Chapter 7, Sykes and Millman suggest that teachers' performance will be enhanced if their role is organized and evaluated at least partially on the basis of student outcomes.

The last three chapters in Part II are concerned with organizing the role of the school administrator. In Chapter 8, Goldring makes the case that the role of the school administrator needs to be organized around the necessity for boundary spanning between the school and its environment. In Chapter 9, Bolman and Heller suggest that the role of school administrator needs to be organized to provide leadership to the rest of the people in schools. In Chapter 10, Ogawa describes how the process of fitting a specific individual to the role of administrator in a specific school can be more effectively organized based on research findings.

In the concluding essay, the editors review the chapters, attempting to understand the actions that comprise the organizing strategies implied in each chapter. Specifically, and at the risk of oversimplifying the subtle arguments of the contributors, we attempt to categorize the chapters in two dimensions according to their answers to the question of who organizes schools and the means by which they are organized.

Acknowledgments

We would first like to thank all of the contributors, who have been patient with us throughout this entire process. Their willingess to rewrite their chapters several times is especially appreciated and undoubtedly makes this a better book. We especially want to thank our friend and colleague Mylan Jaixin, who has always been encouraging. We owe a special thanks to W. Frank Masters, who read many of the manuscripts in early draft form and was generous in his comments about them; there is no doubt that his comments improved the quality of several chapters. We are also grateful to the following people: Gracia Alkema, for supporting us in this project; Don and Helen Mundell, for instilling excitement for the realm of ideas in Bryan and thus making it possible for us to work together; Margaret Gleason, who provided organizational support and without whose patient recordkeeping this project would have bogged down in a morass of lost manuscripts and sporadic correspondence; and Colleen Clausen, who also helped out with communication and correspondence. Others deserving of thanks include Tom Corcoran, Rodney Ogawa, and Bill Altman. Finally, thanks to Anna and Yael for providing the personal support necessary for us to see all of our projects through to completion, and to Carol, for teaching us the feline skills of survival. Finally, we want to emphasize that this project has been a joint work in every respect; the names of the editors appear in alphabetical order.

About the Contributors

Samuel B. Bacharach is Professor of Organizational Behavior at the New York State School of Industrial and Labor Relations at Cornell University, Graduate Professor of Educational Administration at Cornell, and Senior Professor by special appointment to the School of Management at the University of Tel Aviv.

Lee G. Bolman holds the Marion Bloch Chair in Leadership at the University of Missouri–Kansas City. His recent books include *The Path to School Leadership, Becoming a Teacher Leader,* and *Leading With Soul: An Uncommon Journey of Spirit* (all written with Terrence E. Deal).

Krista D. Caufman is a doctoral student in the Center for Politics and Economics at the Claremont Graduate School and is Director of the Writing Center at Harvey Mudd College. Her research interests include the rhetoric of policy reform the role of experts in a democracy, and the history of the social sciences.

Terrence E. Deal is Professor of Education and Human Development at Peabody College, Vanderbilt University. He has coauthored 16 books, including the national best-seller *Corporate Cultures.* His latest book, with Lee G. Bolman, is *Leading With Soul: An Uncommon Journey of Spirit* (March 1995). In addition to his university responsibilities, he consults internationally with business, education, health care, and other organizations.

Ellen B. Goldring is Professor of Educational Leadership and Associate Dean for Academic Affairs at Peabody College, Vanderbilt University. Her research focuses on the organization and control of schools, and their impact on educational leadership and the principalship. Much of her work examines the changing roles of principals and parents. In an international perspective, she has published in such journals as *Educational Administration Quarterly, Educational Policy,* and *Urban Education.* She is coauthor with Sharon F. Rallis of *Principals of Dynamic Schools: Taking Charge of Change* (Corwin Press).

Ann Weaver Hart is Dean of the Graduate School and Professor of Educational Administration at the University of Utah. Prior to her appointment as Dean, she served as Associate Dean of the Graduate School of Education and as a full-time faculty member at the University of Utah. Her research focuses on educational leadership, the design of work in educational organizations, and academic freedom at all levels of education. Recent publications include *Principal Succession: Establishing Leadership in Schools* (SUNY, 1993); *The Principalship: Professional Visualization in Action* (McGraw-Hill, forthcoming); "Work feature values of today's and tomorrow's teachers: Work redesign as an incentive and school improvement policy" in *Educational Evaluation and Policy Analysis* (1994); and "Creating Teacher Leadership Roles: The Impacts of Core Group Support" in *Educational Administration Quarterly.*

Rafael Heller is a doctoral student in education at the University of Michigan. His research focus is English in education, with a particular interest in play as a teaching medium.

Charles Taylor Kerchner is Professor of Education at the Claremont Graduate School. Before coming to Claremont in 1976, he was on the faculty at Northwestern University, where he received his Ph.D., and was a member of the Illinois Board of Higher Education staff. In the early 1990s, he traveled the country studying the relationship of teacher unions and educational reform. That research, largely in central-city districts, is contained in a series of 14 case studies and two books: *A Union of Professionals* (Teachers College Press, 1993) and *Beyond the Barricades* (Jossey-Bass, in press).

Jason Millman is Professor of Educational Research at Cornell University. He specializes in the measurement of human capabilities, in the assessment of testing programs, and in personnel evaluation. Former editor of two professional journals and consulting editor to many more, he has been elected to office of national organizations six times. He is currently the chair or executive committee member on three of the five national advisory boards on which he serves.

Stephen M. Mitchell is Program Director at the National Alliance of Business. Currently, he is serving as Project Director for the National Workforce Assistance Collaborative, a Department of Labor-funded program to create a nationally recognized resource that will help small and midsize U.S. businesses obtain the information and assistance they need to create and retain high-skill, high-paying jobs for American workers. He received his B.A. from Harvard College, and his M.S. and Ph.D. from Cornell University. He has served on the faculty of Cornell, Carnegie Mellon, and SUNY Binghamton.

Bryan Mundell is Coordinator of European Programs and Research for the Smithers Institute at Cornell University, Visiting Professor at Bocconi University, and a faculty member of the Bocconi Graduate School of Business in Milan, Italy. He received his Ph.D. in organizational behavior from Cornell and has published articles in *Educational Administration Quarterly, Journal of Organizational Behavior*, and *Human Relations*. He is also currently an editor of the annual review *Research in the Sociology of Organizations.* He has just completed coediting a volume for that series titled *European Perspectives on Organizational Theory*, and is working on another edited volume on the legacy of colonialism in labor relations systems. Current research interests include the history of American capitalism, organizational deviance, and prosocial behavior.

Rodney T. Ogawa is Professor of Education and Associate Director of the California Educational Research Cooperative at the University of California, Riverside. He received his Ph.D. from Ohio State University. His recent publications include "The Institutional Sources of Educational Reform" (*American Educational Research Journal*) and a chapter with Paula White titled "School-Based Management in Public Schools." His current research employs organization theory to study school-family relations.

Eric Rait is a Ph.D. candidate in organizational behavior at the New York State School of Industrial and Labor Relations at Cornell University. His current research focuses on those factors that influence organizational learning in software development teams. Since completing his Ed.M. at the Graduate School of Education at Harvard University, he has worked on a number of school change projects in Israel and in the United States.

Brian Rowan is Professor of Education at the University of Michigan. He received his B.A. from Rutgers University and his Ph.D. in sociology from Stanford University. His research focuses on issues related to school organization and effectiveness, education policy, and applied social research. Currently, he serves on the editorial boards of the *American Educational Research Journal, Educational Administration Quarterly, Educational Evaluation and Policy Analysis,* and *Educational Researcher* and is a frequent consultant to educational research and development organizations.

Gary Sykes is Professor in the Department of Educational Administration and the Department of Teacher Education at Michigan State University. His interests include educational policy making, research on teaching, and professional education for teachers and administrators. He received his Ph.D. in the design and evaluation of educational programs at Stanford University. He is coeditor with Jon Schaffarzick of *Value Issues and Curriculum Conflicts* and with Lee Shulman of the *Handbook of Teaching and Policy.* Recent publications include "Teacher Education and the Case Idea," with Tom Bird, in *Review of Research in Education,* and "Curriculum Policy," with Richard Elmore, in the *Handbook of Research on Curriculum.*

Part I

Images of Structure

SAMUEL B. BACHARACH
BRYAN MUNDELL

The focus of Part I on the structure of school organizations is both fundamental and timely. It is fundamental because it deals with a long-running debate in both the organizational literature and the research on education—whether organizations (schools) should be structured tightly and bureaucratically, with tight coupling between parts, or whether they should be structured more loosely, leaving teachers the freedom to develop innovative approaches for unique local conditions. It is timely in light of the attention paid during the past 10 years to "school restructuring" and "break the mold schools."

In the first chapter, Rowan makes the trade-offs between different ways of organizing school structure the center of his attention. Rowan contributes to our understanding of school structure by applying theories of organizational design to this debate and discussing the results of experiments in school restructuring with reference to the ultimate objective of schools—student learning. He starts from the stream of organ-

1

izational research during the 1970s, where researchers found that schools were so loosely coupled that they were largely uncontrollable due to the absence of both formal controls (bureaucratic rules) and informal controls (professional norms). Rowan applies Burns and Stalker's typology of organizations as either *mechanistic* or *organic* to explain the two approaches to structural reform that characterized the 1980s. Briefly, advocates of the former aimed at tightening formal bureaucratic controls over teachers, whereas advocates of the latter aimed at loosening such controls and encouraging teachers to develop professional norms to channel their hidden creative energy toward increased student learning.

During the 1970s, the mechanistic strategy seemed to take hold. Teaching was viewed as a technology in which the uncertainty could be wrung out by standardizing and routinizing a set of teacher behaviors. The expected result of tightening bureaucratic controls on teachers so as to force them to consistently use the new methods of "direct instruction" to teach the same material ("curricular alignment") would be so-called instructionally effective schools. The effectiveness of these methods could be measured by standardized tests used to hold teachers accountable for the amount of knowledge that their students learned.

However, during the mid-1980s, the pendulum seemed to swing back toward the organic conception of schools. Advocates of this approach pointed out that teaching is not amenable to routinization because the nature of the inputs (students) is so variable. Variable inputs require judgment and creativity, which are best fostered with more organic forms such as network and participative structures of decision making and the development of collegial and professional cultures rather than bureaucratic rules. Advocates of the organic approach argued that rather than being organized to control teachers directly, schools should be organized to give teachers autonomy and the tools necessary to practice their profession.

After summarizing the research on some important cases where each approach has been implemented, Rowan suggests some tentative ways to pull the most valuable lessons from each to form a more balanced organizational structure. He concludes by suggesting a research agenda based on the investigation of four themes: the nature of teaching as an organizational technology, the relationship of teaching tasks to organizational design, the relationship of organizational design to learning outcomes, and the constraints on organizational design.

In Chapter 2, Kerchner and Caufman categorize the decisions that constitute the actions that occur within schools in response to political forces. They present a typology of decisions that are made around and within schools, depending on the location at which the decision is made and whether the decision will have sudden and discrete effects or only marginal and incremental effects on the organization.

The first dimension of their typology reflects the fact that the location at which a decision is made affects the decision process. Some decisions are made outside the schools through a political process of conflict and resolution between interest groups, followed by institutionalization throughout the field of education. Other decisions are made inside the schools by superintendents and principals who have the hierarchical authority and reputed expertise to do so. Still other decisions are made by groups, some of which are established specifically for the purpose of making a particular decision or type of decision.

The second dimension of their typology is based on the difference between the "big" decisions typically dealt with in the literature on strategic decisions and the more frequent decisions made every day. The former category Kerchner and Caufman label *discrete* decisions, defined as the rare and precedent-setting decisions that are made at recognizable moments in time. The latter category they label *incremental* decisions, which can accumulate in importance if a series of them are made in a similar direction over time, whether each is made independently by different actors or not. Whereas discrete decisions are recognized as important when they are made, incremental decisions may be seen as strategically important only in retrospect. Combining these two dimensions, Kerchner and Caufman then investigate some typical decision processes occurring in each of the six domains of Table 2.1 (p. 45).

The remainder of Chapter 2 is devoted to examining ways that policymakers and practitioners make strategy across the boundaries between the six domains of Kerchner and Caufman's typology. They provide specific examples of various combinations and trade-offs that decision makers face, along with some incisive remarks about other possibilities that naturally follow from their typology.

To sum up, the authors have two overall messages: First, we need to be aware of the differences between different types of decisions because different decision-making mechanisms are appropriate in each domain; second, the most important decisions are really a type of "meta-decisions"—deciding to direct a decision to a particular domain. They integrate the two messages by suggesting that "strategy lies as much in moving a decision to a favorable arena as it does in making the judgment itself" (p. 65). Both policymakers and practitioners recognize the importance of what has been called "problem framing."

Chapter 3 focuses on organizing schools so as to retain the knowledge that is generated within them. Rait's aim is to "map out the factors that may inhibit or support processes of organizational learning in schools" (p. 72). He does that by defining the term *organizational learning,* describing the cognitive and environmental determinants of organizational learning, offering detailed prescriptions for enhancing organizational learning in schools, and analyzing the disincentives for and sources of resistance to organizational learning in schools.

After a thorough review of many different definitions of organizational learning, Rait discusses some commonalities (themes of adaptation and change) and an important difference (whether that change is cognitive or behavioral). The differences are explained in Argyris and Schon's vocabulary of *single-* and *double-loop learning.* Briefly, single-loop learning is simple adaptation of behavior to small changes in generally stable environments. In rational bureaucracies, troubleshooting routines may serve to correct organizational errors. In Rait's words, "the fundamental operating assumptions or governing values of the organization or individuals need not be examined or altered to achieve such change" (p. 74). On the other hand, double-loop learning may be required in more complex situations characterized by systemic error. In such cases, learning must include both reflective inquiry into the fundamental assumptions or values of the organization as well as the action that is indicated by such inquiry.

In the next section, Rait describes the cognitive and environmental determinants of organizational learning. Because individuals cannot possibly process and use all of the information that they are bombarded with, they need some sort of filing system, containing categories that they can prioritize.

This information filing system has been labeled a *schemata*. As data arrive, they must be assimilated into one's schemata.

As Rait points out, this cognitive filing system has benefits and costs. To the extent that organization members have been socialized to have similar schemata, a common basis for action may be in place, while pathologies such as "groupthink" may be observed. To the extent that the schemata of organization members are different, more diverse information is obtained from the environment, while the same data from the environment may create misunderstandings and disagreement over the organization's lessons to be learned. Finally, the modification of the organization's common schemata (i.e., organizational learning) is also affected by environmental factors like the organizational culture, structure, and external climate.

Even in the face of all these complex factors affecting the organization's common schemata, Rait suggests a number of prescriptions for stimulating organizational learning that have been offered by other writers. Rait cites cognitive strategies from the work of Argyris and Schon aimed at generating valid information and free, informed choices by organization members. These strategies include publicly testing individual and organizational tacit assumptions to reduce confusion and misinterpretations, thus encouraging organization members to combine advocacy of their positions with "active inquiry into other interpretations and alternative views" (p. 84). This process is most likely to be fruitful when organization members scrutinize their own practices using experiential data of their own making (e.g., tape recordings of meetings or reconstructed role-plays). Argyris and Schon's Model 2 prescription also emphasizes "the constant monitoring and testing of choices during implementation" (p. 85). In essence, what Argyris and Schon are advocating is collaborative inquiry, which results from multiple cycles of action and reflection (e.g., Lewin's "action research cycle").

On the other hand, to the extent that the organizational schemata is understood differently by different organization members, there is the potential for misunderstanding and conflict. Rait presents Argyris and Schon's ladder of inference as a potential tool for bringing to the surface the differences in interpretations made by different individuals and groups in the organization. By moving down the ladder until agreement is reached, one can identify the source of the misunderstanding. Other tools that Rait cites include problem reframing, systems dynamics, and critical-incidents training.

However, as Rait points out, despite the promise of such tools, organizational learning may not come easy. He presents four levels of resistance to organizational learning in schools. First, stakeholder politics make schools the focus of many ideological struggles and institutionalization attempts, which school organization members may wish to deflect away from what they see as their primary mission.

Second, schools may resist organizational learning due to the strength of their institutionalized culture. Rait describes some of the same historical cultural residues that are documented more completely in Chapter 4 of this book and describes the forces in favor of the status quo. In Rait's words, "risk taking, inquiry, and search behaviors of organizational learning are inconsistent with the attributes of highly institutionalized settings" (p. 92).

Third, the technical nature of teachers' work creates further obstacles to organizational learning. Their isolation from each other in separate classrooms, lack of time for reflection, and constantly expanding societal expectations meet head-on with the realities of fewer resources, inadequate rewards, and uncertain core technologies.

The fourth obstacle to organizational learning in schools that Rait identifies is the inherently conservative nature of our information-processing apparatus. As previously pointed out, there is a substantial amount of inertia in our theories and schemata, and those theories tend to filter out incongruous data and protect us from change. This inertia requires a substantial amount of extra energy to overcome. Teachers must be given incentives to try harder to overcome the limits, structures, and arrangements that inevitably confront them in the social organizations that we call schools.

The remainder of Chapter 3 provides the reader with some prescriptions for how to enhance organizational learning within schools: The first set concerns teachers' participation in schoolwide processes of inquiry and the second concerns other participants in such processes. For teachers to participate in organizational learning, they need to be granted time for the critical thought and reflection necessary for double-loop learning. They also need to be considered as self-learning and peer-coaching professionals rather than order-following bureaucrats.

The second set of prescriptions concerns recent attempts to restructure the governance and decision-making structure of entire school systems by involving the entire community of stakeholders (e.g., New York's Compact for Schools). Committees composed of diverse stakeholders work together to bring to the surface their assumptions and create a consensus for a specific set of changes (e.g., the creation of "family groups").

Rait concludes the chapter with a call for the institutionalization of the process of organizational learning. For this to occur, reinforcement for learning and implementation is crucial, as is modeling of the process by administrators and principals. Although organizational change is often portrayed as a three-stroke cycle of *unfreezing* the old model, *changing* to a new one, and *refreezing* the new model, the model offered here leaves out the third stage. Rather, once the old model is unfrozen, the new model is constantly under scrutiny in a two-stroke cycle of *action* and *reflection*. Such a cycle demands the best of school participants, but will reap rewards that are inconceivable under the current model of school organizations.

Deal focuses on culture—a crucial element in schools. He does this in Chapter 4 by addressing himself to a long-neglected aspect of schools—what they mean to their members and society. Schools are meaningful because people (students, teachers, staff) are able to make sense out of their experiences in school. Deal explains that culture is the set of frames or metaphors that individuals use to make sense out of their experience and behavior. Identifiable and meaningful school cultures emerge to the extent that different participants in the same school make sense out of their experience in similar ways.

Culture can be manifest as so many small pieces of information generated by organization members individually that no one member has access to all pieces. Alternatively, culture can take the form of a few large pieces of information that constitute the core symbols that form the shared definition of reality of all organization members. In either case, these symbols are generated and then either embraced and learned or ignored and forgotten, depending on the interests of each individual or subgroup within the organization.

These symbols are important for understanding behavior in school organizations because they exert an influence on their members' behavior at various levels of cognition. At deeper levels of cognition, cultural symbols are labeled values (e.g., more formal education is better for the child than less) or assumptions (e.g., children should be grouped by age rather than subject area or ability) that are rarely questioned. At somewhat less deep levels are norms and rules for behavior that are allowed to guide behavior even though alternatives to them may be recognized. These norms vary in the strength of their influence. Deal cites Corbett, who distinguishes between strong sacred norms, which anchor the organization's identity, and weaker profane norms, which are more changeable patterns of thought, belief, and action.

Culture is crucial to organizations because cultural symbols fulfill several important functions. For example, cultural symbols tie together three overlapping domains—the organizational history, the current beliefs and patterns of action, and the common vision of the future. Organizations need to create, revive, revise, or transform their myths in order to bring the organization's past up to date and to prepare now for the future. Further, in a strong organizational culture, the members believe in what they are doing, share a common heritage and faith, and dream (aspire) together. In sum, culture provides meaning, spirit, and motivation to what people do while working in organizations.

The most common pattern of sense-making (that is, culture building) within schools during the 20th century has been to see them as collections of people and objects scientifically and rationally constructed and coordinated to achieve certain obvious social purposes. Although the relentless push for scientific management, centralized administration, school consolidation, and so on would seem to prove that the 20th century has been characterized by the triumph of logic over instinct in schools, Deal reminds us that this is not the only pattern of sense-making available to humans. Instead, he argues convincingly that schools resemble tribes, with common values, heroes, rituals, ceremonies, and stories shared by the whole network of diverse cultural players such as priests, storytellers, gossips, and spies. The cultural symbols shared by members of the tribe (school) help to bridge the gap between competing subcultures.

Deal illustrates this line of argument by citing Sapolsky's analysis of a quintessentially rational organization—the Polaris missile development program at the cutting edge of high technology. He suggests that the reason for that program's success had more to do with the web of meaning that the public relations consultants spun about the program than with the achievement of rational criteria of success. The Polaris program was successful because people inside and outside the program *believed* that it was successful.

Note that Deal is not saying that the Polaris missile program was a failure in any technological or rational sense. What he is saying is that the belief that it was successful was created by modern magicians who invoked the sacred icons of rationality and technology. By reenacting the myths of modern management and engineering that dominated America during the 1960s, the spiritual leaders of the Polaris program were able to convince themselves and key representatives of the broader society that the program was a success.

If all this is true for one of the most rational and technological organizations, then Deal infers that it may be true for other types of organizations. According to this reasoning, if we want to make our school organizations more successful, then we should concentrate on making them more *meaningful* rather than more *rational*. His prescription for schools is that their leaders focus on creating, reviving, revising, and transforming their myths.

Deal reminds us that myths are made more by artistic and expressive processes than by rationalist and mechanical ones. Myths are created and transformed not by administrators but rather by archivists, choreographers, and poets. Myths take the form of acts of appreciation, acts of critical reading and interpretations, and displays of the meaning of life.

Based on this perspective, Deal offers more specific strategies for improving school organizations by focusing on cultural manifestations, whether these are expressed verbally or nonverbally. He offers many categories of these strategies: metaphors, poetry, stories, theater, rituals, music, and art. He also suggests that these categories may be combined in interesting ways (e.g., dance is a combination of music and rituals). Finally, he offers the compelling example of the construction of a "mythogram" to help organization members understand their situation.

In short, after a thorough review of the plethora of definitions of organizational culture going back to Barnard's classic *Functions of the Executive*, Deal suggests that the revival of interest in organizational culture during the 1980s was a sort of revival of secular spiritualism. School theorists and practitioners would do well to heed his advice, paying more attention to the webs of meaning that they are spinning while they are organizing people in schools.

ONE

The Organizational Design of Schools

BRIAN ROWAN

This chapter discusses alternative strategies for the organizational design of schools. By organizational design, I mean deliberate attempts by administrators or policymakers to construct or change an organization's structure to meet desired goals. In education, the problem of organizational design has emerged as the subject of lively academic debate in the literature on school restructuring. The topic has also taken on practical importance as state and local policymakers have begun to implement a variety of organizational changes designed to improve student achievement in schools.

A number of observers have noted that two different and potentially incompatible approaches to the organizational design of schools have emerged in the past decade (Bacharach, Bauer, & Shedd, 1986; Kirst, 1988; Passow, 1989). One approach, pioneered by many large urban districts and several state legislatures, addresses the problem of low student achievement by advocating increased bureaucratic controls over curriculum and teaching (Fuhrman, Clune, & Elmore, 1988; Rowan, Edelstein, & Leal, 1983). But this approach has drawn opposition based on the argument that bureaucratic controls are incompatible with the professional autonomy of teachers and potentially damaging to teacher morale (Darling-Hammond & Wise, 1985; Rosenholtz, 1987). As a result, a second strategy for the organizational design of schools has emerged, one that calls for a decrease in bureaucratic controls over schools and the creation of innovative working conditions that enhance the commitment and expertise of teachers (Elmore & Associates, 1990).

These alternative approaches to school reform pose a challenge to research on school organization. Throughout most of the 1970s, organization theorists described schools as loosely coupled systems that lacked both tight bureaucratic controls over teaching and the kind of collegial structures that characterize professional work (Lortie, 1975; March & Olsen, 1976; Meyer & Rowan, 1978; Weick, 1976). This literature constituted a major theoretical advance, both in organization theory generally and in research on educational organizations. However, a continued fascination with loose coupling may be outdated. The educational reforms of the 1980s are deliberately designed to change the organizational conditions that led researchers to label schools as loosely coupled systems, and new models of school organization are needed to guide and assess these reform initiatives.

In this chapter, I use Burns and Stalker's (1961) classic distinction between *mechanistic* and *organic* forms of management to describe these emerging approaches to the organizational design of schools. I argue that both the mechanistic and organic approaches to school design seek to achieve the same organizational goal: increased student achievement. However, I argue that the two approaches rely on different organizational design features and seek to affect different organizational processes to achieve this goal. The mechanistic approach involves the development of an elaborate set of input, behavior, and output controls designed to regulate classroom teaching and standardize student opportunities for learning. A key assumption is that these controls will provide uniform and high-quality instruction in schools. In contrast, an organic approach rejects bureaucratic controls and seeks instead to implement collaborative and participative forms of management that support teachers' decision making and increase teachers' engagement in the task of teaching. The key assumption of this approach is that these innovative working arrangements will improve student achievement by unleashing the energy and commitment of expert teachers.

In the pages that follow, I discuss the theoretical underpinnings of these alternative approaches to organizational design. I then review recent research on schools to consider the extent to which these alternative approaches have been implemented in practice and whether, when implemented, they have the intended effects on teaching and learning in schools. I conclude with a set of questions intended to guide future research on the organizational design of schools.

A Theoretical Perspective on Organizational Design

Organization theorists have developed a variety of perspectives on the organizational design process, but in this chapter I use only one of these to discuss the organizational design of schools. The analysis I present is derived from a theoretical perspective known as contingency theory, particularly that branch of contingency theory that holds that organizational effectiveness results from an appropriate match between an organization's technology and the procedures the organization uses to coordinate and control work. The assertion of a technological imperative in organizational design is grounded in the early work of Woodward (1965), Perrow (1967), and Thompson (1967), but hypotheses derived from this work have proven remarkably robust in research on a variety of organizations (for reviews, see Scott, 1975; Simpson, 1985).

In contingency theory, *technology* is defined broadly as the actions individuals perform, with or without the aid of tools or mechanical devices, to transform inputs into outputs (Perrow, 1967). Using this broad definition, different organization theorists have conceptualized different dimensions of technology (Scott, 1975). However, one dimension has proven remarkably robust in predicting variation in organizational structure. Studies of factory work, office work, and work in professional settings all show that structural arrangements for coordinating and controlling work are closely associated with task uncertainty (Simpson, 1985).

Based on this empirical evidence, contingency theorists have generated a simple set of propositions to serve as guidelines for organizational design. Organizations or subunits operating technologies characterized by high degrees of task certainty are assumed to be most efficient when they develop a mechanistic control structure that features high levels of centralization, formalization, and routine bureaucratic procedure. When tasks are certain, work can be centrally planned and closely supervised, and workers can develop behavioral routines that promote efficiency. On the other hand, as tasks become more uncertain, work requires more flexibility and organizations are assumed to require a more organic form of management to maintain efficiency. Thus, under conditions of task uncertainty, central planning and standardization become inappropriate and organizations instead develop informal and consultative arrangements to cope with the increased problem-solving demands associated with task uncertainty (Perrow, 1967).

Mechanistic and Organic
Designs in Schools

Contingency theory can be applied to the recent literature on school restructuring if one is willing to assume that organizational "technologies" are socially constructed (Berger & Luckmann, 1967). For example, in this chapter I argue that the creation and institutionalization of new technical knowledge about classroom instruction has shaped educational administrators' and policymakers' assumptions about the nature of teaching as an organizational technology and that this, in turn, has led to alternative approaches to the organizational design of schools. Thus I do not assume that the nature of instruction in schools is fixed or immutable. Rather, as the discussion below demonstrates, the nature of teaching as an organizational technology is the subject of debate, with different theorists, policymakers, and practitioners perceiving the work of schools as having a variety of dimensions or properties.

For example, during the 1970s and 1980s, many arguments about the reform of schools were motivated by new developments in research on teaching and by research on instructionally effective schools. Together, these lines of research encouraged many researchers and policy analysts to adopt a highly rationalized view of teaching and school management (e.g., Murphy, Hallinger, & Mesa, 1985). Research on effective schools encouraged the idea that the goals of schooling could be clearly framed and measured in terms of basic skills outcomes (e.g., Edmonds, 1979), and research on teaching led to the view that a routine set of behaviors, typically identified as "direct instruction" (Rosenshine, 1983), could achieve these goals with high certainty. The problem of school reform thus became that of managing this highly routinized technology by implementing tightened controls over teaching. These controls were designed to focus teachers' and students' efforts on reaching clearly defined goals, and they prescribed the appropriate teaching methods and materials teachers should use to reach these goals.

As this view of effective schooling was disseminated, school districts and state legislatures across the country began to develop a host of bureaucratic controls over teaching (Fuhrman et al., 1988; Rowan et al., 1983). For example, the emphasis on basic skills achievement in the effective-schools literature led to the implementation of a strategy of "curriculum alignment" in which standardized textbooks were used as input controls to constrain teachers' decisions about instructional content, and norm- or criterion-referenced tests were used as output controls to assess student achievement and hold educators accountable for student outcomes. Moreover, these input and output controls were often reinforced by the implementation of more stringent behavior controls. Districts began to provide workshops in direct instruction and to train principals in methods of instructional supervision. In many districts, the goal was to develop more uniform approaches to teaching and to tighten supervisory practices (Rowan et al., 1983). More recently, these trends have been reinforced by state-level policies that tighten curricular controls over local schools and set standards of evaluation for teachers (Fuhrman et al., 1988).

By the mid-1980s, however, researchers began to question this strategy. In part, this occurred as research on teaching turned away from the study of routine teacher behaviors and began to focus on the study of teachers as active decisionmakers working in complex classroom environments. What has emerged from this more recent line of research is a view of teaching not as a set of routine behaviors that can be scripted and implemented uniformly in classrooms but rather a view of teaching as a nonroutine technology that relies on teacher judgment and expertise for its success (Berliner, 1986; Brophy & Evertson, 1976; Shulman, 1987).

This revised view of teaching led many researchers and policymakers to call for more organic forms of school organization, especially in the literature on school restructuring and teacher professionalism (Carnegie Task Force on Teaching as a Profession, 1986; Elmore & Associates, 1990; Lieberman, 1988; National Governors' Association, 1986; Tucker, 1988). For example, a common theme in this newer literature has been the call to replace hierarchical structures with network structures of decision making in schools. In this approach, teachers would assume expanded authority in schools, collegial patterns of interaction would be nurtured so that information and advice about teaching could be shared more frequently, and teamwork would be used as an integrative device for the school. In this setting, school leadership would be more widely exercised, with teachers emerging as leaders alongside the school principal, and with advice and information supplanting formal rules and procedures in instructional decision making.

As this brief review suggests, two very different strategies for the organizational design of schools have emerged over the past decade as perspectives about the nature of teaching as an organizational technology have evolved. One strategy is based on a view of teaching as a routine technology and assumes that a mechanistic approach to organizational design can improve school effectiveness. The alternative strategy is based on a view of teaching as a nonroutine technology and assumes that an organic approach to organizational design is needed.

Many observers have concluded that these alternative approaches to school management are incompatible. In large part, this conclusion is based on the observation that the two strategies rely on very different organizational processes to achieve their intended effects. For example, the mechanistic strategy assumes that teaching can be routinized, and as a result, it relies on elaborate controls to constrain teachers' decisions and activities. This approach is consistent with the mechanistic forms of management that have dominated industrial organization for the past century, but organization theorists have come to see that this approach to management can limit workers' commitment to the firm and potentially lead to decreased levels of motivation.

By contrast, the organic approach to school management assumes that teaching is a nonroutine and uncertain form of work. As a result, the organic approach relies on teachers' motivation and commitment to work to obtain effectiveness (Rosenholtz, 1987). That is, given the absence of elaborate controls over teachers' work, an organic approach to organizational design must rely on teachers' problem solving and expertise to improve teaching. Research on organic management in industry suggests that employee commitment and motivation increase when workers have more authority, variety, and collegiality in their work (Porter, Lawler, & Hackman, 1975; Turner & Lawrence, 1964). But more important, the basis of employee commitment changes under organic management. As Burns and Stalker (1961) point out, "The emptying out of significance of the hierarchic command system [in organizations] . . . is countered by the development of shared beliefs about the values and goals of the concern." Thus, with organic management, cultural controls replace formal controls and employees come to base their commitment to organizations on personal identification with the organization's mission and values.

In summary, the two approaches to the organizational design of schools just discussed begin with very different assumptions about the nature of teaching and thus arrive at very different strategies of organizational design. The mechanistic approach assumes that teaching can be routinized. That is, this design strategy seeks to eliminate technical uncertainty through the development of an elaborate set of input, behavior, and output controls intended to standardize and routinize the instructional work of teachers. The organic approach, by contrast, views teaching as a nonroutine activity. As a result, this design strategy tolerates uncertainty in teaching by developing managerial practices designed to cope with it. In the organic approach, teachers are given control over decision making in order to adapt to instructional uncertainties, and collegial controls are put into place in order to increase the amount of knowledge and expertise available to teachers in making these adaptations. The assumption is that uncertainty in teaching is inevitable and that the most effective way to cope with it is to allow teachers considerable autonomy while enhancing their knowledge and expertise.

The Mechanistic Strategy in Practice

In this section, I turn to the problem of whether the two design strategies just discussed can be observed in practice, and whether, when implemented, they have the expected effects on organizational processes. I begin to answer these questions by first reviewing research on the mechanistic approach to organizational design in schools.

Curriculum Alignment

One central feature of the mechanistic approach is curriculum alignment. In theory, this management practice is intended to specify a clear set of instructional goals and to focus the work of teachers and students on the achievement of these goals by developing input and output controls that constrain teachers' content decisions. What follows is a brief review of what is known about the various forms by which these controls are exercised in states and districts and the effects these controls have on teaching practices and teacher commitment.

A useful starting place is two studies conducted in the early 1980s. Goodlad's (1984) massive study of schools found that curriculum controls varied greatly across both states and school districts, but that some school systems had developed tight curriculum controls in the form of subject-specific curriculum guides intended for use in classrooms. Nevertheless, he concluded that "teachers in our sample viewed [these] state and local curriculum guides as of little or moderate usefulness in guiding their teaching" (Goodlad, 1984, p. 49). A study of curriculum controls in school districts located in five states conducted by Floden et al. (1988) offers an explanation for this finding. This study found that a majority of districts in the study had all of the elements needed to engage in curriculum alignment, including a set of districtwide curriculum objectives, mandated texts and teaching time-lines and mandatory districtwide testing systems. However, these researchers found that "districts tend to make unconnected decisions [about curriculum, texts, and testing] that do not lead to any clear curriculum policies" (Floden et al., 1988, p. 104). Moreover, curriculum controls were not reinforced by other control systems. Teachers were neither rewarded for following districts rules about curriculum, texts, and testing nor punished for ignoring them.

Others have studied the state reforms of the early 1980s, which brought about increased graduation requirements and the implemen-tation of competency or proficiency tests for students (Airasian, 1987; Fuhrman et al., 1988). Research on these developments suggests that state controls can have effects on school processes. For example, Clune, White, and Patterson (1988) found that increased graduation require-ments changed student course-taking patterns in a sample of schools and districts within four states. Almost all of the schools studied added math and science courses, and on average, 27% of the students took an additional math class and 34% took an extra science class as a result of these curriculum changes. Moreover, although Clune and colleagues found evidence that some of the new math and science courses were "watered down" versions of academic classes, they also found that teachers felt that state and district curriculum guidelines prevented this from occurring in most instances.

We can only speculate about the effects of changed course-taking patterns on student achievement. Studies generally show a relation-ship between content covered and academic achievement (Carter, 1984; Cooley & Lienhardt, 1980), leading to the prediction that enroll-ment in additional math or science classes will improve achievement in these areas. However, a study by Alexander and Pallas (1984) showed that completion of the kinds of course requirements suggested by recent reform proposals improved the achievement of students on average but had little effect on the achievement of students with low grade point averages. Thus further research is required to demonstrate direct effects of curriculum requirements on student achievement.

Rosenholtz (1987) studied an alternative form of state-level curricu-lar control: competency tests for students. In interviews with a sample of elementary school teachers during the first year of implementation of statewide minimum competency testing, she found that virtually all of the teachers in her sample reported altering the content of their instruction to conform to the content of the state tests. However, the study failed to confirm the idea that this form of curriculum control would have negative effects on teachers' attitudes about work. Only 25% of the 73 elementary school teachers in this study felt that their professional autonomy was compromised by the testing program, and less than 20% thought the testing program would force them to leave teaching. Still, less than 25% of the teachers thought the testing program was helpful.

Other researchers have studied the implementation of curricular controls at the local level and found effects on teachers' practices. For example, in a study of teachers' reactions to districtwide testing practices, Darling-Hammond and Wise (1985) found that almost all of the teachers they interviewed in three large school districts reported altering their curricular emphases and the amount of time spent teaching students how to take tests as a result of these testing programs. This was particularly true in school systems that used what these researchers called competency-based education, an instructional management system that ties student matriculation through a tightly sequenced curriculum to mastery of competency tests. In these systems, teachers reported that the instructional management system greatly affected pacing and content decisions and that it was excessively rigid.

A study by Bullough, Gitlin, and Goldstein (1984) illustrates more clearly the effects of this kind of instructional management system. These researchers found that teachers accepted the tightly sequenced curriculum and the pre- and posttests that determined student progress through the curriculum, believing that they had a measure of autonomy within this tightly structured curricular framework. But they also found that autonomy was defined narrowly as the freedom "to use a different worksheet or create a worksheet of my own, as long as it meets the objective" (Bullough et al., 1984, p. 349). More important, the control system appeared to encourage teachers to adopt what these researchers called a "technocratic mindedness" in which teachers defined students' learning needs in terms of test results and specific learning objectives rather than in holistic terms. Moreover, public inspection of test results encouraged a rapid pace of instruction, a search for teaching techniques that could accomplish learning objectives in a minimum amount of time, and competitiveness among teachers. Despite this, many teachers praised this management system's effects on students and enjoyed the certainty they derived from using the system.

Again, we can only speculate about the effects of such highly rationalized instructional management systems on student achievement.

Much research supports the assumption that tightly sequenced curricula, when accompanied by pre- and posttests and careful attention to the alignment between instructional tasks and test items, can have dramatic effects on student achievement (Block & Burns, 1976; Cohen, 1987). Thus there is apparently some wisdom in teachers' adaptations to these highly rationalized instructional management systems. When teachers are evaluated in terms of student test performance, and when work systems encourage rapid pacing, teachers appear to have discovered the benefits of frequent testing and instructional alignment.

Behavior Controls

In addition to curriculum alignment, a mechanistic design strategy can include an emphasis on behavior controls. Typically, these controls are designed to standardize teaching practices and take the form of in-service training programs in "effective" teaching practices accompanied by increased evaluation of teachers. The research reviewed below suggests that states and local districts are increasingly implementing these kinds of controls.

At the state level, there appears to be a growing recognition that behavior controls represent a useful supplement to curriculum controls. For example, a review of education reform initiatives in six states (Fuhrman et al., 1988) found that states were increasing funding for staff development programs for teachers, for leadership training for principals, and career ladder programs. Thus states were combining behavior controls with other forms of control in a pattern that resembles the mechanistic strategy of organization design.

The most studied state-level initiative in this area is career ladder programs. Although these programs are often thought of as a means of enhancing the professional status of teachers, a critical and controversial component of these programs is the evaluation of teachers. Studies by Fuhrman et al. (1988) and Rosenholtz (1987) demonstrate that when these programs were implemented in Florida and Tennessee, teachers viewed the evaluation procedures used to place teachers at various points in the career ladder as unfair and unreliable. Rosenholtz (1987), for example, interviewed 73 elementary school teachers during the first year of implementation of the career ladder program in Tennessee. She found that nearly two thirds of these teachers challenged the fairness and legitimacy of the evaluation procedures used in the program; only about one third thought the state's method of evaluation was appropriate, objective, or useful; and 82% thought mediocre teachers could be promoted within the system.

Other research suggests that local school systems are becoming more active in the area of teacher evaluation. For example, between 1981 and 1984, data from the High School and Beyond Administrator Teacher Survey show that about 53% of the high schools in the United States changed teacher evaluation practices (U.S. Department of Education, 1988). A study of school districts with reputedly well-developed programs of teacher evaluation conducted by Wise, Darling-Hammond, McLaughlin, and Bernstein (1985) suggests reasons for the changes noted above. In the 32 districts studied by Wise and colleagues, the evaluation systems that preceded the current systems were criticized as being too formal, subjective, inconsistent, and ineffective—the same complaints raised against career ladder programs.

Even in the reputedly well-developed evaluation systems studied by Wise and colleagues (1985), there were obvious weaknesses. Few districts evaluated tenured teachers frequently, and the districts did not integrate teacher evaluation with other control systems, for example, curriculum controls or in-service programs on effective teaching practices. Nevertheless, the researchers did find several districts with exemplary practices. In these systems, teachers viewed evaluation practices as fair, reliable, and valid. This apparently resulted from the use of a few highly trained evaluators, frequent observations, and a focus on minimum—rather than advanced—standards of teaching proficiency.

Research suggests that well-developed evaluation systems can have positive effects on teachers' sense of workplace commitment, morale, and teaching efficacy. For example, in the study by Wise and colleagues (1985), teachers working in districts with exemplary evaluation practices were more committed to evaluation, reported that teacher and administrator communication was good, and became more aware of school goals and alternative classroom practices. A series of studies by Dornbusch and colleagues (Dornbusch & Scott, 1975; Natriello, 1984; Natriello & Dornbusch, 1981) confirm and extend these findings. This work finds that teachers are more satisfied when teacher evaluations and feedback are more frequent, when evaluation standards are uniform and shared, and when teachers feel they have influence in the setting of evaluation standards. Teachers also report increased feelings of efficacy under these conditions.

An alternative behavioral control involves the use of in-service training programs. During the past decade, for example, a large number of districts have implemented training programs based on the direct instruction model of effective teaching (e.g., Good & Grouws, 1979; Hunter, 1983). Findings are beginning to accumulate about the conditions under which these kinds of programs lead to desired changes in teachers' classroom practices. For example, studies by Coladarci and Gage (1984) and Sparks (1986) suggest that teacher behaviors will change as a result of in-service programs only to the extent that staff developers work directly with teachers to encourage commitment to implementation and to the extent that there is extensive follow-up observation of teachers, with peer observation apparently producing the most change in teachers' behavior.

However, these studies only evaluated teacher activities during and shortly after participation in staff development activities and thus provide little evidence of the potential for lasting change in teacher behavior. Thus it is useful to turn to a 4-year study of the implementation of a staff development program reported by Stallings and Krasavage (1986). In this program, teachers were provided with 3 years of training in classroom management and a direct instruction model of teaching, and each teacher received extensive coaching after each training session. Stallings and Krasavage found steady increases in desired teacher behaviors during the 3-year training period as well as evidence of improved student behavior and achievement. However, in the fourth year of the project, when the training and coaching activities were substantially reduced, there were decreases in all of these desirable outcomes.

Robbins (1986) provided useful insights about this study. Apparently project developers hoped that peer coaching and observation would replace the observation and coaching provided by project developers, thereby maintaining desired teaching behaviors. But this did not occur. Still, Robbins asserted that the program had lasting effects. Teachers became more collegial and supportive of experimentation, thought differently about teaching and learning, and began to influence conditions that affected their classroom work. Thus, although specific teacher behaviors were not maintained, there were lasting organizational changes.

Summary

Taken as a whole, research indicates that few districts are currently implementing a mechanistic design strategy in an all-encompassing way. For example, there appear to be few attempts to tie curriculum policies together (Floden et al., 1988) or to link these to other behavioral controls (Wise et al., 1985). Moreover, even various types of behavior controls, such as teacher training and evaluation practices, appear to be unrelated in most districts (Wise et al., 1985).

However, the studies reviewed here do suggest the conditions under which a mechanistic design strategy can affect teachers' conceptions of the task of teaching, teacher behavior in the classroom, students' opportunities for learning, and student achievement. Apparently, intensive controls such as competency-based instructional programs, frequent teacher evaluations, and intensive staff development efforts have the greatest effects. The studies by Bullough et al. (1984) and Robbins (1986) demonstrate how these kinds of controls affect the ways teachers think and talk about teaching, and the studies by Clune et al. (1988), Bullough et al. (1984), and Stallings and Krasavage (1986) demonstrate that intensive application of the mechanistic strategy can affect students' opportunities for learning and student achievement. Thus, when intensive controls are implemented at the school level, there is evidence that they work as intended. The systems increase the alignment between instruction and test content, the pace of instruction, student on-task behavior and content coverage, and student achievement.

The data only partly confirm the idea that intensive controls over teaching damage teacher commitment. Apparently, it is weak and inconsistent application of a mechanistic design strategy that has negative effects, as the studies by Rosenholtz (1987) and Wise et al. (1985) demonstrate. On the other hand, intensive applications of a control-based strategy of school improvement—for example, competency-based instruction, intensive teacher evaluation, and intensive staff development—all were found to have positive effects on teacher morale, efficacy, and cohesiveness (Bullough et al., 1984; Natriello, 1984; Robbins, 1986; Wise et al., 1985).

The Organic Strategy in Practice

Evidence on the implementation of an organic strategy of school design is less systematic than evidence on the mechanistic strategy, in part because the logic of this approach is just now beginning to emerge in education circles. However, research is now being conducted on elements of this approach, and it is this research that is reviewed here. In particular, in this section, I review recent research on teacher participation in decision making; on attempts to develop network structures of coordination and collaboration that support teachers' decision making, and on patterns of school management that rely on communal rather than hierarchical forms of organization to achieve integration. All of these approaches to organizational design seek to enhance teachers' capacities to cope with instructional uncertainties.

Teacher Participation in Decision Making

Organic designs attempt to increase worker participation in decision making as an alternative to hierarchical forms of decision making. Organization theorists argue that moving decision making closer to the technical core can increase the timeliness and quality of decisions, especially in organizations operating nonroutine technologies. They also assume that this kind of participation in decision making increases worker morale and commitment to the firm. Similar arguments have been advanced in the literature on school restructuring. School reformers argue that increased teacher participation in school decision making will enhance both teacher commitment and the quality of decisions made about schooling (e.g., Conley, Schmidle, & Shedd, 1988).

Research demonstrates that decisions about classroom practices in American schools are highly decentralized, but that decisions over other issues, especially budgeting and personnel practices, are highly centralized, especially in public schools (U.S. Department of Education, 1988). Other research shows that teachers desire more participation in school decision making. For example, Bacharach et al. (1986) surveyed 1,789 National Education Association members. They found that the percentage of teachers wanting more participation was 73% for decisions about expenditures priorities, 70% for budget development, and 65% for staff hiring. A large majority of teachers also wanted more participation in decisions about staff development (70%), evaluation practices (63%), and instructional grouping and grading practices (55%). Bacharach and colleagues argue that the survey "demonstrate[s] convincingly that most teachers think they should have considerably more opportunity to be involved in decision making" (p. 251).

Site-based management has arisen as one organizational design strategy for increasing teacher participation in school decision making. As Clune and White (1988) noted, this management approach attempts to increase school autonomy in one or more of the following domains: budgeting, curriculum, or staffing. These researchers studied 31 school districts that were implementing site-based management and found a variety of patterns of implementation. Districts varied in the areas of decision making that were decentralized and in the formal arrangements used to accomplish decentralization. The only constant across all districts appeared to be the establishment of school management councils. However, given the widely varying patterns of implementation across districts, the activities of these councils also varied greatly.

Clune and White's (1988) discussion of school site councils, as well as Malen and Ogawa's (1988) study of school site councils in Salt Lake

City, suggests that this form of participatory management does little to increase teachers' influence in policy formation. Both studies reported that the establishment of school site councils afforded teachers with increased opportunities to participate in decision making. However, traditional school norms and role orientations often persisted, and as a result, site-based management did little to actually change patterns of leadership and decision making in schools.

Despite these findings, there is reason to believe that strategies designed to alter school decision making are worth pursuing. For example, White (1992) studied three of six districts in the Clune and White (1988) study that emphasized decentralization of authority to teachers. This study confirmed that there was only a small change in the amount of authority delegated to teachers in these districts. But this small change was important symbolically to teachers and apparently had positive effects on teachers. In the districts studied by White, teachers reported increased knowledge about school and district policies, more job motivation, enhanced feelings of teaching efficacy, and improved communication among staff. These findings parallel those reported by Newmann, Rutter, and Smith (1985) in a quantitative study of high schools, as well as a great deal of previous research on organizational climates in schools (Miskel & Ogawa, 1988).

Network Structures of Professional Control

A second component of the organic approach consists of calls to create a career ladder with "lead" or "mentor" teacher positions in it (e.g., Carnegie Task Force on Teaching as a Profession, 1986). As we have seen, career ladders are sometimes seen as part of a mechanistic design strategy that emphasizes teacher evaluation, but we have also seen that this emphasis is controversial. An alternative rationale for career ladders is that they can establish a network of professional colleagues in schools. From this perspective, career ladders allow teachers to act as mentors and to support one another outside the system of hierarchical and bureaucratic controls in education. In addition, it is hoped that teachers who assume lead or mentor teacher roles will benefit from the enriched nature of their jobs and be more committed to teaching as a profession (Schlechty, 1989).

In the current education system, teachers already have opportunities to participate in these kinds of extended roles, for example, as grade-level or department chairs, coordinators, consultants, staff developers, teacher trainers, committee chairs, or master teachers. A study by Hatfield, Blackman, Claypool, and Mester (1985) found that teachers who occupy these roles report that their main function is to interact with peers, but that most feel they lack adequate time to perform this function. Still, teachers report deriving satisfaction from this role and feel it is an important part of their career advancement.

Hart (1985, 1987) studied the implementation of a career ladder in a medium-sized district in Utah. The operation of this program was consistent with the principles of organic management. Teachers were given much authority to formulate and implement the program, and the program stressed collegiality. Hart found that faculty interaction increased as a result of program implementation and that both probationary and experienced teachers requested assistance from teacher leaders. However, attitudes about the peer supervision component of the program were mixed, and teacher leaders (who did the supervision) appeared less satisfied than did other teachers. On the whole, however, teacher leaders saw the initiative as leading to career growth.

In summary, it appears that the participation of teachers in extended roles fosters high levels of commitment and satisfaction. Extended roles apparently foster opportunities for career growth and for variety and authority in work, especially when compared to the usual role of teachers. All of this suggests to some observers (e.g., Hart, 1987; Rosenholtz, 1987) that theories of job design developed in the literature on business management could be applied in educational organizations. In this literature, jobs that provide workers with enhanced opportunities for authority, variety, autonomy, and collegiality have been found to affect worker commitment (Porter et al., 1975; Turner & Lawrence, 1964; Walton, 1980). Unfortunately, in a recent review of research on job satisfaction and motivation in education, Miskel and Ogawa (1988) found no studies explicitly designed to test theories of job design in educational settings.

Collegiality Among Teachers

A related theme in the school improvement literature is the call to increase collegiality and collaboration among teachers. The goal of this reform is to break down patterns of teacher isolation stemming from the "cellular" form of organization in schools (Lortie, 1975; Pellegrin, 1976). From the standpoint of organic management, the cellular arrangement of schools and the associated pattern of teacher isolation are problematic because they force teachers to depend on their own resources to resolve curricular, instructional, and management problems that arise during the planning and conduct of instruction. Consistent with organic management, school reformers assume that collaborative arrangements will enhance teachers' capacity for learning and problem solving, build solidarity and cohesiveness within the school, and satisfy teachers' needs for affiliation.

A study by Zahorik (1987) provides useful information about the amount and nature of collegial interaction among teachers in schools. In interviews with 52 teachers in six elementary schools, he found that teachers spent about an hour a day at various times talking with other teachers. About two thirds of this was spent talking about teaching, learning, or other education-related matters. About 10 times a week teachers offered help to other teachers; they received help from other teachers about eight times a week. Helping episodes tended to focus on problems related to materials, discipline, the learning problems of individual students, or classroom activities. Very little help was related to the use of specific teaching techniques, organizational goals and objectives, student evaluation, or room organization.

Zahorik's (1987) study found that two conditions noted by other researchers affect the development of collegiality among teachers: school organization and norms of privacy. On the first point, Zahorik found that teachers working in teaming arrangements gave more help to one another than did other teachers. This is consistent with earlier research by a group of researchers at Stanford University who found that when elementary school teachers worked in team-teaching arrangements and taught reading lessons to multiple reading groups using differentiated reading materials, collaborative arrangements and influential interactions among teachers increased (Cohen, Deal, Meyer, & Scott, 1979; Meyer, Cohen, Brunetti, Molnar, & Leuders-Salmon, 1971). Thus the Stanford studies confirm a major assertion of contingency theory: Teachers who operate more complex forms of instructional technology are more likely to look to colleagues for technical support and information.

Zahorik's (1987) study also confirms Little's (1982) study of the role of faculty norms in promoting collegiality. Little examined six schools that varied in the success of staff development and student achievement and noted that successful schools were characterized by four practices: teachers engaged in frequent talk about teaching, teachers were observed and critiqued, teachers designed and planned teaching materials together, and teachers taught other teachers in various ways. Little explained the development of these practices by reference to faculty norms of collegiality and continuous improvement. The successful schools studied by Little differed from the schools studied by Zahorik. Zahorik noted that in the schools he studied, teachers were satisfied with their teaching and maintained strict norms of privacy.

An important question is whether the development of collaboration and collegiality in schools affects teacher commitment or teaching practices. On this point, research is inconsistent. For example, Zahorik (1987, p. 394) concluded that the information shared by teachers in his study was "shallow" and unlikely to lead to profound changes in teaching practices, even in the schools with the highest levels of interaction. This finding is consistent with a quantitative study conducted by Miskel, McDonald, and Bloom (1983) of 1,500 elementary school teachers in 89 elementary schools. In this study, measures of work system interdependence (e.g., joint teacher planning, use of materials) and teacher-teacher communication failed to have effects on teacher job satisfaction or perceived effectiveness. The Stanford studies discussed above also suggest that collaboration may have weak effects on teaching practices.

However, it is possible that these studies failed to find the expected effects on teacher outcomes because collaboration and collegiality in these schools were too low. In fact, Miskel et al. (1983) noted that variation in measures of work system interdependence and teacher-teacher communication was restricted to the lower end of the scales used in their study. Moreover, neither Cohen et al. (1979) nor Zahorik (1987) noted a general pattern of intensive and persistent collaboration in the schools they studied. On the other hand, when intensive patterns of collaboration are present, researchers have found the expected effects. For example, Intili (1977) used data from the Stanford studies and found that teachers became more reflective in their decision making when their participation in teaming arrangements was persistent and intensive. And Bird and Little's (1985) case study of a junior high school found that when two departments worked intensively over a 5-year period to enrich the classroom environment, teachers made profound changes in their teaching practices.

Thus various factors appear to condition the effects of collegiality and collaboration. Simple attempts at promoting collaboration that allocate small amounts of time and result in limited contact do not appear to have great effects on teacher commitment or teaching practices. Instead, the development of a faculty culture that reinforces the norm of continuous improvement and sustains intensive collegial interactions over a long period of time appears to be required if collegial forms of organization are to produce the intended effects.

Development of Community in Schools

A final theme in the organic approach relates to Burns and Stalker's (1961) insight that in organic management, formal authority structures become less important in directing work, and informal norms or cultural controls guide work and sustain workers' commitment. In part, this entails the development of shared values that unify members of different subunits and orient them to a common purpose. This theme is also found in much writing on effective schools (e.g., Purkey & Smith, 1983; Rutter, Maughan, Mortimore, Outsen, & Smith, 1979). I refer to this process as the development of community within schools.

Understanding of this issue has been advanced in a recent study by Bryk and Driscoll (1988). These researchers used High School and Beyond data to construct an index of communal organization in high schools. The index measured three aspects of this concept: a system of shared values, a common agenda of activities, and collegial relations among adults coupled with a "diffuse" teacher role. According to Bryk and Driscoll, shared values provide a set of clear expectations to motivate and guide the behavior of faculty and students (cf. Metz, 1986). A common agenda of activities unites school members both physically and spiritually. And a diffuse teacher role brings teachers into frequent contact with teachers and students in settings other than the classroom.

Bryk and Driscoll (1988) demonstrated that schools with higher scores on the index of communal organization had more favorable teacher and student outcomes. Communally organized high schools had higher teacher efficacy and satisfaction, higher staff morale, higher teacher enjoyment of work, and lower teacher absenteeism. Students in schools with a higher score on the communal index were more interested in academics, less absent from school or classes, and more orderly. They also had higher student achievement and dropped out of school at lower rates.

There are two cautions about these results. First, as Bryk and Driscoll (1988) note, the values embraced by a school community have important consequences. Obviously, much research supports the notion that high expectations for student success is a critical part of the value system of any school, and this normative dimension was included as part of Bryk and Driscoll's communal index. However, other value systems, even though they are commonly shared, may be detrimental to student performance, as Swidler's (1979) case studies of alternative schools demonstrate. In one school in Swidler's study, the shared values of the school community encouraged students to think of themselves as "bad," and Swidler ably demonstrated the negative effects this had on students.

In addition, Swidler's study suggests a set of conditions in which the diffuse role of teachers noted by Bryk and Driscoll may become overextended. For example, Swidler labeled the alternative schools she studied as "schools without authority" because the lack of a hierarchical structure forced teachers to rely on personal bonds with students to maintain order and motivate learning. Swidler found that teachers who were most successful in this setting were also the most likely to become exhausted and to leave teaching. Thus Swidler's case studies usefully demonstrate the limits of communal forms of organization.

Summary

The research on organic approaches to organizational design leads to a set of conclusions similar to those reached about the mechanistic approach. First, evidence indicates that the organic approach is inconsistently and partially implemented in schools, as studies of site-based management, career ladders, and teacher collaboration demonstrate. More important, we know little about how the various elements of an organic design strategy can be combined, although the work of Bryk and Driscoll (1988) suggests that when the various elements of this approach are combined into a coherent organizational form, the effects on teachers and students can be dramatic.

A second conclusion is that the organic approach, like the mechanistic strategy, appears to work best when applied intensively, although the research reviewed here also suggests some limits to this general rule. Studies of collegiality and collaboration best illustrate the need for intensive application of an organic design strategy. Apparently, only sustained and intensive cooperation among teachers yields the kinds of changes in teaching and the high levels of teacher commitment desired by those who advocate an organic approach to school design. At the same time, Swidler's (1979) work suggests that too much extension of the teacher role, as well as too little reliance on hierarchical authority, can produce teacher stress and burnout, a point also stressed in the more general literature on job design (Porter et al., 1975). Thus an important point for future research might be an examination of the point at which organic forms of management reach diminishing returns.

Finally, the question of how organic management leads to improved school effectiveness requires much more thorough analysis. The studies reviewed here strongly suggest that organic management positively affects teachers' workplace commitment. What is less clear is how organic management affects the nature of teaching and learning in schools. Although it makes sense to assume that teachers who bring more energy to the classroom and who feel more efficacious will perform better, the evidence on this point is disturbingly weak. I will return to this problem in greater detail below.

A Research Agenda on Organizational Design in Schools

The evidence reviewed here suggests that both the mechanistic and organic strategies of organizational design can lead to improved student outcomes, but that neither approach is consistently implemented in most schools. This should not come as a surprise, because the approaches developed here are abstract models. Although it would be interesting and informative to investigate the validity of these models as taxonomies of organizations, decades of organizational research provides little reason to expect that ideal types based in theory will be observed in pure form in practice (e.g., Pugh, Hinings, & Hickson, 1969). As in other complex organizations, traditions of practice, environmental pressures, and community settings hinder the development of preferred or consistent design strategies in schools.

As a result, it seems more appropriate for future research to advance from a stage in which school organization and effectiveness are discussed in terms of abstract models and taxonomies to a stage in which researchers investigate subsidiary issues that would inform the development of organizational design principles for schools. To summarize the results of the preceding literature review and extend the ideas in it, I conclude with a discussion of four such issues that can be used to guide future research.

Nature of Teaching as an Organizational Technology

This chapter began with the assertion that conceptions of teaching as an organizational task varied and that this had implications for the organizational design of schools. The research reviewed here confirms the first assertion. It is clear that teachers' conceptions of task vary from setting to setting. For example, in competency-based instructional programs, there was evidence that teachers viewed their tasks as routine (Bullough et al., 1984), whereas in other settings, for example, the complex and individualized classrooms studied by the Stanford group (Cohen et al., 1979), teachers were apparently confronted with

complex decisions that required support and interaction with colleagues.

Research on schools as organizations has seldom recognized variability in the nature of instruction or considered the origins of teachers'
differing conceptions of task. Instead, there has been a widespread
assumption that teaching is always a complex and uncertain task. This
view is firmly embedded in classic discussions of the school as a formal
organization (e.g., Bidwell, 1965; Meyer & Rowan, 1978; Weick, 1976)
and in more recent discussions of the professionalization of teaching.
However, the literature reviewed here suggests that we need to move
beyond this invarying view of teaching to formulate hypotheses about
the conditions that give rise to differing views of teaching as an
organizational task.

A useful example of this kind of research is a study of over 600 high
school teachers in California and Michigan conducted by Rowan,
Raudenbusch, and Cheong (1992). This study used measures of organizational technology drawn from the broader literature on organizations (Withey, Daft, & Cooper, 1983) to examine the nature of teaching
tasks. The measures used in the study indexed two dimensions of
teaching work: task variety and task uncertainty. The study found little
support for the premise that teaching is characterized by high degrees
of technical uncertainty. In fact, only 17% of the teachers in this sample
reported this to be the case. By contrast, there was more variation in
teachers' reports of task variety. Overall, teachers' task conceptions
tended to fall into two main categories: 47% of the teachers viewed
teaching as having low task variety and low task uncertainty (i.e., as
routine work) and 35% viewed teaching as having low task uncertainty
but high task variety (i.e., as engineering work).

Rowan and colleagues (1992) attempted to explain why teachers
adopted different views of their work. Consistent with the Stanford
studies, they found that instructional grouping arrangements affected
high school teachers' conceptions of task, with teachers working with
mixed-ability classes viewing their work as more uncertain than did
teachers who worked in more homogeneous classrooms. They also
found that task conceptions varied by subject matter specialization,
with math teachers reporting less task variety than other teachers. This
finding is consistent with Stodolsky's (1988) comparison of math and
social studies teaching in elementary schools. She found that "there is
considerable homogeneity in math instruction, whereas variety is characteristic of social studies" (p. 13).

The Rowan et al. (1992) study also demonstrates that teachers'
experience and beliefs affected task conceptions. For example, more

experienced teachers perceived less task uncertainty than did inexperienced teachers, a finding consistent with research on teacher decision making, which finds that experienced teachers establish decision routines to cope with the demands of their work (Shavelson, 1983). In addition, teachers' perceptions of students and views about the purposes of instruction affected task conceptions. For example, in the study by Rowan and colleagues, teachers who perceived variability in students and who held "constructivist" views of teaching tended to report higher levels of task variety and task uncertainty than did teachers who perceived uniformity in students and who reported that a goal of teaching is to pass on a relatively fixed body of knowledge.

Clearly, more research on teachers' perceptions of task is needed. But a general conclusion is warranted from the evidence reviewed here. Organization theorists and policymakers can no longer assert that instruction is inherently nonroutine. Instead, organization theorists need to adopt a more fine-grained approach to the analysis of teaching, one that examines the instructional circumstances in which teachers work and teachers' personal views about the goals of teaching and the qualities of students.

Relationship of Teaching Tasks to Design

There is also a need to examine relationships among the task characteristics of teaching and organization design features in schools. As we have seen, contingency theory asserts a relationship between task characteristics and organizational design, and the evidence reviewed in this chapter provides some support for this theory. In particular, the work of the Stanford group (Cohen et al., 1979) suggests that as the work of teachers becomes more complex and nonroutine, organic forms of management arise in schools.

However, the relationships between task and organizational design may be more complicated than we have assumed thus far. For example, past research usually has failed to distinguish among various dimensions of teaching as an organizational technology, for example, task variety and task uncertainty. Yet the research conducted by Rowan and colleagues (1992) shows that these dimensions of task are not perfectly correlated and that these two task dimensions have different relationships to organizational design features. For example, Rowan and colleagues found a negative relationship between task uncertainty and teacher collaboration, a finding consistent with Rosenholtz's (1989) study of elementary school teachers. Rosenholtz argued that collaboration with other teachers reduces task uncertainty. At the same time,

Rowan and colleagues found that task variety was positively related to teacher collaboration, a finding consistent with Cohen et al.'s (1979) observation that complex grouping arrangements and the use of multiple reading texts—factors that increase task variety—gave rise to teacher collaboration. Thus, in assessing relationships among task characteristics and organizational design in schools, researchers need to recognize various dimensions of task technology.

More important, simple analyses of relationships among task and design variables may not adequately capture the logic of contingency theory. At the heart of contingency theory is the assertion that a match between task and organization design enhances organizational effectiveness. An empirical assessment of this hypothesis requires complex research designs of the sort used in Woodward's (1965) pioneering study of industrial organizations. Unfortunately, similar designs have not been used in studies of school effectiveness. However, these complex research designs may be needed to disentangle a major finding of our review. Apparently, both mechanistic and organic designs can have positive effects on school effectiveness.

One way to explain this seemingly contradictory finding is to assume that the relationship between design form and effectiveness depends on the type of technology operated within an organization. Under this assumption, effective schools with mechanistic designs would have teachers who held routine task conceptions, whereas effective schools with organic designs would have teachers who held nonroutine conceptions of task. Conversely, we would expect organic designs to be ineffective and unneeded when teachers view their tasks as routine and mechanistic designs to be inappropriate and ineffective when teachers view their work as nonroutine. To date, neither the school reform literature nor the literature on school organization has been sufficiently attentive to the contingent relationship between organizational design and school effectiveness.

Relationship of Organizational Design to Outcomes

Still a third line of research is needed to clarify the relationships among characteristics of school organization, teacher commitment, and classroom outcomes. Research on the effects of organizational structure on teacher commitment variables is widely scattered, as our review indicates, and much of the debate about the negative effects of bureaucratic controls in schools, and to a lesser extent, the positive effects of organic designs, is based on impressionistic evidence or research using simple methodological designs. More careful studies, based on explicit theoretical conceptions of organizational structure, teacher commitment, and teacher motivation are needed.

This involves several problems. First, there is a need to conceptualize the organizational structure of schools and to explore how the jobs of teachers can be enriched. For example, common and standardized questionnaires drawn from mainstream research on job design (see, e.g., Miner, 1980, chap. 9) could be used to measure aspects of job autonomy, responsibility, and variety and to assess the extent to which various alternative designs in schools increase or decrease these characteristics of teacher and student roles. Also, there is a need to ascertain the extent to which job characteristics and other school design features affect various dimensions of teacher commitment or other motivational outcomes such as expectations for success or feelings of efficacy. Some research of this sort has recently been conducted (e.g., Reyes, 1992; Rowan et al., 1992), but the research either fails to use standard measures of commitment and/or motivation or contains inadequate measures of organizational design features.

Second, and especially critical for those who assert the efficacy of organic designs, is the need to examine how increases in worker commitment and motivation affect student learning. Here researchers might follow the lead of Ashton and Webb (1986), who argued that motivational variables directly affect teacher behaviors associated with student learning. This is an interesting line of analysis, but Ashton and Webb's research found only inconsistent effects of teacher efficacy—a motivational construct—on measures of teachers' use of direct instruction techniques in their classrooms. Thus a problem for future research will be to specify other motivational constructs and other observable teacher behaviors (or cognitions) to demonstrate how teacher motivation affects student learning.

There is also a need to engage in further studies of the effects of bureaucratization on student learning. Although much research supports the idea that strategies of curriculum alignment, competency-based instructional management, and intensive in-service programs can affect teacher and student behaviors associated with increased basic skills achievement, more research is needed to examine whether these behavioristic and control-oriented strategies can equally affect higher-order thinking and problem solving among students.

Constraints on Organizational Design

Finally, our discussion thus far has focused almost exclusively on what can be called the "technological imperative" in organizational design. That is, I have argued that organizational structures are affected by the nature of the work performed within organizations. Although this theoretical perspective is useful, there is also a need for researchers to turn their attention to other constraints on organizational design. In particular, research on organizations generally suggests that the social environments in which organizations are located and the nature of the people working in organizations also affect organizational designs.

In education, much attention has recently been given to the effects of social environments on school structure. For example, it is becoming increasingly clear that organic forms of school organization are more likely to arise in the private rather than public sector of K-12 schooling (Bryk & Driscoll, 1988; Chubb & Moe, 1990; Rowan, Raudenbusch, & Kang, 1991). There are several possible explanations for this finding, but one persuasive line of argument concerns the inability of public schools to develop the kind of clear and unified mission that is essential to organic management. For example, Bryk and Driscoll's (1988) study demonstrated that the diversity of students in public schools mitigates against the formation of community in schools, and Fuller and Izu's (1986) research showed that the presence of multiple sources of funding, a characteristic of many public schools, further works against the establishment of a unified values system in schools. But more research is needed on how environmental conditions affect organizational design, as is more research on how schools can free themselves of environmental constraints to pursue their own design strategies.

Finally, theories of school design need to consider how design variables interact with the personal characteristics of teachers to affect commitment outcomes. For example, Walton's (1980) studies of "high commitment" work systems in industrial settings suggest that an organic approach to design depends critically on the attitudes and characteristics of workers in the system. A related point is found in the literature on job design, which shows that not all workers prefer to work in enriched jobs (Miner, 1980). As a result, successful work-restructuring efforts in industry have necessarily been accompanied by intensive recruitment efforts that carefully screen employees (Walton, 1980).

Research on schools is beginning to suggest that a similar phenomenon exists in education. For example, studies by Rowan et al. (1991) and Smylie (1992) demonstrate that teachers' willingness to participate in organic forms of management varies greatly within schools as a function of personal beliefs and personal background. However, the dependence of organic management on the preexisting commitment of teachers has not been fully recognized by those who advocate the simultaneous restructuring of schools and professionalization of teaching. Advocates of this approach are aware that failure to implement an organic approach to organizational design can discourage the recruitment of highly able teachers, but they have not given sufficient attention to the idea that successful implementation of an organic approach depends on recruiting particular kinds of teachers or to the reactions of experienced teachers to organic designs. Based on research in business and industry, as well as an emerging body of research in education, not all of today's teachers should be expected to react uniformly and favorably to an organic strategy of organizational design. Thus research that identifies the characteristics of teachers who thrive in organic settings would be useful, not only to bring educational studies in line with more general theories of organizational design but also to guide future recruitment efforts in the teaching profession.

Conclusion

The research reviewed here establishes a new and complex agenda for research on school organization and effectiveness. This agenda arises from a consideration of organization design strategies being advocated in the education policy environment. If researchers are to provide information relevant to practice, it follows that they need to conduct research capable of evaluating these new design strategies. The research reviewed here and the discussion of needed future research suggest a host of issues that need to be examined in this new agenda and provide a conceptual framework for developing theories of the organizational design of schools.

References

Airasian, P. W. (1987). State mandated testing and educational reform: Context and consequences. *American Journal of Education, 95,* 393-412.

Alexander, K. L., & Pallas, A. M. (1984). Curriculum reform and school performance: An evaluation of the "new basics." *American Journal of Education, 92,* 391-420.

Ashton, P. T., & Webb, R. B. (1986). *Making a difference: Teachers' sense of efficacy and student achievement.* New York: Longman.

Bacharach, S. B., Bauer, S., & Shedd, J. B. (1986). The work environment and school reform. *Teachers College Record, 88,* 241-256.

Berger, P. L., & Luckmann, T. (1967). *The social construction of reality: A treatise in the sociology of knowledge.* New York: Anchor.

Berliner, D. C. (1986). In search of the expert pedagogue. *Educational Researcher, 15,* 5-13.

Bidwell, C. E. (1965). The school as a formal organization. In J. G. March (Ed.), *Handbook of organizations.* Chicago: Rand McNally.

Bird, T., & Little, J. W. (1985). *Instructional leadership in eight secondary schools.* Boulder, CO: Center for Action Research.

Block, J. H., & Burns, R. B. (1976). Mastery learning. In L. S. Shulman (Ed.), *Review of research in education* (chap. 1). Itasca, IL: Peacock.

Brophy, J. E., & Evertson, C. (1976). *Learning from teaching: A developmental perspective.* Boston: Allyn and Bacon.

Bryk, A. S., & Driscoll, M. E. (1988). *An empirical investigation of the school as community.* Unpublished manuscript, University of Chicago, Department of Education.

Bullough, R. V., Gitlin, A. D., & Goldstein, S. L. (1984). Ideology, teacher role, and resistance. *Teachers College Record, 86,* 339-358.

Burns, T., & Stalker, G. M. (1961). *The management of innovation.* London: Tavistock.

Carnegie Task Force on Teaching as a Profession. (1986). *A nation prepared: Teachers for the 21st century.* New York: Carnegie Forum on Education and the Economy.

Carter, L. F. (1984). The sustaining effects study of compensatory education. *Educational Researcher, 13,* 4-13.

Chubb, J. E., & Moe, T. M. (1990). *Politics, markets and America's schools.* Washington, DC: Brookings Institution.

Clune, W., & White, P. A. (1988). *School-based management: Institutional variation, implementation, and issues for further research.* Madison, WI: Center for Policy Research in Education.

Clune, W., with White, P., & Patterson, J. (1988). *The implementation and effects of high school graduation requirements: First steps toward curricular reform.* Madison, WI: Center for Policy Research in Education.

Cohen, E. G., Deal, T. E., Meyer, J. W., & Scott, W. R. (1979). Technology and teaming in the elementary school. *Sociology of Education, 52,* 20-33.

Cohen, S. A. (1987). Instructional alignment: Searching for a magic bullet. *Educational Researcher, 16,* 16-20.

Coladarci, T., & Gage, N. L. (1984). Effects of a minimal intervention on teacher behavior and student achievement. *American Educational Research Journal, 21,* 539-556.

Conley, S. C., Schmidle, T., & Shedd, J. B. (1988). Teacher participation in the management of school systems. *Teachers College Record, 90,* 259-280.

Cooley, W. W., & Leinhardt, G. (1980). The instructional dimensions study. *Educational Evaluation and Policy Analysis, 2,* 7-26.

Darling-Hammond, L., & Wise, A. E. (1985). Beyond standardization: State standards and school improvement. *Elementary School Journal, 85,* 315-335.

Dornbusch, S. M., & Scott, W. R. (1975). *Evaluation and the exercise of authority.* San Francisco: Jossey-Bass.

Edmonds, R. (1979). Effective schools for the urban poor. *Educational Leadership, 37*, 15-24.

Elmore, R. F., & Associates. (1990). *Restructuring schools: The next generation of educational reform.* San Francisco: Jossey-Bass.

Floden, R. E., Porter, A. C., Alford, L. E., Freeman, D. J., Irwin, S., Schmidt, W. H., & Schwille, J. R. (1988). Instructional leadership at the district level: A closer look at autonomy and control. *Educational Administration Quarterly, 24*, 96-124.

Fuhrman, S., Clune, W. H., & Elmore, R. F. (1988). Research on education reform: Lessons on the implementation of policy. *Teachers College Record, 90*, 237-257.

Fuller, B., & Izu, J. (1986). Explaining school cohesion: What shapes the organizational beliefs of teachers? *American Journal of Education, 94*, 501-535.

Good, T., & Grouws, D. (1979). The Missouri Mathematics Effectiveness Project: An experimental study in fourth-grade mathematics classrooms. *Journal of Educational Psychology, 71*, 335-362.

Goodlad, J. I. (1984). *A place called school: Prospects for the future.* New York: McGraw-Hill.

Hart, A. W. (1985, April). *Formal teacher supervision by teachers in a career ladder.* Paper presented at the annual meeting of the American Educational Research Association, Chicago.

Hart, A. W. (1987). A career ladder's effect on teacher career and work attitudes. *American Educational Research Journal, 24*, 479-504.

Hatfield, R. C., Blackman, C. A., Claypool, C., & Mester, F. (1985). *Extended professional roles of teacher leaders in the public schools.* East Lansing: Department of Teacher Education, Michigan State University.

Hunter, M. (1983). *Mastery teaching.* El Segundo, CA: TIP.

Intili, J. (1977). *Structural conditions in a school that promote reflective decision-making.* Ph.D. dissertation, Stanford University, CA.

Kirst, M. W. (1988). Recent state education reform in the United States: Looking backward and forward. *Educational Administration Quarterly, 24*, 319-328.

Lieberman, A. (1988, February). Expanding the school leadership team. *Educational Leadership, 45*, 4-8.

Little, J. W. (1982). Norms of collegiality and experimentation: Workplace conditions of school success. *American Educational Research Journal, 19*, 325-340.

Lortie, D. C. (1975). *Schoolteacher: A sociological study.* Chicago: University of Chicago Press.

Malen, B., & Ogawa, R. T. (1988). Professional-patron influence on site-based governance councils: A confounding case study. *Educational Evaluation and Policy Analysis, 10*, 251-270.

March, J. G., & Olsen, J. P. (1976). *Ambiguity and choice in organizations.* Bergen, Norway: Universitetsforlaget.

Metz, M. H. (1986). *Different by design: The context and characteristics of three magnet schools.* New York: Routledge & Kegan Paul.

Meyer, J. W., Cohen, E., Brunetti, F., Molnar, S., & Leuders-Salmon, E. (1971). *The impact of the open space school upon teacher influence and autonomy: The effects of an organizational innovation.* Stanford, CA: Stanford University, Stanford Center for Research and Development in Teaching.

Meyer, J. W., & Rowan, B. (1978). The structure of educational organizations. In M. W. Meyer & Associates, *Environments and organizations* (pp. 78-109). San Francisco: Jossey-Bass.

Miner, J. B. (1980). *Theories of organizational behavior.* Hinsdale, IL: Dryden.

Miskel, C., McDonald, D., & Bloom, S. (1983). Structural and expectancy linkages within schools and organizational effectiveness. *Educational Administration Quarterly, 19,* 49-82.

Miskel, C., & Ogawa, R. (1988). Work motivation, job satisfaction, and climate. In N. Boyan (Ed.), *Handbook of educational administration* (pp. 279-304). New York: Longman.

Murphy, J., Hallinger, P., & Mesa, R. P. (1985). School effectiveness: Checking progress and assumptions and developing a role for the state and federal government. *Teachers College Record, 86,* 615-641.

National Governors' Association. (1986). *Time for results.* Washington, DC: Author.

Natriello, G. (1984). Teachers' perceptions of the frequency of evaluations and assessments of their effort and effectiveness. *American Educational Research Journal, 21,* 579-604.

Natriello, G., & Dornbusch, S. M. (1981). Pitfalls in the evaluation of teachers by principals. *Administrator's Notebook, 29,* 1-4.

Newmann, F. M., Rutter, R. A., & Smith, M. S. (1985). *Exploratory analysis of high school teacher climate.* Madison: Wisconsin Center for Education Research.

Passow, A. H. (1989). Present and future directions in school reform. In T. G. Sergiovanni & J. H. Moore (Eds.), *Schooling for tomorrow: Directing reforms to issues that count* (pp. 13-39). Boston: Allyn and Bacon.

Pellegrin, R. J. (1976). Schools as work settings. In R. Dubin (Ed.), *Handbook of work, organizations, and society.* Skokie, IL: Rand McNally.

Perrow, C. (1967). A framework for the comparative analysis of organizations. *American Sociological Review, 32,* 194-208.

Porter, L. W., Lawler, E. E., & Hackman, J. R. (1975). *Behavior in organizations.* New York: McGraw-Hill.

Pugh, D., Hinings, C. R., & Hickson, D. J. (1969). An empirical taxonomy of structures of work organizations. *Administrative Science Quarterly, 14,* 115-126.

Purkey, S. C., & Smith, M. S. (1983). Effective schools: A review. *Elementary School Journal, 83,* 427-452.

Reyes, P. (1992). *Preliminary models of teacher organizational commitment: Implications for restructuring the workplace.* Madison, WI: Center on Organization and Restructuring of Schools.

Robbins, P. (1986). The Napa-Vacaville Follow-Through Project: Qualitative outcomes, related procedures, and implications for practice. *Elementary School Journal, 87,* 139-151.

Rosenholtz, S. J. (1987). Education reform strategies: Will they increase teacher commitment? *American Journal of Education, 95,* 534-562.

Rosenshine, B. (1983). Teaching functions in instructional programs. *Elementary School Journal, 83,* 335-352.

Rowan, B., Edelstein, R., & Leal, A. (1983). *Pathways to excellence: What school districts are doing to improve instruction.* San Francisco: Far West Laboratory for Educational Research and Development.

Rowan, B., Raudenbusch, S. W., & Cheong, Y. F. (1992, April). *The task characteristics of teaching: Implications for the organizational design of schools.* Paper presented at the annual meeting of the American Educational Research Association, San Francisco.

Rowan, B., Raudenbusch, S. W., & Kang, S. J. (1991). Organizational design in high schools: A multilevel analysis. *American Journal of Education, 99,* 238-266.

Rutter, M., Maughan, B., Mortimore, P., Outsen, J., & Smith, A. (1979). *Fifteen thousand hours: Secondary schools and their effects on children.* Cambridge, MA: Harvard University Press.

Schlechty, P. C. (1989). Career ladders: A good idea going awry. In T. J. Sergiovanni & J. H. Moore (Eds.), *Schooling for tomorrow: Directing reforms at issues that count.* Boston: Allyn and Bacon.

Scott, W. R. (1975). Organizational structure. *Annual Review of Sociology, 1,* 1-20.

Shavelson, R. J. (1983). Review of research on teachers' pedagogical judgements, plans, and decisions. *Elementary School Journal, 83,* 392-413.

Shulman, L. S. (1987). Knowledge and teaching. *Harvard Educational Review, 57,* 1-22.

Simpson, R. L. (1985). Social control of occupations and work. *Annual Review of Sociology, 11,* 415-436.

Smylie, M. A. (1992). Teacher participation in school decision making: Assessing willingness to participate. *Educational Evaluation and Policy Analysis, 14,* 53-67.

Sparks, G. M. (1986). The effectiveness of alternative training activities in changing teaching practices. *American Educational Research Journal, 23,* 217-226.

Stallings, J., & Krasavage, E. (1986). Program implementation and student achievement in a four-year Madeline Hunter Follow-Through Project. *Elementary School Journal, 86,* 117-138.

Stodolsky, S. (1985). *The subject matters.* Chicago: University of Chicago Press.

Swidler, A. (1979). *Organization without authority: Dilemmas of social control in free schools.* Cambridge, MA: Harvard University Press.

Thompson, J. D. (1967). *Organizations in action.* New York: McGraw-Hill.

Tucker, M. S. (1988, February). Peter Drucker, knowledge work, and the structure of schools. *Educational Leadership, 45,* 44-47.

Turner, A. N., & Lawrence, P. R. (1964). *Industrial jobs and the worker.* Boston: Harvard University Press.

U.S. Department of Education. (1988). *High School and Beyond Administrator Teacher Survey (1984): Data file users manual.* Washington, DC: Author.

Walton, R. E. (1980). Establishing and maintaining high commitment work systems. In J. R. Kimberly, R. H. Miles, & Associates, *The organization life cycle.* San Francisco: Jossey-Bass.

Weick, K. E. (1976). Educational organizations as loosely coupled systems. *Administrative Science Quarterly, 21,* 1-19.

White, P. (1992). Teacher empowerment under "ideal" school site autonomy. *Education Evaluation and Policy Analysis, 14,* 69-82.

Wise, A. E., Darling-Hammond, L., McLaughlin, M., & Bernstein, H. T. (1985). Teacher evaluation: A study of effective practices. *Elementary School Journal, 86,* 61-121.

Withey, M., Daft, R. L., & Cooper, W. H. (1983). Measures of Perrow's work unit technology: An empirical assessment and a new scale. *Academy of Management Journal, 26,* 45-63.

Woodward, J. (1965). *Industrial organization: Theory and practice.* London: Oxford University Press.

Zahorik, J. A. (1987). Teachers' collegial interactions: An exploratory study. *Elementary School Journal, 87,* 385-396.

Institutionalism and Strategic Decisions in Education

CHARLES TAYLOR KERCHNER
KRISTA D. CAUFMAN

It is not strange that much of the conceptual interest in the role of institutions in American life comes from scholars interested in education and other public and not-for-profit organizations. These organizations operate in ways that are highly institutionally determined. Indeed, much of the critique of public education in the United States rests on the extent to which institutional arrangements constrain organizational strategy. To portray strategic decision making in education requires an understanding of the ways in which public education as an institution shapes what decisions are made, how they are made, and where they are made (Mansbridge, 1983, 1990; March & Olsen, 1976, 1989). The institutional logic of educational decisions may have little to do with the technical requirements of teaching and learning.

In recent years, there has been renewed attention to the patterning effects of professions, interest groups, national societies, and governmental rule makers. These institutions "penetrate the organization, creating the lenses through which actors view the world and the very categories of structure, action and thought" (DiMaggio & Powell, 1991, p. 11).

Institutions penetrate organizations by creating cognitive constructions (Berger & Luckmann, 1967). They set the criteria for a good decision, and they constrain decision makers by invoking what DiMaggio and Powell (1983) call isomorphism. The patterning effect of isomorphism occurs because of political influences, because of professional or occupational norms that transcend individual organizations, or simply because organizations copy responses to uncertainty from other organizations. These effects are particularly felt in public school organizations, which are highly dependent on external resources and have a weak core technology (Meyer & Rowan, 1978).

Schools make decisions under conditions of ambiguity (Cohen & March, 1974; March & Olsen, 1976). Objectives are not unknown, but the classic goals cited for educational organizations—intellectual and personal development, social integration, and economic growth—"are rarely specified in terms precise enough to be administratively useful" (March & Olsen, 1989, p. 228). When goals are specified in precise and measurable terms, such as increasing test scores, they become problematic and contentious.

Moreover, schools are tied to the environment by politics and due process. For the past 50 years, education's major strategic decisions have been made outside of school organizations. Desegregation was forced on schools by courts rather than school boards. Congress created categorical funding, which externally directed programs and finances. State legislatures adopted collective bargaining statutes, which reordered school authority structures and resource allocations.

Strategic decisions are also made at the classroom level by the two million policy brokers called teachers. Because school decisions are frequently analytically ambiguous, practitioners give meaning to policies through experience and practice. The incremental effects of their time allocations, beliefs, and teaching practices form the meaning of schooling.

These institutional factors in education demand that we enlarge our conception of strategic decision making beyond traditional big decisions, those decisions "made at the top about bigger matters" (Hickson, Butler, Cray, Mallory, & Wilson, 1986, p. 27). To characterize organizational strategy and strategic decision making exclusively as protracted deliberative processes that yield distinct decisions misses much of the richness and much of the reality. To enlarge the discussion of strategy, we divide decision making in educational organizations along three dimensions, shown in Table 2.1:

- Discrete versus incremental decisions
- External versus internal decisions
- Individual versus group decisions

TABLE 2.1 A Typology of Strategic Decisions and Decision Processes

| | External | Internal | |
		Group	Individual
Discrete	Unitary politics: decisions on the basis of commitment to common purpose Interest groups: decisions on the basis of negotiation of preferences Revolutions: decisions on the basis of regime overthrow	Conventional: big organizational decisions on the basis of situationally established routines and legitimated participants	Entrepreneurial: decisions on the basis of cognitive integration of information within a single mind
Incremental	Additive layering of laws, rules, and regulations: decision making on the basis of muddling through	A series of incremental decisions on the basis of continuous improvement	A series of individual role-taking decisions on the basis of individual discretion

The conventional literature defines strategic decisions as those at the center of things. Other decisions may echo it, but the big decision sets the precedent for the smaller decisions that follow. *Precursiveness* and *rarity* are the terms used by Hickson et al. (1986, p. 41). However, as we have indicated, strategic direction is not always determined by discrete decisions. Often, it is the result of either a series of decisions linked by time and feedback or a cluster of decisions made relatively independently. The strategic importance of these incremental changes may be only recognized in retrospect (March & Olsen, 1976). For example, the cumulative effect of categorical funding programs, each enacted to advance and protect a class of students, may be to formalize the organization and make timely student service delivery difficult.

Second, internal and external decisions differ. Powerful external decisions follow a political logic of interest organization and articulation. In contrast, internal decisions follow an organizational logic in which access is determined by hierarchical position and reputed expertise.

Group and individual decisions also have different logics. The literature frequently considers decisions made by groups, sometimes groups established specifically to make big decisions (Allison, 1969, 1971; Keller, 1983). Some groups operate under governmental or corporate secrecy, such as John F. Kennedy's crisis council during the Cuban missile crisis. Some operate in the open, such as the National Commission on Excellence and Education, whose report, *A Nation at Risk* (1983), focused the country's attention on the condition of the educational system. In both cases the organization and the participants recognize the locus of the decision, the legitimacy of the decision makers, and the fact that a decision will emerge.

Other strategic decisions are made much more privately, centering around single individuals who may or may not lead organizations. Autocrats, entrepreneurs, and treaty negotiators make decisions with organizations in mind, but the process of making such decisions differs markedly from that used in group decision making.

These divisions give us the six domains in Table 2.1. The division is of theoretical interest and practical importance because different decision mechanisms apply in each domain. Different decision mechanisms require different process criteria, include different legitimate participants, and yield different types of decisions. In a practical sense, the overarching strategic questions for both administrators and policymakers come in directing decisions toward or away from an arena.

Policymakers recognize this import when they discuss different policy mechanisms. The instruments they choose to translate policy goals into concrete actions can determine the success or failure of the policy. In the process of studying educational reform, McDonnell and Elmore (1987) identified four categories of instruments that policymakers employ: mandates, inducements, capacity building, and system changing. McDonnell and Elmore argue that policymakers rely on mandates because they lack systematic knowledge about the relative effectiveness of alternative mechanisms. Their framework of alternative policy instruments outlines some of the "key relationships among problem definition, instrument choice, organizational context, implementation, and effect" (McDonnell & Elmore, 1987, p. 149). In particular, they note differences in resources available (rules, money, or authority), expected outcomes, major costs and benefits, and time horizons.

Practitioners recognize that there are different arenas too. For the practitioner, making strategic decisions is as much a matter of knowing how to move decisions from one cell to another as it is of acquiring craft knowledge of techniques within a cell. The qualitative dimension that underlies "strategic decision making" is what to decide and where to decide it. Thus the argument in this chapter rests partly on the work of problem framing (Allison, 1971; Bolman & Deal, 1984, 1991).

Individual decisions connote biases, worldviews, and cognitive frames. Group decisions involve the problem of combination or synthesis. External decisions involve more explicit political calculation and maneuvering. It is the combination of these approaches that gives us a full view of strategy (Schwenk, 1988a, 1988b).

In the following sections of this chapter, we explore each of the cells shown in Table 2.1. First, we illustrate discrete decision making, which occurs both internally and externally. Then, description turns to incremental decisions. These descriptions of discrete and incremental decision making lay the groundwork for a closing discussion about strategy making through directing decisions to different arenas.

Strategy as Discrete Decisions

As the top half of Table 2.1 shows, discrete decisions may take on vastly different characteristics depending on the nature of the decision.

Conventional Big Decisions: The Gang's All Here

Conventional big decisions are decided through a system of unitary authority. These decisions are made at the top because the participants at the top are legitimated to make them. They use routines of information gathering and inspection that are generally preapproved and understood. In what is probably the most thorough study of its kind, Hickson and his colleagues (Hickson et al., 1986) extracted the most important elements of big decisions by studying more than 150 major managerial decisions in 30 British organizations ranging from 100 to more than 57,000 employees.

They describe three different group decision processes:

Sporadic: often multiyear processes beset with disrupting delays and interruptions, more sources of expertise with greater variance in the confidence placed on information and views, more informal interaction, and final authority at a higher level than the decision participants.

Fluid: relatively speedy processes handled in relatively formal settings, much discussion channeled through prearranged subgroups, and fewer disruptions.

Constructed: less scope for negotiation, made at a level below highest management, generally relying on internal rather than external experts, and usually less complex with less activity.

The complexity and politicality of decisions statistically mapped on the three decision types produce three classifications:

Vortex-Sporadic Decisions. Vortex decisions are infrequent, weighty, and controversial matters from which "eddies run throughout the higher echelons to suck everyone and everything into swirls of activity" (Hickson et al., 1986, p. 174). These decisions tend to be complex although not necessarily precursive or determinant of future decisions. They involve contentious political interests and may be influenced externally.

School districts can create vortex-sporadic decision arenas by marking a decision as highly strategic. The San Diego Unified School District used this technique to initiate its reform and restructuring agenda in the 1980s (Payzant, 1992). However, it is more common for unplanned events to pull a district into a spin of decision making that can often disrupt normal operations. Large-scale labor conflicts have this effect, as do situations defined as emergencies. The shootings of children in the Stockton, California, schools and the deadly hurricane that destroyed both schools and housing in Miami, Florida, had a vortex effect.

Tractable-Fluid Decisions. Tractable decisions are less complex and serious, but they often have diffuse consequences. These decisions are rare, but appear to have consequences for the future. Politically, they are noncontentious. Fewer specialists from the organization are involved and fewer are called in from outside.

Conventional contract negotiations, for either land or labor, have this characteristic. They are usually handled by internal experts with only marginal participation by others, yet the results set patterns for the future, a consequence that gives these decisions the precursiveness mentioned by Hickson and colleagues.

Familiar-Constructed Decisions. Familiar decisions concern more recognizable and limited questions. They are the least complex or unusual, and their consequences are limited. These decisions follow standard operating procedures. "Management can guide this sort of decision along constructed pathways which have been traveled by its predecessors" (Hickson et al., 1986, p. 185).

It is in these decisions that standard operating procedures become the most evident. Allison's (1969, 1971) description of standard operating procedures during the Cuban missile crisis is most telling.

Individual Strategy: The Single Informed Mind

In an entrepreneurial setting, or in other organizational settings subject to close personal control, a leader's schemata or worldview becomes the organization's strategy-making mechanism. Mintzberg and Waters (1982) tracked strategy making at Steinbergs, a Canadian retailer led for more than a half century by one person, Sam Steinberg, who guided the business from a mom-and-kids enterprise to a multidivisional corporation with sales of more than $1 billion. Over the course of 57 years there were only six strategic shifts, three major ones. After concluding their studies, Mintzberg and Waters argued, "The conception of a novel strategy is an exercise in synthesis, which typically is best carried out in a single, informed brain" (p. 496).

From Drucker's (1976) case examples to Peters and Waterman's (1982) heroic managers, we are presented with pictures of individuals who so deeply "knew" their organization that they could walk confidently into an uncertain future even when things looked bleak. As Mintzberg and Waters (1982) said of Sam Steinberg, "No other mode of strategy making can provide the degree of deliberateness and of integration of strategies with each other and with the environment. None can provide so clear and complete a vision of direction, yet also allow the flexibility to elaborate and rework that vision" (pp. 495-496).

Because schools are not proprietorships, the parallels to individual ownership are not exact, but the stories of so-called turn-around schools frequently feature a dominant individual, often a school principal. Lightfoot's (1983) chronicles of "good schools" portray Norris Hogans as the authoritarian and visionary leader of George Washington Carver High School in Atlanta. The bullhorn-toting Joe Clark (Clark & Picard, 1989) and the reclusive Doc Littky (Kammeraad-Campbell, 1989) carved quite different images for themselves, but each effectively ruled his organization. Each also ran afoul of higher authorities.

Looking at the set of decisions that typify corporate strategic planning, we are struck by the extent to which relatively few of these decisions are available to educational organizations. Unlike private companies, school districts are highly restricted in decisions about entering or leaving different markets and in the ability to flee from adverse situations. For example, troubled urban areas host many schools but few shopping centers. There are no school district analogies to W. R. Grace's abandonment of the shipping business or R. J. Reynolds's transmutation beyond tobacco.

In many ways, individual school districts are more like franchises than like corporations. Their core activities and many of their operating requirements are defined externally. Although school districts explore coordinated children's services and the addition of specialty magnet schools, they are not generally free to decide that "special ed looks like a loser; let's close down the programs."

Although there is great variation by state, school districts generally are fiscally constrained. Most lack independent taxing authority. Most are highly limited in charges they can make for fees and services. Unlike corporations, they do not issue stock and their ability to take on debt is limited.

Bomb Throwers, Pressure Groups, and the Public Good

All these factors increase the importance of external strategic decision making. External decision making requires a political logic that varies according to the type of politics involved.

Unitary Politics—Reform in the 1980s

In the first decades of this century, school districts were formed around an assumption of a unified public interest. Defining public education in this way allowed school districts, particularly the large ones, to create a tightly integrated pyramid structure and a strong unity of command (Weeres, 1992). The organization that we recognize as a strong, centralized public bureaucracy arose because of relatively widespread agreement among community elites that educational expertise could be politically neutral and thus should be independent of city governments and political machines.

This historical period ushered in the strong school superintendency and the application of scientific management principles to schooling

(Callahan, 1962; Tyack & Hansot, 1982). It also ushered in the idea that public policy surrounding schools should have broad-based support, which requires prominent, powerful, and public sponsorship. Koppich (1990) calls this "high politics" and illustrates its application to the major pieces of legislation enacted over several decades. In the case of the Elementary and Secondary Education Act (ESEA), the president and high-ranking congressional leaders, as well as civil rights groups and religious and labor organizations, sponsored the measure (Koppich, 1990).

How is high politics created? First, there is a belief that something beyond individual interest both exists and is powerful. Within the past few years, authors from different disciplines have rediscovered that aspect of public life that goes beyond self-interest (Mansbridge, 1990). Psychologists have become interested in "prosocial behavior" and political scientists have been fascinated by situations in which public officials cast votes against the apparent self-interest of their constituents.

Second, consent has to be generated. This requires "that the political argument inevitably must be formulated in terms broader than that of the self-interest of the individual or the group making the claim" (Kelman, 1987, p. 93). Relative to most other nations, the United States is a highly heterogeneous nation that relies on what Greider (1992) calls its "civic faith" to overcome vast differences among its people (p. 15).

Most urban school reforms of the 1980s began with an effort to identify and mobilize public interest around reforming the schools. In Rochester, Cincinnati, Louisville, San Diego, and other cities, a carefully cultivated civic agreement served as a precursor to reform and allowed groups with strong interests to look toward overarching goals (Hill, Wise, & Shapiro, 1989; Kerchner & Koppich, 1993). In Pittsburgh, Superintendent Richard Wallace made extensive use of school and community surveys and meetings to forge consensus around six goals that guided the district for a decade (Kerchner, 1993b) Thus high politics maintains the possibility of unitary interests and consensus around the common good.

Interest Group Politics—Legitimating Collective Bargaining

Interest group politics does not require an assumption of overriding public good. A good decision is a bargain that results from negotiations—lobbying, campaigning, and otherwise representing competing legitimate interests. Educational strategy thus becomes the balancing of interests.

Interest group politics are, of course, not exclusive to decisions made external to school organizations. Like other organizations, schools possess well-established competing interests. But the established routines and the internal hierarchy of organizations dampen explicit displays of individual or departmental interest. In external settings, the strategy of decision making quickly recognizes the presence and legitimacy of competing interests and those stakeholders attached to particular interests.

Parents supporting special education, the caucus of Latino principals, and the religious opponents of sex education are representative of the hundreds of organized interests found in public education. The logic of strategic decision making through interest representation is found in political systems models such as Easton's (1965), where the political process aggregates individual groups around articulated demands on the system. Strategic decisions emerge in the form of rules, laws, contracts, and regulations (Johnson, 1983; Kerchner & Mitchell, 1988; Shedd & Bacharach, 1991).

Nowhere is the operation of interest politics more visible than in the development of collective bargaining arrangements for school employees and particularly for teachers. The adoption of collective bargaining legitimated the idea that employees possessed interests that diverged from those of school managers and board members and that employees had the right to pursue those interests.

Although, as we discuss in following sections, collective bargaining agreements often produce incremental change, contracts also signal discrete changes in educational strategy. In 1987, Jefferson County Public Schools and the Jefferson County Teachers Association contract legitimated pursuit of substantial decentralization through what the contract calls "participative management" (Jefferson County Board of Education, 1988). As has been the case in other school districts, the contract allowed teachers to vote to assume substantial decisional participation in the school's personnel, program, and budget.

Gaining support for the contract involved articulating a problem—in the Jefferson County case, improving school performance and responsiveness. Then, both union leaders and managers needed to aggregate support for the idea. On the union side, teachers needed to become convinced that voting for participative management would not destroy the strong union they had built. Managers and school board members needed to become convinced that the schools would not fly out of control. All sides needed to believe that the contract addressed their interests.

Revolutionary Politics—Regime Overthrow

The object of revolutionary politics is not to reach agreement and find mutually acceptable solutions, but to overthrow the existing order. Much of educational politics in the 1980s and 1990s has been revolutionary in character, an effort to deliver a set of "system shocks" to the existing institution. Vouchers, tax credits, and privatization schemes are explicit attempts to decrease the internal control of existing schools and districts.

Small-regime overthrows are common in public education. The work of Iannaccone and Lutz (1970) tracks the relationship between involuntary turnover among school board members and the departure of school superintendents. These periodic changes result in what they call the dissatisfaction theory of politics (Iannaccone & Lutz, 1978) that has been extended to turning-point elections in national politics (Iannaccone, 1988).

Whereas most school reforms do not represent regime overthrows, some do, the largest and most vivid case being the Chicago school reforms beginning in the late 1980s. The Chicago Public Schools, tagged by then Secretary of Education William Bennett as "the worst in America" (Hess, 1991, p. 6), became the target of a massive coalition between business interests, legislators, the mayor's office, and established critics of the schools.

In response, Illinois Governor James Thompson signed the Chicago School Reform Act, creating strong local school councils composed of parents, teachers, citizens, and principals at each school house. Power was to shift from a large central office to each school site, and a bureaucratic, command-oriented system was to yield to a decentralized and democratic model. The traditional pyramid-shaped organizational structure was to be inverted. The existing insiders, particularly the central administration and the Chicago Teachers Union, found their traditional sources of influence circumscribed. Ayres (1993) calls the change "Chicago's Perestroika."

Similar externally driven changes can be found in Detroit, where a school reform board has attempted to redefine authority downward in the system ("Will Empowerment Weaken Teachers?" 1992), and in Denver, where Governor Roy Romer intervened in a labor dispute to produce an agreement that redefined authority in ways that neither the teachers' union nor the central administration wished (Murphy, 1992).

Regime overthrow produces a classic conflict cycle, a change in the social system that is hardly ever thought of as strategic decision making by those within the existing ruling coalition (Cyert & March, 1963). But one would be hard pressed to understand educational change without knowing the history of how insiders and outsiders battled for position (Dahrendorf, 1959; Ravitch, 1983).

Strategy Through Incremental Decisions

Discrete decisions are essentially calculatively rational, whether the rationality is driven by political, economic, or cultural values. Incremental decisions follow an adaptive logic. "An action is taken; the world responds to the action; and the individual [or collective] infers something about the world and then adapts" (Lave & March, 1975, p. 248). Adaptive rationality rules the world of mouse mazes and pigeon cages, of falling in love and of learning the ropes at a new job.

Adaptive rationality is consistent with modern organizational theory, which rests on recognizing limits to cognitive rationality. The inability to optimize separates Simon's (1957) "administrative man" from economic rationality. If one cannot be calculatingly rational, then one can, in Lindblom's (1959) words, "muddle through." Lindblom recognized the inherent value of small, measured steps that solve immediate problems. Small steps lead to an intertwining of values and empirical analysis. "The idea that values should be clarified, in advance of examination of alternative policies, is appealing." But often there are "no preferences in the absence of public discussion sufficient to bring an issue to the attention of the electorate" (Lindblom, 1959, p. 81).

"Little Tries" and TQM

Adaptive rationality makes particular sense in organizations, such as schools, that have a weak technology. With a weak technology, it has been historically difficult to link changes in inputs with changes in outputs and determine a production function (Odden, 1992).

Under these circumstances, Gage's (1985) findings about progress apply: Few reforms will yield huge outcome effects, but many will yield a 2% to 3% difference. Programs that aim at easy targets can quickly become part of a school's repertoire. Making many changes insulates schools from the accusation that any single change has failed. Reformers in Jefferson County, Kentucky, have adopted Schlechty's phrase "little tries" to express this philosophy. Individually, changes need not be particularly heroic or radical, but the combined effect is significant (Kerchner, 1993a).

Although strategies developed on the basis of successive changes carry the danger of circularity (Arrow, 1950), they also present the possibility of continuous improvement. The underlying idea behind Deming's work and the total quality management (TQM) movement is that cycles of analysis and improvement carried out at low levels in an organization can reveal systemic problems that could be addressed by discrete large-scale strategies (Deming, 1986; Gitlow & Gitlow, 1986; Mann, 1986; Sherkenbach, 1986; Walton, 1986). Only attention to the details of service or production can create the needed insights. TQM processes are similar to the constructed-familiar type of discrete decisions in that they become an organizational routine, but they operate continually. Deming's process can also trigger discrete decision processes. His statistical method distinguishes between "ordinary" and "special" causes of quality variation. Ordinary causes occur at the individual and work group levels and workers respond directly to them. However, special causes of variation lie outside of direct intervention by workers, who, under Deming's philosophy, are not responsible for correcting the system. That is management's job.

TQM is beginning to be infused in schools across the country. The American Association of School Administrators and the National Education Association have begun training teams of teachers and administrators in its principles. Statistical controls help employees to know when to intervene in a process and when to leave it alone. For example, students in Mount Edgecumbe High School in Alaska monitored teachers to determine how they spent their time in class. Although teachers believed they were encouraging experiential learning, the data showed that they spent more time lecturing. As a result, the school altered its schedule from seven 50-minute periods to four 90-minute periods to provide more time for active learning (Olson, 1992).

The Pinellas County (Florida) School District has wholeheartedly pursued the philosophy of total quality management. The district, which is one of the largest in the United States, began to move toward site-based management in the 1980s. It redoubled its efforts in 1991 when the state mandated that all schools use site-based management by 1993-1994. Pinellas officials recognized that the sheer size of the district (125 schools, 14,000 employees, almost 96,000 students) would require an overarching management strategy to avoid chaos (Lytle, 1990).

The rediscovery of Deming's work in the United States effectively fused statistical techniques pioneered in America with the Japanese management tradition, providing a means to connect reflection and work-site calculation with organizational-level decision making. In particular, the *Ringi* system emphasizes participation in organizational decision making by encouraging consensus among all concerned members of the organization. By circulating proposals both horizontally and vertically in the hierarchy, an initiator attempts to attain an informal agreement before formal procedures begin. This preliminary discussion and approval often reduce the problems associated with implementation.

To achieve the same effect in American schools, the participants often have to be trained in consensus building. In Louisville, Kentucky, the Gheens Professional Development Academy provided a safe haven for teachers and administrators to explore consensus decision making (Kerchner, 1993a). In Glenview, Illinois, the teachers' union and the school recognize that consensus decision making is not simply a vague phrase; it is a new process (Smylie, 1993). They incorporated the concept into their constitution: "Consensus means general agreement and concord. For consensus to exist, it is not necessary for every participant to agree in full, but it is necessary for every participant to be heard and, in the end, for none to believe that the decision violates his or her conviction. It is not necessary that every person consider the decision the best one." Thus, for consensus decision making to be effective in schools, it must be legitimated and protected by the contract, and the decision participants must be trained in its techniques.

"Muddling Through"

Comprehensive rational policy formulation, advocated by some analysts, is impossible in actual practice. Because the underlying values and objectives of a policy are frequently unclear or contested, the initial step of the formulation process is thwarted. And because no policymaker can grasp, let alone anticipate, all the consequences of a particular policy choice, a systematic comparison of the alternatives is also impossible. Instead, policymakers must "muddle through" the complex problems they encounter.

Because policymakers face numerous constraints—political, legal, financial, cognitive, and otherwise—they must restrict their attention to a small number of political values and policy alternatives. These constraints require policymakers to engage in "successive limited comparisons" (Lindblom, 1959). Limited comparisons consider only those ways in which a proposed policy differs from the status quo. Thus, rather than reinventing the wheel with each policy proposal, the policymakers can concentrate on the facts relevant to the marginal differences between the alternatives.

This approach is particularly appropriate in policy arenas where the values are vague or disputed. Although policymakers may not agree on the criteria for evaluating the alternatives, they can often agree on the specific proposals. Lindblom (1959) argues that this agreement on the policy itself is the only test of its "correctness." By limiting the debate about the values and objectives of a policy, the incremental approach decreases the policymakers' need for information about these elements. Again, they need only consider the marginal differences in the policy alternatives.

By making limited comparisons and incremental changes, policymaking becomes "a process of successive approximation of some desired objective in which what is desired itself continues to change under reconsideration" (Lindblom, 1959, p. 413). Incremental change intimates the probable consequences of a policy if it is pursued further and allows policymakers to remedy errors quickly. It does not require accurate predictions or full-blown theories, which Lindblom contends are impossible anyway.

Critics of Lindblom's method argue that incrementalism is trapped in its own framework. Policymakers can continue to choose policies that are foolish or ineffective, and they can overlook good policies that develop outside the accepted chain of command and are therefore "politically irrelevant" or policies that make nonincremental changes and are therefore "politically impossible."

The pattern of muddling through is clearly seen in the pattern of school district and court responses to desegregation since the *Brown* decision over 40 years ago. The decision's phrase "all deliberate speed" set up a situationally specific requirement that courts fashion a remedy that fit the circumstances of each city. Thus, in different locations across the country, courts approved plans to bus children, provide interdistrict transfers, create magnet schools, and expend additional resources on schools where it was impractical to decrease racial isolation.

In virtually all cases, the decisions were disjointed and incremental, the subject of multiple hearings and rulings. Indeed, over the decades, the underlying issue appeared to change. As Colton and Uchitelle (1992) argue, until the mid-1970s the politics of desegregation were almost exclusively focused on racial balance with the most heated issue being "forced busing." However, by the mid-1970s many urban school districts served populations that were largely children of color. The issue changed from balance to educational adequacy. In a 1990 case involving the Kansas City Schools, the U.S. Supreme Court held that the school district could be ordered to levy taxes to pay for remediation of segregation even though the taxes were in excess of the state's tax limitation statutes (*Missouri v. Jenkins*, 110 S.Ct. 1651).

Dreeben and Barr's (1983) description of school desegregation and special education implementation draws the distinction between an effective civil rights remedy and changes in the way schools operate. Access does "not necessarily guarantee that schools will operate differently to provide, in a technological and productive sense, better learning" (Dreeben & Barr, 1983, p. 87).

Strategy Making Behind the Classroom Door

The inability of school hierarchies to effectively control their internal environments has long been recognized (Bidwell, 1965). As a consequence, strategic decisions are often effectively made by individual teachers in their classrooms, and ironically, the ability of teachers to make strategic decisions *increases* as the number of external mandates and rules rises.

Teachers become what Lipsky (1980) calls street-level bureaucrats, essentially choosing which of a large and internally conflicting set of rules they will follow. Lipsky's street-level bureaucrats—the teachers, police officers, social workers, court officers, and many other public employees—live in a "corrupted world of service" (Lipsky, 1980, p. xiii). They, like Horace, the high school teacher in Sizer's (1984) work, make compromises within a world of constraints where there is a severe mismatch between the job to be done and the resources available. Thus they acquire substantial discretion in determining the nature, amount, and quality of services rendered to any particular client. "Judges decide who shall receive a suspended sentence and who shall receive maximum punishment. Teachers decide who will be suspended and who will remain in school, and they make subtle determinations about who is teachable" (Lipsky, 1980, p. 13).

In a system suffering from severe resource inadequacies, teachers and principals continue to muddle through and make the system work. By knowing the ins and outs of the system, principals in Chicago were able to increase their resources despite the cutbacks that accompanied the financial crisis in 1979 (Morris, Crowson, Porter-Gehrie, & Hurwitz, 1984). So the street-level bureaucrats endure, often making decisions based more on survival than on strategy. As the financial situation worsens and the infrastructure falters, "even greater confusion and 'anarchy' seem to prevail in city decision making" (Crowson & Boyd, 1991, p. 90).

Individuals also set strategies through socialization. Teachers largely learn how to teach from other teachers, not from their formal training. Teachers spend up to 10,000 hours as children in the presence of teachers, and this experience has a powerful effect on their ideas about what teaching is and their image of a good teacher (Lortie, 1975).

The socialization to teaching is made even more important by the relative isolation of the act of teaching from other adults. As Kidder (1989) so aptly titled it, teaching is an occupation carried out *Among Schoolchildren*. It is not surprising, then, that much of the critique of teaching rests on its inability to examine, make explicit, and hand down the *accumulated* wisdom of generations of teachers. In strategic terms, teaching is blighted by a lack of institutional memory and an inability to engage in incremental group decision making. The isolation of teaching provides room for creativity, but it prevents the aggregation of teacher lore into occupational wisdom (Little, 1985; Lortie, 1975; Shulman & Sykes, 1983).

Strategy Making Across the Boundaries

As we have shown, the logic of decision is different for each of the major types of strategy making. Given a different decision logic and process, strategies decided in one setting are likely to differ from those made in other settings. If this is the case, then the important strategic decision arises in one's ability to move decisions from one arena to another.

Empowering Individuals Versus Groups

Strong business owners and strong principals illustrate the strength of individual decision making. Street-level bureaucrats illustrate their ability to persevere in situations where organizations are in decline. However, individualism also carries a price. A single unified mind approaching a decision has no limits other than its own. When entrepreneurial decisions are wrong, they are often gloriously and dramatically wrong. Schwenk (1988b) writes of the decisional schema acquired by John DeLorean at General Motors and carried into the ill-fated vehicle that bore his name. High production and exciting cars made DeLorean successful at GM. It also led him to scale production of his own cars at a rate six times that which marketing firms estimated initial sales potential to be, and ultimately to attempt rescue of his firm through illegal means.

Creating proprietorships is a prime means of individualizing strategic decisions, and much of the critique of current school bureaucracy is aimed toward strategic individualization. When Chubb and Moe (1990) speak of schools that understand what they are, they are speaking of strongly empowering individual leaders by removing external constraints. They envision a system where "schools control their own admissions—they set their own criteria and make their own decisions about programs, methods, structure, and virtually everything else pertaining to the kind of education they provide; and with teachers running their own shops, many of the preexisting formal rules imposed through collective bargaining and democratic control have either been waived or ignored" (Chubb & Moe, 1990, p. 213).

School-based management schemes that vest control in the principal are prime examples. Perhaps the most powerful of these are the charter initiatives in the United States that would make individual schools fiscally independent of school districts. This change is exactly the force of the 1988 Educational Reform Act in Britain, which allows individual schools to opt out of the management of the local school authority and receive grants directly from the central government.

Professionalization is also a means to individualization. Traditionally, professionals have been allowed to exercise significant social control and discretion because of the specialized knowledge or skills they command. Recognizing teachers as professionals increases their autonomy and discretion, effectively empowering them as individuals (e.g., Shedd & Bacharach, 1991).

Paradoxically, many decentralizing reforms move decisions from individuals to groups. School site management plans in Miami, Pittsburgh, Chicago, and Jefferson County, Kentucky, vary markedly, but each endorses group decisions (Kerchner & Koppich, 1993). Teachers who greet reforms with visions of individual empowerment are often dismayed by the extent to which previously closed doors—such as their classrooms—become the object of group decisions. Frequently, these teachers recoil, complaining of "process paralysis" or simply a need to be left alone (Malen, 1992; Malen, Ogawa, & Kranz, 1990).

Adaptive influence on strategy, the kind that is present among street-level bureaucrats, can also be increased or decreased. Organizational anarchists know that one way to gain discretion is to overload the system. Cases of extreme financial stress generally decrease supervision of individual service providers. Central office personnel reductions in Chicago and Los Angeles, for example, have created islands of relatively uninspected autonomy in the schools.

The opposite effect, decreasing individual ability to strategize, occurs when service responses are to be standardized. Either direct supervision or process-specific rules markedly decreases the ability of individuals to respond to school problems. Tyack's (1974) "one best system" characterization of urban schools in the United States arose through the external engineering of curriculum, lessons, and school management.

Marketization Versus Socialization of Services

Over the past decade no public policy option has proven more controversial than that of marketizing education. Marketizers argue that the current system is dysfunctionally rule-bound, the result of cycles of interest group intervention followed by enforcement mandates. The present institution of education, Chubb and Moe (1990) argue, "tends to promote organizational characteristics that are ill-suited to the effective performance of American schools" (p. 21). Marketization, on the other hand, would allow schools to become more flexible and responsive to changing preferences. Thus Chubb and Moe advocate choice as a panacea. "Taken seriously, choice is not a system-preserving reform. It is a revolutionary reform that introduces a new system of public education" (Chubb & Moe, 1990, p. 217).

Introducing market forces into education is often thought of as radical decentralization (Chubb & Moe, 1990; Friedman, 1955). But structuring represents very high-level strategizing. "Structuring the market to serve a public purpose is in fact the opposite of leaving matters to the 'free market'—it is a form of *intervention* in the market" (Osborne & Gaebler, 1992, p. 283).

Finding the right combination of bureaucratic and market mechanisms to deliver an educational service requires consideration of the characteristics of each as an alternative policy mechanism. Both bureaucratic and market solutions can be found to promote the four core values in education: choice, equity, excellence, and efficiency (Kerchner & Boyd, 1988).

To increase client choice in education, policymakers can pursue "demand-side" interventions, which use the market, or "supply-side" interventions, which work through the bureaucracy. Supply-side interventions include administrative decentralization, magnet schools, and transfer regulations, whereas demand-side interventions include vouchers, tax credits, and independent contractors. Supply-side reforms can promote equity in education by increasing the bureaucracy's ability to respond to client demands. On the other hand, equity in education can be promoted by increasing the ability of individual clients to gain access to the education they want.

Bureaucratic reforms pursue excellence by defining a single, unified standard of education, whereas a market approach would support multiple standards, educational "brand names" that cater to quite different ideas of quality. Ultimately, the question of efficiency in education comes down to the advantages of regulating the market versus managing the bureaucracy.

Kerchner and Boyd (1988) identified three policy clusters that blend these social values.

Market professionalism concentrates on establishing teachers as professionals and pays little attention to schools as organizations. Professional teachers maintain a monopoly over service provision, and quality is controlled through professional associations that enforce rigorous training and entrance examinations. Schools are responsible for attracting and retaining students.

Bureaucratic entrepreneurship centers on establishing diversity within existing school districts. Schools "differentiate themselves according to learning style, educational philosophy, and organizational structure" (Kerchner & Boyd, 1988, p. 112). As a result, both schools and students participate in the marketplace. However, the overall structure remains fairly bureaucratic. This policy cluster is most commonly played out in school-site management reforms.

Community democracy views schools as "membership benefit districts" that could be organized geographically or based on common values. Schools would operate as "very small governments, much like an owners association in a condominium or co-operative apartment building" (Kerchner & Boyd, 1988, p. 113). This option combines political and economic interests into a single marketplace. However, it creates serious concerns about equity and civil rights.

These policy clusters demonstrate that markets and bureaucracies are not incompatible. Tools from each tradition can be used to structure schools and to provide educational services.

Crisis Versus Standard Operating Systems

Some organizational crises, such as a fire in a school or a riot at a football game, are recognized spontaneously. Others are declared. For example, *A Nation at Risk* was worded and presented to deliberately create a crisis in public education. Its bellicose rhetoric, "the rising tide of mediocrity" and "an act of war" by an unfriendly power, were phrases intended to spur alarm and response. It clearly succeeded. In a matter of months, public education moved from obscurity to the center of public debate. The educational reform movement of the 1980s and 1990s sustained public attention of much greater intensity and duration than the 18 months that are usual for a public issue.

Deliberately elevating an issue to crisis proportions is a powerful intervention (Kerchner & Schuster, 1982). Crisis legitimates a chief executive's personal involvement in matters that would normally be subordinated, allows lower level subordinates to deliberate with top managers, and creates an expectation of path-breaking change.

The management of crisis proceeds under its own rules (Caplow, 1983). Once a crisis is declared, a manager or responsible official must appear on the scene personally. To declare a crisis and not to respond to it personally is to invite harsh criticism and retribution. A crisis council may be formed, resources mobilized, and a plan enacted.

The National Commission's declaration of crisis was a deliberate choice intended to seize a place for education on the public policy agenda (Cobb & Elder, 1972). Secretaries of Education Terrel H. Bell and William J. Bennett made masterful use of the bully pulpit to gain media attention and reshape the public policy agenda (Boyd, 1990; Clark & Astuto, 1986; Jung & Kirst, 1986).

Politically, the strategy was perfectly attuned to that of the Reagan administration, calling attention to the failings of education and placing responsibility on the states for a response (McNeil, 1985). The states responded with extensive legislation in nearly all cases and hefty budget increases in many. The effect was both to increase the public policy attention given to education and to recast educational policy from the equity criteria that had guided it from the mid-1960s to concern for excellence and standards (Boyd & Kerchner, 1988; Clark & Astuto, 1986).

Unfortunately, enactment or recognition of a crisis also requires response and a declaration that the crisis has been solved. In the case of the 1980s education crisis, as in the case of the 1960s War on Poverty, no declaration of success leading to a logical end of the crisis was possible. Unresolved crises lead to disillusionment and disaffection.

However, not declaring a crisis or otherwise suspending the rules allows organizational routines and standard operating procedures to take hold and govern decision patterns. (This assumes, of course, that routines exist for the problem at hand.) Managers who seek stability create and intensify these routines. Each of the same school districts that created external mandates to initiate their reform efforts also created internal restructuring councils to *routinize* the changes. Notably, Pittsburgh, Miami, and San Diego schools created such entities. These reforms illustrate the importance of moving between discrete and incremental decisions in the same reform process. As Starbuck and Nystrom (1981) note, "A well designed organization is not a stable solution to achieve, but a developmental process to be kept active" (p. xx).

Mandates and Revolutions

Although by no means absolute, managers can strongly influence a decision's discreteness or incrementalism through structuring the decision process. In general, the more familiar the decision, the more moderate the process. Routine, periodic decisions, such as setting the annual budget, are unlikely to produce novel ideas or bold departures from the past. Although the decisions may involve serious issues, such as budget cutbacks, they are unlikely to produce new direction or leadership. Preplanned organizational routines take over (Allison, 1971; Hickson et al., 1986).

When these organizational routines take over, process criteria are frequently substituted for outcome criteria. The question becomes "Did the group use a good decision process?" rather than "Was the decision successful?" Public bureaucracies, in particular, show a marked tendency toward judging decision participants based on procedural propriety. Organizations adopt or accept criteria that are independent of the efficient coordination and control of production activities (Meyer & Rowan, 1978). This universal process has been defined as "the iron law of ossification" (Peterson, 1981, p. 72).

However, a manager can transform the incremental decision into a discrete decision in at least two ways:

Create a Mandate. Managers can bind themselves and their organizations to making large, discrete decisions by creating an external mandate for change. Virtually all of the school districts that have taken on large-scale restructuring or revitalization in the past decade used prestigious external boards or commissions to declare that change was necessary (Hill et al., 1989; Kerchner, Koppich, King, & Weeres, 1990). The schools in both Cincinnati and San Diego created external commissions to create a change agenda.

Define a Large Decision. Less dramatic and more internal, chief executives can create ad hoc committees specifically to take on large decisions. In higher education, this device has been used to address problems that proved intractable through faculty senates, administrative councils, or other conventional means (Keller, 1983).

Conclusion

Strategic decisions in education extend beyond big organizational decisions and frequently occur outside of rationalized processes, such as strategic planning. Strategic decisions occur outside school organizations as well as inside, and at the individual level as well as among groups. Decisions made in each of these arenas take on different characteristics. They have different decisional logics, and the rules and processes for participation vary. Moving decisions from one decision arena to another yields a different decision process and quite likely a different outcome. Strategy lies as much in moving a decision to a favorable arena as it does in making the judgment itself.

The institution of education as we know it is the product of different decisional arenas and the ability of institutional constituents to establish and control the rules for decisions in them. Labor statutes and a canon of practice powerfully influence the arena of collective bargaining and the extent to which educational strategy issues from labor contracts and derivative decisions. Accrediting agencies and disciplinary associations, such as the National Council of Teachers of English, define the boundaries of acceptable practice and create the cognitive structures under which teachers strategize in their own classrooms. State and federal statutes, thousands of them, create a web of constraints and powers that, in effect, turn compliance into strategic enactment. Much grand strategy in education is found in the construction of these arenas.

References

Allison, G. T. (1969). Conceptual models and the Cuban missile crisis. *American Political Science Review, 63,* 689-718.

Allison, G. T. (1971). *Essence of decision.* Boston: Little, Brown.

Arrow, K. (1950). A difficulty with the concept of social welfare. *Journal of Political Economy, 58,* 4.

Ayres, W. (1993). Chicago: A restless sea of social forces. In C. T. Kerchner & J. E. Koppich (Eds.), *A union of professionals: Unions and management in turbulent times* (pp. 313-343). New York: Teachers College Press.

Berger, P. L., & Luckmann, T. (1967). *The social construction of reality.* New York: Doubleday.

Bidwell, C. E. (1965). The school as a formal organization. In J. G. March (Ed.), *Handbook of organizations* (pp. 972-1022). Chicago: Rand McNally.

Bolman, L. G., & Deal, T. E. (1984). *Modern approaches to understanding and managing organizations.* San Francisco: Jossey-Bass.

Bolman, L. G., & Deal, T. E. (1991). *Reframing organizations: Artistry, choice, and leadership.* San Francisco: Jossey-Bass.

Boyd, W. L. (1990). How to reform schools without half trying: Secrets of the Reagan Administration. In S. B. Bacharach (Ed.), *Education reform: Making sense of it all* (pp. 42-51). Needham Heights, MA: Allyn and Bacon.

Boyd, W. L., & Kerchner, C. T. (Eds.). (1988). *The politics of excellence and choice in education: Yearbook of the Politics of Education Association.* Philadelphia, PA: Falmer.

Brown v. Board of Education of Topeka, 347 U.S. 483 (1954).

Callahan, R. E. (1962). *Education and the cult of efficiency: A study of the social forces that have shaped the administration of the public schools.* Chicago: University of Chicago Press.

Caplow, T. (1983). *Managing an organization.* Orlando, FL: Holt, Rinehart & Winston.

Chubb, J. E., & Moe, T. M. (1990). *Politics, markets and America's schools.* Washington, DC: Brookings Institution.

Clark, D., & Astuto, T. (1986, October). The significance and permanence of changes in federal education policy. *Educational Researcher,* pp. 4-13.

Clark, J., & Picard, J. (1989). *Laying down the law: Joe Clark's strategy for saving our schools.* Washington, DC: Regnery Gateway.

Cobb, R. W., & Elder, C. D. (1972). *Participation in American politics.* New York: Holt, Rinehart & Winston.

Cohen, M., & March, J. G. (1974). *Leadership and ambiguity: The American college president.* New York: McGraw-Hill.

Colton, D., & Uchitelle, S. (1992). Urban school desegregation: From race to resources. In J. G. Cibulka, R. J. Reed, & K. K. Wong (Eds.), *The politics of urban education in the United States: The 1991 yearbook of the Politics of Education Association* (pp. 137-148). Washington, DC: Falmer.

Crowson, R. L., & Boyd, W. L. (1991). Urban schools as organizations: Political perspectives. In J. G. Cibulka & K. K. Wong (Eds.), *Politics of Education Association yearbook* (pp. 87-103). New York: Falmer.

Cyert, R. M., & March, J. G. (1963). *A behavioral theory of the firm.* Englewood Cliffs, NJ: Prentice Hall.

Dahrendorf, R. (1959). *Class and class conflict in industrial society.* Stanford, CA: Stanford University Press.

Deming, W. E. (1986). *Out of the crisis.* Cambridge: MIT Center for Advanced Engineering Study.

DiMaggio, P. J., & Powell, W. W. (1983). The iron cage revisited: Institutional isomorphism and collective rationality in organizational fields. *American Sociological Review, 48,* 147-160.

DiMaggio, P. J., & Powell, W. W. (1991). Introduction. In W. W. Powell & P. J. DiMaggio (Eds.), *The new institutionalism in organizational analysis* (pp. 1-38). Chicago: University of Chicago Press.

Dreeben, R., & Barr, R. (1983). Educational policy and the working of schools. In L. Shulman & G. Sykes (Eds.), *Handbook of teaching and policy* (pp. 81-94). New York: Longman.

Drucker, P. (1976). *Management.* New York: Harper & Row.

Easton, D. (1965). *A systems analysis of political life.* New York: John Wiley.

Friedman, M. (1955). The role of government in education. In R. A. Solo (Ed.), *Economics and the public interest* (pp. 123-144). New Brunswick, NJ: Rutgers University Press.

Gage, N. L. (1985). *Hard gains in the soft sciences: The case of pedagogy.* Bloomington, IN: Phi Delta Kappa.

Gitlow, H., & Gitlow, S. J. (1986). *Deming guide to achieving quality and competitive position.* Englewood Cliffs, NJ: Prentice Hall.

Greider, W. (1992). *Who will tell the people: The betrayal of American democracy.* New York: Simon & Schuster.

Hess, G. A., Jr. (1991). *School restructuring, Chicago style.* Newbury Park, CA: Corwin.

Hickson, D. J., Butler, R. J., Cray, D., Mallory, G. O., & Wilson, D. C. (1986). *Top decisions: Strategic decision-making in organizations.* San Francisco: Jossey-Bass.

Hill, P. T., Wise, A. E., & Shapiro, L. (1989). *Educational progress: Cities mobilize to improve their schools.* Santa Monica, CA: RAND Center for the Study of the Teaching Profession.

Iannaccone, L. (1988). From equity to excellence: Political context and dynamics. In W. L. Boyd & C. T. Kerchner (Eds.), *The politics of excellence and choice in education: Yearbook of the Politics of Education Association* (pp. 49-66). Philadelphia, PA: Falmer.

Iannaccone, L., & Lutz, F. W. (1970). *Politics, power and policy: The governing of local school districts.* Columbus, OH: Charles E. Merrill.

Iannaccone, L., & Lutz, F. W. (1978). The dissatisfaction theory of governance. In F. W. Lutz & L. Iannaccone (Eds.), *Public participation in local school districts.* Lexington, MA: D. C. Heath.

Jefferson County Board of Education. (1988). *Agreement between the Jefferson County Board of Education and the Jefferson County Teachers Association: 1988-1992.* Louisville, KY: Author.

Johnson, S. M. (1983). Teacher unions in schools: Authority and accommodation. *Harvard Educational Review, 53,* 309-326.

Jung, R., & Kirst, M. (1986). Beyond mutual adaptation, into the bully pulpit: Recent research on the federal role in education. *Educational Administration Quarterly, 22*(1), 80-109.

Kammeraad-Campbell, S. (1989). *Doc: The story of Dennis Littky and his fight for a better school.* Chicago: Contemporary Books.

Keller, G. (1983). *Academic strategy: The management revolution in American higher education.* Baltimore, MD: Johns Hopkins University Press.

Kelman, S. (1987). Public choice and public spirit. *The Public Interest, 87,* 80-94.

Kerchner, C. T. (1993a). Louisville: Professional development drives a decade of school reform. In C. T. Kerchner & J. E. Koppich (Eds.), *A union of professionals: Unions and management in turbulent times* (pp. 45-76). New York: Teachers College Press.

Kerchner, C. T. (1993b). Pittsburgh: Reform in a well-managed public bureaucracy. In C. T. Kerchner & J. E. Koppich (Eds.), *A union of professionals: Unions and management in turbulent times* (pp. 77-108). New York: Teachers College Press.

Kerchner, C. T., & Boyd, W. L. (1988). What doesn't work: An analysis of market and bureaucratic failure in schooling. In W. L. Boyd & C. T. Kerchner (Eds.), *The politics of excellence and choice in education: Yearbook of the Politics of Education Association* (pp. 99-116). Philadelphia, PA: Falmer.

Kerchner, C. T., & Koppich, J. E. (1993). *A union of professionals: Unions and management in turbulent times.* New York: Teachers College Press.

Kerchner, C. T., Koppich, J. E., King, B., & Weeres, J. (1990, October). *This could be the start of something big: Labor relations reforms in the 1990s.* Paper presented at the annual meeting of the University Council for Educational Administration, Pittsburgh, PA.

Kerchner, C. T., & Mitchell, D. (1988). *The changing idea of a teachers' union.* New York: Falmer.

Kerchner, C. T., & Schuster, J. H. (1982). The uses of crisis: Taking the tide at the flood. *Review of Higher Education, 5*(3), 121-141.

Kidder, T. (1989). *Among schoolchildren.* Boston: Houghton Mifflin.

Koppich, J. (1990). *Educational reform as high politics: Toward a political theory of school reform movements.* Unpublished doctoral dissertation, University of California, Berkeley.

Lave, C. A., & March, J. G. (1975). *An introduction to models in the social sciences.* New York: Harper & Row.

Lightfoot, S. L. (1983). *The good high school: Portraits of character and culture.* New York: Basic Books.

Lindblom, C. E. (1959). The science of muddling through. *Public Administration Review, 19*(2), 79-88.

Lipsky, M. (1980). *Street-level bureaucracy: Dilemmas of the individual in public services.* New York: Russell Sage.

Little, J. W. (1985). *What schools contribute to teachers' professional development.* San Francisco: Far West Laboratory.

Lortie, D. C. (1975). *Schoolteacher: A sociological study.* Chicago: University of Chicago Press.

Lytle, V. (1990, November). The sky's the limit. *NEA Today,* pp. 4-5.

Malen, B. (1992). *Bellevue: Renewal and school decision making* (Project Report). Claremont, CA: Claremont Graduate School, Claremont Project VISION.

Malen, B., Ogawa, R. T., & Kranz, J. (1990). What do we know about school-based management? A case study of the literature—A call for research. In W. H. Clune & J. F. Witte (Eds.), *Choice and control in American education volume 2: The practice of choice, decentralization and school restructuring* (pp. 289-342). New York: Falmer.

Mann, N. (1986). *The keys to excellence: The story of the Deming philosophy.* Santa Monica, CA: Preswick.

Mansbridge, J. J. (1983). *Beyond adversary democracy.* Chicago: University of Chicago Press.

Mansbridge, J. J. (Ed.). (1990). *Beyond self-interest.* Chicago: University of Chicago Press.

March, J. G., & Olsen, J. P. (1976). *Ambiguity and choice in organizations.* Bergen, Norway: Universitesforlaget.

March, J. G., & Olsen, J. P. (1989). *Rediscovering institutions: The organizational basis of politics.* New York: Free Press.

McDonnell, L. M., & Elmore, R. F. (1987). Getting the job done: Alternative policy instruments. *Educational Evaluation and Policy Analysis, 9*(2), 133-152.

McNeil, L. (1985). Teacher culture and the irony of school reform. In P. G. Altbach, G. P. Kelly, & L. Weis (Eds.), *Excellence in education: Perspectives on policy and practice* (pp. 183-202). Buffalo, NY: Prometheus.

Meyer, J. W., & Rowan, B. (1978). The structure of educational organizations. In M. W. Meyer & Associates, *Environments and organizations* (pp. 78-109). San Francisco: Jossey-Bass.

Mintzberg, H., & Waters, J. A. (1982). Tracking strategy in an entrepreneurial firm. *Academy of Management Journal, 25,* 465-499.

Morris, V. C., Crowson, R. L., Porter-Gehrie, C., & Hurwitz, E., Jr. (1984). *Principals in action: The reality of managing schools.* Columbus, OH: Charles E. Merrill.

Murphy, M. J. (1992). *School reform and labor relations—Denver style* (Project Report). Claremont, CA: Claremont Graduate School, Claremont Project VISION.

National Commission on Excellence in Education. (1983). *A nation at risk: The imperative for educational reform, a report to the Secretary of Education.* Washington, DC: U.S. Department of Education.

Odden, A. (1992). Discovering educational productivity: An organizational approach. *Educational Evaluation and Policy Analysis, 14,* 303-305.

Olson, L. (1992, March 11). Schools getting swept up in current of business's "quality" movement. *Education Week,* pp. 1, 25-27.

Osborne, D., & Gaebler, T. (1992). *Reinventing government: How the entrepreneurial spirit is transforming the public sector from schoolhouse to statehouse, city hall to the Pentagon.* Reading, MA: Addison-Wesley.

Payzant, T. W. (1992). *Restructuring San Diego City schools: The myths and realities of systemic change* (Symposium Report No. 1). Claremont, CA: Claremont Graduate School, Institute for Education in Transformation.

Peters, T. J., & Waterman, R. H., Jr. (1982). *In search of excellence: Lessons from America's best-run companies.* New York: Harper & Row.

Peterson, R. (1981). Entrepreneurship and organization. In W. H. Starbuck & P. C. Nystrom (Eds.), *Handbook of organizational design* (pp. 65-83). New York: Oxford University Press.

Ravitch, D. (1983). *The troubled crusade.* New York: Basic Books.

Schwenk, C. R. (1988a). The cognitive perspective on strategic decision making. *Journal of Management Studies, 25*(1), 41-56.

Schwenk, C. R. (1988b). *The essence of strategic decision making.* Lexington, MA: Lexington Books.

Shedd, J. B., & Bacharach, S. B. (1991). *Tangled hierarchies: Teachers as professionals and the management of schools.* San Francisco: Jossey-Bass.

Sherkenbach, W. W. (1986). *The Deming route to quality and productivity: Roadmaps and roadblocks.* Milwaukee, WI: American Society for Quality Control.

Shulman, L. S., & Sykes, G. (Eds.). (1983). *Handbook of teaching and policy.* New York: Longman.

Simon, H. (1957). *Administrative behavior* (2nd ed.). New York: Macmillan.

Sizer, T. R. (1984). *Horace's compromise: The dilemma of the American high school.* Boston: Houghton Mifflin.

Smylie, M. (1993). Glenview, Illinois: From contract to constitution. In C. T. Kerchner & J. E. Koppich (Eds.), *A union of professionals: Unions and management in turbulent times* (pp. 174-206). New York: Teachers College Press.

Starbuck, W. H., & Nystrom, P. C. (1981). Designing and understanding organizations. In W. H. Starbuck & P. C. Nystrom (Eds.), *Handbook of organizational design.* New York: Oxford University Press.

Tyack, D. (1974). *The one best system: A history of American urban education.* Cambridge, MA: Harvard University Press.

Tyack, D., & Hansot, E. (1982). *Managers of virtue: Public school leadership in America, 1820-1980.* New York: Basic Books.

Walton, M. (1986). *The Deming management method.* New York: Dodd, Mead.

Weeres, J. G. (1992). *The organizational structure of urban education systems.* Unpublished manuscript, Claremont Graduate School, Claremont, CA.

Will empowerment weaken teachers? (1992, September 5). *Detroit Free Press,* p. 8A.

THREE

Against the Current

ORGANIZATIONAL
LEARNING IN SCHOOLS

ERIC RAIT

Engaging in organizational learning may be as natural as "talking shop" with a fellow worker about how to repair an especially testy machine, or as tortuous as a collective search for a tacit assumption that is invisibly influencing a group's work practices. Organizational learning suggests a wide range of meanings, from the exotic-sounding notion of double-loop learning to seemingly straightforward acts of adaptation to a changing environment. The revival of interest in creating learning organizations that is currently sweeping through public and private institutions points to the compelling appeal of the promise of an organizational fountain of innovation and adaptive capacity.

Such seduction, though, masks many of the problems of realizing organizational learning. Approaches to planned organizational change are often like a single spotlight that illuminates the contours of an issue from a single angle. When one shines a sole beam of light on an object, one invariably enshrouds part of that phenomenon in shadow, and

AUTHOR'S NOTE: I thank Robert Stern, Tove Hammer, Ann Martin, and the editors of this book for their thoughtful and insightful comments.

within those darkened areas may exist powerful forces that need be acknowledged and considered as well. Accordingly, assessing the viability of organizational learning methods in schools involves positioning a series of spotlights at different angles to illuminate all of the contours, including the potential sources of resistance. Establishing such a three-dimensional field of vision will facilitate the accurate and honest assessment of the challenge of organizational learning in schools.

This chapter will map out the factors that may inhibit or support processes of organizational learning in schools. First, a comprehensive definition of organizational learning will be offered. Second, a pragmatic description of the formal methods for enhancing organizational learning will ground this chapter in sufficient detail so that the reader may grasp the practical dimensions of such activity. Third, the tightly packed layers of resistance to organizational learning will be scrutinized, for they provide potent disincentives for such activity. Finally, examples will demonstrate that in spite of the many impediments along the way, the techniques of organizational learning are valuable tools for implementing change in the complex, equivocal environment of schools.

Definitions of Organizational Learning

Competing perspectives have prevented the adoption of a single definition of organizational learning. It has been defined as the detection and correction of error (Argyris & Schon, 1978), the generation of new insights or knowledge (Hedberg, 1981), feedback from previous experience that is used to choose among present alternatives (Levitt & March, 1988; March & Olsen, 1976), the adoption of new action-outcome maps (Duncan & Weiss, 1978; Meyer, 1982), and the successful restructuring of organizational problems (Simon, 1971). Huber (1991) suggests that an "entity learns if, through its processing of information, the range of its potential behaviors is changed" (p. 89).

Organizational learning occurs when organization members acquire information from the environment and generate appropriate responses to organizational issues. Such learning is distinctly organizational when it relies on the combined experiences, perspectives, and capabilities of a variety of organization members. This process is mediated by three variables that regulate the flow of information among members: the repertoire of individual cognitive strategies available, the organization's informal web of culture and norms, and the organization's formal structure. These factors determine the degree to which members will be capable of scanning, accurately interpreting, and using information in the service of concerted action (Daft & Weick, 1984). These search behaviors demand cognitive processes that extend beyond the capabilities of a single individual, for the act of sharing information requires a mutual process of translating events, developing common meanings, and assembling acceptable conceptual schemes and rules. The fact that close friends who have no competing agendas may inadvertently become entangled in this operation of shared understanding points to the challenges of such activity in more dynamic organizational settings.

Organizations embody a theory of action composed of norms, strategies, structures, and operating assumptions. Implicit within an organization's theory of action is a map of the environment and inferences about causal relations (Schon, 1986). This theory of action may be disrupted as novel situations arise for which no precedents exist. Contexts for change or learning thus result from stress, dysfunctionality within the system, or other novel situations (new technologies, structural shifts, etc.). Because most organizations cannot allocate resources in order to continually scan their environments to predict and control for the natural modulations of organizational life, learning is usually triggered by scarcity of resources, conflict, or substandard performance (Hedberg, 1981).

Cangelosi and Dill (1965) suggest that organizational learning is generally ignited by three different kinds of stress, all of which are familiar to school professionals. Discomfort stress describes the costs required by organizational members to scan and understand the environment so that the organization can make predictions about the future; how many schools have the resources to invest in such proactive searching? Performance stress is rooted in an organization's sensitivity regarding success and failure and the brittleness that often results from such concerns; how many teachers wonder whether their work is efficacious? Disjunctive stress results from divergence and conflict in the behavior of organizational members and subgroups; how many different interest groups tug at schools to achieve their desired ends? These three sources of stress may result in a gap between an organization's desired and actual performance; this chasm is the natural setting for organizational learning.

And herein lies a fundamental paradox of organizational learning. Organizations encounter situations that demand learning, which may be an arduous and disturbing process, when they are already weakened by stress and tension. Reflecting on organizational processes and events when objectives are being met and members are immersed in success is a far simpler matter than undertaking a process of inquiry when members are frustrated and the organization is in crisis.

The stress that results from the misalignment of operations and goals may be functional, for it alerts the organization to the necessity of learning and reassessing standard procedures (Hirschman, 1970). Faced with suboptimal performance, organization members may choose the "voice" option and actively seek to improve their actions. That, however, is but one response. Organization members may also choose to exit (Hirschman, 1970) from the organization or silently comply (Kolarska & Aldrich, 1980) with its reality.

Organizational learning results from inquiry, formal or informal, that mediates the shift from one theory of organization to another (Schon, 1986). This integrated cycle of reflective thought and action (Dewey, 1938) may lead to generating alternative solutions to problems, reflecting on previously unquestioned assumptions, experimenting, scanning the environment for salient information, or other activities that enable organization members to restructure their organizational knowledge base. Organizational learning is therefore the expansion of the knowledge base at the discretion of an organization or groups within the organization. Newly acquired knowledge may result in shifts in behavior and practices or in the generation of new action-outcome formulas that will determine future practices. Because new insights or capabilities may not cause any immediate effects, learning need not leave an immediate behavioral footprint.[1]

The variety of formulations of organizational learning above contain a common rhetoric of adaptation and change, but a significant discrepancy among the definitions should be noted. Whether organizational learning concerns behavioral or cognitive change is a primary point of contention. Some scholars (Levitt & March, 1988; March & Olsen, 1976) have suggested that learning occurs when a new behavioral outcome is produced, whereas others (Argyris, Putnam, & Smith, 1985; Argyris & Schon, 1974, 1978) contend that such adaptive behavior may constitute single-loop learning, which is appropriate only in stable environments characterized by a high degree of control and a rational system of organization. Under such conditions, routinized troubleshooting procedures may be effective mechanisms for correcting organizational errors.[2] The fundamental operating assumptions or governing values of the organization or individuals need not be examined or altered to achieve such change.[3] Double-loop learning is required in complex situations that demand that the governing variables directing organizational action be examined to assess whether they are contributing to the generation of systemic error

(Argyris & Schon, 1978). Learning therefore comprises both reflective inquiry and action.

To illustrate the difference between single- and double-loop learning (see Figure 3.1), consider a manufacturing unit that is switching over to a team-based system of organization. A week of training is provided to all the team members to enhance information sharing and problem-solving capabilities among organizational members. Following the training, no significant changes are noted in the communication dynamics of the team. At this juncture, single- or double-loop responses may emerge. A single-loop response would be to increase the amount of training and coaching provided to members. No further assessment of the situation would be necessary. On the other hand, a double-loop process would begin with a stage of problem setting in which the circumstances within which the team operates are examined. Such an inquiry may begin with a question like, "Are other organizational features (e.g., supervisor style, organizational structure, the reward system) creating a situation in which information sharing is considered risky?" or "What is preventing team members from using what they learned in the training program?"

Distinguishing between those situations that require single- and double-loop learning is not always a simple matter. Divergent perspectives among organization members may lead one person to believe that a certain scenario requires the rote implementation of standard operating procedures, whereas another may assert that only double-loop inquiry will reveal a problem's roots and enable proper treatment of the situation. That two people may offer such different interpretations points to the necessity of using learning frameworks in which both positions can be weighed.

Limits of Learning From Experience in Organizational Settings

It has been said that experience is the best teacher. No manual, no videotape, and few parents or friends can substitute for what a child learns when he gets up on two wheels and integrates his sense of balance and visual perception in an effort to ride his bicycle down the sidewalk. A simple learning cycle of feedback from previous behavior informs the child's behavior—he is positively reinforced for staying on the bike and punished by the sidewalk for falling off. Similarly, a working adult accumulates experience by repeatedly engaging in a series of practices over time. By storing these practices and precedents

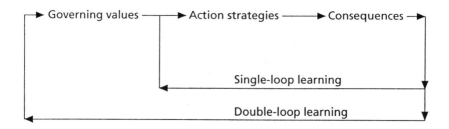

FIGURE 3.1. Single-Loop and Double-Loop Learning

and then recalling them, organization members evidently learn from their experience base. However, such learning differs from getting up on a bicycle in a number of ways.

Skinner's (1953) behavioral conceptualization of learning suggests that organization members would learn sufficiently from their experience if organizational contingencies and reinforcements were arranged in rational, consistent patterns. Every action would produce a response that would provide feedback, signaling whether the actor's behavior has achieved the desired objective. This stimulus-response cycle would supply organization members with all of the information needed to smoothly adjust their practices to the internal and external modulations of organizational life. What prevents organizations from providing the kind of immediate feedback that the sidewalk provides for the novice bicycle rider?

First, most research on learning has been conducted within the controlled environment of the psychological laboratory. Participants generally perform linear functions and tasks, and consequences in the form of feedback are immediate and unambiguous (Huber, 1991). Furthermore, most behavioral research has focused on eliciting behaviors determined by the experimenter. Contrast a laboratory setting with an organizational environment. Organizations are often characterized by multiple goals (that may compete with one another), often operate within complex and turbulent environments, encounter unanticipated alternatives, provide lagged and incomplete feedback to members, and comprise numerous influential social networks (professional, hierarchical, departmental, etc.).

In schools, the internal and external environments weaken school professionals' abilities to achieve the control required for a stimulus-response cycle of learning. Disparate objectives among various stakeholder groups (teachers, parents, principals, superintendents, state officials, and students) further muddle the process of setting goals, for their divergent agendas cannot be collapsed neatly into a unified plan. Furthermore, pupils, the "raw materials" being transformed, are unpredictable to a degree that few engineers could tolerate in their materials. Can one imagine what building a bridge would be like if architects, engineers, and construction workers could not assume a constant tensile strength of steel? In spite of these constantly shifting forces, schools are expected to define specific goals and perform in accordance with them.

In summary, lab studies based on producing predetermined modes of behavior in participants may be similar to organizational processes based on clear routines and unambiguous procedures, but they have little relevance for the intricate work processes of schools (and many other types of organizations) that require cognitive complexity and the exercise of judgment by members. The intended rationality of organizations is impaired and bounded (March & Simon, 1958) by incomplete information, imperfect feedback loops, and ignorance of alternatives. These organizational properties undermine the possibility that a comprehensive, smoothly functioning stimulus-response cycle of antecedents, behaviors, and consequences could be realized in a complex, real-life setting. If the links between actions and environmental responses are distorted, disturbed, or delayed, organization members will not always be capable of assessing the efficacy of their behavior.

Importing the behaviorist language of learning into the literature on organizational learning, Hedberg (1981) distinguished between two models of learning environments, labeling them "complete" and "incomplete" learning cycles. In a complete learning cycle, each action adds information, strengthening or weakening input-outcome linkages. Cyert and March's (1963) theory of decision making suggests that organizations comprise complete cycles of feedback loops (see Figure 3.2). Members receive feedback from the environment that enables them to present alternatives and modify their practices accordingly. Thirteen years later, March and Olsen (1976) reassessed that model and argued that systemic disruptions in the cycle obstruct people's ability to learn from experience alone. They describe four kinds of "incompleteness" in organizational learning cycles. Role constrained learning occurs when standard organizational procedures or role-based constraints weaken the connections between individual beliefs and actions. The crucial link between knowledge and practice is thus severed. Superstitious learning occurs when an organization's responses are poorly aligned with the environment, which may result from particularly complex organization-environment relations. Audience learning

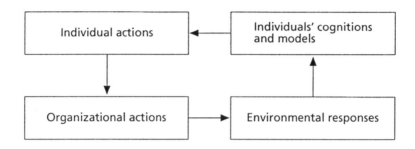

FIGURE 3.2.
SOURCE: Cyert and March, 1963.

results from weak ties between individual and organizational action, due to poor individual inferences about effectiveness, organizational politics, and resistance to change in organizations. Learning under ambiguity results from members' being unclear about organizational events and incapable of assessing why.

Schools contain both complete and incomplete learning cycles. Teachers may know that certain curricular activities will produce certain reactions in their students, and students may know that a given number of unexcused absences will have grave implications. Alongside these complete learning cycles are a multitude of incomplete ones: the principal who is unsure of the effects of a given policy on her staff, the teacher who wonders about the efficacy of small-group activities in the classroom, the superintendent who wrestles with a new budget, and so on. Incomplete learning cycles, which cripple an organization's ability to learn and adapt through the simple accrual of experience, are probably more common in schools than are complete cycles.

Cognitive and Environmental
Determinants of Organizational Learning

As discussed above, learning is both an individual and a collective phenomenon. Scrutinizing the individual and social components of learning reveals a complex aggregate of factors that determine the degree to which organizational learning is a possibility.

The most characteristic thing about mental life, over and beyond the fact that one apprehends the events of the world around one, is that one constantly goes beyond the information given. (Bruner, 1957)

Whether silently gazing across a desert landscape, arguing a new budget proposal, or having a drink with friends, the individual is engaged in a cognitive act of information processing. Thousands of stimuli confront us every day, igniting chain reactions of mental activity—information is received, filtered, and ordered. The speed and frequency with which people perform this seemingly straightforward procedure of "information administration" suggests that we are efficient clerks. We make decisions, impose order on chaos, and try to maintain our sanity in the face of it all.

However, Bruner and others (Fiske & Taylor, 1984; Nisbett & Ross, 1980) suggest that people do both *more* and *less* than simply receive, file, and use that continual stream of information. When "going beyond the information given," perceptions and cognitions often modify the nature of incoming stimuli. Information is received and interpreted through a screening process of inferential procedures that facilitate quick responses and quantitative efficiency. Uncertainty is thus converted to resolve. People make more inferences and assumptions in situations where they have little information on which to base a judgment (Cantor & Mischel, 1977); it is as though inference enters the vacuum created by a shortage of data. Inferential reasoning thus enables people to do quite a bit *more* than merely receive and file incoming information.

What is the source of human inferences? Cognitive researchers have suggested that people develop knowledge structures, or schemata, that function as an information filing system. These mental devices consolidate large volumes of information into categories of knowledge that are more accessible and user friendly. Our cognitive filing systems are miserly, minimalist, category-based arrangements into which new bits of information must be assimilated. Referred to as top-down or theory-driven information processing, this procedure assumes that new information must align itself with what is already in place. Nisbett and Ross (1980) state that "objects and events in the phenomenal world are almost never approached as if they were *sui generis* but rather are assimilated into preexisting structures in the mind of the perceiver" (p. 36).

Neisser (1976) defines schemata as "the portion of the entire perceptual cycle which is internal to the perceiver, modifiable by experience, and somehow specific to what is being perceived" (p. 54). Perception is subsequently influenced by personal expectations. Neisser's perceptual cycle (see Figure 3.3) suggests an interactive process between the available information in a given environment, an individual's schemata, and that person's perceptual exploration. For example, a certain

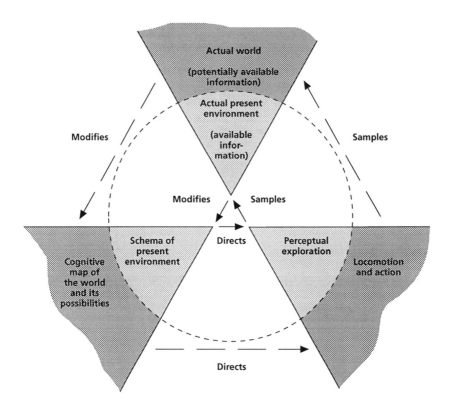

FIGURE 3.3. Schemata as Embedded in Cognitive Maps

SOURCE: Neisser, 1976. From *Cognition and Reality* by Ulric Neisser. Copyright © 1976 by W. H. Freeman and Company. Used with permission.

amount of information about a new personnel policy may be available to teachers through school bulletins and union newsletters. A teacher's reaction to the available information will be influenced by a number of factors beyond the content of the new policies. Experiences with previous policies and procedures and the degree to which that teacher actively seeks out information in the environment thus contribute to the schemata that mediates the person's contact with new information. Schemata are patterns of action that reflect both the historical nature of their content and potential directions for action in the future (Neisser, 1976). Therefore, because information is generally processed through preexisting structures, we filter and thereby do *less* than consider all incoming stimuli.[4]

Schemata combine to form cognitive maps that delineate likely sequences of actions or scenarios (Neisser, 1976). Weick and Bougon

(1986) refer to cognitive maps as epistemological structures. Through reflection, a person imposes meanings on events, connects such events together, and then imposes meanings on the emerging concepts. When cognitive maps are linked together, they form theories of action—a set of road maps and directions for navigating myriad situations, from how to drive on an icy road to how to deal with an unruly pupil. Such a cognitive orientation leaves little room for random behavior—an implicit theory buttresses every act.

Much contemporary social-psychological research has focused on knowledge structures, schematic representations, and people's ability to coherently and accurately interpret their environment. People rapidly process large amounts of information with the assistance of a number of heuristics (Nisbett & Ross, 1980). Data-rich environments may make these cognitive shortcuts necessary, but they also make us error prone on a number of levels. In processing new data, we are misled by our previous theories and may subsequently distort new information. We recall previously existing knowledge structures more easily from our memories, and they provide us with biased interpretations (Cantor & Mischel, 1977). We often haphazardly infer causality between objects. Finally, a belief-perseverance effect makes us reluctant to modify those theories that underlie our cognitive schemata; this reluctance is expressed by our tendency to discount contradictory evidence.[5]

Our comprehension of events and subsequent actions are thus guided by the layout of our schemata. The table below outlines the costs and benefits of the schematic structure of knowledge:

Benefits	*Costs*
Imposes structure on experience	Encourages stereotypical thinking
Allows interpretation of ambiguous situations	Fills data gaps with typical, not veridical information
Speeds up information processing and problem solving	Ignores discrepant, possibly important information
Supplies missing information through default option	Discourages departure from conventions and norms
Enables prediction of future events and outcomes	Inhibits creative problem solving

SOURCE: Adapted from Sims, Gioia, & Associates, 1986.

The composite picture that emerges from recent social-psychological research is one of strong mechanisms for the maintenance of belief systems. Although prospects for flexibility in such an atmosphere of

cognitive conservatism may sound bleak, our knowledge structures
are in fact always being modified in small increments. As a critical mass
of "discrepant" information accrues, we begin to see it as less discrepant and reassess the appropriate schema (Higgins & Bargh, 1987).
Furthermore, when people are motivated to be more accurate in their
analysis, they will expend extra effort to modify their knowledge
structures (Chaiken, 1980).

Cognitive structures may complicate the possibility of concerted organizational action. Individuals retain cognitive schemata as varied as
their biographies and experience bases. School professionals draw on
schemata for topics like classroom discipline, rewards, teaching methods,
and administration. Divergent schemata may engender disagreements
and volatile conflicts among professionals with different theories of education. Two school principals may bring discrepant experiences and
subsequent plans for action to an evolving crisis with the school board, and
this split may cripple their ability to act in concert to defuse the situation.

Conversely, processes of organizational socialization (Van Maanen
& Schein, 1979) may cause individuals' schemata to converge over
time. Sorokin (1966) observed:

> When the same occupational operations are performed from day
> to day for many years, they effectively model the mental, moral,
> social, physiological and anatomical properties of their members
> in accordance with the nature and requirements of occupational
> work. Each occupation tends thus to make its members in its own
> image. And the longer an individual stays in the same occupation
> the deeper is the transformation. (p. 211)

Organization-level cognition will also be affected by bits of causal
reasoning about organizational contingencies described as "distilled
ideology" (Porac & Salancik, 1986); such configurations of information
describe global causal relations through an economical method of
retaining only the memory of the conclusion reached. The raw evidence used to calculate a response to a given situation is preserved in
simple snapshot form. Thus the minimization of cognitive expenditure
is a prominent strategy in organizational as well as personal life.[6]

Environmental factors like organizational culture, structural properties, and an organization's external climate also affect the ability of
organizational members to learn. Neisser (1976) elucidated the nature
of macrolevel forces on microlevel processes as follows:

> Note that the chessmaster does not control my behavior by any
> psychological device. He simply makes legal moves which have

the effect of changing my environment and the possibilities it offers. Indeed, this is almost always how behavior is controlled. Changing the world is a very powerful way of changing behavior; changing the individual while leaving the individual intact is a dubious proposition. (p. 183)

Analyzing an organizational process in purely individual terms would be as foolhardy as describing the chessmaster's game without referring to his opponent's moves. Just as the chessboard demarcates options for movement of chess pieces, an organization's visible and invisible structural properties fundamentally influence individual practices and behaviors.

If an organization's formal structures (organizational chart, electronic mail system, cross-functional teams, etc.) provide opportunities for information sharing and collaborative problem solving, then the opportunities for organizational learning will be enhanced. Similarly, a normative system and culture in which collaboration and exploration are seen as nonessential luxuries will not cultivate learning activities.

An organization's culture embodies an informal structure and normative system that influence information flow and other organizational processes. Culture may implicitly or explicitly delineate the boundaries of what is considered proper and improper action. As a mechanism of normative control (Kunda, 1992), culture may in fact decrease an organization's capacity to learn by reducing the amount of permissible deviance in information (Weick, 1979). As actions are aligned and habituated patterns evolve, stasis may supplant learning.

An organization's ability to learn will also be influenced by the nature of its external environment. A moderate amount of stress will be more likely to generate learning than overly stable or turbulent environments (Emery & Trist, 1965). Placidity will attenuate search behaviors and experimentation and lower incentives for improving performance (Hedberg, 1981), whereas an overly dynamic setting will result in a deterioration of learning, due to the high costs of search and experimentation. The analysis of schools and their environments later in this chapter demonstrates the potency of macrolevel variables as key determinants of organizational learning.

Organizational Learning Illustrated

Conceptualizations of organizational learning range from naturalistic descriptions of informal adaptation processes (Brown & Duguid, 1991) to normative prescriptions for formal efforts to enhance learning (Argyris & Schon, 1974, 1978). The most detailed and comprehensive descriptions of formal learning are those of Argyris and colleagues in their writings on action science.

Argyris and Schon (1978) assume that organizations are perpetually involved in dynamic transactions with both internal and external environments. This dialectic of multiple and potentially conflicting objectives held by organization members may accentuate the necessity of developing the ability to engage in double-loop learning, but people may alternatively adopt defensive skills aimed at avoidance of threatening or embarrassing situations. As previously noted, double-loop learning involves the modification of organizational norms and policies and challenges the stabilizing features of organizations. A clear trade-off between organizational control and the license to challenge and reflect on those sources of equilibrium leaves organization members who wish to create learning organizations caught in a precarious bind. This tension is not lost on Argyris and Schon, who openly acknowledge the fact that critical inquiry cannot be separated from issues of power and control in organizations.

Argyris and Schon (1974, 1978) have focused on the interpersonal arena of organizational inquiry. Drawing on cognitive research and case studies, they have argued that solving complex organizational problems often requires overcoming obstacles on the interactional level.[7] Their research suggests that certain cognitive strategies facilitate the generation of valid information and free, informed choices by organization members. If individual and organizational tacit assumptions are publicly tested, then fewer inferences (that may lead to confusion and misinterpretation) will be made. Organizational processes that are less muddled with untested hypotheses will contain fewer misunderstandings among members and facilitate concerted action. Argyris and Schon suggest that a central component of learning is the coupling of explicit advocacy of one's position with active inquiry into other interpretations and alternative views. Such an approach increases the chances that all relevant data will be weighed and that the collective information base of an organization will grow. Figure 3.4 describes the ramifications of different patterns of advocacy and inquiry in human interactions.

Organizations learn when people detect and correct errors in the dominant norms, strategies, and procedures of their organizations. At the heart of action science are the skills of double-loop learning. Argyris and Schon (1978) contend that most organizations embody Model 1 learning systems, which offer few opportunities for double-loop learning. Model 1 learning systems are characterized by the following governing values: Unilateral (not collaborative) definition of organiza-

		Inquiry: Low	Inquiry: High
Advocacy	High	Telling Imposing	Dialogue Mutual Learning
	Low	Withdrawing Observing	Interviewing Easing in

FIGURE 3.4. Advocacy and Inquiry
SOURCE: Action Design Associates, 1993.

tional goals; win-lose dynamics, which foster an aggressive environment and result in defensive behaviors; and an appearance of cool rationality, maintained to prevent people from expressing dissent or becoming too emotionally involved in organizational matters. Model 1 dynamics result in face-saving behaviors, the repression of difficult topics of discussion, and limited, single-loop learning systems.

Argyris and Schon's Model 2 prescription emphasizes the salience of decision-making processes based on a weighing of all valid information, free and informed choice by participants, and the constant monitoring and testing of choices during implementation; collaborative inquiry generates double-loop learning, which is the crux of their approach. The difficulties individuals face when trying to enact Model 2 behaviors cannot be overstated. People are highly experienced and skilled in Model 1 dynamics and may be more comfortable preserving the status quo of a Model 1 system, for Model 2 represents risk and, for many, a threatening level of organizational candor. Action science idealistically charges people with the task of transforming their deeply ingrained interaction patterns.[8] Fortunately, their works provide detailed trail maps for learning the skill of double-loop learning in inflexible and contentious environments. Organizational learning is most likely to take place when individuals examine their own practices using data from actual organizational events, whether in the form of tape recordings of meetings, reconstructed conversations, or role-plays. Through these experiential media, people bring their theories of action

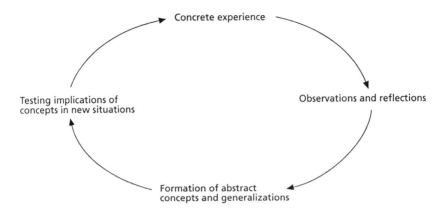

FIGURE 3.5. The Lewinian Experiential Learning Model

SOURCE: Kolb, David A., EXPERIENTIAL LEARNING: Experience as the Source, © 1984. Reprinted by permission of Prentice Hall, Inc., Englewood Cliffs, NJ.

to the surface. Collaborative inquiry results from multiple cycles of action and reflection (Dewey, 1938).

Lewin's (1951) important contribution, the action research cycle (see Figure 3.5), is another powerful representation of the process of organizational learning. Lewin maintained that learning is best facilitated in an environment of tension between concrete experience and analytic detachment. Through the testing of new organizational actions, learning may lead to validation or shifts in practice. Such a process facilitates a groundswell of pertinent information that might otherwise remain unexpressed.

The ladder of inference (Argyris et al., 1985; Argyris & Schon, 1974, 1978) is another very helpful heuristic. Organizational processes based on highly inferential communication patterns may be effective and economical among close colleagues who understand each other's meanings and nuances, but in broader settings they can lead to misunderstandings. When people unknowingly attribute different meanings to the same events or objects, the conflicts and suspicions that ensue often hamper information sharing and concerted action. Individuals and groups can refer to the ladder (see Figure 3.6) to recognize the multiplicity of interpretations held by organization members. By examining the inferential chain that links observable (or agreed on) data to variant conclusions, organization members critically scrutinize their individual and collective cognitive processes. Misunderstandings are not

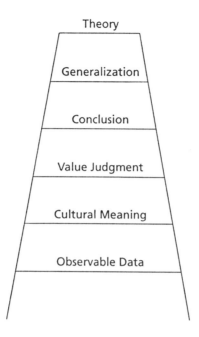

FIGURE 3.6. The Ladder of Inference

necessarily repaired, but they are at least identified by moving down the ladder to the point where divergent interpretations converge.

Other scholars have developed methods for improving organizational learning skills. Because every organizational event has a number of characteristics and can subsequently be seen through a number of prisms, reframing a problem may alter the meanings attributed to a situation. A well-known act of reframing was Tom Sawyer's recasting the chore of whitewashing his fence into an amusement that had few parallels on a hot summer afternoon in Mississippi (Watzlawick, Weakland, & Fisch, 1974). Bolman and Deal (1984) have argued that reframing organizational issues through human resource, political, symbolic, and structural frames enriches organizational analysis and improves subsequent action.

Senge (1990) has resurrected the conceptualization ([Katz & Kahn, 1966; Weick, 1979] of the organization as an interconnected system) and developed a series of valuable learning tools based on systems dynamics. By conceiving of organizations as being based on interconnected, recursive loops rather than linear processes, the organization member redefines organizational action in terms of loops, interrelationships, and processes rather than linear equations.

As a training or development tool, the use of critical incidents from work life enables people to explore their underlying assumptions and engage in critical reflective processes. When asked to recall an event that symbolized satisfaction and achievement (or failure), people describe a set of observable actions; embedded within such an incident is a tacit theory of professional action that, with the help of a colleague, may be reformulated as a set of organizational beliefs and assumptions.

Resistance to Organizational Learning in School Systems

The concepts and tools outlined above sound promising. The prospect of assessing and repairing organizational action, greater organizational flexibility, innovation, and improvement conjure up images of an organizational fountain of youth and vitality. However, organizational learning may not occur so easily. The model of levels of resistance (see Figure 3.7) to organizational learning in schools graphically reveals four levels of obstacles presenting systemic opposition, ranging from the macro environment of schools to the micro strategies employed by organization members.

Stakeholder Politics

Schools are batted back and forth between numerous constituencies engaged in ideological struggles over the nature of our society; the players in this struggle range from our nation's highest elected officials to the local church. The National Defense Education Act of 1958 sought to compensate for the national embarrassment and jealousy caused by Sputnik in 1957. Change has been mandated via the court system (Sarason, 1971), leaving schools no choice about whether to accept the modifications imposed from above. As our nation's most pervasive social institutions, schools are subject to a continual stream of state and federal legislation. Sirotnik and Oakes (1986) describe the external environment's influence:

> Schools have evolved to their present forms precisely as adaptations to a sociopolitical context that is incompatible with the best of our educational intents. In other words, schools have yet

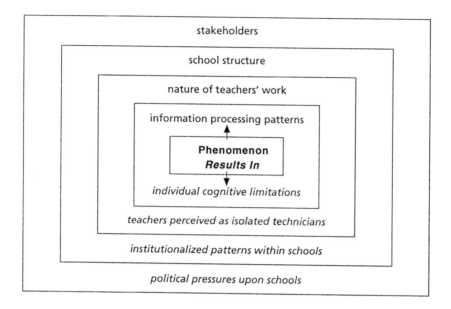

FIGURE 3.7. Levels of Resistance to Organizational Learning in Schools

another set of goals, usually unspoken ones, that place themselves in a central role that maintains society in its currently
functioning forms. When we acknowledge this more implicit set
of goals, schools' resistance to interventions becomes more easily
understood. These goals that direct schools to maintain the societal status quo run counter in many ways to innovations directed at
the development of individuals to their fullest potential. . . . The usually tenuous compromise is that individual development proceeds
only to the point where it begins to threaten the status quo. (pp. 4-5)

The politics of school systems are well documented elsewhere (e.g.,
Bacharach, 1990); what is of concern here are the consequences of a
highly politicized environment for organizational learning. Deciding
who should be involved in the process of determining what schools
should teach and how they should operate is but one of the frequent
quagmires that schools encounter as a result of their turbulent sur-
roundings. On the one hand, the traditional concept of an encapsulated
system has left key parties like parents and teachers out of decision-
making processes but allows district and state officials with bureaucratic authority to exert great influence on school activities. A more

extensive list of groups and parties interested in school affairs would include businesspeople, the clergy, and a plethora of others, for nearly everyone has a stake in what goes on in our schools. Sarason (1971) asks: "Does it make sense to talk about schools as if they are part of a closed system that does not include groups and agencies outside that system?" (p. 11).

These different stakeholders will inevitably seek different outcomes. Because schools cannot be everything to everyone, frustration and bitter struggles often characterize policy debates. Should an urban district support the principles of excellence or equality? Should contraceptives be distributed in high schools? How should the story of Christopher Columbus be taught? Decisions on these topics necessarily please some and anger others. Subsequently, criticism of schools flows voluminously.

Being at society's center stage for so long has made many school professionals feel like they are in a war of attrition. Such turmoil has resulted in a threat-rigidity effect (Staw, McKechnie, & Puffer, 1981), meaning that perceived environmental threats have resulted in a rigidification of behavior among school professionals. Two main implications stem from this: Information is restricted, by narrowing the field of attention and reducing the number of channels used, and control is tightened, by concentrating power and influence. Threat-rigidity is a dynamic that proponents of organizational learning must contend with, for it is both common and antithetical to the notion of learning based on inquiry and exploration.

Institutionalized Culture of Schools

Explicit and implicit theories of organization and administration undergird and give form to an organization's structure. Architects of school administration in the first part of the 20th century sought to mirror the efficiency perspective as espoused by Taylor (1911) in his program for scientific management. This perspective, borrowed directly from industry, prescribed task descriptions, division of labor, and an emphasis on performance standards. These structures have long survived their architects at the beginning of the century. Weick (1979) identified the assumptions that underlay such a system of administration:

1. The presence of a self-correcting rational system among closely linked and interdependent people
2. Consensus on goals and means

3. Coordination by dissemination of information
4. Predictability of problems and responses

Although Weick's conclusion that schools are managed with the wrong model in mind may be true, it is important to identify why this system has sustained itself in spite of decades of attempts at reform. This very same web of forces has impaired and will continue to influence the feasibility of organizational learning in schools. Unless all traces of our past system (e.g., school books, education journals, physical plants, and personnel) vanish, the firm imprint of the past on the present cannot be ignored. Like the layers of artifacts at an archaeological site, an institution's earlier norms and patterns of organization provide the base on which new edifices are built. Cast in concrete and reified in textbooks, bulletin boards, and teachers' lounges, these forms have both functional and symbolic value.

Structure extends external and internal legitimacy to an organization. For insiders, it provides a rational map that elucidates issues of authority, responsibility, and proper performance. For outsiders, structure suggests a functioning machine with discernible, interconnected parts that contribute to the process of transforming inputs to outputs. Just as our individual cognitions are built around categories and structures that interpret and reduce the ambiguity of a plethora of stimuli, an apparent organizational structure performs a similar deviance-reducing function (Meyer, 1982). We expect our organizations to ha ve clear purposes. In situations with unclear technologies and outcome definitions, formal organizations develop simple, standardized outcomes that will be easily communicable and appear to be certain and clear. To establish these mechanisms of rationality in their unpredictable settings, school must decouple their structures from their activities. Such a process of buffering (Meyer, 1982) enables an organization whose work encompasses domains of ambiguity to appear accountable and rational. Barth (1990) has referred to the emergence of "list logic," which enables school officials to appear to be in cool control of their charges, providing political cover from authorities further up in the educational hierarchy.

Many of the foundation papers of the latest wave of works on institutional processes in organizations document American schools (Meyer, Scott, & Deal, 1981; Meyer & Rowan, 1977, 1978; Rowan, 1981, 1982; Scott & Meyer, 1988). Schools have been described as loosely coupled (Weick, 1976) in terms of the technical methods of education, but they are tightly coupled in terms of their culture and structure

(Meyer et al., 1978; Sergiovanni & Moore, 1989). Sarason (1971) addressed the isomorphism of school structure through the prism of
behavioral and programmatic regularities:

> The significance of an existing regularity is that it forces, or
> should force, one to ask two questions: *What is the rationale for the
> regularity?* and *What is the universe of alternatives that could be
> considered?* Put in another way: Can the existing regularity be
> understood without considering its relationship to the alterna-
> tives of which it is but one possibility? (p. 64, italics in original)

Such queries could form the basis for a school embarking on a program
of formal organizational learning, but more often than not, they would
be considered capricious.

This is the iron cage (DiMaggio & Powell, 1983) of institutional
isomorphism; state standards and policies become goals in and of
themselves, rather than means to achieving goals. The structural regularities and institutionalized norms of behavior that characterize schools
are central elements in school culture, enveloping teachers, administrators, students, and the systems that they share. Schools often embody
the dynamic conservatism that Schon (1971) has described as a "tendency to fight to remain the same" (p. 32). Of interest here is the degree
to which such a system will be amenable to organizational learning
and fundamental change. Because these structures provide legitimacy
and a rationalizing structure, their resilience cannot be overstated.
Schon (1971) continues:

> Because of its dynamic conservatism, a social system is unlikely
> to undertake its own change of state. Because it sees every effort
> of transformation as an attack, transformation becomes a kind of
> war. Major shifts in the system come about in response to the
> system's failure or to the threat of failure. (p. 55)

In sum, the risk-taking, inquiry, and search behaviors of organizational learning are inconsistent with the attributes of highly institutionalized settings and thus comprise a second layer of inherent
resistance to learning.

Teachers' Work: The Technology of Schooling

A number of recently published books (Johnson, 1990; Shedd &
Bacharach, 1991) have analyzed what teachers do and how they feel

about their work. Because teachers are the front-line professionals of our schools, their propensity to engage in organizational learning is crucial and cannot be understood independently of the content, context, and concerns regarding their work.

> Everyone's an expert on education. Everyone's been in school and everyone thinks they know what does and doesn't work. . . . I tell people, "You're an expert on studenting, not teaching. You know what's it's like to be one of twenty-five students facing a teacher. You don't know what it's like to be a teacher facing twenty-five students." (A teacher quoted in Shedd & Bacharach, 1991, p. 13)

Nonteachers have a hard time comprehending the complexity of the work performed by teachers. In seeking to generate an appropriate occupational comparison for the work performed by teachers, Shedd and Malanowski (1985) repeatedly faced limiting definitions and functions. Eventually, their descriptive inquiry identified the work processes of civil engineers and television news directors as being structurally similar to teaching. The primary constructs of all three jobs are managerial/supervisory and technical/professional, demonstrating a fusion of two sets of skills and competencies. Lieberman and Miller (1991) interpret the work of teachers along different parameters, citing universal/cognitive (based on a repertoire of skills about groups and the transmission of knowledge) and particular/affective (motivation based) skills. Both typologies of teachers' work demonstrate that a panoply of skills is used by teachers in and around the classroom.

In addition, teachers make about 200 pedagogical decisions per class hour. Each decision may shift the focus of the class and its activities; hence active implementation is accompanied by continuous cycles of planning and evaluation. When do teachers find the time to evaluate but a handful of their decisions in such a busy environment?

The elusive link between teaching and student learning is a fact of life in the classroom; no technical culture (Perrow, 1970; Thompson, 1967) maps out unfailing processes for accomplishing school goals (Rosenholtz, 1989). Uncertainty also springs from changing student needs, interaction with groups rather than individuals, and ambiguous, conflicting goals. Finally, students are ethnically and socioeconomically diverse, possessing a range of intelligences, skills, and competencies that the teacher must somehow fit into an equation with a huge number of unknown variables. Thus the web of managerial and professional responsibilities is woven with threads of variable raw materials.

Other conditions of teachers' work add more challenge. Low salaries combined with the lack of opportunities for formal advancement within the profession and the lack of recognition by parents and administrators preclude teachers from sensing clear organizational reinforcement for their work (Johnson, 1990). Scarce resources attenuate a teacher's ability to function, let alone innovate. Johnson (1990) remarks:

> Teachers who work in unsound or dirty buildings and lack adequate, up-to-date supplies are like manufacturers whose plants are poorly ventilated, dentists whose drills are dull, lawyers whose casebooks are dated, architects without pencils, or physicians who can secure only enough polio vaccine to inoculate one-third of their patients. (pp. 58-59)

Teachers remain largely isolated from one another; only 2 of the 16 activities that teachers engage in on a daily basis involve contact with other adults (Shedd & Bacharach, 1991). The atomized structure of schools has made it hard to develop norms of collegiality among teachers. Barth (1990) adds:

> In schools, like sandboxes, the benefit of parallel play is isolation from others who might take our time, challenge our practice, steal our ideas, or have us do things differently. The price of parallel play is, of course, that we ward off those who might help us do things better and with whom together we might do grander things than either could do alone. And the price is isolation from other adults. (p. 18)

In summary, a number of obstacles to engaging in organizational learning activities are inherent features to the work of teachers. Isolation from other adults, crushing time constraints, and expanding societal expectations are exacerbated by shrinking resource bases, meager reinforcement, and indeterminate core technologies. These are not the raw materials from which organizational learning can be easily forged. Although the necessary stress is present, the teacher's world is void of extra time and other resources that could nurture learning efforts. Consequently, the essential element of reflection in action may be a scarce commodity in the teacher's satchel.

Social Cognition and School Work

As explained earlier, the inherently conservative nature of our information-processing apparatus is itself a significant barrier to learning. We are biased in favor of perceiving data consistent with our schemata and use those schemata to interpret ambiguous data. Old theories persevere, and our belief in a stable state (Schon, 1971) protects us "from apprehension of the threats inherent in change" (p. 11). If schools cannot offer incentives for change, teachers may not be sufficiently motivated to modify their practices. Greene (1984) suggests that teachers who bring an interest and commitment to their work inevitably experience a rude awakening: "We become sharply aware of limits, of structures and arrangements that cannot easily be surpassed" (p. 7).

Organizational Learning in Schools— Can It Be Achieved?

Having defined organizational learning, described some of its methods, and tempered the reader's optimism with a pragmatic appraisal of systemic resistance in schools and other organizations to such activity, this chapter now turns to specific applications within schools. Two primary foci for organizational learning activity in schools will be considered. The first centers on teachers, for they are the primary service providers in schools. As such, teachers potentially play a key role in making schools more effective learning organizations. The second sphere of organizational learning encompasses schoolwide issues of improvement, including governance and decision-making processes. Linking organizational learning activity in the two arenas is essential, for each recursively reinforces the other. If school professionals engage in processes of reflection and exploration and examine their practices and norms on the schoolwide level, then teachers may perceive that such inquiry is indeed safe and legitimate; this may reinforce teachers' efforts to do the same at the classroom level.[9] Conversely, teacher-level learning reinforces the need for schoolwide inquiry and learning, for a school's organization and structure inevitably spill over into the classroom; teachers will identify numerous schoolwide policies and issues that affect their classroom capabilities. When Barth (1990) talks about building a community of learners, he is referring to such a multilevel process of engagement.

Educational researchers and practitioners may read the following sections and think, "Isn't this what good professional development activities are all about?" The answer is yes, with an important addendum. Teachers (and others) engage in organizational learning when they cross the invisible line that separates their classroom (or office) from the rest of the school and contribute to the collective knowledge of the school (Levitt & March, 1988). This may occur through schoolwide inquiry, recommendations for the establishment of new structures that institutionalize and legitimize their learning, collaboration with fellow colleagues, or expansion of their knowledge (and subsequent communication to other interested parties) of their students' home lives. Teacher development programs often result in important individual learning, but organizational learning demands that learning and change be situated in the organizational (schoolwide) arena.

Teachers and Teaching

The problems of learning from individual experience have been described earlier. Richert (1991) summed them up well when he stated that "having an experience does not constitute learning from it; having an experience and then thinking about it to make sense of it does." Time-out for the evaluation of even a few of those 200 decisions made every hour is not considered to be an integral element of teachers' work in most public schools. A model of teacher development aimed toward organizational learning depends on the adoption of a professional rather than bureaucratic definition of teachers' work. Like lawyers and doctors, teachers are professionals who must maintain and enrich their reserves of professional knowledge. Schaefer (1967) explains:

> Teaching, more than any other vocation, perhaps, ought both to permit and to encourage the pursuit of meaning beyond any current capacity to comprehend . . . teachers have not been freed to study their craft rigorously and dispassionately. . . . If assignments to schools were to be structured so as to combine the investigation of tough problems with on-going teaching efforts, the psychic rewards available to individual instructors would be enormously increased. (p. 59)

A reformulation of teacher-school relations (Shedd & Bacharach, 1991) based on the proposition that professional inquiry is an integral element of the job will result in systemic reinforcement for organizational learning for teachers. With support and safety from retribution within schools, teachers are capable of being their peers' best teachers. The lonely profession (Sarason, 1971) would thus cease to be as lonely as it has been in the past.

Replacing the norm of isolation with a norm of collaboration among teachers may be an important step ahead for organizational learning in schools. A recent National Education Association survey (1988) provides vital information concerning which kinds of contact with other adults teachers find to be the most effective sources of teaching knowledge and skills (see Table 3.1). Teachers speak with one voice on this point: Besides the unmediated learning derived from hours at the head of a classroom, teachers most highly value their interactions with other teachers—not with trainers, researchers, or administrators. Rather than relying on outsiders for answers and unintentionally reinforcing the norm of teacher as technician or bureaucrat, teachers maintain that their professional knowledge is the most important resource in schools; however, these resources, like veins of coal deep in the earth, are often hidden from view. Their tacit nature requires a mining process in which knowledge is brought to the surface, inspected, and converted to fuel for the future.

By reclaiming knowledge about teaching, teachers both acknowledge and question the socially constructed nature of schools and their technologies. Teachers engage in double-loop learning when they ask, "Where do my ideas come from?" (Smyth, 1987). Through processes of critical thought, teachers exercise their ability to free themselves from taken-for-granted ways of acting in the world and begin to entertain alternatives (Berlak & Berlak, 1981). Berlak and Berlak have identified a series of 16 dilemmas through which teachers may reflect on their past and present practice. They suggest that by assessing action through the prism of historical and biographical forces, professionals may discover the roots of those assumptions that underlie their practices.

Learning and development activities for teachers based on reflection and inquiry are not simple tasks. Perceptual norms learned earlier in life are resilient mechanisms designed to protect the individual. The individual and subjective nature of our perceptions makes it difficult to share basic assumptions and educational philosophies. Assumptions and philosophies are also tacit, which makes them especially hard to lay out and inspect in the presence of others. In a workshop taught by the author a few years ago, a teacher responded to my introductory remarks with the incisive comment: "You're asking me to look into a mirror. What if I don't like what I see?"

Ironically, the formidable obstacles to teacher learning via reflection are the very reasons why such inquiry is necessary. The norms that

TABLE 3.1 Effectiveness of Different Sources of Teaching Knowledge and Skills

Source	Percentage Indicating Definitely Effective
Direct experience as a teacher	91.5
Consultation with other teachers	52.2
Your observation of other teachers	49.5
Study and research pursued on your own	46.1
Graduate courses in field of specialization	36.7
Consultation with grade-level or subject-level specialists	31.5
Undergraduate course in field of specialization	30.7
Professional conference and workshops (other than in-service training)	23.9
Professional journals	19.7
Graduate courses in education	19.0
Formal evaluation of your performance	16.0
Consultation with building-level administrators	14.9
Undergraduate education courses	13.0
In-service training provided by your school district	12.9

SOURCE: National Education Association (1988).

dictate against such interaction have ossified over time and resulted in systemic isolation of teachers from one another. Rosenholtz (1989) explains that ambiguous goals, infrequent evaluation, and a lack of defined common purpose among teachers results in high levels of self-reliance. An absence of professional interaction has spawned a culture of apprehension about "thinking out loud" and openly discussing teaching practices. Such self-sealing processes are characteristic of single-loop learning systems. If the perceived costs of collaborative inquiry are great, then discussing pedagogy and educational philosophy with peers who may not share basic assumptions can be stressful and threatening. The concepts and methods of double-loop learning described above may minimize the volume of defensive reactions among colleagues.[10]

Shedd and Bacharach (1991) have noted that when teachers begin to learn new skills and improve their work, they are making a transition from treading water to swimming. But for how long will teachers be able to maneuver amid the currents of their schools without any changes in their environment that would facilitate their swimming? Learning of this nature will not be sustained unless it is part of a wider effort aimed at improving the organization's operation. If such activity is relegated to the occasional in-service or summer seminar, it will not be perceived as an integral element of a teacher's responsibilities and will wither.

Schoolwide Learning

The second arena for organizational learning activity in schools is the entire school. Schools are in flux across the nation; in New York State, for example, schools are forging new plans for restructuring through shared decision-making processes as part of the Compact for Schools, a mandated program that demands far-reaching changes in school organization and operating procedures. Groups of parents, teachers, administrative support staff, and in some cases, students are forming school committees and hammering out plans that will fundamentally alter school governance structures.

Fine and Vanderslice's (in press) account of a project in a Philadelphia high school provides specific examples of what it means for a school to become an "inquiring community." Teachers, students, and others collected and interpreted an extensive range of data and modified school policies as a result of their findings. At an early stage, teachers were given demographic, attendance, and achievement data and asked to interpret it as though they were school planners; such data collection and analysis had been traditionally conducted at the district or state level. Data were also collected on other restructuring efforts in urban schools via principal and teacher visits from other school systems in the nation. Additional qualitative data were collected through a number of venues through teacher and parent interviews of students, school staff, and community members. Fine and Vanderslice (in press) write: "The process of doing these interviews allowed educators who had worked together for an average of fifteen years to construct a unified yet complex picture of the many dimensions of the school's community and students' lives." Third, the schoolwide committee charged with restructuring began a reflective process of bringing to the surface and scrutinizing their individual and organizational assumptions about their school. The data collection process itself ignited the committee's motivation and moved them toward a reframing of the changes they sought. As a result of their data collection, teachers and others decided that they were interested in further studying pupil absences and attendance.[11] Their choice of a topic stemmed from a basic concern among school professionals: How can one properly teach when pupil attendance fluctuates so sharply?

Such environmental scanning is an activity of central importance in organizational learning, for it enables an organization to expand its interpretive powers (Daft & Weick, 1984). By actively intruding into the external environment, collecting data, and making sense of them, an organization discovers vital information, whereas passive indifference to such data collection results in constrained, routine explanations and stasis.

One tangible outcome of the process has been the creation of "family groups" in the school, which consist of 8 to 15 students (of different ages) and one adult, who meet 2 to 5 times weekly:

> The family group concept captured the sense of the staff that students would benefit from more intensive and regular contact with at least one adult, and that adult would be in a good position to learn what kinds of assistance individual students needed and know how to access appropriate resources.

Another example of schoolwide learning and adaptation is the initiative of a parent on a school-restructuring committee in an elementary school in central New York. Frustrated that most teacher-parent meetings occurred only in the uncomfortable and problematic context of student disciplinary problems, she organized a series of informal breakfast meetings for parents and teachers. Dozens of parents and teachers have met informally over coffee and doughnuts at 7:00 a.m. This seemingly simple idea illustrates the potential for learning when new groups are brought into the decision-making process. Her initiative is an excellent example of how reframing the relationship between parents and teachers can engender new approaches to old problems.

Back to the Basics of Learning

A basic tenet of any learning situation (Skinner, 1953) is that behavior will be shaped by its consequences. More specifically, desired states or behaviors will not recur if some form of reinforcement does not follow. In this regard, organizational learning is no different from learning to ride a bicycle. It will not be sustained if reinforcements do not follow. How long will that parent be willing to pay for a few dozen doughnuts out of her own pocket for the weekly parent-teacher meetings? Can the family group concept sustain itself if it remains an ancillary activity rather than an element in a school professional's job description? Why should teachers engage in potentially stressful processes of inquiry if the school principal does not? Teacher reflection on teaching practices will not be sustained over time if the organization continues to reward rigid accountability and control; these norms fundamentally contradict the ethos of professional inquiry. Schools must develop systems of reward for such learning to sustain such efforts over time. Principals who model these processes for their teachers and demonstrate that teachers will be safe from retribution will have taken a significant step toward creating a community of learners.[12]

When structures and reinforcement systems support the practice of organizational learning, architects of schools will have rearranged key elements in the formal organization. One would expect that these modifications would gradually shape the informal organization, and learning behaviors would evolve into organizational norms. The simple techniques described above may serve as incremental training strategies that "prime the pump" toward the development of organizational learning competencies. Shifting structures, new schedules of reinforcements, and effective communication channels will assist in the process of internalizing the language and actions of inquiry.

Many organizational change efforts involve a cycle of unfreezing (creating motivation for change), changing (introducing a new model), and refreezing (helping the client to integrate the new point of view) (Schein, 1987). Organizational learning differs from this cycle in that there is no stage of refreezing. There usually is not a clear new model or specific system to adopt. Organizational learning suggests a more fluid, dynamic approach to change. Consequently, it is also crucial that programs aimed at generating organizational learning determine clear indicators of success. Vague objectives like improved communication among staff members or quality education will not provide specific metrics with which to evaluate whether learning has taken place. They may leave organization members with nothing more than an ambiguous feeling about whether changes are being sustained over time. In a districtwide intervention in 1992-1993, the author observed that the districtwide committee's process of determining behavioral indicators of organizational learning was, in and of itself, an effective vehicle for inquiry and learning.

The theory of organizational learning is an appropriate model for school change on a number of levels. First, it uses the resources and experience base of school professionals, rather than relying on the import of change models from the outside. As such, it reinforces and affirms the competencies of school professionals, rather than denigrating them in the face of an inorganic model of practice. Second, organizational learning acknowledges the salience of structural, normative, and cognitive factors in the complex process of organizational change. Finally, just as John Dewey (1916) suggested that the "self is not ready-made, but something in continuous formation through choice of action" (p. 408), organizational learning isolates a similar constellation of forces in organizations. The weaving together of practices with reflection enables organization members to configure their organization's processes and objectives and realistically consider alternatives.

Notes

1. If learning is to be considered organizational and not individual, shifts in an organization's theory of action must be collectively evaluated. New practices must be carried out repeatedly by numerous members. New learning may be incorporated into standard operating procedures or conveyed to new members via stories or norms of practice.

2. It has been has argued that even the most sophisticated repair manuals and documentation, which may be considered single-loop learning tools, do not provide sufficient assistance to technicians. Rather, technicians rely heavily on informal interpersonal communication with other technicians.

3. Hedberg (1981) has drawn a similar distinction between learning and adaptation. Learning involves delineating the associations between past actions, the effectiveness of those actions, and future actions. Adaptation is strictly behavioral and may subsequently not lead to more effective action in future situations.

4. The origins of these knowledge structures and schemata are many—life experiences, the norms and culture of the environment in which the individual is embedded, media images, ideologies, and ethical codes all contribute to the generation of cognitive schemata. In most cases, people are unaware of the intricate cycle of activity that characterizes their perception; after all, it happens automatically.

5. Nisbett and Ross (1980) support a "cold-cognitions" argument, meaning that these knowledge structures are a function of perceptual and cognitive machinery, rather than being motivationally based. Although knowledge structures may be "coolly" established, one's attachment to a particular schema can warm up over time and grow to resemble a fierce commitment. People may consequently respond defensively (and hotly) when their cognitive maps are challenged (Argyris & Schon, 1974).

6. Organizational processes may benefit from the convergence of numerous opinions and schemata. Shrivastava and Schneider (1984) refer to such individual assumptions and maps as frames of reference. They contend that

aggregate assumptions that represent "logically integrated clusters of belief" become organizational frames of reference among organizational members. Such shared maps may facilitate problem solving and decision-making processes, as they are the vehicle for collective understanding. However, the cohesion and uniformity may reduce the legitimacy of divergent views and lead to a rigidification of response (Shrivastava, 1983) or groupthink (Janis, 1972).

7. Hackman and Morris (1974) have also pointed out the salience of group interaction processes as important mediators of individual, group, and task characteristics.

8. Argyris (1964) has written extensively about the lack of fit between the characteristics of organizations and human nature, and Schon (1971) has written about human resistance to change and the dynamic conservatism of organizations.

9. Social theories of learning (Bandura, 1986; Lave & Wenger, 1991) emphasize the salience of imitation and vicarious processes; optimally, the school principal should model the process for his or her staff.

10. Techniques of teacher reflection, mentoring, and collaboration are hardly new to the educational environment. Teachers have used case studies (Richert, 1991), action research programs, and microteaching techniques. These approaches cast the teacher as a continuing learner who is capable of both investigating and improving educational practice.

11. The author worked on a similar project in a Boston high school in the late 1980s; coincidentally (or not), the teachers there also studied absence patterns after determining that it was a major obstacle to their work.

12. Much of what has been described above demands collegiality between teachers and administrators. Collegiality requires that principals enunciate clear statements of cooperative expectations, facilitate the behavior via release time and/or resources, and protect those who take risks.

References

Action Design Associates. (1993). *Organizational learning in action*. Newton, MA: Author.

Argyris, C. (1964). *Integrating the individual and the organization*. New York: John Wiley.

Argyris, C. (1993). *Knowledge for action*. San Francisco: Jossey-Bass.

Argyris, C., Putnam, R., & Smith, D. (1985). *Action science*. San Francisco: Jossey-Bass.

Argyris, C., & Schon, D. (1974). *Theory in practice: Increasing professional effectiveness*. San Francisco: Jossey-Bass.

Argyris, C., & Schon, D. (1978). *Organizational learning; A theory of action perspective*. Reading, MA: Addison-Wesley.

Bacharach, S. B. (1990). *Education reform: Making sense of it all*. Boston: Allyn and Bacon.

Bandura, A. (1986). *Social foundations of thought and action: A social cognitive theory.* Englewood Cliffs, NJ: Prentice Hall.

Barth, R. (1990). *Improving schools from within.* San Francisco: Jossey-Bass.

Berlak, H., & Berlak, A. (1981). *Dilemmas of schooling.* London: Methuen.

Bolman, L. G., & Deal, T. E. (1984). *Modern approaches to understanding and managing organizations.* San Francisco: Jossey-Bass.

Brown, J., & Duguid, P. (1991). Organizational learning and communities of practice. *Organization Science, 1,* 40-57.

Bruner, J. (1957). Going beyond the information given. In H. Gulber et al., *Contemporary approaches to cognition.* Cambridge, MA: Harvard University Press.

Cangelosi, V., & Dill, W. (1965). Organizational learning: Observations towards a theory. *Administrative Science Quarterly, 10,* 175-230.

Cantor, N., & Mischel, W. (1977). Traits as prototypes: Effects on recognition memory. *Journal of Personality and Social Psychology, 35,* 38-48.

Chaiken, S. (1980). Heuristic vs. systematic information processing and the use of source vs. message cues in persuasion. *Journal of Personality and Social Psychology, 39,* 752-766.

Cyert, R., & March, J. (1963). *A behavioral theory of the firm.* Englewood Cliffs, NJ: Prentice Hall.

Daft, R., & Weick, K. (1984). Toward a model of organizations as interpretive systems. *Academy of Management Review, 9,* 284-295.

Dewey, J. (1916). *Essays in experimental logic.* Chicago: University of Chicago Press.

Dewey, J. (1938). *Logic: The theory of inquiry.* New York: Holt, Rinehart & Winston.

DiMaggio, P., & Powell, W. (1983). The iron cage revisited: Institutional isomorphism and collective rationality in organizational fields. *American Sociological Review, 48,* 147-160.

Duncan, R., & Weiss, A. (1979). Organizational learning: Implications for organizational design. In B. M. Staw (Ed.), *Research in organizational behavior* (Vol. 1, pp. 75-123). Greenwich, CT: JAI Press.

Emery, F., & Trist, E. (1965). The causal texture of organizational environments. *Human Relations, 18,* 21-32.

Fine, M., & Vanderslice, V. (in press). *Collaborative action research: Reflections on method, politics and critical conversations.*

Fiske, S., & Taylor, S. (1984). *Social cognition.* Reading, MA: Addison-Wesley.

Greene, M. (1984). How do we think about our craft? *Teachers College Record, 86,* 55-67.

Hackman, J., & Morris, C. (1974). *Group tasks, group interaction performance, and group performance effectiveness: A review and proposed integration* (Tech. Rep. No. 7). Yale University, School of Organization and Management.

Hedberg, B. (1981). How organizations learn and unlearn. In P.C. Nystrom & W. H. Starbuck (Eds.), *Handbook of organizational design* (Vol. 1, pp. 9-11). New York: Oxford University Press.

Higgins, E., & Bargh, J. (1987). Social cognition and social perception. *Annual Review of Psychology, 38,* 369-425.

Hirschman, A. (1970). *Exit voice and loyalty.* Cambridge, MA: Harvard University Press.

Huber, G. (1991). Organizational learning: The contributing processes and the literatures. *Organization Science, 1,* 88-115.

Janis, I. (1972). *Victims of groupthink.* Boston: Houghton Mifflin.

Johnson, S. M. (1990). *Teachers at work: Achieving success in our schools.* New York: Basic Books.

Katz, D., & Kahn, R. (1966). *The social psychology of organizations.* New York: John Wiley.

Kolarska, L., & Aldrich, H. (1980). Exit, voice and silence: Consumers' and managers' responses to organizational decline. *Organization Studies, 1,* 41-58.

Kolb, D. A. (1984). *Experiential learning: Experience as the source.* Englewood Cliffs, NJ: Prentice Hall.

Kunda, G. (1992). *Engineering culture: Control and commitment in a high-tech corporation.* Philadelphia, PA: Temple University Press.

Lave, J., & Wenger, E. (1991). *Situated learning.* Boston: Cambridge University Press.

Levitt, B., & March, J. (1988). Organizational learning. *Annual Review of Sociology, 14,* 319-340.

Lewin, K. (1951). *Field theory in social science.* New York: Harper & Row.

Lieberman, A., & Miller, L. (Eds.). (1991). *Staff development for education in the 1990s.* New York: Teachers College Press.

March, J., & Olsen, J. (1976). *Ambiguity and choice in organizations.* Bergen, Norway: Universitetsforlaget.

March, J., & Simon, H. (1958). *Organizations.* New York: John Wiley.

Meyer, A. (1982). Adapting to environmental jolts. *Administrative Science Quarterly, 27,* 515-537.

Meyer, J., & Rowan, B. (1977). Institutionalized organizations: Formal structure as myth and ceremony. *American Journal of Sociology, 83,* 440-463.

Meyer, J., & Rowan, B. (1978). The structure of educational organizations. In M. W. Meyer & Associates, *Environments and organizations* (pp. 78-109). San Francisco: Jossey-Bass.

Meyer, J., Scott, W. R., & Deal, T. (1981). Institutional and technical sources of organizational structure: Explaining the structure of educational organizations. In H. Steen (Ed.), *Organizations and human services: Cross-disciplinary perspectives.* Philadelphia, PA: Temple University Press.

National Education Association Research Division. (1988). *Conditions and resources of teaching.* Washington, DC: Author.

Neisser, U. (1976). *Cognition and reality.* San Francisco: Freeman.

Nisbett, R., & Ross, L. (1980). *Human inference: Strategies and shortcomings of social judgement.* Englewood Cliffs, NJ: Prentice Hall.

Perrow, C. (1970). *Organizational analysis: A sociological view.* Belmont, CA: Wadsworth.

Porac, J., & Salancik, G. (1986). Distilled ideologies: Values derived from complex reasoning in complex environments. In H. Sims, D. Gioia, & Associates (Eds.), *The thinking organization* (pp. 75-101). San Francisco: Jossey-Bass.

Richert, A. (1991). Using teacher cases for reflection and enhanced understanding. In A. Lieberman & L. Miller (Eds.), *Staff development for education in the 1990s* (pp. 113-132). New York: Teachers College Press.

Rosenholtz, S. (1989). *Teachers' workplace: The social organization of schools.* New York: Longman.

Rowan, B. (1981). The effects of institutionalized rules on administrators. In S. B. Bacharach (Ed.), *Organizational behavior in schools and school districts* (pp. 47-75). New York: Praeger.

Rowan, B. (1982). Organizational structure and the school environment: The case of public schools. *Administrative Science Quarterly, 27*, 259-279.

Sarason, S. (1971). *The culture of school and the problem of change.* Boston: Allyn and Bacon.

Schaefer, R. (1967). *The school as a center of inquiry.* New York: Harper & Row.

Schein, E. (1987). *Process consultation.* Reading, MA: Addison-Wesley.

Schon, D. (1971). *Beyond the stable state.* New York: Norton.

Schon, D. (1986). Organizational learning. In G. Morgan (Ed.), *Beyond method: Strategies for social research* (pp. 114-128). Beverly Hills, CA: Sage.

Scott, W., & Meyer, J. (1988). Environmental linkages and organizational complexity: Public and private schools. In H. Levin & T. James (Eds.), *Comparing public and private schools* (pp. 128-160). New York: Falmer.

Senge, P. M. (1990). *The fifth discipline: Mastering the five practices of the learning organization.* New York: Doubleday.

Sergiovanni, T., & Moore, J. (Eds.). (1989). *Schooling for tomorrow: Directing reform to issues that count.* Boston: Allyn and Bacon.

Shedd, J. B., & Bacharach, S. B. (1991). *Tangled hierarchies: Teachers as professionals and the management of schools.* San Francisco: Jossey-Bass.

Shedd, J. B., & Malanowski, R. (1985). *From the front of the classroom: A study of the work of teachers.* Ithaca, NY: Organizational Analysis and Practice.

Shrivastava, P. (1983). A typology of organizational learning systems. *Journal of Management Studies, 20,* 1-28.

Shrivastava, P., & Schneider, S. (1984). Organizational frames of reference. *Human Relations, 37,* 795-809.

Simon, H. (1971). Designing organizations for an information-rich world. In M. Greenberger (Ed.), *Computers, communications and the public interest* (pp. 37-53). Baltimore: Johns Hopkins University Press.

Sims, H., Gioia, D., & Associates. (1986). *The thinking organization.* San Francisco: Jossey-Bass.

Sirotnik, K., & Oakes, J. (1986). *Critical perspectives on the organization and improvement of schooling.* Boston: Kluwer Nijhoff.

Skinner, B. (1953). *Science and human behavior.* New York: Macmillan.

Smyth, J. (1987). *Educating teachers: Changing the nature of pedagogical knowledge.* London: Falmer.

Sorokin, P. (1966). *Sociological theories of today.* New York: Harper & Row.

Staw, B., McKechnie, P., & Puffer, S. (1981). Threat rigidity effects in organizational behavior: A multi-level analysis. *Administrative Science Quarterly, 26,* 501-524.

Taylor, F. (1911). *Principles of scientific management.* New York: Harper & Row.

Thompson, J. (1967). *Organizations in action.* New York: McGraw-Hill.

Van Maanen, J., & Schein, E. H. (1979). Toward a theory of organizational socialization. In B. M. Staw (Ed.), *Research in organizational behavior* (Vol. 1, pp. 209-264). New York: JAI.

Watzlawick, P., Weakland, J., & Fisch, R. (1974). *Change.* New York: Norton.

Weick, K. (1976). Educational organizations as loosely coupled systems. *Administration Science Quarterly, 21,* 1-19.

Weick, K. (1979). *The social psychology of organizing.* New York: Random House.

Weick, K., & Bougon, M. (1986). Organizations as cognitive maps. In H. Sims, D. Goia, & Associates (Eds.), *The thinking organization.* San Francisco: Jossey-Bass.

Symbols and Symbolic Activity

TERRENCE E. DEAL

The Oglala believe the circle to be sacred because the great spirit
caused everything to be round except stone. Stone is the implement
of destruction. The sun and sky, the earth and the moon are round
like a shield, though the sky is deep like a bowl. Everything is round
like the stem of the plant. Since the great spirit has caused
everything to be round, mankind should look upon the circle as
sacred, for it is a symbol of all things in nature except stone. . . . For
these reasons, the Oglala make their tipis circular, and sit in a circle
at all ceremonies.

Geertz, 1973, p. 128

To a so-called primitive people, such as the Oglala, there is an intimate
connection among myths, beliefs, ceremonies, symbols, and everyday
life. In their distant past, the circle was somehow infused with meaning
and spirituality. Faith in the circle and disdain for stone represents and
shapes the Oglala's immediate experience. It bonds individuals in a
common quest, creating inner harmony and meaning within the tribe.
The circle is their totem, the stone their taboo.

Modern people often believe they have ventured far from such
primary roots. We conduct ourselves and construct our institutions

around sound reasoning and facts rather than intangible symbols. Modern versions of human organizations are designed to accomplish specific goals and objectives. To maintain high levels of effectiveness and efficiency, they are intentionally governed by rationality and a formal chain of command. As a consequence, accountability, control, specialization, and authority are uppermost on the minds and agenda of modern managers. Intuition, spirituality, and a belief in the divine or supernatural are the mystical province of magic or religion. Spirituality falls far outside official boundaries of businesses, armies, hospitals, or schools. Even affiliative organizations such as communities, families, and churches look to rational, rather than spiritual, principles for solutions to human problems.

Can we conclude that logic has triumphed over instinct and tradition? Most would agree that instrumental patterns and practices make more sense than those of their early expressive forerunners. But what seems self-evident may be a contemporary form of self-deception. Easy-to-draw conclusions themselves rest on an alternative set of beliefs and an abiding faith in modern management. Where the Oglala believe in the circle, today's managers believe in rationality and technology. Emotionality or spirituality are like stone to the Oglalas—taboo. Buildings, rituals, ceremonies, and other aspects of everyday life reflect rational icons just as the Oglala's tipis and traditions represent the circle.

Consider a well-known example. Sapolsky's (1972) analysis of the success of the Polaris missile project shows how rational processes can serve as expressive symbols. Polaris's "magical management cures" were initially believed to be the ingredients of its phenomenal success (a government-funded effort completed successfully on time and under budget). Management practices did not make effectual contributions to the project's progress, however. Rather, the regular meetings, "Pert" charts, computer-aided planning, and well-integrated systems signified something else. They created a mystical world not unlike that of the Oglala, although held together by a different set of values and beliefs:

> An alchemous combination of whirling computers, bright-colored charts, and fast-talking public relations officers gave the Special Project Office a truly effective management system. It mattered not whether the parts of the system functioned, or even existed. It mattered only that a certain people, for a certain period of time, believed that they did. (Sapolsky, 1972, p. 129)

Not only did those management practices encourage and motivate those within the project, they also projected its shared occultism to outsiders bolstering their faith and confidence. Members of Congress, impressed with the management magic, left the project alone. The myth was highly contagious. It traveled across oceans. The British Admiralty heard about the project's success and sent a team to see what the English could learn from the U.S. Navy. They recognized that functional contributions of management systems were not what mattered. They realized that the expressive forms mirrored accepted management myths and rituals to external audiences. Outsiders, as well as participants inside, believed in the project's efficacy and had faith that it would succeed. The team returned and recommended that Her Majesty's Navy adopt similar practices.

If Sapolsky's conclusions are valid (and they are supported by studies in other settings), then we have drawn the wrong lessons from the success of Polaris. Rather than struggling to make organizations more rational, we should be trying to make them more meaningful. Public schools, in particular, may profit from a modern adaptation of the Oglala or Polaris experience in which sacred beliefs are represented in shared mythical godlike symbols, reinforced in rituals, ceremonies, and stories. Cultural elements give all human organizations internal meaning, purpose, and cohesion. In Geertz's words, "Man is an animal suspended in the webs of significance he himself has spun" (p. 5). If so, we need to pay more attention to what we are spinning. Culture shapes human experience. Therefore, heeding the lyrics of a popular country song quite literally may be in order: Be careful of what you dream because your dreams will soon begin dreaming you.

We need to attend to an organization's identity. We must also consider the symbolic images conveyed to external constituencies. The image an organization projects must be isomorphic with prevailing myths about what makes an organization effective (Meyer & Rowan, 1983). Rational theorists contend that organizations are judged on the basis of results. Institutional theorists argue that the key issue is sustaining faith, belief, and confidence. Support is anchored on the congruence of an organization's appearance with prevailing societal myths (Meyer & Rowan, 1983).

From a cultural or institutional perspective, the main issue in maintaining internal cohesion and confidence of external constituents is symbolic rather than instrumental. Although goals, accountability, authority, and other structural concepts are important, they are not the driving force or bonding glue in any organization—particularly in those where mission and impact are ambiguous and hard to determine.

Drawing on literature from a variety of disciplines as well as anecdotes and cases from divergent fields, this chapter will explore: (a) historical foundations for the renewed interest in the symbolism of organizations; (b) current conceptions of the term *culture*; and (c) expressive strategies to restore faith and confidence in American education, business, and health care.

The Revival of Secular Spiritualism

Visiting a foreign country jolts the traveler with a bewildering array of novel assumptions and unfamiliar ways. At a superficial level, these manifest themselves in different customs and rituals. Japanese bow and exchange business cards. Saudi men who are friends rub noses. Americans shake hands. Beneath these outward behavioral exchanges are even more radical differences in the way social groups view cosmology, epistemology, theology, and other pillars of human experience. When we enter another country, we are literally passing into another universe.

In the early 1900s, such variations in constructed universes were explained by a concept called culture. An ephemeral term, culture enjoys as many definitions as there are people who study it. Several years ago, Kluckholn noted 164 different definitions. The list grows longer each year as researchers struggle to label and explain symbolic forces that make people different from one another and allow some to succeed under conditions where others fail.

Culture is not only applied to different societies or across national boundaries. The term has become popular in the field of organizational theory and behavior. Culture is used to explain and analyze differences across organizations—within the same societal context. Corporations, as modern counterparts of primitive tribes, are viewed widely through a symbolic or spiritual lens. The shift in paradigms occurred for the same reasons that stimulate scientific revolutions (Kuhn, 1970). Anomalies appear that the reigning paradigm cannot explain. In the field of organizational theory, rational conceptions were not working. They were unable to explain or control human behavior in organizations. In countries like Japan, corporations were attending to cultural matters. Their productivity and financial reward seemed greater than those in America where structure and strategy ruled the day. Second, a competing alternative paradigm begins to emerge. In the 1970s, a series of books captured the fancy of corporate America. *In Search of Excellence, Corporate Cultures,* and others renewed the interest in culture and symbols as a key factor in successful performance.

This was old hat to anyone familiar with the historical literature. There is nothing new about focusing on the symbolic or spiritual side of a human enterprise. The supposed discovery was actually a redis-covery of aged vintages. Barnard gave us a hint of what was to be refound in the appendix of *Functions of the Executive* (1938):

> To understand the society you live in, you must feel organizations—which is exactly what you do with your non-logical minds about your university, church, community, and family . . . the feeling is in our marrow, but not yet emerged into articulate form. (p. 306)

Arnold (1938), one of Barnard's contemporaries, made the point even more forcefully. Although (or because he was) a professor of law, he was especially appreciative of the powerful role symbols play in human experience: "The words, ceremonies, theories, and other sym-bols man uses make him believe in the reality of his dreams and thus give purpose to his life" (p. 3).

In more recent times, Selznick (1949) echoed similar views: "To create an institution, we rely on many techniques of infusing day-to-day behavior with meaning and purpose. One of the most important of these is the elaboration of socially integrating myths" (p. 151).

Each of these early commentators reinforces the ways and lessons of the Oglala and Polaris. In every organized activity, it is important that people believe in what they are doing, share a common heritage and faith—and dream together. This provides meaning and spirit to fuel what they do with passion and purpose. Whatever their form, symbols bind a people together, bond them in a common quest, and help convey their spirit to others.

Old knowledge in new skins applies also to emerging ideas in specialized studies of schools as organizations. The roots of symbolic ideas go back a long way. In 1932, Waller observed:

> Schools have a culture that is definitely their own. There are, in the school, complex rituals of personal relationships, a set of mores, folkways and irrational sanctions, a moral code based on theme. These are games which are sublimated wars, teams, and an elaborate set of ceremonies concerning them. There are tradi-tionalists waging their world-old battle against innovators. There are laws and there is the problem of enforcing them. (p. 103)

More recently, Sarason (1971) reinforced Waller's observations, al-though his point of departure was quite different. Sarason (1971) focused on behavioral regularities, showing how a culturally restricted universe of options makes it difficult to alter the educational status quo:

The problem of change is inherent in the fact that history and tradition have given rise to roles and regulations, to interlocking ideas, practices, values, and expectations that are "givens" not requiring thought or deliberation. These "givens" [like other categories of thought] are far less the products of characteristics of individuals than what we call culture and its traditions . . . One of the most major problems in our schools is recognizing that the major problem in our schools inheres far less in the characteristics of individuals than it does in its culture and systems charac- teristics in that one cannot see culture and systems the way that one sees individuals. Culture and systems are not concrete, tan- gible, and measurable the way individuals are. (pp. 227-228)

From a still more recent perspective, Swidler (1979) reinforces both Sarason's and Waller's insights through her studies of alternative schools, those designed intentionally to break away from established traditions and practices:

Watching teachers and students in free [experimental] schools, I became convinced that culture, in the sense of symbols, ideolo- gies, and a legitimate language for discussing individual and group obligations provides the substrata on which new organiza- tional forms can be erected. . . . Organizational innovations and cultural change are constantly intertwined, since it is culture that creates the new images of human nature and . . . symbols with which people can move one another. (p. viii)

The role of symbols in organizations is not a new concept. We are currently witnessing a revival—of ideas that have informed our knowl- edge of tribes, societies, or organizations for a long time. Like other scientific rediscoveries, it took some internal anomalies and tragedies, some victories outside America's boundaries, and a reemerging para- digm to refocus our attention on the symbolic side of organizations. We needed a reminder that spirituality, belief, and faith are not issues that progress and modern people have moved beyond or outgrown.

The revival of interest in culture has inherited a plurality of concepts and competing intellectual camps. People disagree about what culture is. There is also contention over whether (a) a culture is something an organization has or is, (b) an organization has a unified culture or competing subcultures, (c) people find meaning in organizational or professional membership, (d) culture can be measured, (e) culture affects performance, or (f) culture can be shaped or changed. The list of disputes goes on and on. There is little reason to suspect that disagreements will be settled soon. Nor will any attempt be made here to provide a novel synthesis. Divergent ideas accumulated over several decades, like the federal deficit, are not going to be resolved easily or quickly. The objective at hand is to sketch briefly the intellectual topography as it currently exists in both the business and educational literatures. No attempt has been made to be exhaustive or all inclusive. Others have or will eventually undertake such important work.

The Culture of Business Organizations

In Search of Excellence, Corporate Cultures, and other works in the early 1980s were icebreakers opening a passage for a convoy of ideas about the role of culture in modern business. Breaking the ice did not clear the way for consensus about what culture is or why it matters. Most would agree that every business has a feel, a tone, a climate—or something in the air readily felt but difficult to describe. The problem is trying to define in specific terms a qualitative sense that is inherently elusive, ephemeral, and difficult to pin down. Schein (1985) was the most aggressive in trying to give substance to something that can otherwise mean nothing or everything. His definition stakes out a definite conceptual claim. To him, culture is "the pattern of basic assumptions that the group invented, discovered in learning to cope with its problems of external and internal integration" (Schein, 1985, p. 90).

Others also provide a definitive rendering of what culture is. Aligned against Schein's elegant definition is Webster's (Deal & Kennedy, 1982): "The integrated pattern of human behavior that includes thought, speech, action, and artifacts, and depends on man's capacity for learning and transmitting knowledge to succeeding generations" (p. 4); or Bower's (Deal & Kennedy, 1982): "The way we do things around here" (p. 4). Although lacking a sophisticated conceptual elegance, both definitions provide a parsimonious, easily accessible version. Many executives find them easier to digest and apply in capturing the existential underpinnings of everyday practice.

Smircich (1983) makes an important distinction between whether culture is something an organization *has* as opposed to a quality that an organization inherently *is*. She sees language, myths, stories, and rituals not as inert artifacts or assumptions but as active agents,

> generative processes that yield and shape meanings that are fundamental to the very existence of the organization. When

culture is a root metaphor, the researcher's attention shifts from concerns about what do organizations accomplish and how the organization is accomplished to what does it mean to be organized? (Smircich, 1983, p. 353)

Other researchers dispute the notion of a monolithic or shared symbolic universe amid diverse business functions. How can abstract values be shared across R&D, administrative operations, sales, or marketing subcultures—all well known for putting a unique imprimatur on their subspecialty?

Another issue arises around whether culture can be measured. Kilmann and Saxton (1983) argue that it can. They developed a Cultural Gap Survey to pinpoint discrepancies between reality and what desired levels are in four normative areas:

Task support: norms for sharing information, helping other groups, and being concerned with efficiency; for example, "Support the work of other groups" versus "Put down the work of other groups."

Task innovation: norms for being creative, being rewarded for creativity and doing new things; for example, "Always try to improve" versus "Don't rock the boat."

Social relationships: norms for socializing with one's work group and mixing friends and business; for example, "Get to know the people in your work group" versus "Don't bother."

Personal freedom: norms for expressing one's self, exercising discretion, and pleasing one's self; for example, "Live for yourself and your family" versus "Live for your job and your career." (Kilmann & Saxton, 1983, pp. 363-364)

Cultural gap analyses typically identify differences in perceptions based on position in the formal hierarchy. Those at the top see far fewer cultural gaps than those at the bottom of the formal hierarchy.

Others agree that culture can be captured in quantitative terms (Beck & Moore, 1983, 1984; Martin & Powers, 1983; O'Reilly, 1983; Ouchi & Johnson, 1978). Instruments are developed around similar assumptions (e.g., Sashkin, 1987).

A fifth strand of controversy centers on the link between a cohesive culture and financial performance. Many of these studies are cross-sectional, looking at the relationship between cultural cohesion and the bottom line within a limited time period. A recent publication (Kotter & Hesklett, 1992), however, provides longitudinal evidence that ties a distinctive culture to various measures of performance over a 10-year period (return on investments, stock price, etc.). Their work documents a strong relationship between culture and perform-ance, mediated by two factors: (a) the congruence between cultural patterns and the business environment and (b) the extent to which adaptability (through leadership) is woven into the nest of cultural assumptions.

A final controversy exists between two contentions: (a) culture is an aspect of organizational life that can be shaped by those in leadership positions, and (b) leaders are themselves shaped by cultural patterns and practices. Schein (1985) offers the most powerful argument for the former: "There is a possibility underemphasized in leadership research that the only thing of real importance that leaders do is to create and manage culture and that the unique talent of leaders is their ability to work with culture" (p. 2). Pfeffer (1981) agrees: "One of the crucial tasks of management involves the construction and maintenance of systems of shared meaning and culture. Language, symbolism, rituals, are important elements in the process of shared meaning and should become the focus of administrative work" (p. 5).

Just how this cultural shaping can occur is less obvious. Some argue that the leader's vision infuses the organization with meaning and purpose. Others maintain that the leader creates culture by sending signals through words and deeds. Still others would focus on a more subtle interaction between leaders and followers that creates a sense of meaning and purpose in a more organic, collaborative way.

The Culture of Schools

Recent intellectual endeavors to study the culture of schools parallel those in business and industry. For example, how culture is defined varies widely. Erickson (1987) sees culture as knowledge or as idea-tional, as a set of interpretive frames or metaphors for making sense of experience and behavior. Within this realm, he identifies three distinct conceptions. The first pictures culture as many small chunks of infor-mation, generated by a group, although no one has access to the entire repertoire. The second sees culture as a more limited set of chunks organized into core constructs or symbols that are widely shared and accepted as reality. The third conception treats culture as arising from the conflict among various interest groups within a given social sys-tem. Small or large chunks of information are generating constantly and either learned, forgotten, embraced, or ignored, depending on a group's position in a social order (pp. 13-14).

Erickson's third conception has been developed more fully by Bates (1987):

> It is only within such an understanding of the struggles between cultures in the wider society, of their historical development and the structures of domination and subordination that exist among them, that we can begin to understand the complex features of the cultures of schools, the linkages that exist with the various cultures in the wider society and the limits and possibilities of administration in the development and modification of such culture. The notion of the corporate culture offered by advocates of the managerial tradition is an impoverished substitute for such understanding. (p. 92)

Corbett, Firestone, and Rossman (1987) accept Wilson's (1971) definition of culture as "symbolically shared and transmitted knowledge of what is, and what ought to be, symbolized in art and artifact" (p. 37). They distinguish between two kinds of qualities and norms. *Sacred norms* are immutable anchors of an organization's identity. *Profane norms*, on the other hand, although strategically important, are susceptible to change as new knowledge, practices, or products are made available. Together, sacred and profane norms support ingrained patterns of thought, belief, and action.

Saphier and King (1985) suggest cultural norms that affect school improvement, including collegiality, caring, celebration, humor, and traditions.

Deal (1987), paralleling the imagery in Deal and Kennedy (1982), suggests that schools resemble tribes insofar as they evolve values, heroes and heroines, rituals, ceremonies, stories, and an informal network of cultural players (priests/priestesses, storytellers, gossips, and spies). These symbolic elements interweave to create meaning and commitment. Schools that encourage shared symbols and symbolic activity are able to build organic webbing across competing subcultures of teachers, students, parents, and administrators.

The notion of subcultures extends beyond functional role groups. Lortie (1975) and others argue that a distinctive subculture develops within the profession of teaching. Although its uniformity is disputed, for better or worse, teachers are acculturated into a professional worldview that is different from that of administrators (Wolcott, 1977). Whether these differences are more clearly drawn than functional differences in business and industry is open to speculation.

Various studies have also probed the connection between culture and productivity in education. Evidence suggests that school culture (ethos or cohesiveness) is related to student performance (Chubb, 1988; Purkey & Smith, 1983; Rutters, Maughan, Mortimer, Ouston, & Smith, 1979). If one compares public with private schools, the link between cohesion and various outcome measures—absenteeism, morale, disruptiveness, or achievement—is even more evident (Bryk & Driscoll, 1988; Hannaway & Abromowitz, 1985).

In the education literature, determining culture's measurability is even more complicated than in business. One reason is that in education, the concept of climate has dominated the field. The conceptual overlap between climate and culture is another hotly contested issue. School effectiveness researchers have recently incorporated cultural ideas and a symbolic language into their formulations (Brookover & Lezotte, 1979; Purkey & Smith, 1983). But they have stopped short of adopting a specific cultural approach to school improvement.

As in business, the question of whether culture can be shaped or managed is up for grabs. Bates (1987), for example, sees it one way:

> Culture is constituted and expressed through institutions, social relations, customs, material objects, and organizations. To this extent, culture is observable; empirical descriptions can be provided of the ways in which the meanings, values, ideas, and beliefs of social groups are articulated through various cultural artifacts. These artifacts constitute the structures through which individuals learn their culture.

Deal and Peterson (1991) advocate the other view:

> One of the most significant roles of leaders (and of leadership) is the creation, encouragement, and refinement of the symbols and symbolic activity that give meaning to the organization (p. 13).
>
> Principals can and do help create an ethos of respect, affection, and achievement every day by understanding the "subtext" of schooling. (p. 3)

Moving Toward Areas of Agreement

Business and educational writers agree that history plays a powerful role in determining cultural patterns. Although they might disagree on how the evolution takes place—or the degree of influence administrators have on its course—consensus forms around the idea that people are constantly making and remaking culture. There is also accord that deep-seated cultural myths, assumptions, and beliefs become manifest in rituals, ceremonies, and artifacts, as well as in both human and nonhuman symbols. There may be a meeting of the minds on the assumption that social collectives all need a sense of hope and a vision of the future.

Juxtaposing past, present, and future creates an elongated view of culture, connecting it to historical roots and projecting it forward to dreams unfulfilled. As Cox (1969) observes about modern people:

> Their burning desire for a better future world can sometimes prevent them from savoring this present one. In certain festive and fanciful movements history allows us to taste in the present the first fruits of what we hope for in the future. (pp. 118-119)

From this longitudinal perspective, school improvement has three overlapping symbolic domains: (a) history; (b) current cultural values and patterns expressed in heroes/heroines, rituals, ceremonies, and stories; and (c) a vision of what the future might become. Owen (1987) sees this process as myth making, "creating a likely story arising from the life experience of any group, through which they come to experience their past, present, and potential" (p. 16).

Owen implies that organizations need to create, revive, revise, or transform the myths that provide collective spirit and vitality. Although creating myths is the work of a given group or organization, the process typically requires a source of moral support. We typically label this energy as leadership. Symbolic leadership is different from conceptions based on personality, position, or authority. Its moral mantle can be assumed by anyone who emerges as an archivist, symbol, choreographer, or poet (Deal & Peterson, 1991).

To approach organizational improvement symbolically, we need a more expressive, artistic way to proceed:

> Organizations are representations of our humanity, like music or art; they can be known through acts of appreciation ... organizations are symbolically constituted worlds; they can be known through acts of critical reading and interpretation ... organizations are symbolic forms, like religion and folklore; they are displays of the meaning of life. (Smircich, 1983, p. 66)

This requires strategies that embrace the expressive side of human experience: art, poetry, music, rituals, ceremonies, dance, metaphors, and humor.

Symbolic Strategies for
Improving Organizations

Organized human activity creates as many problems as benefits. There are many reasons for the divided balance sheet. One is that potential payoffs are undercut by an undying faith in the efficacy of rationality. We assume that rational is better. Rational tenets are widely embraced by those who try to improve businesses or schools. They share a common belief. If we can eliminate irrational noise, create clearer goals, and integrate efforts through vertical coordination, organizations should work better and be more efficient. In this view, human needs, political interests, and existing normative patterns are seen as irrelevant obstacles, intractable problems, or impediments to change (Bolman & Deal, 1991).

Organizational culture highlights other assumptions. The driving potency in organizations now becomes the invisible, taken-for-granted, informal patterns and rules created through time (Schein, 1985). These, not policies or formal rules, determine day in and day out what people actually do (Deal & Kennedy, 1982).

Improving organizations, therefore, requires a focus on values, rituals, ceremonies, and other manifestations of culture. This is a shift from traditional paradigms, mindsets, and language that guide reform efforts. If culture is the largely invisible, deeply held web of beliefs and assumptions of an organization, to understand the opaque depths requires a look beneath the tip of the existential iceberg. We need a way to capture and communicate elusive and intangible meanings and values. Thankfully, long ago our ancestors crafted symbolic forms that apprehend the powerful, elusive, intangible subcurrents of human experience. These expressive forms have always been a part of religion, art, and theater. The renewed interest in culture makes these forms applicable to modern organizations. If we array these expressive windows to apprehend the deeper side of organizations on a continuum from verbal to nonverbal, they include metaphors, poetry, stories, theater, rituals, music, and art.

A metaphor is a language form that helps us see one thing in terms of another (Brown, 1976; Manning, 1979; Morgan, 1980; Reddy, 1979). The "as if" nature of a metaphor makes strange things familiar and familiar things strange. It captures patterns that otherwise remain hidden below the realm of conscious thought. Thinking about an organization as a tree, an animal, or a book can help people express, identify, or clarify complex issues or qualities that lie below the surface (Gordon, 1961; Schon, 1979).

Poetry is a linguistic form that allows people to communicate on a level below ordinary language. A poem invites interpretation and allows people to express and enjoy the warmth, sorrow, and joy of human experience. Through poetry we experience emotions and values not otherwise easy to articulate. Thinking about policies as poetry, memos as metric, or routine as rhyme illuminates what is hidden well below and beyond our conscious grasp.

Stories have always served as a vehicle for communication and human bonding (Enderud, 1976; Martin, 1980; Martin & Powers, 1983; Mitroff & Kilmann, 1975; Wilkins, 1976). Grounding intangible issues and values in personalized examples helps pass important moral lessons from generation to generation. Telling stories provides a medium for sharing and appreciating the rich texture of life. Hearing stories is the primary way that people learn what to do. Analyzing stories provides still another avenue for understanding what a culture values and wishes to maintain.

Theater has traditionally provided an important stage for human expression (Brissett & Edgley, 1974; Mangham & Overington, 1987; Manning, 1979; Turner, 1982). In theater, deep dilemmas are shared, appreciated, and sometimes resolved. The inherent tension between reality and fiction makes drama an engaging paradox. In the theater, people see themselves; they laugh, cry, and experience a shared emotional catharsis (Aristotle, 1982). Bringing everyday life on stage provides a dramatic medium through which both players and audience share deep emotions and contradictions. Theater creates an opportunity for people to express hidden, intangible values and issues.

Rituals enable people to act out and reaffirm their values and beliefs (Manning, 1979; Moore & Meyerhoff, 1977). Unlike theater, rituals have no audience. People themselves are the players. The repetitious, stylized sequence of moves helps them to experience and share important, subtle meanings and emotions (Blum, 1961; Trice & Beyer, 1984). In a ritual, one experiences the myths and values of a culture (Geertz, 1973; Owen, 1987; Trice, Belasco, & Alutto, 1969).

Music is another expressive medium that allows people to communicate and share things below the level of ordinary consciousness. Melodies create meaning and mental images that transport people to a deeper plane. Lyrics add another dimension by putting poetry into rhythm and harmony. Adding music to rituals creates the dance.

Visual images and pictures provide a final avenue for human expression. Through art, people are able to see, share, and interpret their experience. In modern organizations, a picture can literally be worth a thousand words.

These expressive forms encourage a level of human dialogue and activity below and beyond ordinary, everyday happenings. Metaphors, poetry, stories, theater, rituals, music, and art allow people to communicate about what is going on in the realm of spirit. On a deeper plane, these expressive forms provide an avenue for identifying, framing, and transforming issues that distract from effective performance. They provide a safe medium through which people can discuss taboo subjects. More important, they provide an outlet for issues and dilemmas that lie at the cusp of consciousness.

Although many efforts are trying to incorporate cultural ideas into traditional problem-solving formats, others are using expressive activity as an alternative means of organizational improvement.

Using Metaphors

As noted, a metaphor is a linguistic device to capture complex, elusive ideas and to penetrate and apprehend meaning hidden below or behind ordinary comprehension. Everyday communication would be impossible without metaphors. Sports metaphors such as "He's a team player," "You have him playing your game now," "Let's get the ball rolling," and "We'll have to do an end run to get our point across" enhance communication. They also lead to a root metaphor of organization as team (Lakoff & Johnson, 1980). Inclusion and influence are often heavily dependent on one's ability to understand and use appropriate metaphors.

Metaphors can also be used more intentionally. In one large teaching hospital, for example, important conflicts among competing goals of research, teaching, and patient care were not being addressed openly. Management was either unwilling or unable to recognize the root issues. A fruitful discussion was stimulated by a question, "Suppose you were to think of the hospital as if it were a tricycle; which would be the front wheel: research, teaching, or patient care?" The query sparked a frank 3-hour exchange. In its latter stages, the group agreed that although teaching and research were very important, the hospital's top priority had to be top-quality patient care. Without quality patient care, the other two goals could not be realized. Letting patient care dip below the hospital's high standards of quality would jeopardize its mission. The management group concluded the discussion with a commitment to refocus attention on patient care. The meeting ended on a humorous note, when a physician noted: "But have you ever watched an adult trying to ride a tricycle?" Humor also has an important expressive role to play in organizations (Hansot, 1979).

In a meeting, a school board and superintendent struggled to pinpoint the cause of chronic communication problems. Each person was asked to write on a card a metaphor that would capture the essence of where the group was. The cards were collected and the metaphors were read aloud. Although each was different, all pointed to a common theme: "a puzzle still in the box," "the states before the Articles of Confederation," and "a flower that hasn't opened." The group realized that its problem could be solved by pulling the separate pieces together or blossoming into a more integrated form. Negotiations forged new agreements for how the various roles could work together more organically.

A year later, the group reconvened. Once more each person contributed a metaphor to capture the essence of where they were. All the metaphors were either boats or ships—all in a stormy sea and off course. The group had come together, but it realized that to move ahead it now had to "chart a course" and "sail unified into the wind." Some steps were outlined for developing a districtwide philosophy.

Metaphors stimulate a meaningful exchange that would otherwise be impossible. Deeper revelations help to develop inventive strategies for dealing with underlying causes instead of focusing on superficial symptoms.

Using Poetry

Like metaphors, poetry tenders intangible, emotional issues for appreciation and enlightenment. Poems are memorable as well as enjoyable. At one of Fairfax county school's management conferences, subgroups of 1,500 administrators were asked to contribute poems, songs, or skits to capture the essence of the district. After lunch, each subgroup shared its self-anointed creative masterpiece. One subgroup invited a retiring administrator to come on stage and asked him to lie down. A bouquet of flowers was placed on his chest as one of the group's members read the following poem:

Ode to Barney Jones, a Bearded Priest

After lunch, we felt rather sedate—

Because we chose too much to masticate.

We looked at Barney, one of our priests,

A symbol of change, to say the least.

From a country of excellence, sensitivity, and care,

We hope for others like Barney to share.

Barney, 'tweren't no bureaucratic vulture;

He believed in a cohesive culture.

Present through so much rapid change,

Barney's personality has remained the same.

Barney often with good cheer was heard to mumble,

"That's the way we do things 'round he-ah."

Barney has always been down homey

And never stood on ceremony.

Seeing progress and growth since '62,

He prepares to leave us knowing we've much to do.

In the prose and between the lines, many deep-seated issues were expressed in such a way that they could be shared, understood, appreciated, and ultimately resolved. A retiring cultural priest was recognized and sent on his way into retirement with style.

Using Stories

Around campfires, stories bond people together and pass lore and wisdom from one generation to the next. Although people rarely sit around campfires anymore, organizations gather once or twice a year to celebrate and mark the passage of time. During such gatherings, story-telling is a powerful method of connecting newcomers with history or signaling a new tribal direction.

A principal in New York, for example, has changed the school's new teachers' orientation from a personnel policies and benefits briefing to a cultural "boot camp." Rather than learning rules and procedures, new teachers spend a half day with their older colleagues. The newcomers listen; the old-timers tell it as it was. According to the principal, the stories have made a real difference—for both groups. She has concluded that having stories to tell and no one to hear them is just as bad as not hearing them.

Stories can also be useful in redefining transitions. A new, aggressive chief executive took the helm of a large corporation. Particularly when compared to his predecessor, Frank was blunt, demanding, and not at all hesitant to redress poor performance publicly. An initial search for positive stories was fruitless. He was well known for "taking names and kicking ass." He was seen as arbitrary and capricious. Finally, one vice president shared privately a story about Frank with an unusual twist. A vice president took one of the company's top salespeople to Colorado for a ski vacation as a reward for exceeding his yearly quota. While both were shopping for a new parka for Harold, he suddenly disappeared. The vice president found him, eventually. He was cowering behind a rack of parkas. "What are you doing?" the vice president asked. "It's Frank," he responded in a muffled whisper. "He's here. He'll see me. I know we shouldn't have come. He'll nail my butt to the wall again like he always does." Frank spotted the two standing by the parka rack. "Well, well!" he said. "Fancy meeting you here. Come on, enough hanging around inside, you lounge lizards. We're going to hit the slopes!" He led them to the expert run. Frank was a superb skier; the other two were novices.

"All right," he told Harold. "You follow me down. Keep your nose glued to my rear, otherwise you won't have enough speed to make it across the chasm at the end of the run!"

The two sped down the run and made the jump across the crevasse with space to spare. After they came to a stop, Harold looked Frank in the eye and remarked, "That's what you always do to me. You force me to perform well above where I think my limits are."

Told publicly before a large sales meeting a month later, the story was received positively by a group of people who now saw their president in a new light. The story helped reframe his behavior.

Using Theater

Theater exists in the hazy space between truth and falsehood. In this gray area, drama helps an actor and audience communicate. Deeper aspects of the human experience become obvious without necessarily becoming real. As with metaphors, the "as-if" quality of theater helps make the strange familiar or the familiar strange. Theater helps us appreciate and resolve human dilemmas, without trying to change what is ultimately an unalterable human dilemma.

In a recent meeting of 200 managers—administrators, physicians, nurses, technicians, and support groups—a large hospital departed from its usual nuts-and-bolts retreat format. The meeting began with a 2-hour recitation of history from its founding, over seven decades ago, to the present. A spokesperson from each decade recounted key events, important characters, and illuminating stories. For 2 hours, the entire group was engrossed in the unfolding pageantry. A newcomer remarked afterward, "I feel a part of this place for the first time." An older nurse noted, "It's the first time we've ever shared many of these issues publicly. I now know why we're where we are and have some ideas about where we need to go."

After lunch, each person was assigned randomly to one of six groups. Each group was to discuss one of the hospital's issues. They were asked to share their insights through any form of "symbolic representation" they chose. After an hour and a half, each group presented a one- to three-act play. During the 3 hours, the audience responded with laughter, tears, applause, and "aha"s. Nearly every issue that had been either a taboo subject or difficult to pinpoint was expressed in the skits. Even touchy secrets were brought to conscious awareness in the drama. The hospital's problems and dilemmas were, for the first time, revealed and widely shared. At the end of the first day, the hospital's chief executive "knighted" the new chief operating officer (COO), giving him the title Sir Roland and formally relinquishing to him authority for all operational decisions. This cleared up the confusion about who was in charge of everyday events.

After action plans were formulated the second day, senior management suddenly appeared in formal tuxedos and gowns. During the first day's theater, they learned their widely known nickname: the "suit people" operating behind the "gray doors." They earned this designation because of their formal attire and the fact that the administrative suite was closed off from the rest of the hospital by doors—painted gray and always closed. To the delight of everyone, the group did a takeoff on a classic 1950s song, "Green Door." They changed the lyrics to refer to "Gray Door. . . . What's that secret you're keeping?" When the group returned to the hospital that evening, the gray doors had been removed.

Using Rituals

Shared participation in a ritual bonds people to shared values and to each other. In the Catholic Church, repeating the liturgy, taking communion, and crossing one's self provide physical connections to sacred values, link the Catholic community together, and differentiate the congregation from other faiths.

In secular organizations, rituals play a similar role. In addition, the use of rituals in transition can help people let go of old patterns and mindsets and embrace more effective new ones. On a beach in Seattle, a school principal convened her staff for an evening event. Each person had been asked to write on a wooden board or plank something that was necessary for them to give up to create a better place for children. Around a large bonfire, each read what was written on his or her plank and threw it into the fire. The principal then commented on the relinquished behaviors such as "excessive bitching and moaning," "not caring enough about students," or "doing only what I have to do to get by." As the fire burned bright, consuming the negativity, the principal shared poetry written by students and parents highlighting their hopes and dreams for a better school.

A Texas elementary school now begins each day with opening exercises. The principal recognizes teachers and students who have done something of merit. Together they sing the school song. The opening ritual provides a daily transition from family to school and is a physical reminder of what the business of schooling is really all about.

At Tandem Computer, executives and employees gather each Friday for beer and popcorn. Jim Treybig, the CEO, is often visible and accessible. As beer and popcorn are consumed, communication patterns move above, below, and outside formal channels. More deeply, the ritual expresses the participative values that have made the company a tight community and a tough competitor.

Using Music

If you can't say it, can you sing it? At first blush, this aphorism seemingly has very little to do with life inside a modern organization. Yet a number of corporations use music to convey values and virtues to managers and other employees. Target Stores, for example, communicates its history to new (and experienced) employees through a contemporary "rap" format. The words and music powerfully express the company's character and do it in a lyrical form, communicating subtle messages that are far below a conscious level.

At an annual meeting in a large teaching hospital, people were asked before lunch to write down a song that would capture the unique character of the place. During lunch, 200 independent nominations were sorted into piles. Most of the responses clustered around three songs: "Nine-to-Five," "Take This Job and Shove It," and "The Impossible Dream." A choir was assembled after lunch. Every subgroup was represented by someone in the ensemble. The choir sang all songs that had been contributed, focusing on the top three. Discussions following the performance identified the hospital's dilemmas and concentrated on making their common dream "more possible."

Representatives from federal agencies were asked, as part of the seminar's format, to return from lunch prepared to sing a song that would communicate a particular agency's mission. Initially grumbling about the assignment, the group returned excited and energetic. A representative from each agency sang a song. The Internal Revenue Service chose "I've Got You Body and Soul." A representative from the Bureau of the Mines sang "Dark as a Dungeon." The National Parks group gave a rendition of "America the Beautiful." The Federal Aviation Administration sang a verse from Peter, Paul and Mary's "Leaving on a Jet Plane." At the end of the hour's performance, they were asked what had been learned from the experience. All responded that choosing and singing the song had helped them reconnect with the core mission of their respective agencies. An observer remarked, "And as a taxpayer, I had not realized until now the important contribution that each of you make to the general welfare of our country."

Using Art

When asked for metaphors to describe their organization, people often draw diagrams or pictures. Through visual forms, they seem able to capture and convey issues that neither words nor activity can express.

A conference in New England hosted teams from local school districts. Each team consisted of a principal, parent, teacher, board member, and superintendent. As one of several activities, each team was asked to collectively decide on and draw an image of the district. "Portraits" were then displayed and described by each team. One district's picture was especially poignant. It showed several children of all ages in a cart. Ringed around the cart were depicted stick figures representing teachers, parents, administrators, and board members. Each figure was tugging on a rope attached to the cart. All were pulling hard—in opposite directions.

It was at that moment, the superintendent reported later, that "we saw what various interest groups were doing to children." Later, the team hosted a series of activities designed to unify the system around "What's best for our kids."

Using Multiple Forms

Owen (1987) shows how various expressive approaches can complement each other in transforming an organization. Delta Corporation is a small, high-technology engineering firm. Its founder, Harry

Smith, was a creative genius whose inventions quickly captured the market. He surrounded himself with other entrepreneurial research and development types. The company experienced phenomenal success and ultimately went public. Although the first public stock offering was very successful, the distant horizon portrayed a dim future. Three years thereafter the company's performance had deteriorated to such a degree that Harry was fired and replaced by a new CEO. She quickly distilled the core problem in a succinct metaphor: "What I really need is engineers who can fly."

With the help of an external consultant, a "Mythogram" was constructed using a complicated array of stories from different parts of the company.

The Mythogram of Delta Corporation CEO—"We need engineers who can fly" History—Going Down Hill

Level	Finance	R&D	Production
Exec	Killing of '82	Old Harry	Making the Quota
Mid	Cashflow Kid	Golden Fleece	Reuben
Shop	In Praise of Wilbur	Serendipity	The Zebra
		Sam/Leper Colony	

SOURCE: (Owen, 1987, p. 152).

The mythogram captures the deep divisions among the various subcultures that presented the challenges and opportunities of making a transition from a downhill slide to a group of "engineers who could fly": Together the stories revealed a divisive situation.

Stories within the finance division exemplified the "new breed," analytic types brought in after Harry's demise and departure. The "Killing of '82" told of a new vice president of finance who sold so many tax losses incurred under Harry's management that he managed to make a profit. The "Cashflow Kid" was a new arrival in middle management whose expertise in managing cashflow garnered a solid return on short-term deposits. "In Praise of Wilbur," a story at the operating level of the finance group, was actually about an in-house computer. "The story of Wilbur was rather strange in that no one spoke of what Wilbur did for the corporation, only how elegant he was in his performance" (Owen, 1987, p. 152).

As one might expect, the stories in the research and development division were notably different. At the executive level, "Old Harry" stories recalled the creative accomplishments of the former CEO. Middle-management stories focused on the "Golden Fleece" award given monthly behind the scenes to the researcher who developed an idea with least bottom-line potential. Two stories were commonly shared among those "on the benches." "Serendipity Sam" was the researcher who accumulated the most "Golden Fleece" awards, whose exploits continued the legend of excitement and innovation from Harry's regime. The "Leper Colony" was the rest of Harry's contemporaries who had chosen, or been pushed into, a semiretirement colony.

The production side of Delta also had its stories. "Making the Quota" exemplified an executive value putting numbers over quality. "Reuben" was a tale of a politically sensitive supervisor whose ability to cover himself and impress his superiors led to a series of promotions. On the shop floor, most of the lore focused on "The Zebra," a local bar where people gathered after hours. Those who attended formed a tight cabal in opposition to their superiors. Rather than having a company-wide story, Delta Corporation was a collection of independent cultural cells, each with its own story and values. Across the levels and divisions the stories clustered into two competing themes: the management orientation of the new arrivals and the innovative traditions of the company.

The new CEO recognized the importance of blending old and new into a company where "engineers could fly." She summoned 35 people from across the company to a management retreat. Her strategy surprised everyone:

> She opened with some stories of the early days, describing the intensity of the Old Harry and the Garbage Gang (now known as the Leper Colony). She even had one of the early models of Harry's machine out on a table. Most people had never seen one. It looked rather primitive, but during the coffee break, members of the Leper Colony surrounded the ancient artifact, and began swapping tales of the blind alleys, the late nights, and the breakthroughs. That dusty old machine became a magnet. Young shop floor folks went up and touched it, sort of snickering as they compared this prototype with the sleek creations they were manufacturing now. But even as they snickered, they stopped to listen as the Leper Colony recounted tales of accomplishment. It may have been just a "prototype," but that's where it all began. (Owen, 1987, p. 172)

After the coffee break, the CEO divided the group into several subgroups to share their hopes and dreams for the company. When they returned, the chairs had been arranged into a circle with Old Harry's prototype in the center. With everyone now facing each other, the CEO led a discussion, linking the stories from the various subgroups. Serendipity Sam's report came in an exalted torrent of technical jargon. The members of the Leper Colony quickly jumped in to add details and elaborate the theme. Before long, they and Sam were engaged in an animated conversation.

> The noise level was fierce, but the rest of the group was being left out. Taking Sam by the hand, the CEO led him to the center of the circle right next to the old prototype. There it was, the old and the new—the past, present, and potential. She whispered in Sam's ear that he ought to take a deep breath and start over in words of one syllable. He did so, and in ways less than elegant, the concept emerged. He guessed about applications, competitors, market shares, and before long the old VP for finance was drawn in. No longer was he thinking about selling losses, but rather thinking out loud about how he was going to develop the capital to support the new project. The group from the shop floor forgot about The Zebra and began to spin a likely tale as to how they might transform the assembly lines to make Sam's new machine. Even the Golden Fleece crowd became excited, telling each other how they always knew that Serendipity Sam could pull it off. They conveniently forgot that Sam had been the recipient of a record number of their awards, to say nothing of the fact that this new idea had emerged in spite of all their rules. (Owen, 1987, pp. 173-174)

In one intense memorable event, part of the past was buried as the company's spirit was resurrected and revised to fit the new set of circumstances. The disparaging themes and stories were merged into a company where "engineers could fly"—in a profitable way. In the Delta case, expressive strategies not only helped to identify the problem, an expressive event helped to get the organization back on track, blending new and old together in a new shared enterprise.

Symbols and the Appearance of Change

Symbols can play a significant, direct role in organizational improvement and performance. There is also another possibility. Earlier in the case of the Polaris missile system example, symbols and symbolic activity not only promoted internal cohesion, their influence extended to outside constituents. Because the project's management systems gave the appearance of an efficient and well-run operation, important groups outside the inner perimeter believed that everything was under control and moving along. Their confidence kept them from interfering and engaging in oversight activities that are notorious for distracting energy from the ongoing operation.

This possibility is consistent with the arguments of institutional school theorists. From this perspective, all organizations maintain the faith and confidence of outsiders through a symbolic facade that incorporates current societal myths about what a good organization should look like. When the organization's appearance is isomorphic with these prevailing beliefs, a logic of confidence promotes belief and faith in the organization's effectiveness.

As Meyer and Rowan (1983) point out: "By designing a formal structure that adheres to the prescriptions of myths in the institutional environment, an organization demonstrates that it is acting on collectively valued purposes in a proper and adequate manner. . . . The incorporation of institutionalized elements provides an account of its activities that protects the organization from having its conduct questioned. The organization becomes, in a word, legitimate, and it uses its legitimacy to strengthen its support and secure its survival" (p. 31).

When inconsistencies are noticed, then the logic of confidence breaks down and external constituencies press for hard evidence of effective performance. This sets up a reversal of the logic of confidence, a vote of no-confidence, which sets up a downward spiraling self-fulfilling prophecy—unless the organization can respond.

One of the most common responses is the well-known rhetoric and ceremony of change and reform.

> People may picture the present as unworkable, but the future as filled with promising reforms of structure and activity; but, by defining the organization's valid structure as lying in the future, this strategy makes the organization's current structure illegitimate. (Meyer & Rowan, 1983, p. 38)

This requires organizations to emphasize public displays of pomp and circumstance broadcasting to both insiders and outsiders that everything is working, workers are happy, things are under control, and everything is going to get even better. As noted earlier, to the extent that such public displays are isomorphic with prevailing mythology, the organization is able to maintain faith and confidence. To the extent they are not, the organization engages in change and reform.

As managers try to improve organizations, they must respect the Janus-like nature of an organization's activities. On the one hand, changes can bring actual improvement. On the other hand, carried out with attention to its important symbolic character, the act of changing maintains faith and belief in the enterprise—even though nothing ever really changes.

Spirituality in Organizations

We need to reincorporate spirituality into organized human activity. In our quest to become more modern, we have embraced rationality as the most promising route to take. Along the way, we have forgotten that when it comes to matters of the spirit, we are primitive people dressed in modern costumes, working in contemporary tribal units. We, like the Oglala and Polaris, need our totems, myths, rituals, stories, and ceremonies. Otherwise, life in organizations loses its meaning. When it does, people inside lose their faith and hope. Those who count on the organization for products and services likewise lose their confidence and withdraw their support.

We are now on the crossroads of some important decisions. We can choose to regain our sense of spirit and breathe new life into our businesses, hospitals, and schools. Or we can continue to experience the human toll exacted by treating our organizations solely as instruments of efficiency and rationality. Cox (1969) vividly makes the case:

> We have pressed [modern man] so hard toward useful work and rational calculation, he has all but forgotten the joy of ecstatic celebration, antic play, and free imagination. His shrunken psyche is just as much a victim of industrialization as were the bent bodies of those luckless children who were once confined to English factories from dawn to dusk. . . . Man is essentially festive and fanciful. To become fully human, Western industrial man, and his non-Western brother insofar as they are touched by the same debilitation, must learn again to dance and to dream. (p. 12)

References

Aristotle. (1982). *Aristotle's poetics* (J. Hutton, Trans.). New York: Norton.

Arnold, T. W. (1938). *The folklore of capitalism.* New Haven, CT: Yale University Press.

Barnard, C. I. (1938). *Functions of the executive.* Cambridge, MA: Harvard University Press.

Bates, R. J. (1987). Corporate culture, schooling, and educational administration. *Educational Administration Quarterly, 23*(4), 79-115.

Beck, B., & Moore, L. (1983). *The influence of corporate image on manager style.* Paper presented at the conference on Organizational Folklore, Santa Monica, CA.

Beck, B., & Moore, L. (1984). *Linking the host culture to organizational variables.* Paper presented at the Conference on Organizational Culture on Meaning of Life Workplace, Vancouver, B. C., Canada.

Blum, A. (1961). *Company organization of insurance management.* New York: American Management Association.

Bolman, L. G., & Deal, T. E. (1991). *Reframing organizations: Artistry, choice, and leadership.* San Francisco: Jossey-Bass.

Bower, M. (1982). The will to manage. In T. E. Deal & A. A. Kennedy (Eds.), *Corporate cultures.* Reading, MA: Addison-Wesley.

Brissett, D., & Edgley, C. (1974). *Life as theater: A dramaturgical sourcebook.* Chicago: Aldine.

Brookover, W. B., & Lezotte, L. W. (1979). *Changes in school characteristics coincident with changes in student achievement* (Occasional Paper No. 17). East Lansing: Michigan State University, Institute for Research on Teaching.

Brown, R. H. (1976). Social theory as metaphor. *Theory and Society, 3,* 169-197.

Bryk, A. S., & Driscoll, M. E. (1988). *The high school as community: Contextual influences and consequences for students.* Chicago: National Center for Effective Secondary Schools.

Chubb, J. E. (1988). Why the current wave of school reform will fail. *Public Interest, 90,* 28-49.

Corbett, H. D., Firestone, W. A., & Rossman, G. B. (1987). Resistance to planned change and the sacred in school culture. *Educational Administrative Quarterly, 23*(4), 36-59.

Cox, H. (1969). *The feast of fools.* Cambridge, MA: Harvard University Press.

Deal, T. E. (1987). The culture of schools. In L. Sheive & M. Schoenheit (Eds.), *Leadership: Examining the elusive. 1987 yearbook of the ASCD* (pp. 3-15). Alexandria, VA: ASCD.

Deal, T. E., & Kennedy, A. (1982). *Corporate cultures.* Reading, MA: Addison-Wesley.

Deal, T. E., & Peterson, K. P. (1991). *The principal's role in shaping school culture.* Washington, DC: U.S. Department of Education.

Enderud, H. G. (1976). The perception of power. In J. G. March & J. Olsen (Eds.), *Ambiguity and choice in organizations.* Bergen, Norway: Universitetsforlaget.

Erickson, F. (1987). Conceptions of school culture: An overview. *Educational Administration Quarterly, 23*(4), 11-24.

Geertz, C. (1973). *The interpretation of cultures: Selected essays.* New York: Basic Books.

Gordon, W. J. (1961). *Synectics, the development of creative capacity.* New York: Harper.

Hannaway, J., & Abromowitz, W. (1985). Public and private schools: Are they really different? In G. Austin & H. Garber (Eds.), *Research on exemplary schools.* Orlando, FL: Academic Press.

Hansot, E. (1979). *Some functions of humor in organizations.* Unpublished paper, Kenyon College, Ohio.

Kilmann, R. H., Saxton, M. J. (1983). *The Kilmann-Saxton culture gap survey.* Pittsburgh, PA: Organizational Design Consultants.

Kotter, J. P., Hesklett, J. L. (1992). *Culture and performance.* New York: Free Press.

Kuhn, T. (1970). *The structure of scientific revolutions.* Chicago: University of Chicago Press.

Lakoff, G., & Johnson, M. (1980). *Metaphors we live by.* Chicago: University of Chicago Press.

Lortie, D. C. (1975). *Schoolteacher: A sociological study.* Chicago: University of Chicago Press.

Mangham, I. L., & Overington, M. A. (1987). *Organizations as theater: A social psychology of dramatic appearances.* Chichester, UK: Wiley.

Manning, P. (1979). *Police work: The social organization of policing.* Cambridge: MIT Press.

Martin, J. A. (1980, July). *Stories and scripts in organizational settings* (Research Report 543). Stanford, CA: Stanford University School of Business.

Martin, J. A. & Powers, M. E. (1983). Truth of corporate propaganda: The value of a good war story. In L. R. Pondy, P. M. Frost, G. Morgan, & T. C. Dandridge (Eds.), *Organizational symbolism* (pp. 93-108). Greenwich, CT: JAI.

Meyer, J. W., & Rowan, B. (1983). Institutionalized organizations: Formal structure as myth and ceremony. In J. W. Meyer & W. R. Scott, *Organizational environments* (pp. 21-44). Beverly Hills, CA: Sage.

Mitroff, I. I., & Kilmann, R. H. (1975). Stories managers tell: A new tool for organizational problem solving. *Management Review, 64*(7), 18-28.

Moore, S. F., & Meyerhoff, B. (1977). *Secular ritual.* Assen, Amsterdam, Netherlands: Van Gorcun.

Morgan, G. (1980). Paradigms, metaphors, and puzzle solving in organization theory. *Administrative Science Quarterly, 25,* 605-622.

O'Reilly, C. A. (1983). *Corporations, culture, and organizational culture: Lessons from Silicon Valley firms.* Paper presented at the Academy of Management meetings, Dallas.

Ouchi, W. G., & Johnson, J. B. (1978). Types of organizational control and their relationship to emotional well-being. *Administrative Science Quarterly, 23,* 292-317.

Owen, H. H. (1987). *Spirit: Transformation and development in organizations.* Potomac, MD: Abbott.

Pfeffer, J. (1981). *Power in organizations.* Marshfield, MA: Pitman.

Purkey, S. L., & Smith, M. S. (1983). Effective schools: A review. *Elementary School Journal, 83*(4), 427-452.

Reddy, M. (1979). The conduit metaphor. In A. Ortony (Ed.), *Metaphor and thought.* Cambridge, UK: Cambridge University Press.

Rutters, M., Maughan, B., Mortimer, P., Ouston, J., & Smith, A. (1979). *Fifteen thousand hours.* Cambridge, MA: Harvard University Press.

Saphier, J., & King, M. (1985). Good seeds grow in strong cultures. *Educational Leadership, 42*(6), 67-74.

Sapolsky, H. (1972). *The Polaris system development.* Cambridge, MA: Harvard University Press.

Sarason, S. B. (1971). *The culture of the school and the problems of change.* Boston: Allyn and Bacon.

Sashkin, M. G. (1987, April). School culture assessment questionnaire. In *Leadership and culture building in schools: Quantitative and qualitative understandings.* Paper presented at the annual meeting of the American Educational Research Association, Boston.

Schein, E. H. (1985). *Organizational culture and leadership: A dynamic view.* San Francisco: Jossey-Bass.

Schon, D. A. (1979). Generative metaphor and social policy. In A. Ortony (Ed.), *Metaphor and thought.* Cambridge, UK: Cambridge University Press.

Selznick, P. (1949). *TVA and the grass roots.* Berkeley: University of California Press.

Smircich, L. (1983). Concepts of culture and organizational analysis. *Administrative Science Quarterly, 28*, 339-358.

Swidler, A. (1979). *Organization without authority.* Cambridge, MA: Harvard University Press.

Trice, H. M., Belasco, J., & Alutto, J. A. (1969). The role of ceremonials in organizational behavior. *Industrial and Labor Relations Review, 23*, 24.

Trice, H. M., & Beyer, J. M. (1984). Studying organizational culture through rites and ceremonies. *Academy of Management Review, 9*(4), 653-669.

Turner, V. (1982). *Celebration: Studies in festivity and ritual.* Washington, DC: Smithsonian Institution Press.

Waller, W. (1932). *The sociology of teaching.* New York: John Wiley.

Wilkins, A. (1976). *Organizational stories as an expression of management philosophy: Some implications for social control in organizations.* Dissertation, Stanford University, Stanford, CA.

Wilson (1971). *Sociology: Rules, roles, and relationships.* Homewood, IL: Dorsey.

Wolcott, H. F. (1977). *Teachers vs. technocrats: An educational innovation in anthropological perspective.* Eugene, OR: Center for Educational Policy and Management.

Part II

Images of Roles

SAMUEL B. BACHARACH
BRYAN MUNDELL

In Part II, we move away from the focus on school *structures* as various modes of organizing behavior and toward a focus on changing *roles* as modes of organizing behavior in schools. Hart begins this section by challenging us to rethink what it means to be an effective teacher and, ultimately, to reorganize the teaching role itself. Despite the widespread diffusion of microcomputers throughout the public school system during the past 10 years, there has been little systematic research of the effects of that technology on teaching and learning. In Chapter 5, Hart begins to address that issue by carefully documenting how one computer-based instructional innovation—called Math Smart—could and should be used as an opportunity to rethink the role of the teacher in the process of learning. Using the existing literature on social relationships at work and job redesign, she offers a thoughtful analysis of the effects of Math Smart on the learning process and the teaching role.

Chapter 5 begins with a description of Math Smart as a 2-year project carried out with students in the fifth and sixth grades of a lower-middle-class elementary school. The goal of Math Smart is to change the children's approach to math; instead of just memorizing procedures, they are taught to think conceptually, putting problems into categories and devising methods by which they can tell the computer to solve them. The role of the teacher changes; instead of being a dispenser of knowledge, the teacher becomes a facilitator, problem poser, skeptic, and questioner.

Math Smart involves several stages. First, physical materials are used to represent symbolic relationships. Second, the children learn to convert word problems into equations. Third, the children use a computer program called HyperTalk® to tell the computer to solve the problem according to rules that they themselves generate. Fourth, the children tell the computer to generate new and harder problems of the same general type. Finally, the children write an essay about what they have done.

Hart points out that although the students who used Math Smart performed better on standardized tests, there are significant obstacles to its implementation, mainly due to several pressures that Math Smart puts on existing social structures. First, Math Smart requires teachers to reconstruct their own knowledge of mathematics using objects. Second, the need for access to lots of computers requires coordination with computer labs. Third, the teachers and students must both learn HyperCard®, getting accustomed to using computers as problem-solving tools rather than merely machines for drilling and memorizing. Fourth, teachers must reconceptualize their role in the learning process, which is very difficult. Fifth, teachers must reframe outcome measures toward concepts and understanding. Sixth, Math Smart will create the need for new methods of teacher evaluation.

In short, Hart argues that Math Smart requires that the role of the teacher in the learning process be entirely redesigned. In other words, Math Smart is an example of what Hart calls "instruction-based teacher work redesign." Because it involves the redesign of work, Hart argues that Math Smart should be examined carefully for its effect on the social systems and structure of schools. If instruction-based work redesign is imposed without such an examination, then dissatisfaction and burnout among teachers is likely to result. The remainder of Chapter 5 is therefore divided into four conceptual categories: the work structure, the characteristics of the school's social system and organizational environment, individual characteristics, and social information processing.

In the first section, Hart applies two theoretical frameworks to an analysis of Math Smart's effects on the work structure in schools. First, she applies Hackman and Oldham's well-known job characteristics model, carefully discussing the effects of Math Smart on the job characteristics of the teacher. Next she applies the sociotechnical structures approach, which suggests the need for constant compromise between the imperatives of technical efficiency and the social needs of the workers.

The second conceptual category to be subjected to Hart's scrutiny comprises the characteristics of the school's social system and organizational environment. Here she argues that a number of dynamic factors at each particular school affect educational outcomes. According to Hart, these factors include the following: a dozen or so organizational resources that are affected by Math Smart and, in turn, affect outcomes; the norms, expectations, and values of teachers; intraorganizational politics; the tension between role ambiguity and work routinization; organizational inertia; and leadership. She gives specific examples of how each of these factors may play out for instruction-based work redesign based on Math Smart.

Hart's third conceptual category is composed of the individual characteristics of teachers. This category is subdivided into personal traits and previous teaching experiences. Personal traits include variables such as: job involvement; organizational commitment; personal self-concept; and needs for growth, achievement, and autonomy. Previous teaching experience variables include the number of years spent in the classroom, age, professional socialization, and role or career transitions passed through.

The fourth and final category examined by Hart is social information processing. Here she reminds us that the interpretation of work redesign is crucial, for what we call reality is the result of a joint process of social construction. She cites a number of examples: First, the social environment can give each individual teacher cues as to which dimensions are relevant in characterizing his or her work environment; second, the social environment affects the way that the teacher weighs the importance of each of these dimensions; third, the specific social context affects the way that others evaluate the various dimensions; and fourth, the social context affects the organizational climate, which determines whether teachers will experience a positive or negative visceral reaction to the specific change, which can be rationalized later as more data arrive.

Hart's application of the voluminous research on work redesign to Math Smart has broad implications. Instruction-based redesign holds great potential as an innovative way to improve the efficacy of teachers' and students' work, and Hart provides a well-thought-out framework for the use of the existing research on work design in schools. Furthermore, Hart's analysis provides some possible reasons for the slow integration of computer technologies into schools despite massive expenditures on hardware and software. It suggests that all technologies introduced into the school be examined for structural, group, individual, and interpretive effects.

In Chapter 6, Mitchell also focuses on the role of the teacher as a point of departure for reforming the schools, suggesting ways to improve the performance of the organization by better motivating the teachers. He begins by explaining two key assumptions behind his analysis—that organizations are systems with vertical and horizontal linkages and that individuals are crucial to organizational performance.

Mitchell sets Chapter 6 up in a goal-setting framework, using an input-process-output model to manage the performance of individual teachers so as to achieve the desired organizational goals. That framework has three components: specifying the desired organizational results and determining the individual teacher performances that will lead to the desired organizational results; establishing a work environment that will motivate teachers to perform; and focusing on the continuous improvement of quality.

For Mitchell, specifying the desired organizational results involves a two-stage, three-step process. The first stage occurs at the organizational level. First, based on the sources of variability in outcomes, *standards* of excellence, effectiveness, quality, or performance must be identified (e.g., high achievement of students). The second step in specifying desired organizational results is to establish *indicators* or measures of each standard. The third step in the process of specifying organizational results is to develop *objectives* for each indicator.

The second stage in specifying results occurs at the individual level. In schools, this involves determining the individual teacher performances that will lead to the desired organizational results. Essentially, this process is similar to the process outlined above (involving standards, criteria, and objectives), but is applied to individual performance instead of organizational outcomes. Mitchell provides a list of helpful samples of standards and indicators for individual performance. Setting performance objectives for each individual should be based on (a) an organization (or department) plan established to achieve *its* objectives (so that the performance objectives of each individual add up to the organization or department objectives); (b) a review of the core responsibilities of the individual position and the employee's strengths and weaknesses; and (c) the employee's long-term career objectives, preparing for future jobs or possibilities.

After providing guidance in specifying desired organizational results in terms of individual performance, Mitchell moves on to the second component of his framework—how to establish a work environment that will motivate teachers to perform at the desired level. His argument is that such a motivating work environment must have three linked components: the belief that the exertion of effort will lead to the desired performance, the belief that the desired performance will lead to a desired reward, and the feeling that the rewards are worth exerting the effort for. Mitchell considers each component.

In the final section of Chapter 6, the author reminds us that sustaining high-quality organizational performance is more than a one-shot cure—it requires continual improvement, as the quality-control literature maintains. Mitchell suggests that a switch in focus from student outcomes to a simultaneous focus on inputs, outputs, and the learning process would enable better quality control in schools, thus obviating the need for corrective action after it was too late. Technologies that permit continuous monitoring of the learning process would facilitate that switch in focus. If that is to work, individuals must not be afraid to identify areas where improvement could occur. The culture of educational organizations must change from finger-pointing and blaming to constructive criticism aimed at improvement.

Taken together, Mitchell's three components offer a road map for those who would improve schools by managing the performance of individuals who work within them. Specifying desired results at the organizational and individual levels, establishing a motivating work environment, and changing the culture from one emphasizing accountability and blame to one emphasizing the continuous improvement of quality are all important.

Yet Mitchell points out that performance management is not a panacea—it should be part of an integrated district plan to improve quality. Such a plan should start with a vision, be articulated into a mission statement, and provide clear priorities at the district, school, and individual levels. Mitchell provides a clear example of such an integrated plan and how the plans can be improved by involving the key frontline organizational actors—the teachers. When performance management becomes institutionalized as part of a districtwide integrated plan, then a large step will have been taken toward the improvement of school organizations.

Sykes and Millman consider an alternative method of organizing the performance of teachers in Chapter 7—the evaluation of teachers based on evidence of student learning. Like Mitchell, they identify their work as one part of a broader issue—in this case, how work should be controlled in complex organizations. Chapter 7 is an attempt to draw some conclusions about (and derive some principles for) the use of evidence of student learning to evaluate teachers. Their conclusions and principles are drawn from three types of evidence gathered by Sykes and Millman and presented in this chapter: six prominent cases; the prevailing views held by the public, teaching professionals, and the testing experts; and the impact that the current reform movement is having on teaching, learning, and assessment.

The first case examined by Sykes and Millman is what has been called *performance contracting*, where the organization conducting the teaching gets paid according to the results that students achieve on standardized tests. The belief was that paying for results would focus instruction, motivate the teachers, and promote modern and effective methods of instruction. Unfortunately, performance contracting did not work—there were no statistically significant differences between the test scores of test and control groups. There was some evidence that instruction was more focused in the test groups, but that evidence was also bad news—the control groups were found to do better in content areas that were not part of the experiment. Apparently, more focused instruction did not improve test scores in the area focused on, but reduced learning in areas not focused on.

Sykes and Millman's second case is the use of *teaching performance tests*. These tests are assessments and attitude scales given to students, the results of which indicate the teacher's performance. Teachers are given a mini-lesson of unfamiliar material (e.g., scoring a shuffleboard result), time to prepare, and a specified length of time to teach the material. Students are then tested on material similar to that provided in the mini-lesson. The packets of mini-lessons and kits were marketed as Teaching Improvement Kits. Teaching performance tests never took hold for two main reasons. First, they were unreliable—a teacher might score well on one mini-lesson and poorly on another. Second, because the mini-lessons are designed to be unrelated to the content matter normally studied in schools, teaching and learning was trivialized and decontextualized—in today's jargon, their ecological validity approached zero.

The third case considered by the authors is that of *merit pay*. Most attempts have failed due to the difficulty in determining criteria for excellence in teaching. The problem is that teachers do not have any confidence in data that they believe do not represent the complexity of their work environment and are too susceptible to manipulation and distortion. There is an unavoidable tension evident here; if teachers are offered choices and participation in the determination of merit, then they accept the results of the plan, but unless the plan is standardized (removing teacher choices), then biases inevitably creep in. Merit pay also suffers from another problem: It tends to cause teachers to "teach to the test," making performance on the test a more important goal than student learning.

Teacher goal setting is the fourth case explored by Sykes and Millman and has been defined as involving five steps: teacher self-evaluation, the teacher drafting a performance contract, the teacher and the evaluator discussing it and finalizing it, both teacher and evaluator monitoring the progress toward the specified goals, and both discussing which goals have been met and which have not been met. Goals are categorized as general (for the whole class) or specific (for a subset or an individual), academic or nonacademic. After providing a list of strengths and weaknesses of this approach, Sykes and Millman conclude that goal setting is useful because of its inherent flexibility to variable inputs. Teachers have a lot of latitude in making judgments about the specific situation and students that they face, and they can adjust their goals accordingly. However, because of this flexibility, goal setting should not be used to compare individual teachers directly with one another.

The demand for accountability in education during the past 25 years has resulted in the fifth case explored by the authors— *student testing for school accountability.* On the positive side, the use of standardized tests to measure the performance of schools and school districts certainly clarifies the goals and focuses teachers' attention on the specific targets set. However, Sykes and Millman quote Shepard's list of six negative effects: political pressure leading to score inflation; narrowing of the curriculum; misdirected instruction; the application of outmoded "drill and practice" learning theory; a bias against the harder-to-teach kids; and the "deskilling" of teachers. In addition, the authors provide another list of negative effects on individual teachers. Once again, Sykes and Millman point out that these effects are supported by the general organizational behavior theory and literature. They conclude by suggesting that the use of testing for accountability and organizational control is bound to have negative effects, but that such testing is probably inevitable. In light of that, probably the best that can be done is to try to increase the positive benefits of such testing.

To demonstrate some possible positive benefits, the sixth and last case considered in Chapter 7 is that of the Prospect School in North Bennington, Vermont. This private school operated between 1965 and 1990, based on the philosophy that assessment should support teaching and learning rather than be oriented to external record keeping and standardized testing. The idea is that teachers' formal and informal methods of observing and documenting children's development over time are central to good teaching.

In the Prospect School, children were put in classes with many different ages, allowing them to remain with the same teacher and classmates for up to 3 years. Prospect also founded an archive of children's work that documented their growth over periods of up to 10 years. The assessment methods relied on a formal method that they called a descriptive review of the child, combining observation, documentation, and interviews. Over time, teachers were encouraged to build on the natural interests of each individual child toward the achievement of a formal education.

The record at Prospect School provides evidence that learning is an idiosyncratic process, and development should be broadly defined to include physical, emotional, and social as well as intellectual dimensions. These conclusions have important implications for the use of student testing in the evaluation of teachers, as will be apparent in the remainder of Chapter 7.

The second type of evidence gathered by Sykes and Millman is the views of the public, teaching professionals, and the testing experts. To put it briefly, they suggest that there is a wide gulf between all three groups on the issue. Generally, the public wants simple accountability by and for the numbers, believing that we can judge teachers based on their own performances indirectly by judging their effects on students. On the other hand, teachers know that their profession involves complexity and uncertainty, and even the best and most motivated teachers do not entirely control how much their students learn. As the authors point out, this is consistent with Merton's comment that laymen tend to judge professionals based on the outcome, whereas professionals themselves judge their results relative to the possibilities that they control. Generally, the psychometricians and testing experts come down on the side of the teachers, opposing the use of student learning as a measure of teacher effectiveness except under laboratory conditions. They point out that there are too many variables out of the control of the teacher, multiple-choice tests are too limiting, and the validity and reliability of existing measurement instruments is too low.

The third type of evidence that Sykes and Millman present in Chapter 7 is the effect of the current education reform movement on teaching and learning. They discuss three trends: new goals for learning, new conceptions of teaching, and the shifting face of student assessment. First, there seems to be a consensus emerging around a set of ambitious goals. Psychological theories of learning are changing; no longer do we need to teach basic skills first. The new "fourth R"—reasoning—is best studied in the traditionally academic disciplines. There is a need for curriculum and policy coherence. Second, there are new conceptions of teaching emerging. If these new ambitious goals are to be attained, teachers will have to be innovative and not afraid to take risks in "break the mold" schools. Generic competencies (e.g., classroom management) are not enough. They have been replaced by two aphorisms—the subject matters and the context counts. The content of teachers' knowledge is important, and the situation is also important. Excellent teachers both have a rich command of the subject matter and are able to adapt to diverse situations. Third, fundamental beliefs about student assessment are coming into question. The psychometric paradigm is being challenged with fundamental questions about the nature of validity and intelligence and the negative results of excessive testing. As a result, there is a search for new forms and approaches. A new term, "authentic achievement and assessment," has entered the vocabulary. Standardized multiple-choice tests are being supplemented by professional portfolios, and people are insisting that they be rewritten so as to be sensitive to context and individual.

All three types of evidence collected (cases, views of the experts, and the impact of reform) lead Sykes and Millman to propose some principles for a student learning component for the National Board of Professional Teaching Standards. They present the case for such a component and propose some design principles based on the evidence discussed in their chapter. They present those principles in the form of answers to four basic questions: What evidence should be obtained from students? What methods of data collection should be included? How much standardization should be built into the process of selecting learning goals and of collecting, assessing, and submitting the student-provided evidence? How much weight should the student-based evidence carry in the total assessment? The answers to those questions sum up Chapter 7 better than could be done here.

One of the key factors that Hart identified in her analysis of efforts to redesign the role of the teacher is the necessity for strong and consistent leadership in fostering such change. Consistent with that necessity, the next three chapters focus more clearly on the key role played by administrators of school organizations. In Chapter 8, Goldring focuses on the boundary-spanning part of their role—that is, how they manage the school's environment. As she points out, during the past 20 years, theories of organizational behavior have tended to consider organizations in general, and schools in particular, more as open systems than as closed ones. This means that the roles spanning the boundary between the organization and the environment have also become more important.

Boundary spanning is also important because schools do not generate their resources internally. Like all organizations, schools are tied to their general environment by the need to procure inputs (students and resources) and dispose of outputs (graduates). They are tied to elements in their specific environment to obtain specific resources (e.g., schools must convince voters that they are doing an acceptable job to win approval for their proposed budgets).

Goldring notes that the boundaries around school organizations are particularly permeable—that is, marginal outsiders (e.g., parents) have a lot of influence on school activities. Because schools are public institutions, outsiders such as parents cannot generally be excluded from them, so the only way for school organizations to manage their environment is to regulate the conditions and procedures by which such outsiders can influence the organization. Principals generally set the policy and manage many of the relationships, so Goldring argues persuasively that it is important to study their roles as boundary spanners.

The growing importance of the environment means that leaders of organizations must either manage (i.e., manipulate) it or else adapt to its changing demands. Goldring's basic premise is that organizational leaders in general, and school principals in particular, have some, but limited, latitude for making choices. Principals are dependent on the central district headquarters for resources, so they are constrained to adapt to central office demands. At the same time, they need enough autonomy and flexibility to adapt to local conditions. The challenge to principals is to make the right choices so as to strike an appropriate balance that affords the school both enough resources and autonomy to function properly.

According to Goldring, boundary-spanning roles involve macro and micro components; the macro level includes the environmental map of an organization and strategies for managing that environment, whereas the micro level includes the perceptions of the environment and the power tactics that actors acquire through environmental contingencies. Each level is explored in turn. Goldring divides the environment into elements of the *general environment* that are not dealt with on a daily basis but remain potentially relevant to the school (e.g., employers and the armed forces) and elements of the *specific environment* that are relevant all the time (e.g., teacher unions, the state and federal departments of education, and parents of the students).

Goldring also points out that the nature of school environments can vary greatly along four dimensions: volatility (stable versus dynamic), resource capacity (abundant versus scarce), clustering (structured versus anarchic), and complexity (homogenous versus heterogenous). *Uncertainty* is a problem for the school administrator to the extent that a school faces an environment that is volatile, has scarce resources, is anarchic, and is heterogenous. Based on a distinction between three types of uncertainty (state, effect, and response), Goldring discusses how uncertainty and dependence have independent and combined effects on the strategies that are available to school administrators.

Goldring then explains three potential strategies for reducing dependence: *competitive* strategies wherein principals seek to find alternative sources of the desired resources (e.g., special grants); *public relations* strategies designed to manipulate the environment's image of the school by scanning the environment for and collecting, filtering, and rebroadcasting information; and *voluntary responsiveness* strategies, wherein the school administrators do more than is asked of them in order to build trust and increase their usefulness to (and thus their power over) key elements in the environment.

This last strategy also fits well with Goldring's discussion of strategies aimed at adapting to the environment. In essence, these strategies seek to decrease the environment's *relative power* over the school by selectively increasing *interdependence* between school and environment. Strategies of this type include implicit cooperation, explicit contracting, co-optation, coalition building, and designing the organization in specific ways to adapt to the environment.

If either of these first two sets of strategies (manipulating or adapting to the environment) are impossible or prohibitively expensive, then boundary spanners may employ a strategy of changing the environment or redefining their organization's legitimate domain within that environment. An example of this might be a school changing its mission by becoming a magnet school for one specific area (e.g., the arts).

Goldring then moves to the micro level with an examination of boundary spanning and how members of the organization perceive the environment. This is in line with the tendency of modern researchers to view reality as subjectively enacted by the perceiver, rather than objective and independent of the perceiver. As the mediator between ordinary members of the organization and the environment, the boundary spanner (e.g., the principal) has a substantial amount of flexibility in "enacting" or "constructing" the environment that other organization members perceive.

In the remaining section of the chapter, Goldring discusses the power available to boundary spanners in attempting to control the uncertainty that they must inevitably deal with. She identifies three power tactics: control of key resources (e.g., money, materials, and intangibles such as expertise); using one's centrality in the network of internal decision makers to exert control over the premises of decision making (for more on this, see Chapter 2); and using one's legitimacy and connections with external actors in the environment.

Chapter 8 concludes by integrating the macro- and micro-level arguments across the two ends of the dependence continuum. Figure 8.2 displays some sample strategies by which school administrators manage their boundary-spanning responsibilities at both levels in a way that makes for an appropriate balance between the need to stay tuned in to the environment and the need to maintain enough elbowroom to operate effectively.

Whereas Goldring's analysis of the boundary-spanning nature of the role of the school administrator focused on one important facet of that role, Bolman and Heller take a broader approach, maintaining that administrative leadership is the key to organizing behavior in schools. They begin Chapter 9 by decrying the lack of leadership displayed by school administrators and providing a useful review of research that may help administrators to provide more leadership by helping them to understand, evaluate, and choose among their various options.

This stocktaking begins with a short history of American research on educational administration. They discuss the emergence of the role of administrator as distinct from that of teacher as the urban schools grew beyond the capacity of teachers to manage. Bolman and Heller review the successive importation by educational administrators of scientific management, the human relations era, and the theory movement, respectively.

According to these authors, the present era in educational theory began in 1974. It is characterized by the lack of a consensus on a particular model; underlying contemporary organizational theories include the new institutionalism, organizational culture, and the study of organizations as garbage cans and loosely coupled systems. Epistemologically, theories of educational administration moved away from the notion that social reality was objectively out there, with laws that awaited discovery by those who studied. On the conceptual-analytic level, *the critical theory* movement demonstrated that the theory-making process and theories are subjective; the role of the theoretician should be to bring assumptions behind theories to the surface. On the prescriptive-pragmatic level, *the effective schools movement* sought to understand what it is about this social reality that makes some schools (and leaders) more effective than others, so that similar social realities could be constructed in currently less effective schools.

The authors then review the history and development of various conceptions of leadership. Ideas of what it means to be a leader have evolved in several dimensions: from autocrat to analyst and social architect; from good father to catalyst and servant; from great warrior to negotiator and advocate; from hero as destroyer of demons to hero as creator of possibilities. They reflect two changes—the belief that leadership should be exercised by and for the many instead of by and for the few, and a shift from individual leaders as unilateral to leaders as influencers of relationships. The authors argue that leadership theories need to reflect the new conception by focusing less on identifying the characteristics of superheroes and more on identifying how leaders can better serve their followers, so that their followers will in turn become better servant-leaders.

From that perspective, Bolman and Heller next review the trends in school leadership research. They argue that the specific behaviors identified as good leadership need to be understood as contingent on a variety of variables such as timing, constituents' meaning making, and conditions in the school and community. Although the effective schools research has identified a set of specific behaviors that make for effective school leaders, this research has been based largely on standardized test scores in reading and mathematics, which many claim are inadequate measures of educational achievement.

As in other eras, there has been a tendency for educational administrators to import theories from other types of organizations. The "management revolution" that has been occurring since the 1980s in the private sector has resulted in many calls in the literature on school leadership for decentralized decision-making authority, risk taking and entrepreneurship, collegiality, and local flexibility. Bolman and Heller suggest that these ideas need to be carefully examined in the context of education (e.g., "Will total quality management improve schools? . . . Is total quality management simply an updated way to legitimize hierarchy and control?") (p. 343).

In the remainder of the chapter, Bolman and Heller examine six different, and partially overlapping, conceptions of leadership: vision, passion, and moral leadership; the leader as versatile diagnostician; the leader as politician; management and leadership; equity and leadership; and leadership in an organizational and institutional context. They conclude that leadership is necessary to help us cope with uncertainty and conflict, two characteristics of modern schools. Instead of being locked into obsolete views of heroic leadership and scapegoat leaders who do not deliver superhuman performance, we need better leadership theories to guide practitioners.

The previous two chapters focus on what makes school administrators effective leaders. The unstated assumption is that not all administrators have the ability or desire to be effective boundary spanners or effective leaders. In Chapter 10, Ogawa takes this a step further by maintaining that the characteristics of individuals must be matched to the demands of their role, and that the nature of roles must be matched with the organizational context. Ogawa deals with the issue of "fit" as part of any effort to organize behavior in schools. This chapter provides an analysis of the literature on administrative succession in the private sector and develops a research agenda for the study of administrator succession in schools.

Ogawa organizes his chapter around five categories of factors associated with administrator succession: organizational outcomes, organization members' responses to succession, successor/organization fit, conditions of the succession process, and antecedents to succession. He tracks these five categories of factors backward from organizational outcomes to the antecedents to succession to produce a map (Figure 10.1) characterizing plausible linkages between variables related directly and indirectly to administrative succession.

In the first category, two types of *organizational outcomes* have been studied. Regarding *organizational performance*, there have been studies of for-profit corporations, athletic teams, and school administrators. The research suggests that there is either no link or a negative link between succession and organizational performance. In other words, the replacement of the coach, manager, or administrator either did not affect performance or was related to a decline in performance. Regarding *organizational change*, the studies (all of school organizations) report mixed results. However, the research is consistent in reporting that successor superintendents can produce changes in their districts.

The second category of variables that Ogawa investigates is the *organization members' responses to succession*. Negative responses reported include disruptions in lines of communication, power relationships, decision-making processes, and the equilibrium of operations. In addition, five studies of diverse types of organizations reported an increase in conflict and tension among organization members. For example, after a brief "honeymoon," most teachers became insecure and mistrustful of the new principal. Unfortunately, there is little research evidence that the responses to administrator succession are related to organizational outcomes such as performance and change.

Ogawa next discusses a third category of variables—*the impact of successor/organization fit on the response of organization members*. The belief is that a good fit will cause a positive response, whereas a poor fit will cause a negative response. A good fit will minimize the disruptive effects of change; a poor fit will maximize those disruptive effects. When successors fail to adhere to organizational norms, conflict and tension increase, and when successors show concern for their subordinates while demonstrating their expertise (two dimensions often identified in the general organizational behavior literature as characterizing good leadership behavior), the subordinates will respond favorably to the new administrator.

The determinants of the successor/organization fit are likely to be found in the characteristics of the successor and the conditions under which the succession occurs. Ogawa points to two conditions of the succession process that appear to affect the frequency of the succession and the source of the successor. Generally, the more frequent the succession in a particular organization, the more disruptive the succession. Regarding the source of the successor, outsiders generally performed worse than insiders but were better at changing their organizations and show more concern for their subordinates.

The last category of succession-related variables are *the antecedents to the succession process.* Three variables are potentially relevant here: the size of the organization, the previous performance of the organization, and the environmental conditions facing the organization. Although the research findings on size are unclear, research clearly validates the common-sense notion that poor organizational performance is likely to result in administrative succession. In addition, the defeat of incumbents in school boards is likely to result in the selection of an outsider successor, and state educational policies are likely to influence the direction of organizational changes initiated by successors.

In the remainder of Chapter 10, Ogawa summarizes the pattern of results reported on, and discusses the implications of, his map of succession-related variables for policy, practice, and research. Specifically, he suggests some tentative implications for both school boards and administrative successors.

FIVE

The Impacts of Mathematics and Computer Technology on the Core Assumptions and Practices of Teaching

ANN WEAVER HART

Arising from the human resource management tradition, work redesign initiatives in organizations seek to improve people's work satisfaction and performance by making all aspects of work more fulfilling and motivating and to improve the quality and quantity of outcomes. Early in its development, this scholarship focused narrowly on discrete, structural job design features (Hackman & Oldham, 1980). As it developed, the research sought to understand relationships among work structures and individual and group characteristics. Personal and social system variables were found to affect perceptions about the work and its outcomes in isolation of objective characteristics of the work.

AUTHOR'S NOTE: I wish to thank Kerrie Naylor for her assistance with the review of literature and the application of work redesign concepts to the instructional imperatives of Math Smart.

Although generally isolated from the work redesign research, teacher work reform inquiry includes variables found to be crucial in other disciplines. Complicated by the school work context, which must address the work of children along with the work of adults, school reform presents a unique case. In *no other work context* do children and adults labor side by side. Their goal: to help each child learn.

Over the past decade, school reformers drew on research, beliefs, and stories about work and incentives valued by intelligent and talented teachers (Johnson, 1990a, 1990b). Hoping to attract and retain the best possible pool of teachers, they designed programs such as career ladders, mentor teachers, site-based management, and shared decision making (Little, 1990b). The majority of policy initiatives restructuring teacher work and the governance of schools, however, did not address the instruction of children—the work of schools—even as their designers asserted that instructional improvement was a major goal (Clarridge, 1988). Although many advances have been made in knowledge about effective instruction (including the use of sophisticated computer technology to improve learning), restructuring reforms continue to be dominated by political forces seeking to increase parental control and choice and by teacher professional groups seeking to improve the conditions and status of teaching work (Bacharach, 1990; Hart, 1990b). The history of education reform recounts policies and initiatives targeting work redesign for teachers (Bacharach, 1990; Murphy, 1990). Yet policy goals may not be clear, policymakers often do not know what they want, and stated goals frequently are inconsistent, unstable, and ambiguous. In this unstable environment of change, negotiation, and uncertainty, work redesign for teachers continues to capture attention and stimulate reform. At the same time, many fundamental teaching and learning questions that are coupled with the career satisfaction of the best teachers receive little attention.

This chapter offers one perspective on work redesign in schools, applying research on work redesign in organizations to an analysis of an instructional reform that affects fundamental work structure, social interaction patterns, and authority relationship. Research and theory on work redesign are used to frame an examination of the work structure and social systems affecting an innovative, cognition-based, and computer-assisted approach to mathematics instruction. This instructional approach (Math Smart) uses computers as tools in the learning process (rather than as tools for drill and practice). It affects the core technology of schools, challenging assumptions about the relevance and importance of fundamental tasks and relationships.

How Math Smart affects the redesign of teaching is discussed, and the concept of schools as organizations for learning is explored.

Despite the promise of increased learning that computers seem to offer, when research and development models for the use of computer technology in education are imposed on schools with no attention to their impact on the work structures of adults and children and the social systems of schools, they have an abysmal success rate. These (and other reform failures) have led some to recommend the critical examination "of the teaching profession *in the context of a general examination of schooling itself*" (Sirotnik, 1985, p. 68, italics in original). Reinforcing this recommendation, researchers find that people take satisfaction in the nature of work; their work fundamentally affects their attitudes about and the outcomes of their jobs (Kerber & Campbell, 1987). In the sections that follow, I describe the Math Smart program and review recent theoretical and research literature on work redesign. In the last section, I analyze the implications of Math Smart (and similar reforms) for the redesign of teachers' and pupils' work in restructured schools.

Math Smart: Computer-Assisted Conceptual Change in Mathematics

The mathematics instruction model on which this chapter relies was developed and tested in a 2-year project designed to change the way children conceptualize mathematics. It sought to change their approach to math: Rather than solving problem after problem using memorized procedures, children are taught to place problems in conceptual categories, understanding and analyzing the nature of the problem as they seek solutions (Connell & Peck, 1991). The instructional program began with 24 low-ability fifth-grade pupils. In the second year, 36 upper-ability fifth- and sixth-grade pupils were added, all in a lower middle-class elementary school.

The explicit goal of Math Smart instruction is to bring about conceptual change. It helps children internalize mathematically meaningful structures by posing problems for them to solve. Physical materials are used to represent symbols and symbolic relationships and to develop problem-solving strategies. For fractions, for example, children use egg cartons, rulers, clock faces, meter sticks, cakes (actual and drawn), graph paper chunks of various sizes, and sketches to represent the proportional relationships they study. In the process, children learn to translate problems into mathematical terms, internalize concepts rather than memorize algorithms (set procedures), and engage in "thought experiments" (Connell & Peck, 1991).

After they are comfortable with these physical materials, and children are functioning well at the level of sketches and manipulation, the teacher poses problems using worksheets, handouts, or templates; the children then physically construct the problem using familiar physical objects or sketches. Each class generates its own templates or models because each class tends to construct slightly different versions of physical representations of underlying mathematical constructs, and they do not automatically transfer from one class to another.

Children then use HyperTalk®[1] to instruct a computer to perform explicit steps to solve problems based on general concepts developed by them. They construct word problems of their own and learn to tell the problem in mathematical terms. The teacher may ask the children to pose a problem that they can solve, but which they believe no one else can solve. These problems often look much like those they have encountered in class but, according to Connell, "much nastier."[2] The children must master procedural *and* conceptual knowledge and be able to frame mental problems and understand mathematical, conceptual processes to tell the computer what to do.[3] They also must have regular access to computers, not just intermittent work in a school computer lab.

The tasks and roles of teachers and pupils also are altered by Math Smart. Adults serve as problem posers, question askers, and general skeptics. They do not explain and demonstrate. Children solve, explain, and justify their solutions and methods. Once children have overlearned math concepts (as measured by their explanations and justifications), they then instruct the computer via HyperTalk to compute additional, new, and specific problems that are examples of the mathematics they have generalized. This process accomplishes two goals: (a) It builds a bridge between children's/learners' physical experiences and the abstract formalisms of mathematics (leading to algebra); and (b) it requires that children/learners create an exact language to describe what they are doing. The children write for 10 minutes at the end of each lesson, recording what they have learned that day, the connections of the day's learning with concepts learned in the past, and impressions of the learning experience. This process allows them to draw on the benefits of deliberately structured experiential learning (Boud, Keogh, & Walker, 1985).

This instructional method changes assessment and evaluation, too. Drill and practice in which children try to solve problems and increasingly rely on rote memorization are de-emphasized (Connell & Peck, 1991).[4] Rather, the method capitalizes on successive internalization and abstraction of mathematical experiences and strives to help children develop self-generated rules for math computation. In addition to improved accuracy, a major goal of the Math Smart method is to increase pupils' attempts to solve problems based on a newly found confidence that they can be successful.

The following principles guide Math Smart instruction (Connell & Peck, 1991; Peck & Connell, 1991; Peck & Connell, in press):

1. The instructor does not explain but serves as a problem poser, skeptic, and question asker, focusing on pupil explanations. The traditional roles of instructor and pupil are reversed.

2. Meanings are defined using physical objects that pupils can manipulate. The meanings and mathematical relationships defined by this process are associated with arithmetical symbols and operations.

3. Instructors help children internalize and abstract their experiences by working with problems in the absence of the physical materials with which they learn new concepts.

4. Instructors use a meaning-centered evaluation rather than counting the number of problems computed correctly by pupils on assignment worksheets. This approach for assessing mathematical knowledge has long been reserved for advanced levels of study—algebra, geometry, trigonometry, and calculus—after many pupils have given up on math.

5. Using established programs, pupils instruct computers to solve problems based on the methods they develop. Pupils use the computer as a tool to construct methods of dealing with problems. They identify and select the data to be included in a problem, set goals, and choose appropriate procedures and control statements to obtain and verify results. They then instruct the computer to carry out the operations they define. Children learn there are many ways to solve a problem. The method capitalizes on "the computer's infinite patience and need for exactness of logic and clarity of expression" (Connell & Peck, 1991, p. 11).

Studies measuring learning outcomes support the efficacy of the Math Smart method. In the pilot study described above, children's correct responses on standardized tests increased significantly. In addition to this increase in correct answers, their ability to solve problems beyond the immediate topics of study increased. Although geometry and statistics were not taught, scores increased in these areas, with the greatest gains in pre-algebra, problem-solving, and estimation. Children's attempts to solve problems also increased. Low levels of performance decreased. In addition, children continued to use many different learning processes in the search for solutions (Connell & Peck, 1991).

Like other instructional innovations, Math Smart faces obstacles when educators attempt to implement it in schools. The social system and learning environment is not experimentally controlled and is firmly established. The Math Smart innovation exerts pressure on the work and social structures of teachers and children in a number of ways. It requires that:

1. Teachers become learners who must often reconstruct their own understanding of mathematics. They must learn to use physical objects rather than abstract symbols to pose questions that children must solve. The program challenges the assumption that teachers who are provided with innovative curricula (and shown how to use them) will be able to effectively implement them in their classrooms (Stoddart, Connell, Stofflett, & Peck, 1991).

2. Computers be available to pupils at all times during mathematics instruction, increasing the need for cooperation and coordination in computer labs.

3. Pupils and teachers know how to use established programs (HyperCard® in this example) to tell computers what steps to follow. They also must reconceptualize their view of computers as tools to solve problems rather than as drill-and-practice machines.

4. Teachers reconceptualize their role and adopt new activities. Teachers change from tellers and evaluators to problem posers, questioners, and skeptics and use physical objects to pose mathematical problems. This experience often contradicts the thousands of hours teachers have spent in classrooms as learners and fundamental expectations that the teacher will be the giver and explainer of knowledge. (Some will chastise them if they adopt this new role, arguing that they must remain expert givers of knowledge.)

5. Teachers, school and district administrators, and state evaluators reframe pupil outcome measures to include measures of conceptual understanding.

6. Teacher evaluation methods and criteria be modified. Currently popular observation instruments (Acheson & Gall, 1987) will be miserably out of date.

Instruction-Based Teacher Work Redesign

Good quality computer-assisted Math Smart instruction challenges many conventional assumptions and customs of work in schools. It changes the teachers' tasks, their control over students' tasks, the kind of feedback teachers and students receive, and notions of autonomy. The structure of work (for children and teachers) within the social system of schools received little or no attention in school reform literature until the Carnegie Forum report of 1986. Yet talented people recruited to teaching who find a working environment that fails to promote their success will become disillusioned and leave the profession regardless of their qualifications (Bacharach, Conley, & Shedd, 1986). Teacher mentor programs, for example, disrupt and are vulnerable to the social system of teaching (Little, 1990a). Likewise, the tasks children perform are shaped as much by convention as by good practice. Recent research provides convincing evidence that the school organization, not the individual teacher or child, should be the level of analysis in the search for antecedents of satisfaction and outcomes of work in schools (Smylie, 1992; Smylie & Denny, 1990; Smylie & Smart, 1990).

In addition to having demonstrable benefits for children, Math Smart joins an almost overwhelming number of initiatives that would redesign the work of teachers and learners. Some of these problems address the contents and processes of student learning; some develop in response to related teacher career needs and the conditions of work in schools (Hart, 1990a, 1990b). Cunningham (1983), for example, concluded after reviewing the literature on teacher burnout that it was in part attributable to the social and structural design of work. Other writers (Little, 1982, 1990a, 1990b) also emphasize the importance of teacher work structure.

Work redesign literature provides insights into complex structural and social factors that influence the work of teachers and pupils. Redesign seeks to "improve an organization's coordination, productivity, and overall product quality and to respond to employees' needs for learning, challenge, variety, increased responsibility, and achievement" (Cunningham & Eberle, 1990, p. 56). This focus provides a useful framework for understanding the dynamics that shape what people do in schools. The following discussion is organized around conceptual categories drawn from work redesign literature (Hart, 1990b): (a) work structure, (b) group characteristics of the social system and the organizational environment, (c) individual differences, and (d) social information processing influencing the interpretation of the innovation. These factors combine to create the perceived work characteristics people frame as pupil/teacher outcomes.[5] These conceptual categories help build a view of work for the people who spend their time and expend their creative effort in schools. Scholars of work redesign often conclude that work structure alone will not predict outcomes (Griffin, 1985). When the unique interactions among the work of children (or youth) and teachers are considered, education presents an intriguing and unusual case. Task structures, pupil and teacher assessment, the social structure of a school, content, and elegant technologies must affirm any innovative approach to instruction before it can become a productive part of the whole. The Math Smart innovation can bring improved outcomes for children. In part, its success depends on the ability of those who work in schools to understand the interaction of technical imperatives, work structure, and the social environment.

Work Structure

Interest in structures of work shaped the earliest efforts at work redesign. Instructional innovations such as Math Smart affect the fundamental structure of teachers' and pupils' work. Two prominent frameworks for understanding work structure to which educators can turn are the job characteristics model and the sociotechnical approach to work design.

The Job Characteristics Model

The structural framework driving much of the research and development on work redesign in recent years was developed by Hackman and his colleagues (Hackman & Oldham, 1980). Although shortcomings remain in the model's power to predict causal relationships among work structures, intervening psychological states, and the motivating potential of work, the basic elements continue to retain their explanatory value in subsequent research. The job characteristics model posits that elements of task, autonomy, and feedback can predict the motivating potential of work. A linear relationship, leading to the motivating potential of a job (MPS), is central to the model:

(skill variety + task identity + task significance) ×
autonomy × feedback = tested MPS.

The elements of task (variety, identity, and significance) are hypothesized to affect a perception that the work is meaningful with significant moderating effects exerted by a person's individual needs for growth (growth-need strength). Elements of the job are hypothesized to result in meaningfulness (from task features), knowledge of results (from feedback), and responsibility (from autonomy). This body of research defines skill variety as the need for a broad and distinct body of knowledge and skills necessary to accomplish the work; task identity as the ability to complete a task or a discrete piece of work; task significance as the effect of the job on other people or their jobs in the organization; autonomy as freedom, independence, and discretion in scheduling and completing work and influence on the knowledge and resources necessary to complete the work; and feedback as information about performance that comes from the work itself rather than from supervisors (Brief, Wallace, & Aldag, 1976; Green & Novak, 1982).

At present, the most significant challenges to the linear relationships in the job characteristics model center on causality—from job characteristics to psychological states to motivating potential (see Figure 5.1). These challenges question the simplicity of the model; the discrete meaning of task identity, autonomy, and meaningfulness; and the model's dependence on information about tasks and relationships in the workplace (Walsh, Taber, & Beehr, 1980). Additional questions about the power and discrete effects of the intervening psychological states remain (see Figure 5.1). Some studies support the conclusion that meaningfulness may supersede the other factors (Wall, Clegg, & Jackson, 1978). The model may need to include task interdependence as a sixth core dimension (Kiggundu, 1981). Role clarity, challenge (Walsh et al., 1980), job longevity (Kemp & Cook, 1983), need for achievement (Steers & Spencer, 1977), and work context (Champoux, 1981) have been suggested by various scholars as powerful work design factors that function as intervening and moderating variables. Other research suggests that autonomy may be the most crucial of the core job characteristics (Breaugh & Becker, 1987; Loher, Noe, Moeller, & Fitzgerald, 1985).

Another challenge to the model has been mounted by critics who see significant cross-study variance in result. Fried and Ferris (1987),

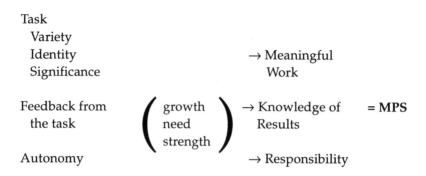

FIGURE 5.1. Elements of Structure: The Job Characteristics Model

in a meta-analysis of almost 200 relevant studies, concluded that most of this variance is attributable to statistical artifacts. Given the complexity and nature of the factors contributing to work attitudes and resulting performance, they concluded that the model stands fairly well against some of the major challenges. However, their results suggest that experienced meaningfulness and experienced responsibility could be integrated into a single dimension and that feedback from the work may motivate through all three of Hackman and Oldham's critical psychological states. Their major concern about the use of the model to assess actual work redesign emanates from a weak relationship between the psychological states as intervening variables and work performance established by their analysis.

Educational researchers seeking direct support for a job characteristics model of teaching work find that the model generally holds. Charters (1984) found that the Job Diagnostic Survey could not discriminate among the work of teachers in different subject and grade-level assignments. This research, conducted prior to the decade of reform just drawing to a close, revealed job dimension patterns that parallel those in Hackman and Oldham's (1980) samples. However, the model revealed no significant differences between teachers teaching different subjects, leading the researchers to conclude that it was not useful for distinguishing between teachers in the sample and that teachers' core job characteristics were essentially the same.

The structural features of the model, however, have been found to parallel structures in teachers' work and to predict motivating potential. Barnabe and Burns (1991), in a major test of the model, found that Hackman and Oldham's original research on various kinds of work could be replicated for teaching work. One major difference in their findings deserves note. The teachers in their sample demonstrated a dramatically lower experienced responsibility for outcomes, even when they described their work as high in autonomy (the structural characteristic hypothesized by the model to predict responsibility for outcomes). Given the argument by some scholars that autonomy may be the most significant of the core job characteristics and given the lack of a connection between autonomy and responsibility for outcomes in the Canadian sample, any change in structures that increases teachers' feelings of responsibility might cause a major improvement in teachers' motivation.

Education researchers also have found that important environmental and school-level factors affect teachers' responses to changes in their work designed to improve student outcomes. Smylie and Smart (1990), for example, found that teachers' support for career enhancement structures varies with their perceptions about various dimensions of the work such as the evaluation system and administrative burden, particularly in reference to their professional working relationships with other teachers.

Math Smart and other innovations affect the core work technology in schools, altering teachers' and students' tasks, the nature of the feedback they receive, and the autonomy and interdependence of teachers. Students gain more control over tasks, and teachers' control and autonomy becomes less indirect. In addition to the job characteristics just discussed, subject content fundamentally shapes the structure of teaching (Porter & Brophy, 1988). Thus math instruction reforms require a new cognitive structure as well as new technologies. The pressures Math Smart exerts on work structures illustrate this need. It restructures much of the teachers' job along all five core dimensions of the job characteristics model and adds interdependence (with technologies and with students). First, it requires an increase in skill variety from teachers. Teachers need to master computer skills far beyond the word-processing and drill-and-practice chores needed for more conventional computer technology initiatives in schools. The job characteristics model suggests that this increase in skill variety will make the job more motivating than before. Second, task identity may decrease—teachers are more dependent than ever on pupils' ability to define questions and advance the problem-solving process. Third, task significance should increase. Each time the teacher asks a question or stimulates student exploration, the impact on other pupils and on their mastery and abstraction is enhanced. The effects of Math Smart on autonomy and feedback are unpredictable and could be ambiguous. Certainly, feedback from students expands in form and substance, but the kind of feedback received adds an ambiguity that sometimes is difficult to tolerate when teachers are used to simple, right-and-wrong answers to mathematical problems. The core technologies of other professions that depend on client outcomes, such as social services, demonstrate similar relationships (Ashford & Cummings, 1985; Eisenstat & Felner, 1984).

Effects on teachers' feelings of responsibility for outcomes, experienced meaningfulness, and knowledge of results, for example, may follow changes in core technologies and in teacher and student tasks. Yet the relationships among job characteristics and psychological states for teachers require further exploration (Barnabe & Burns, 1991), and innovations may further complicate these relationships. Autonomy, a valued (though nebulously defined) feature of teachers' work, appears to strongly affect both job satisfaction and experienced responsibility for outcomes. At the same time, preliminary research on teacher work structure (Barnabe & Burns, 1991) and on the outcomes of Math Smart suggest areas of potential conflict. First, student outcome goals change substantially. Standardized and criterion-referenced achievement tests on which the number of correct answers to established problems is used to assess success will be inappropriate. Second, teachers' roles will require alteration, and they may need assistance in establishing clear roles (and behaviors) as problem posers, questioners, and skeptics. The legitimacy of these new roles in the eyes of other teachers, parents, and the community may also be in question, and negative judgments about the appropriateness of the new roles may exert pressure to return to the less productive, traditional methods. Participation in the decision to implement and in the logistics of implementing Math Smart also may play a critical part. If Elmore (1980) is correct, this program will not succeed if mandated from above. Attention to these variables will help planning and intervention strategies to optimize the positive impacts of instructional reform.

Sociotechnical Structures

Sociotechnical models provide a slightly different view of work structures than the model of job characteristics does. These models focus on the requirements of technical effectiveness in combination with the social and psychological needs of people. The sociotechnical approach (Cherns, 1987; Trist, 1974, 1981) to work redesign emphasizes the compromises necessary between work design and social imperatives. It also acknowledges that techniques used to structure work depend on both the job and the organizational culture, and the processes by which technology and structure affect people's performance and satisfaction require constant reconsideration (Jones, 1984). Given the nature of computer assisted instruction used by Math Smart in which teachers' answer-giving relationship with students changes significantly, these considerations take on added importance. For all kinds of work, "the dramatic transformation of traditional types of work that has accompanied the introduction of computer-based control technologies has brought the matter of job design very much into the policy domain" (Albin, 1985, p. 703). One scholar in the tradition of sociotechnical design asserts that "the most effective organizations will be those in which the technology and the organization structure and social processes are designed to fit together" (Whyte, 1991, p. 97).

Cherns (1987) provides insight into the principles of sociotechnical design. He suggests that redesigners should consider crucial principles that make it possible to develop work configurations grounded in individual work groups and supported by the social structure. These central principles are summarized in Table 5.1.

Cherns's principles promote an integration of the social and technical work worlds, the support of information work groups, and the development of transition structures that facilitate change (Fincham, 1989). "Teachers should collectively control technical decisions about the structure, form, and content of their work" (Darling-Hammond, 1986, p. 544). Math Smart requires that teachers' beliefs about the "right" way to structure instruction will require careful reassessment in light of each new technical development.

Research tracing emerging outcomes of some educational restructuring and reform efforts affirms the interdependence of social systems and structure suggested by sociotechnical theories of work structure. Hart (1990a, 1992) found that the social interaction patterns and beliefs about appropriate and right activities in schools significantly affected teachers' responses to various work structures associated with teacher career ladders and site-based decision-making programs. Malen and Ogawa (1988) and Ogawa and Malen (1991) uncovered similar patterns related to site-based decision making and shared governance plans. Rather than providing social structures that support leadership roles for teachers, mentors, and more participative decision structures in schools, these researchers found that the social system worked against the new structures. Either established definitions of appropriate social relationships caused such discomfort that some teachers were unwilling to continue in new roles or else the established social structures overcame planned changes in authority relationships (such as those expected in site-based decision making), and principals and

TABLE 5.1 Principles of Sociotechnical Design

Principle	Purpose
Compatibility	Optimization of social and technical systems
Minimum specification	Facilitates informal work groups
Minimum variance export	Groups fill many supervisory functions
Boundaries facilitate sharing	Spreads information, knowledge, and learning
Information flow	Facilitates work accomplishment
Access to resources and the authority to use them	Maximum advantage of equipment, materials, and other resources
Management of general functions	Protects against remote firefighting
Element adjustments	Maximizes organizational integration and adjustment to environment
Support congruence	Promotes integration
Adjustment period for organizational design	Formation of transition to support social and technical adjustments
Change and redesign are technical and social	Accommodates rapid permanent innovation

other conventional authority roles continued to so dominate the decision process that no real change was apparent.

The sociotechnical approach to work structure calls attention to tensions that could result if technical imperatives are imposed on instruction. In the case of Math Smart, not only are instruction and work dependent on computers but the "telling" role of teachers virtually disappears. Sociotechnical analyses raise additional issues for the redesign of teacher and pupil work that deserve attention in Math Smart. First, the dependence on technology opens up a whole new set of issues related to the context and to interactive work with computers by teachers and children. Second, the conceptual, social, and technological aspects of instruction involving teachers and children require careful and mutually supportive designs. Those implementing the innovation should take specific steps to (a) avoid overspecification of ways in which the methods should play out in classrooms; (b) protect it from other aspects of the school based on different assumptions and methods; (c) promote the sharing of information, knowledge, and learning among children and teachers and the free flow of information about the program in the community; (d) make necessary adjustments to the school (such as scheduling) to accommodate the innovation; and, perhaps most important, (e) provide for the development of a "transition organization," acknowledge its unique part in the overall implementation, and be tolerant and supportive of the pressures that are unique to the transition period.

Group Characteristics: The School Social System and the Organizational Environment

Work redesigners need repeated reminders that work reform takes place in real settings filled with people. Schools are a specific kind of workplace (Bacharach & Mitchell, 1991; Johnson, 1990a). Research on work redesign in education yields evidence that dynamic factors at each school significantly affect the nature of educational outcomes (Hart, 1990a). These factors include organizational resources; norms, expectations, and values; intraorganizational politics and power; perceptions of work and of role routinization and clarity; inertia; and leadership.

Organizational *resources* are the most visible feature of the environment affecting the outcomes of work redesign. Resources can limit impacts because of scarcity (Peters & O'Connor, 1980) or provide avenues for intervention (Mitchell, 1986). Writers agree that resources affecting the outcomes of work design include (a) information; (b) materials, supplies, or clients; (c) budget; (d) human support services; (e) training or knowledge; (f) time; (g) work environment and space; (h) tools and equipment; and (i) authority (Bacharach & Mitchell, 1991; Hart, 1990b). Of these resources, only four depend on money. The reallocation of existing resources might be used to create more attractive work structures, increase teacher growth opportunities, and provide incentives to teachers to rethink and reorganize their work (Lipsky, 1976; Mitchell, 1986), mitigating some of the negative effects of resource scarcity (Lipsky, 1976). Every one of the eight is affected by Math Smart.

The *norms, expectations, and values* of the group exert a second strong influence over interpretations and outcomes of work redesign in schools. Although studies on the sociology of teaching (Johnson, 1990a, 1990b; Lortie, 1975; Waller, 1932) describe a profession in which civility, equality, and privacy dominate rules of teacher interaction, evidence is mounting that significant differences also may be rooted in work subgroups such as schools (Hart, 1990a; McKelvey & Sekaran, 1977;

Van Maanen & Katz, 1976). School-level social expectations and norms should have a profound impact on interactions and outcomes as work is socially constructed (O'Connor & Barrett, 1980).

The frame of reference from which people judge the relative desirability of job structures in part depends on the norms, values, and expectations of the group to which they belong, especially if they have positive memories of their membership and experiences. Some writers find significant additions to explained variance in people's descriptions of their work from their frame of reference, professionalism, and affect or attitudes (O'Reilly, Parletter, & Bloom, 1980). "Past experiences, present roles, and socialized expectations, may result in different perceptions and definitions of the same job" (O'Reilly et al., 1980, p. 119). Others find that a person's position in an organization's central communication network, involvement with outsiders, and other forms of social interaction affect her or his ability to see the work differently from the strongly accepted insider group perspective (Dean & Brass, 1985).

Research in schools supports predictions that social system dynamics will exert a powerful influence on work redesign. Hart (1990a) found that social interactions at the school level either suppress or ratify widespread professional norms chronicled most recently by Johnson (1990b). In a comprehensive comparative case study of two similar schools undergoing work redesign, she observed teachers in a supportive social group redefining the importance of status and pay differentiation, interdependence, and change. Teachers attempting changes in a different school in which norms of equality, privacy, and civility (defined as nice, cordial, placid) were enforced were ostracized and suffered intensely. The redesigned work was halted. Little (1982) described dynamics in effective schools in which norms of experimentation and collegiality exerted primary influence. She also found powerful social forces affecting instruction and the interventions and assistance offered by teacher leaders and mentors under school reform plans (Little, 1982, 1990a, 1990b).

Math Smart also challenges schools' norms, expectations, and values. Teachers and children do very different things and valued outcomes differ substantially. Explanations are not valued; skepticism and questioning are valued. Evaluation relies on assessment of meaning rather than counts of correct responses. Children have as much impact on the selection of the problems completed as do teachers.

A third aspect of a work group affecting redesign is *intraorganizational politics*. Bacharach, Bamberger, and Conley (1990) point out that we must acknowledge the power of the environment, the reality of organizations as negotiated political systems, and the cyclical historical patterns of schools. When these factors in the nature of schools as organizations are adequately understood, they exert influence on strategies for redesign and reform that seesaw back and forth between professional and managerial demands and "are tacitly negotiated" between administrators and teachers. Under the current environment, strategies for the solution of school problems are more likely to use "crisis" and "paper clip" approaches than systematic instructional change like Math Smart. Power balances among teachers and between teachers and pupils will shift if control over process is a power issue.

The micropolitical reality of power relationships, coalitions, and bargaining effects on actual work outcomes is well established in organizational theory and research. Bacharach and Mundell (1993), for example, provide a comprehensive analysis of the impacts of political interactions at the group and school levels on multiple organizational outcomes, definitions of reality, and attitudes about the relative desirability of a work situation in education.

A fourth aspect of schools as social work groups emerges from studies on how features of the workplace such as *role ambiguity or work routinization* affect teachers. Interest continues to grow in the unique features of the job that contribute to teachers' attitudes about their work. Conley, Bacharach, and Bauer (1989) studied 42 elementary and 45 secondary schools, finding that role ambiguity and routinization are associated with teacher career dissatisfaction. Teachers, like other professionals working in bureaucracies (Organ & Greene, 1981), appear willing to accept bureaucratization if it clarifies their roles in the organization (without making their work routine and mundane). For elementary school teachers, routinization followed role ambiguity in adding to career dissatisfaction; for secondary school teachers, supervision was the second most powerful predictor of dissatisfaction.

Routinization, ambiguity, and supervision are affected by Math Smart. For example, the transition from traditional to new instructional norms may leave teachers feeling ambiguous about valued behaviors, and their supervisors could quickly undermine Math Smart by relying on assessments of defined direct-teaching behaviors. Those working to implement the method and technology will need to understand the existing "implicit theories" dominating a school (Brief & Downey, 1983). These implicit theories can limit the consideration given a new instructional design such as Math Smart. Teachers may be accused by their colleagues of "not teaching" (Peck, 1987; Peck & Connell, 1991, in press).

These pressures have been predicted. Chubb (1988) and Chubb and Moe (1988) point out that improvement efforts at the work-site level must acknowledge the institutional nature of schools that have interdependent parts, governance by well-established rules and behavioral norms, and adaptations promoting stability. They assert that the organization as a whole—its goals, leadership, followership, and climate—will have more effect on outcomes than policy. Among the strongest of the prevailing group pressures that must be recognized are "institutionalized expectations about the nature of education . . . and the entrenched roles of education participants" (Angus, 1988, p. 30).

Fifth, a factor described as organizational *inertia* or resilience affects the success of work redesign. Brief and Downey (1983) showed that "wrong" views (such as those supporting less effective instructional methods) can be resilient and long lasting:

> The fact that "incorrect" implicit theories may continue to serve a social glue function does not mean that other dysfunctional consequences may not also flow simultaneously to the organization or its members. . . . In some cases, the more embattled the organization, the greater the organization members' perceived need to preserve the traditional arts. (Brief & Downey, 1983, p. 1079)

Redesigners cannot afford to ignore these group effects, however, because "affective responses to work are predominantly associated with organizational characteristics rather than individual ones" (O'Reilly & Roberts, 1975, pp. 148-149).

Organizational inertia is a powerful factor in organizational change. Even in the face of major environmental threats and potential failures such as those currently faced by education, firmly established organizational structures and procedures exhibit resilience against change in strategy or structure:

> When the connections between means and ends are obscure or uncertain, carefully designed adaptations may have completely unexpected consequences. Moreover, short-run consequences may often differ greatly from long-run consequences. In such cases, it does not seem realistic to assume a high degree of congruence between designs and outcomes. (O'Reilly & Roberts, 1975, pp. 148-149).

Examples of inertia in work redesign in education can be found in research on career ladders, mentor teacher programs, and school site management (Hart, 1987, 1990a; Hart & Murphy, 1990; Little, 1990a; Malen & Ogawa, 1989). Teachers often re-create relationships and tasks in conventional ways. Mentors remain in their own classrooms during school hours, so they have trouble seeing new teachers at work. Positions often are awarded on the basis of seniority or rely on a within-school talent pool to avoid competition among teachers. Principals emerge as the primary power center in school site councils.

Elmore (1987, p. 61) argues that policy intersects with content and pedagogy in schools. He attributes the "roots of resistance or inertia" to the prevalence of processes through which policies are implemented from the top down in schools. This undermines the foundations of teachers' authority with children and results in teacher resistance and pupil disengagement. He asserts that any new instructional method changing the design of work also must respect the students' part in the authority structure of schools. Rather than merely reflecting adult expectations of their teachers' roles in the system, students should contribute their own consent to the legitimate authority of teachers. Elmore suggests a programmatic rather than a regulatory view of implementation, supporting instructional innovations.

Math Smart may meet many of Elmore's criteria for reforms with high potential. It depends, for example, on a transfer of conceptual authority and power to students. Teachers are questioners, framers, and inquirers. Students must accept their own authority and responsibility to successfully construct math concepts and instruct computers.

Finally, *leadership* can be conceptualized as a group characteristic affecting work redesign (Hart, 1993; Ogawa & Bossert, 1990). (The importance of leadership in the reform of schools is addressed by Bolman and Heller in another chapter in this book.) Some writers point out that many approaches to work design and redesign neglect the role played by supervision (e.g., Cordery & Wall, 1985). Three interrelated propositions link work properties and first-level management: (a) autonomy and feedback are particularly crucial elements in work design; (b) supervisory practice is a major determinant of these job characteristics; and (c) designing work to enhance autonomy and feedback requires commensurate consideration of the supervisory role (Cordery & Wall, 1985, p. 425). Lack of attention to supervisory issues can contribute to inadequate anticipation of potential problems encountered during work redesign (Cordery & Wall, 1985). If the supervisory role becomes "boundary management"—coordinating the relationship between the primary work group and other work groups—a principal will have to construct and monitor new arrangements for understanding the work. A principal may also need to provide clear boundaries that limit discretion. Supervisors must manage definitions of good work, for example, that conform to the technological and cognitive imperatives of good instruction under Math Smart. This must occur outwardly (for the community) and inwardly, so that activities can be changed and supervision modified (Cordery & Wall, 1985).

The preceding group factors all can be predicted to affect innovations like Math Smart. First, work and role clarity may suffer during the transition from traditional instruction to Math Smart instruction. Ambiguity and routinization are strong predictors of teacher dissatisfaction, and Math Smart may initially increase ambiguity and decrease routinization, autonomy, and perceptions of teacher authority.

Second, norms, expectations, and values long established as accepted and right in schools will come under examination. Implicit theories about teachers as the givers of knowledge and children as learners of algorithms and proofs will be challenged. The existing norms resulted from strong socialization of teachers as both learners and teachers and from widespread acceptance in the society at large of well-established norms (such as how to teach mathematics), goal definitions (number of correct responses on repeated and numerous problems), purposes (correct answers versus abstract understanding of the underlying mathematics concept), beliefs (mathematics is a set of procedures), and habits (explain, give example, make assignment, and help with seat work). Elmore (1987) reminded us that content and pedagogy are both crucial to teachers; changes will spark further resistance and inertia if teachers are excluded from the entire process of implementation—from the original decision to final institutionalization. Peck and Connell found the same dynamics—if Math Smart is to work, it *cannot* be imposed. The method imposes on the culture of authority from child to teacher, changing fundamental interaction patterns. Both pupils and teachers reframe their expectations, and some pupils and parents may initially feel that the teachers are not teaching. The work of children changes fundamentally; they construct concepts, reflect, and seek to structure their own algorithms. This work differs markedly from traditional mathematics assignments—problem after problem in which pupils perform a set of steps taught to them by the teacher in order to find "the answer."

Third, inertia will play into the resistance to change in other ways. Predictions in the organizational inertia literature lead to the conclusion that we may be unwilling to trade old ways of doing math for new, untested and unpredictable mathematics performance resulting from Math Smart. Performance on multiplication tables and geometry proofs is easily measured by counting the number of right answers. This count is a familiar and secure outcome measure. Peck and his colleagues have established that traditional, algorithm-driven methods conventionally used to teach mathematics leave children obsessed with memorizing correct procedures rather than understanding mathematics. They report that children return to these methods whenever they are asked to use mathematics principles learned the old way. Teachers, too, revert to habitual ways of solving problems.

Those hoping to redesign math instruction also must attend to a fourth factor—the organizational realities of isolation, hierarchy, accountability pressure (evaluation techniques), ambiguity and overload, situational uniqueness, and fixed resources identified as characteristic of teaching. Each school will present a unique combination of these group features with which educators and learners must contend.

Perceptions cannot be ignored. The Math Smart initiative can be evaluated using a number of outcomes—children's attitudes toward math, ability to describe abstract mathematical relationships and provide rationales for computation choices, scores on standardized tests, and problem-solving attempts. Teachers' perceptions will, however, determine whether they persevere with the program and facilitate its exportation to new settings. A number of writers have assailed the use of self-reported affective judgments about work to assess redesign (Roberts & Glick, 1981). In the face of this challenge, other writers mount a response: If the relative value of work redesign and people's commitment to it rests on perceptions of its value, then one can only assess success by tapping these perceptions, for it is upon their own judgments that teachers will act (Terborg & Davis, 1982):

> When the intent is to predict or understand employee attitudes or behavior at work . . . , employee ratings of the job dimensions are *preferable* to use, since it is an employee's own perception of the objective job that is causal of his [sic] reactions to it. (Hackman & Oldham, 1976, p. 261)

Finally, school leadership will be changed by the redesign demanded by Math Smart. Chubb (1988) says that leadership in high-performing schools is "more pedagogical and less managerial" (p. 33). It is also stronger, more forceful, and retains a focus on communication and the pursuit of vision. Decision making is more democratic and relationships among teachers and principals more cooperative. He maintains that one can find a general belief among teachers that they have more impact on schoolwide policy and on teaching and discipline in effective schools, and he emphasizes the importance of school-level autonomy. All these features are identified as important aspects of successful work redesign.

School leaders also must respect teachers' goals and the protection of their work boundaries. Teachers' autonomy can be violated if they feel that principals have dictated an instructional method to them (Cordery & Wall, 1985). The question is how might a principal introduce Math Smart (an instructional method) without negatively influencing teachers' perceptions of their work: By working directly with teachers who want to adopt new methods and by bringing along those who are reserving judgment by providing them experiences observing and working with the new processes.

Pressures on leadership will emerge in other areas. Measurement of outcomes, for example, will require quantitative and qualitative data (Connell & Peck, 1991). Low standardized test scores and the availability of technology funds to pay for the computers often drive the initial implementation of innovations such as Math Smart. Outcome scores will play an ongoing part in evaluation. But one also must measure children's ability to explain the mathematical concepts in words and in precise language to a computer, so evaluation requires interviews, journals, and observation of children's interactions with the computers. The measurement of attempts to solve a problem (because an increase in the number of attempts is an important long-range goal as it measures children's attitudes about their likelihood of success with mathematics) and attitude changes have long-term impacts. Principals and district-level administrators will need to provide clear articulation of the program within the school and to those outside the school who may not understand it. Parents will not see pages of homework problems for the children to practice and practice, nor will they see large numbers of scores to be averaged by the teacher to produce grades. All these changes in evaluation will require an environmental reframing and reinterpretation.

Leaders will need to focus on evaluating the teachers' tasks, not the individual. Teachers will be closely studied and will need reassurance that the *method*, not their ability and performance, is being evaluated. This requirement will force us to take seriously rising calls to abandon the practice of spending "disproportionate amounts of time . . . appraising the *individual* rather than evaluating the *task*" (Bacharach & Conley, 1986, p. 12). Evaluation issues reignite questions about teachers as technicians versus teachers as professionals. "Most people will name their best and worst teachers without hesitation, basing these choices not on how much they learned but on the procedures that these teachers followed in their classrooms. . . . As a general principle . . . you prefer that a technician not take on problems that cannot be solved readily and efficiently, but you want a professional to take on *any* problem—regardless of the probable result" (Soar, Medley, & Coker, 1983, p. 240).

Leadership and the supervision of Math Smart programs thus will place very real pressures on principals. Many work redesign approaches neglect supervision, impeding research and practice (Cordery & Wall, 1985). Pressure can come from misinterpretations of the conceptual and work challenges of Math Smart, and policymakers could cripple the innovation through the continued insistence that those using the method comply with outcome measures and behavioral requirements inappropriate to the method. For example, grants and appropriations often include the provision that all money must go directly to hardware and pay for teachers, leaving no resources for training and staff support (Hart, 1991). Peck and Connell often donate their time teaching side by side with teachers in schools in which they work, but this method of support is impractical on an ongoing basis. Studies in other settings revealing administrative failures could well serve as a caution. Among observed failures that could easily affect Math Smart are (a) failure to follow through on efforts that heightened expectations of teachers for pupil performance in mathematics and access to technology for other subjects; (b) unwillingness to increase teachers' influence in crucial decisions related to instruction and failure to integrate Math Smart with other work redesign or school restructuring efforts such as site-based management and career ladders; (c) failure to reduce turnover, making it difficult for the necessary pool of teachers who understand the new conceptualizations of mathematics and have the ability to use computers as a tool to help children master abstract mathematics' concepts; (d) principals' lack of ability to cope with the expansion of work and new challenges, including the scheduling challenges, supervision and evaluation of teachers, and pupil evaluation; and (e) inability to resist pressures from those who do not understand the conceptual basis of Math Smart to go back to the greater predictability and certainty of drill-and-practice methods of math instruction.

Individual Characteristics

Many individual teacher characteristics confound the outcomes of work redesign (O'Connor & Barrett, 1980; Schneider, 1985). Some scholars find that the evidence for a within-person, cognitive consistency interpretation of work design is more compelling than the evidence for a person-situation interpretation (Roberts & Glick, 1981, p. 204). Researchers have investigated a panoply of individual characteristics as moderators of the effects of work redesign (Hart, 1990b), and personal traits or psychological disposition and past work experiences are seen as the most powerful. Because these individual characteristics can affect responses to work redesign by moderating the relationship between task characteristics (like interest, stimulation, etc.) and responses (Gardner, 1986), the link between individual differences and work redesign in teaching becomes important (Staw, Bell, & Clausen, 1986).

Personal Traits

Although dispositional factors moderate the outcomes of work redesign interventions, these factors are largely outside the direct control of administrators and policymakers, except as a focus of attraction, selection, and retention incentives. Consequently, this discussion will focus on a few individual factors that seem to be most malleable to intervention during the implementation of innovations such as Math Smart. First, job involvement and organizational commitment continue to interest scholars in education, in part because the way in which a teacher identifies psychologically with the job reflects on her or his involvement and commitment. This psychological state (related to work features in structural models) appears to affect absenteeism and turnover, as well as the way teachers see themselves. DeLong (1982) found that teachers differ in their career orientations and that responses to the work and to incentives may depend on how they see themselves. Like other individually measured characteristics, professional or personal self-concept may in part result from past performance and from social or group conceptions about worthy work activities. Rewards valued by high-performing teachers provide evidence that they come to value future growth over immediate rewards, preferring further professional growth opportunities over cash. Frase (1989) found this to be the case in Arizona, where high-performing teachers were more likely to choose opportunities for growth and professional travel than cash rewards in a career ladder program. Professional travel provided more opportunities for job enrichment and more recognition from peers.

Needs for personal and professional growth seem to be among the most important of individual traits moderating the effects of work redesign (Gangster, 1980; Hackman & Oldham, 1980). Growth-need strength, need for achievement, need for autonomy, and desire for enriched work seem to exert considerable influence over responses to work redesign (Cherrington & England, 1980; O'Connor, Rudolph, & Peters, 1980; Roberts & Glick, 1981). General ability also moderates outcomes. Although it contributes to the need for growth and overall performance, it also makes people more subject to frustration as a result of organizational constraints (Peters & O'Connor, 1980). Some argue that given the opportunity to learn, teachers attack classroom problems with renewed enthusiasm and that growth opportunity is a powerful source of motivation and satisfaction (Banner, 1985). Because many educational reforms aim to improve the attraction of teaching work for people who possess these characteristics, the job features valued by these people are the focus of much attention.

The desire for professional growth emerges as a strong motivating factor in teachers' support for reforms and thus could play a major part in the success of innovations like Math Smart. Smylie and Smart (1990) found that teachers who support significant changes in their work do so because they see opportunities for their own professional learning. They concluded that "perceived effects on work are more important to teacher support of both merit pay and career ladder programs than is any program characteristic" (p. 149). The major worries teachers in their sample expressed related to possible negative effects of reforms on relationships with other teachers.

Researchers look for individual change in the classroom practices of teachers, in their beliefs and attitudes, and in pupil learning as a result of innovations and interventions. Guskey (1986, 1988) asserted that staff development that results in changes in teachers' classroom practices and has a positive impact on pupil learning will change teachers' beliefs and attitudes. Citing ethnographic evidence from observations of classrooms and other studies of dissemination efforts supporting educational change, he identified three principles that support a linear model predicting outcomes from staff development: (a) recognize that change is a gradual and difficult process for teachers, (b) ensure that teachers receive regular feedback on pupil learning progress, and (c) provide continued support and follow-up after the initial training. Guskey also cautioned that perceptions about the importance of a new practice, its difficulty of use, and congruence with present teaching and philosophy will affect judgments about its worth. Efficacy (general, individual, and teaching) also affects these judgments, and the most able teachers may be more likely to be using effective methods and be interested in new methods. Tying the panoply of individual characteristics together, Guskey pointed out that teacher efficacy, teaching affect, and teaching self-concept significantly relate to teachers' attitudes regarding the congruence, difficulty of use, and importance of redesigned and recommended practices (Guskey, 1988). Also, researchers "have found that the more highly implemented practices tend to be perceived as congruent with the philosophies of individual teachers" (Stein & Wang, 1988, p. 175).

These research findings reinforce early experiences with Math Smart. Teachers must feel confident that their activities are worthwhile, that students learn well and benefit from their efforts, and that they will be evaluated on new criteria congruent with the work structure of Math Smart and the skills children exhibit. Whatever a teacher's original beliefs about worthwhile instructional practice, she or he will need support that affirms the professional value of the new technology and an instructional method that affirms her or his professional self-image as an expert and valued teacher.

Experiences

Work history, education, and training experiences also influence attitudes toward redesign related to teaching. Researchers find "strong early experience effects on attitudes" (Vance & Biddle, 1985, p. 262).

First, years of experience affect attitudes about work, and this experience factor is confounded by age (Kalleberg & Loscocco, 1983; Katz, 1978; O'Reilly et al., 1980). Researchers have found that with increased experience, information about a new work design will have less impact on task-related attitudes and on behavioral intentions (Vance & Biddle, 1985). Newer teachers will value feedback from respected colleagues and authorities, knowledge of results, and opportunities to learn and grow in their own teaching (Hall, 1976). But they also will experience work norms—competent teachers do not ask for help. "You don't ask for help, or people will think that you're no good" (Hart, 1990a, p. 52).

Experience in a profession also socializes people to accept conventional definitions of good work and worthy activities (Turner, 1988), a second experience factor affecting work redesign. People with experience in schools have strong beliefs about the tasks and relationships that identify good teaching in a particular subject (Freiberg, 1985; Griffin, 1985; Little, 1990). Teachers lack preparation for changes in their work that new programs bring; parents, socialized as pupils to expect different behaviors from teachers, lack criteria on which to judge the new relationships, technologies, and relationships; work definitions established over years of socialization omit differentiating features for master versus other teachers; principals lose status; a paucity of experience means that no research base exists on which to judge programs; thoroughly socialized teachers who control teachers' organizations oppose differentiation; and new authority structures compete with conventional school supervisory authority and methods (Freiberg, 1985). As an illustration of the conflict that develops over the redesign of a teaching role, Griffin (1985) poses two very different conceptions of the master teacher. The first conceives of master or mentor teachers as better than others at the same activities. The second defines masters/mentors as doing more than others; the mentor may or may not engage in conventional teaching activity but performs specialized functions in schools and classrooms.

Role and career transitions exert influence on professional identities and norms formed in early career experiences (Nicholson, 1984; Van Maanen & Schein, 1979). Major changes in the way work is done cause people to reframe and redefine themselves. One useful way of conceptualizing readiness for transition was identified by Oldham and Hackman (1980), who classified people at work as overstretched, fulfilled, or growing. Under this classification, teachers who are overstretched by Math Smart will have difficulty processing new information and the new conceptualizations of their work required by the method. Fulfilled teachers may need help framing reasons for the change even if it makes them more effective teachers. Growing teachers will want to push new designs, stretch consultants (as Connell and Peck have discovered), and demand increased knowledge to go along with their new experiences. New roles and unfamiliar boundaries between teachers and students and among teachers are created (Latack, 1984). Experiences also affect work redesign by shaping perceptions of self, efficacy, and success (Stein & Wang, 1988). Co-workers implementing an innovative program often draw on perceptions of self-efficacy and the value of the program. Additionally, teachers assess the likelihood of students' reactions to a new instructional method on the basis of "how students will react to the change . . . and how well the innovation appears to fit the teacher's situation (e.g., is this program workable in my classroom?)" (Stein & Wang, 1988, p. 175).

Like personality, experiences may affect Math Smart implementation. Job involvement and commitment measures may identify teachers likely to be interested in undertaking this major instructional change. Those with high job involvement and commitment to the school should be more successful at making the necessary professional changes. Implementers also can help enhance success: Efficacy can raise teachers' expectations of success; desire for autonomy, creativity, and variety may also have a positive impact because the most powerful moderating variable in work redesign research continues to be growth-need strength or some other similar higher order need. But commitment and the ethics of professional standards could cause problems with Math Smart because a teacher might have difficulty giving up the telling and explaining functions central to many conceptualizations of teaching. If "standards" or "rules" seem to conflict with the new method, they, too, could cause problems. Teachers need professional and personal support interpreting these pressures and coming to grips with the changes in their professional self-concepts that the instructional innovation requires. Without this support, the new pedagogies may never achieve legitimacy within existing professional norms.

Experience also affects attitudes. Teachers who are fulfilled or overstretched in their current teaching may have trouble with the role and work transitions required by Math Smart. Experience causes "overlearning" to which we return. In their pilot program, for example, Connell and Peck (1991) and Stoddart et al. (1991) found that teachers' and children's experiences learning the rules that result in the correct answer to a math problem can contaminate their ability to capitalize on the learning advantages of Math Smart, forcing them to fall back on old methods of problem solving. A correct answer is very comforting.

Social Information Processing—
Interpreting Work Redesign

Regardless of the "objective" reality of work structure, group features, and individual differences, reality is constructed by the sharing and interpretation of information in the social environment. Increased interest in the socially constructed reality of organizations stimulated much of the interest in social information-processing interpretations of work redesign. Smircich (1983) contends that organizations are cultures with deeply embedded beliefs and assumptions about the way things are done and the fundamental meaning of the group. These beliefs about meaning and purpose shape all interpretations of redesigned work. Schein (1985) further asserts that culture is embedded in underlying, preconscious assumptions that participants have trouble identifying by themselves. Were this not the case, these beliefs would not be features of culture. They are fundamental beliefs about reality, its nature and content, and have long since ceased to be subject to examination by those who accept them.

Consequently, Salancik and Pfeffer (1978) offered social information processing as an alternative explanation for observed effects of work redesign emanating from interpretations and meaning rather than objective work features. Differences among people and settings shape interpretations of work redesign in isolation of any objective features of the work or workplace (Adler, Skov, & Salvemini, 1985). This explanation provides a framework for combining structure, group differences, and individual characteristics as information subject to group processing and resulting in the eventual definition of the redesigned work. People evaluate information according to personal relevance and use people similar to themselves as a baseline for comparison. Three information sources shape attitude and need statements during work redesign: (a) individual perceptions and judgments of the desirability of the work setting, (b) information from the social context about appropriate attitudes, and (c) self-perception mediated by past behavior and by the attributions people use to explain it. Pfeffer (1981) provides insight into this view:

> First, the individual's social environment may provide cues as to which dimensions might be used to characterize the work environment. . . . Second, the social environment may provide information concerning how the individual should weight the various dimensions—whether autonomy is more or less important than variety of skill, whether pay is more or less important than social usefulness or worth. Third, the social context provides cues concerning how others have come to evaluate the work environment on each of the selected dimensions. . . . And fourth, it is possible that the social context provides direct evaluation of the work setting along positive or negative dimensions, leaving it to the individual to construct a rationale to make sense of the generally shared affective reactions. (p. 10)

Direct research in work organizations supports Pfeffer's (1981) contention that the saliency and consistency of information cues from the immediate work environment affect definitions and descriptions of work characteristics (Dean & Brass, 1985; O'Reilly et al., 1980). The experimental research supporting this contention reports the effects of artificially constructed social cues on people's job attitudes, and field studies also affirm the power of social information processing. Dean and Brass (1985) found, for example, that position in central communication networks, opportunities to span intraorganizational boundaries, and frequent work at the organization's boundaries (and with outsiders) result in a "convergence or fine tuning of perceptions and a resultant similarity to observable reality" represented by outsiders' assessments of the work characteristics.

Those applying a social information-processing framework to the analysis of work redesign say that information processing affects the way people describe and structure their actual tasks as well as their satisfaction and beliefs. Research in education supports this contention (Hart, 1990a). Teachers in schools engaged in work redesign affirm or reject tasks such as direct assistance with instruction, observation of teaching, supervision of beginning teachers, leadership of decision making, or curriculum writing on the basis of the meaning and legitimacy they come to attach to the tasks. These outcomes appear in schools independent of the formal structure of the redesigned work, be it a career ladder, a mentor teacher program, or a site-based decision-making and management initiative (Hart, 1990a; Little, 1990a; Malen & Ogawa, 1989).

One also must attend to the amount, vividness, and timing of information related to work redesign to understand its impact (Blau & Katerberg, 1982) because belief changes relate to past experiences. Changes in beliefs related to redesigned tasks have been found to be inversely proportional to the amount of information accumulated prior to a work redesign and a direct function of the discrepancy between currently held beliefs and new information (Blau & Katerberg, 1982; Saltiel & Woelfel, 1975). A social information-processing approach to work redesign may relieve some of the perceptual and instrumentation problems that have developed in job characteristics research (Ferratt, Dunham, & Pierce, 1981; Thomas & Griffin, 1983). In the absence of explanations provided by information processing, outcomes of experimental research and field applications of work structure models appear idiosyncratic and inexplicable.

The impact of formal leaders on information processing amplifies other leadership effects on work redesign. Experimental research affirms that significant differences in the ways in which people describe their work and in performance gains can be manipulated by information from a formal leader or supervisor (Green & Novak, 1982). Because they occupy an important formal role in the organization, leaders often have disproportionate impacts on the meaning and interpretations people assign to important organizational events (Schein, 1985; Smircich, 1983). In schools, too, researchers have found that principals have an impact on assessments and perceptions about work redesign far greater than that of any other single member of the school organization (Hart, 1990a; Hart & Murphy, 1990). Principals interpret, judge, praise, and subvert redesigned work through many avenues.

Interpretations of redesigned instruction will also be affected by the judgments of co-workers (Caldwell & O'Reilly, 1982). Experimental designs have yielded results suggesting that the "comments of co-workers [are] a more powerful motivating force than the actual properties of the task" (White & Mitchell, 1979, p. 8). The more frequent, extended, and intense cues about the importance, meaningfulness, and potential of an instructional innovation from other teachers in a school, the more powerful their impacts will be on the outcomes of the program. Under highly salient work conditions, the effect of cues can be crucial. In one setting, people who were told that their group was highly satisfied later described their group and the work situation in more positive terms than people who were told their group was not satisfied (Adler et al., 1985). Studies of university professors support these findings in an education setting. In one study, professors who had decided to remain in their present jobs justified their decisions using objective criteria—valued rewards. But an analysis of these explanations revealed that the decision to remain may have preceded the search for explanations. The researchers concluded that once committed to a job, people describe the rewards they value as the rewards available (Pfeffer & Lawler, 1980).

When educators face important decisions about whether to pursue a major instructional innovation such as Math Smart, they must determine who will participate in making the decision. Participation in important decisions is a major work redesign feature touted in education, and this work feature appears to influence social cues exchanged and the interpretations assigned by people to their newly redesigned work (Hart, 1991). But participation remains a complex variable moderated by many situational factors (Sorensen, 1991). One crucial component found to affect the impact of participation, the salience of tasks being redesigned for those who must complete them (Jans, 1985), will affect many outcomes. Others include the stage of participation, the level of participation (input into the information stage versus final choice) and the organizational domain in which the decision falls (strategic, operational, organizational, or personal).

Objections can be raised against the overreliance on participation as a mechanism for stimulating commitment to work redesign (Locke & Schweiger, 1979). The "ethical imperative" (Sashkin, 1986) vested in participative decision making should be met if it is a crucial value in the work setting, however.

Evaluations of a job's motivating potential may be influenced by social information processing or by nonsocial cues such as the office or school setting (Kulik, 1989). This effect can emerge as social cues at any particular time or as global social assessments that the newly redesigned job fits into a highly valued category. Some evidence exists that a group's evaluation of a job's motivating potential is based on the features of the job and alternative category prototypes. "Social cues can activate features that are strongly associated with prototypical features of a positively (or negatively) evaluated job category. . . . Thus, if redesigning a job alters some prototypical features and results in recategorization to a more positive category, the redesign is 'successful.' However, if the redesign effort does not alter prototypical features, little impact will be observed" (Kulik, 1989, pp. 70-71). This evidence strongly suggests that Math Smart's promoters need to pay a great deal of attention to the attitudes, conversations, and actions of all faculty members to provide ongoing support.

Social information processing may also be useful in preserving ambiguity when the possibility of reaching consensus on work redesign is remote. Consensus on goals and strategies or tactics to achieve those goals may be unrelated to organizational performance (Dess, 1987). Although consensus on either objectives or methods is positively related to performance, when issues are controversial, or difficult, a common method for securing policy support (at the school level for the school in the study) is to increase the ambiguity of the proposed policy (i.e., to resolve conflict by leaving it unresolved, open to interpretation).

> A critical lesson of research on educational change, a lesson often unheeded, is that no education policy is developed or implemented in a social and normative vacuum. Planned change inevitably implicates prevailing patterns of beliefs, assumptions, and practices that define teachers' work and their relationships with children, administrators, and other teachers. These patterns determine, in large part, teachers' responsiveness to innovative ideas and practices. . . . [Findings] suggest that these ideas must take into account the importance that teachers place on their professional relationships with other teachers, their own professional learning and development, and their work in classrooms with students. (Smylie & Smart, 1990, pp. 151-153).

Although social information processing provides insight into observed outcomes of work redesign, some researchers challenge a purely interpretive view (Blau & Katerberg, 1982; Thomas & Griffin, 1983). Looking for an integrated perspective on perceptions of tasks and reactions to them, Griffin, Bateman, Wayne, and Head (1987) stated: "It appears that perceptions of tasks are, in fact, partially determined by their objective properties and partially determined by social cues in

workplaces" (p. 505). They concluded that "managers and organizations can benefit from the evidence that (1) task characteristics and
social cues combine to affect people's reactions to jobs, and (2) introducing constructive changes in an existing work environment can
produce those reactions" (Griffin et al., 1987, p. 517).

A social information-processing view of attitude helps reconcile the
dispositional and situational approaches to outcomes of work redesign
(Calder & Schurr, 1981). It does this by showing how perceptions and
interpretations guide new thoughts and the interpretation of information in conceptualizing attitudes. Although an overreliance on interpretive explanations for work redesign outcomes is not justified, practitioners and researchers should attend to a number of important
factors: (a) the relationships among task features, information cues in
the immediate work setting, and affective responses by those involved;
(b) the social processes involved in people's perceiving, evaluating,
and reacting to social cues related to their work; (c) the relationships
among social cues and past and current socialization processes in
which important norms are recognized, respected, and internalized,
even as they are subject to modification (Thomas & Griffin, 1983); (d)
the interaction of conflicting social cues (Blau & Katerberg, 1982); and
(e) attention to judgments in the setting about the affective and psychological reactions to the new work design that the setting deems
"appropriate" (Hogan & Martell, 1987).

When structural, group, and individual factors have been considered in planning for the redesign of instructional work, the feature of
work redesign through which it is given value exerts final say over its
worth and acceptance. A school will interpret Math Smart for its
members. The nature of the school as a workplace will influence
outcomes (Rosenholtz, 1989). Attention to issues such as teacher participation is justified, if only because resistance, disruption, and intran-
sigence related to Math Smart in the early stages of the innovation can
kill Math Smart (or any work redesign initiative) regardless of its
potential for improving the performance of schools.

People's perceptions of their jobs affect judgments they make about
the job (Sandelands & Calder, 1987; Staw, 1984), and these judgments
are bound to affect Math Smart. Researchers focusing on the relationships between perception processes and judgments have found that
perceptual organization (unit formation—the way in which parts of
the job are organized perceptually by a person) can be influenced by
changes in the job and in turn can influence higher order judgments
about the task. "Objectively, work consists of an ongoing stream of
behavior, but its meaning and significance depend on how it is percep-

tually organized according to its parts" (Sandelands & Calder, 1987, p. 288), and many aspects of perception "lie outside the pale of self-awareness" (p. 290). Perceptions and emerging beliefs appear to fall into units according to relationships among tasks, behaviors, and performance. Evidence continually mounts that people organize their perceptions of work according to their own higher order cognitive processing and their judgments about task attributes. In turn, these judgments shape decisions to persist. One ignores this process at the risk of endangering an innovation. For example, outcomes of Math Smart will hinge in part on the role stress that develops for teachers and pupils in the form of ambiguity, overload, and conflict (Biddle, 1979; Hart, 1987). Research in schools shows that teachers in redesigned work (leaders and mentors) often wonder what to do even when given elaborate job descriptions (Hart, 1987, 1990a; Little, 1990a).

Pressure to grow conceptually and to grow in their ability to use physical objects as analogies for mathematical relationships will be felt by Math Smart teachers simultaneously with pressure to develop their roles as question posers and skeptics (Nicholson, 1984; Nicholson & West, 1987). Peck and Connell envision the new method providing opportunities for teachers to engage in cumulative learning through frequent and regular training. This training may include serial learning with those proficient with Math Smart working side by side with others as role models; it may also include divestiture (a math teacher giving up the role of teller and explainer). All these transition characteristics predict the personal development of teachers. But role ambiguity and overload will result (Toffler, 1981). Teachers will face pressure to prove themselves, a common feature of redesigned work in a new role (Schein 1971). Role conflict also may be a problem, with conflict between the teachers' role as giver of knowledge (in other subject areas untouched by the innovation) and their role as skeptic and questioner. Evidence mounts that if teachers see Math Smart as a way to improve their work, they will give their support. If not, they may see it as interfering with their work (Firestone & Bader, 1990).

Whatever the actual benefits of Math Smart, the program is unlikely to become a permanent part of mathematics instruction unless positive ties are forged between "objective" features of the work structure (the core technology) it requires and perceived features and outcomes. As the preceding discussion illustrates, these perceptions can be conceptualized as emerging from the interaction of work structures, group/social characteristics, and individual characteristics interpreted through social information processing. Perceptions about the salutary features of work intervene between action and outcomes, interacting with information cues, individual and social system differences, and ongoing revisions in the structure of the work (Caldwell & O'Reilly, 1982).

Summary and Implications

The voluminous research on work redesign[6] provides insight into crucial structural, group, individual, and interpretive factors that influence the outcomes of instructional innovation in schools. The elements of formal organizational structure and the structure of teachers' core tasks are fundamentally changed by many instructional as well as structural and governance innovations in schools. The slow integration of technology into schools despite large infusions of resources into hardware and software may in part have resulted from a failure to recognize the sociotechnical nature of these innovations. The social structure of work in schools is also affected by changes in instructional technology.

These changes shape teachers' perceptions of their work and the work of their students. Innovations are judged and reshaped by group and individual differences in each school in which they are implemented. Attitudes about new work designs like Math Smart also change over time as experience with the new forms accumulates and judgments spread. People exchange opinions; influential information sources alter people's attitudes; and people make sense of their experiences as they talk with others, work under the new structures, and watch outcomes emerge.

Consequently, information cues shape perceptions of and responses to instructional innovation as much as objective structures. Ultimately, implicit theories about the core teaching technology, school structures, and the schooling process can be traced and their effects influenced as they interact with and help shape the outcomes of instructional reform. These impacts are illustrated by instructional innovations like Math Smart.

Because Math Smart assaults many firmly established norms of mathematics instruction, challenges teachers' own understanding of underlying rationales for choosing mathematical procedures, places new demands on children as learners, and requires a reframing of the role of the teacher from dispenser of knowledge to resident questioner and skeptic, critical work characteristics will be reframed and restructured. Because instruction, not ideology, is the driving force behind the redesign, those engaged in the Math Smart innovation will challenge the adult world of work by assailing their values and conventions and appealing to their most noble impulses. Scholars and practitioners alike can use the knowledge gained through decades of research on work redesign to enhance the likelihood that promising instructional innovations like Math Smart will succeed.

Work redesign theory holds potential as an organizing framework for the implementation of innovative instructional techniques designed to improve the work of teachers, children, and youth in schools. First, structural theories of work redesign reveal important dimensions of the tasks people perform, their impacts on the psychology and perceptions shaping the work, and eventual effects of the potential of the work itself for enticing and motivating effort on the part of the adults and children who must do the work. Sociotechnical theories provide an integrated perspective on the work and social structure in intersection and a realistic view of the potential, value, and challenges inherent in all major instructional reform efforts.

Second, the sociology of schools as workplaces for adults and young people and the characteristics of each work group provide clues to the interventions needed to promote instructional innovation. Group characteristics shape outcomes. The norms, expectations, and values of those who will teach and learn must not be taken lightly. Intraorganizational politics will determine in part what is valued and what is discarded. Roles will be reshaped, and the ambiguity that accompanies change deserves attention. Simple inertia is a fact of organizational life that warrants no blame, but must not be ignored. Finally, leadership provides information, resources, and interpretations that label an innovation worthy for a specific school, for specific children.

Third, the personal traits, needs, and experiences of the people involved in instructional innovation shape outcomes. Knowledge and preferences vary, and people bring different personal needs to their work. Teachers' needs for professional growth differ—between individuals and at different stages of their personal and career lives. Work redesign theories provide frameworks for understanding the interplay of individual characteristics and instructional innovation efforts and for designing interventions that respect the integrity of the people involved and the innovation.

Finally, instructional work redesign is a social process. Information processing in this social environment results in judgments of value, creates perceptions about "objective" reality, and shapes the actions that follow. Until teachers and children see the merits of instructional innovation for themselves in their context, the relative value of change is academic—for someone else in some other place. People will discount research reports touting miraculous learning outcomes if they fail to see how they might use the new methods in their own schools and classrooms.

Each of these four factors in work redesign—task, group, and individual characteristics and social information processing—profoundly affects the outcomes of instructional innovation. Work redesign theory provides a framework from which educators can approach instructional improvement with sensitivity to both social and technical reality. This theoretical perspective offers insight into the real world in which change must be accomplished, guarding against the disillusionment that may come from attempts to change schools and schooling from exclusively technical perspectives.

Notes

1. HyperTalk is a computer language useful for instructing computer hardware (from mainframes to personal computers) to use the main language of computation, HyperCard. The children use HyperTalk to tell their PCs what to do; their PCs understand HyperCard.

2. The following example illustrates how children build word problems. One group of children had a great deal of practice with physical materials; they were very comfortable with problems posed using sketches. As part of their work to construct meaning, they generated a method of comparing fractions. They found that when comparing two fractions, one fraction would either represent more, less, or the same amount as the other.

With this background, one child developed the following problem: "If I am sharing a cake with seven people, how many shares would I need to keep for myself to have the same amount of cake as I do when I share the cake with six people and keep five shares?" In mathematical terms this would translate to the following:

$$x/7 = 5/6$$

As it turns out, this problem is not trivial. The answer requires that $X = 5\frac{5}{6}$. This is not an answer children typically encounter when beginning to study fractions. The meaning the children constructed early in their learning enabled them to deal with the problem.

3. They do not need to program computers.

4. For details on the rationale, development, and testing of the mathematics instructional method described in this chapter and its implications for teacher education, see Connell and Peck (1991); Peck (1987); Peck and Connell (1991); Peck and Jencks (1981); and Stoddart, Connell, Stofflett, and Peck (1991).

5. This distinction between learning by children and effort by teachers is not made lightly. Outcomes in education are unique; no other endeavor by human beings is so tied to the perceptions, beliefs, and effort of more than one person simultaneously. Although their knowledge, power, and status differ substantially, teachers and students must acknowledge their interdependence, and scholars must acknowledge the power of this interdependence for knowledge about learning in schools to progress.

6. Much of the research reviewed for this chapter was not included in the references. The economies of space made it impossible to refer to every publication read.

References

Acheson, K. A., & Gall, M. D. (1987). *Techniques in the clinical supervision of teachers: Preservice and inservice applications* (2nd ed.). New York: Longman.

Adler, S., Skov, R. B., & Salvemini, N. J. (1985). Job characteristics and job satisfaction: When cause becomes consequence. *Organization Behavior and Human Decision Processes, 35,* 266-278.

Albin, P. S. (1985). Job design, control technology, and technical change. *Journal of Economic Issues, 14,* 703-730.

Angus, L. B. (1988, April). *School leadership and educational reform.* Paper presented at the annual meeting of the American Educational Research Association, New Orleans, LA.

Ashford, S. J., & Cummings, L. L. (1985). Proactive feedback seeking: The instrumental use of the information environment. *Journal of Occupational Psychology, 58,* 67-79.

Bacharach, S. B. (Ed.). (1990). *Education reform: Making sense of it all.* Needham Heights, MA: Allyn and Bacon.

Bacharach, S. B., Bamberger, P., & Conley, S. (1990). Work process, role conflict, and role overload. *Journal of Work and Occupations, 17,* 199-228.

Bacharach, S. B., & Conley, S. C. (1986, April). *Educational reform: A managerial agenda.* Paper presented at the annual meeting of the American Educational Research Association, San Francisco.

Bacharach, S. B., Conley, S. C., & Shedd, J. B. (1986). Beyond career ladders: Structuring teacher career development systems. *Teachers College Record, 87,* 563-574.

Bacharach, S. B., & Mitchell, S. M. (1991). The school as a workplace: Examining the teacher's work environment. In M. Alkin (Ed.), *Encyclopedia of education research.* Englewood Cliffs, NJ: Prentice Hall.

Bacharach, S. B., & Mundell, B. (1993). Organizational politics in schools: Micro, macro, and the logics of action. *Educational Administration Quarterly, 29,* 423-452.

Banner, J. M., Jr. (1985, November). The master teacher's greatest reward. *Educational Leadership,* pp. 74-76.

Barnabe, C., & Burns, M. L. (1991). *A test of the utility of the job characteristics model for diagnosis of motivation in education.* Unpublished paper, University of Toronto.

Biddle, B. (1979). *Role theory: Expectations, identities, and behaviors.* New York: Plenum.

Blau, G. J., & Katerberg, R. (1982). Toward enhancing research with the social information processing approach to job design. *Academy of Management Review, 7,* 543-550.

Boud, D., Keogh, R., & Walker, D. (1985a). Promoting reflection in learning: A model. In D. Boud, R. Keogh, & D. Walker (Eds.), *Reflection: Turning experience into learning* (pp. 18-40). New York: Nichols.

Breaugh, J. A., & Becker, A. S. (1987). Further examination of the work autonomy scales: Three studies. *Human Relations, 40,* 381-400.

Brief, A. P., & Downey, H. K. (1983). Cognitive and organizational structures: A conceptual analysis of implicit organizing theories. *Human Relations, 36,* 1065-1090.

Brief, A. P., Wallace, M. J., & Aldag, R. J. (1976). Linear vs. non-linear models of the formation of affective reactions: The case of job enlargement. *Decision Sciences, 7,* 1-9.

Calder, B. J., & Schurr, P. H. (1981). Attitudinal processes in organizations. In B. Staw (Ed.), *Research in organizational behavior* (Vol. 3., pp. 283-302). Greenwich, CT: JAI.

Caldwell, D. F., & O'Reilly, C. A., III. (1982). Task perceptions and job satisfaction: A question of causality. *Journal of Applied Psychology, 67,* 361-369.

Champoux, J. E. (1981). The moderating effect of work context satisfaction on the curvilinear relationship between job scope and affective response. *Human Relations, 34,* 503-515.

Charters, W. W. (1984). *Feasibility studies of teacher core job characteristics.* Eugene: University of Oregon, Center for Educational Policy and Management.

Cherns, A. (1987). Principles of sociotechnical design revisited. *Human Relations, 40,* 153-162.

Cherrington, D. J., & England, J. L. (1980). The desire for an enriched job as a moderator of the enrichment-satisfaction relationship. *Organizational Behavior and Human Performance, 25,* 139-159.

Chubb, J. E. (1988). Why the current wave of school reform will fail. *Public Interest, 90,* 28-49.

Chubb, J. E., & Moe, T. M. (1988). *What price democracy? Politics, markets and American schools.* Washington, DC: Brookings Institution.

Clarridge, P. B. (1988, April). *Determining the effectiveness of career ladder plans.* Paper presented at the annual meeting of the American Educational Research Association, New Orleans, LA.

Conley, S. C., Bacharach, S. B., & Bauer, S. (1989). The school work environment and teacher career dissatisfaction. *Educational Administration Quarterly, 25,* 58-81.

Connell, M. L., & Peck, D. M. (1991, April). *Report of a conceptual change intervention in elementary mathematics.* Paper presented at the annual meeting of the American Educational Research Association, Chicago.

Cordery, J. L., & Wall, T. D. (1985). Work design and supervisory practice: A model. *Human Relations, 38,* 425-441.

Cunningham, J. B., & Eberle, T. (1990, February). A guide to job enrichment and redesign. *Personnel,* pp. 56-61.

Cunningham, W. G. (1983). Teacher burnout—Solutions for the 1980s: A review of literature. *Urban Review, 15*(1), 37-51.

Darling-Hammond, L. (1986). A proposal for evaluation in the teaching profession. *Elementary School Journal, 86,* 531-551.

Dean, J. W., Jr., & Brass, D. J. (1985). Social interaction and the perception of job characteristics in an organization. *Human Relations, 38,* 571-582.

DeLong, T. J. (1982). Reexamining the career anchor model. Reprinted from *Personnel.* AMACOM Periodicals Division, American Management Associations.

Dess, G. G. (1987). Consensus on strategy formulation and organizational performance: Competitors in a fragmented industry. *Strategic Management Journal, 8,* 259-277.

Eisenstat, R. A., & Felner, R. D. (1984). Toward a differentiated view of burnout: Personal and organizational mediators of job satisfaction and stress. *American Journal of Community Psychology, 12,* 411-432.

Elmore, R. F. (1980). *Complexity and control: What legislators and administrators can do about implementing public policy.* Washington, DC: National Institute of Education.

Elmore, R. F. (1987). Reform and the culture of authority in schools. *Educational Administration Quarterly, 23*(4), 60-78.

Ferratt, T. W., Dunham, R. B., & Pierce, J. L. (1981). Self-report measures of job characteristics and affective responses: An examination of discriminant validity. *Academy of Management Journal, 24,* 780-794.

Fincham, R. (1989). Natural workgroups and the process of job design. *Educational Researcher, 11*(6), 17-22.

Firestone, W. A., & Bader, B. (1990). *Merit or job enlargement? Cases of job differentiation in teaching* (Research report prepared for CPRE). Rutgers, NJ: CPRE.

Frase, L. E. (1989). Effects of teacher rewards on recognition and job enrichment. *Journal of Educational Research, 83*(1), 52-57.

Freiberg, J. (1985). Master teacher programs: Lessons from the past. *Educational Leadership, 42*(4), 16-21.

Fried, Y., & Ferris, G. R. (1987). The validity of the job characteristics model: A review and meta-analysis. *Personnel Psychology, 40,* 287-322.

Gangster, D. C. (1980). Individual differences and task design: A laboratory experiment. *Organizational Behavior and Human Performance, 26,* 131-148.

Gardner, D. G. (1986). Activation theory and task design: An empirical test of several new predictions. *Journal of Applied Psychology, 71,* 411-418.

Green, G., & Novak, M. A. (1982). The effects of leader-member exchange and job design on productivity and satisfaction: Testing a dual attachment model. *Organizational Behavior and Human Performance, 30,* 109-131.

Griffin, G. A. (1985). The school as a workplace and the master teacher concept. *Elementary School Journal, 86*(1), 1-16.

Griffin, R. W., Bateman, T. S., Wayne, S. J., & Head, T. C. (1987). Objective and social factors as determinants of task perceptions and responses: An integrated perspective and empirical investigation. *Academy of Management Journal, 30,* 501-523.

Guskey, T. R. (1986). Staff development and the process of teacher change. *Educational Researcher, 15*(5), 5-12.

Guskey, T. R. (1988). Teacher efficacy, self-concept, and attitudes toward the implementation of instructional innovation. *Teaching and Teacher Education, 4*(1), 63-69.

Hackman, J. R., & Oldham, G. R. (1976). Motivation through the design of work: Tests of a theory. *Organizational Behavior and Human Performance, 16,* 250-279.

Hackman, J. R., & Oldham, G. R. (1980). *Work Redesign.* Reading, MA: Addison-Wesley.

Hall, D. T. (1976). *Careers in organizations.* Pacific Palisades, CA: Goodyear.

Hart, A. W. (1987). A career ladder's effect on teacher career and work attitudes. *American Educational Research Journal, 24,* 479-504.

Hart, A. W. (1990a). Impacts of the school social unit on teacher authority during work redesign. *American Educational Research Journal, 27,* 503-532.

Hart, A. W. (1990b). Work redesign: A review of literature for education reform. In S. B. Bacharach (Ed.), *Advances in research and theories of school management and educational policy* (Vol. 1, pp. 31-69). Greenwich, CT: JAI.

Hart, A. W. (1991). A work redesign view of career ladders in Utah. In L. Frase (Ed.), *Teacher compensation and motivation* (pp. 363-412). Lancaster, PA: Technomic.

Hart, A. W. (1992, April). *Work feature values of tomorrow's teachers: Work redesign as an incentive and school improvement policy.* Paper presented at the annual meeting of the American Educational Research Association, San Francisco.

Hart, A. W. (1993). *Succession dynamics: The organizational socialization of school leaders.* Albany: State University of New York Press.

Hart, A. W., & Murphy, M. J. (1990). New teachers react to redesigned work. *American Journal of Education, 98,* 224-250.

Hogan, E. A., & Martell, D. A. (1987). A confirmatory structural equations analysis of the job characteristics model. *Organizational Behavior and Human Decision Processes, 39,* 242-263.

Jans, N. A. (1985). Organizational factors and work involvement. *Organizational Behavior and Human Decision Processes, 35,* 382-396.

Johnson, S. M. (1990a). Redesigning teachers' work. In R. F. Elmore & Associates (Eds.), *Restructuring schools: The next generation of educational reform.* San Francisco, CA: Jossey-Bass.

Johnson, S. M. (1990b). *Teachers at work: Achieving success in our schools.* New York: Basic Books.

Jones, G. R. (1984). Task visibility, free riding, and shirking: Explaining the effect of structure and technology on employee behavior. *Academy of Management Review, 9,* 684-695.

Kalleberg, A. L., & Loscocco, K. A. (1983). Aging, values, and rewards: Explaining age differences in job satisfaction. *American Sociological Review, 48,* 78-90.

Katz, R. (1978). The influence of job longevity on employee reactions to task characteristics. *Human Relations, 8,* 703-726.

Kemp, N. J., & Cook, J. (1983). Job longevity as a moderator of the perceived task characteristics-job satisfaction relationship: Further evidence of the instability of moderator effects. *Human Relations, 36,* 883-898.

Kerber, K. W., & Campbell, J. P. (1987). Component structure of a measure of job facet satisfaction: Stability across job levels. *Educational and Psychological Measurement, 47,* 825-835.

Kiggundu, M. N. (1981). Task interdependence and the theory of job design. *Academy of Management Review, 6,* 499-508.

Kulik, C. T. (1989). The effects of job categorization on judgments of the motivating potential of jobs. *Administrative Science Quarterly, 34,* 68-90.

Latack, J. C. (1984). Career transitions within organizations: An exploratory study of work, nonwork, and coping strategies. *Organizational Behavior and Human Performance, 34,* 296-322.

Lipsky, M. (1976). Toward a theory of street-level bureaucracy. In W. Hawley et al. (Eds.), *Theoretical perspectives on urban politics* (pp. 196-213). Englewood Cliffs, NJ: Prentice Hall.

Little, J. W. (1982). Norms of collegiality and experimentation: Workplace conditions of school success. *American Education Research Journal, 19,* 325-340.

Little, J. W. (1990a). The mentor phenomenon and the social organization of teaching. In C. Cazden (Ed.), *Review of research in education* (Vol. 16, pp. 297-353). Washington, DC: American Educational Research Association.

Little, J. W. (1990b). The persistence of privacy: Autonomy and initiative in teachers' professional relations. *Teachers College Record, 91,* 509-536.

Locke, E. A., & Schweiger, D. M. (1979). Participation in decision making: One more look. In B. M. Staw & L. L. Cummings (Eds.), *Research in organizational behavior* (Vol. 1, pp. 265-339). Greenwich, CT: JAI.

Loher, B. T., Noe, R. A., Moeller, N. L., & Fitzgerald, M. P. (1985). A meta-analysis of the relation of job characteristics to job satisfaction. *Journal of Applied Psychology, 70,* 280-289.

Lortie, D. C. (1975). *Schoolteacher: A sociological study.* Chicago: University of Chicago Press.

Malen, B., & Ogawa, R. T. (1988). Professional-patron influence on site-based governance councils; A confounding case study. *Educational Evaluation and Policy Analysis, 10*(4), 251-270.

McKelvey, B., & Sekaran, U. (1977). Toward a career-based theory of job involvement: A study of scientists and engineers. *Administrative Science Quarterly, 22,* 281-305.

Mitchell, S. M. (1986, April). *Negotiating the design of professional jobs.* Paper presented at the annual meeting of the American Educational Research Association, San Francisco.

Murphy, J. (1990). *The educational reform movement of the 1980s: Perspectives and cases.* Berkeley, CA: McCutchan.

Nicholson, N. (1984). A theory of work role transitions. *Administrative Science Quarterly, 29,* 172-191.

Nicholson, N., & West, M. A. (1987). *Managerial job change.* Cambridge, UK: Cambridge University Press.

O'Connor, E. J., & Barrett, G. V. (1980). Informational cues and individual differences as determinants of subjective perceptions of task enrichment. *Academy of Management Journal, 22,* 697-716.

O'Connor, E. J., Rudolf, C. J., & Peters, L. H. (1980). Individual differences and job design reconsidered: Where do we go from here? *Academy of Management Review, 5,* 249-254.

Ogawa, R. T., & Bossert, S. T. (1990, April). *Leadership as an organizational characteristic.* Paper presented at the annual meeting of the American Educational Research Association, Boston.

Ogawa, R. T., & Malen, B. (1991). Towards rigor in revisions of multivocal literatures. *Review of Education Research, 61*(3), 265-286.

Oldham, G. R., & Hackman, J. R. (1980). Work design in the organizational context. In G. R. Oldham & J. R. Hackman (Eds.), *Research in organizational behavior* (Vol. 2, pp. 247-278). Greenwich, CT: JAI.

O'Reilly, C. A., III, & Roberts, K. H. (1975). Individual differences in personality, position in the organization, and job satisfaction. *Organizational Behavior and Human Performance, 14,* 144-150.

O'Reilly, C. A., III, Parletter, G. N., & Bloom, J. R. (1980). Perceptual measures of task characteristics: The biasing effects of differing frames of reference and job attitudes. *Academy of Management Journal, 23,* 118-131.

Organ, D. W., & Greene, C. N. (1981). The effects of formalization on professional involvement: A compensatory process approach. *Administrative Science Quarterly, 26,* 237-252.

Peck, D. M. (1987). Children derive meaning from solving problems about physical materials. *Proceedings of the second international seminar on misconceptions and educational strategies in science and mathematics* (Vol. 3, pp. 376-385). Ithaca, NY: Cornell University Press.

Peck, D. M., & Connell, M. L. (1991, April). *Developing a pedagogically useful content knowledge in elementary mathematics.* Paper presented at the annual meeting of the American Educational Research Association, Chicago.

Peck, D. M., & Connell, M. L. (in press). Using physical materials to develop mathematical intuition. *Focus on learning issues in mathematics.* Albany: State University of New York Press.

Peck, D. M., & Jencks, S. M. (1981). Conceptual issues in the learning and teaching of fractions. *Journal of Research in Mathematics Education, 12,* 339-348.

Peters, L. H., & O'Connor, E. J. (1980). Situational constraints and work outcomes: The influences of frequently overlooked constructs. *Academy of Management Review, 5,* 391-398.

Pfeffer, J. (1981). Management as symbolic action: The creation and maintenance of organizational paradigms. In L. L. Cummings & B. M. Staw (Eds.), *Research in organizational behavior* (Vol. 3, pp. 1-52). Greenwich, CT: JAI.

Pfeffer, J., & Lawler, J. (1980). Effects of job alternatives, extrinsic rewards, and behavioral commitment on attitude toward the organization: A field test of the insufficient justification paradigm. *Administrative Science Quarterly, 25,* 38-56.

Porter, A. C., & Brophy, J. (1988, May). Synthesis of research on good teaching: Insights from the work of the institute for research on teaching. *Educational Leadership,* pp. 74-85.

Roberts, K. H., & Glick, W. (1981). The job characteristics approach to task design: A critical review. *Journal of Applied Psychology, 66,* 193-217.

Rosenholtz, S. J. (1989). *Teachers' workplace: The social organization of schools.* White Plains, NY: Longman.

Salancik, G., & Pfeffer, J. (1978). A social information processing approach to job attitudes and staff design. *Administrative Science Quarterly, 23,* 224-253.

Saltiel, J., & Woelfel, J. (1975). Inertia in cognitive processes: The role of accumulated information in attitude change. *Human Communications Research, 1,* 333-344.

Sandelands, L. E., & Calder, B. J. (1987). Perceptual organization in task performance. *Organizational Behavior and Human Decision Processes, 40,* 287-306.

Sashkin, M. (1986). Participative management remains an ethical imperative. *Organizational Dynamics, 14,* 62-75.

Schein, E. H. (1971). Occupational socialization in the professions: The case of the role innovator. *Journal of Psychiatric Research, 8,* 521-530.

Schein, E. H. (1985). *Organizational culture and leadership.* San Francisco: Jossey-Bass.

Schneider, B. (1985). Organizational behavior. *Annual Review of Psychology, 36,* 573-611.

Sirotnik, K. A. (1985, November). Let's examine the profession, not the teachers. *Educational Leadership,* pp. 67-69.

Smircich, L. (1983). Concepts of culture and organizational analysis. *Administrative Science Quarterly, 28,* 339-358.

Smylie, M. A. (1992). Teacher participation in school decision making. *Educational Evaluation and Policy Analysis, 14*(1), 53-68.

Smylie, M. A., & Denny, J. W. (1990). Teacher leadership: Tensions and ambiguities in organizational perspective. *Educational Administration Quarterly, 26,* 235-259.

Smylie, M. A., & Smart, J. C. (1990). Teacher support for career enhancement initiatives: Program characteristics and effects on work. *Educational Evaluation and Policy Analysis, 12*(2), 139-155.

Soar, R. S., Medley, D. M., & Coker, H. (1983, December). Teacher evaluation: A critique of currently used methods. *Phi Delta Kappa,* pp. 239-246.

Sorensen, N. B. (1991). *Participative decision making in public schools: The effects of structural and process properties on decision equilibrium in four decision content domains.* Unpublished dissertation, University of Utah, Department of Educational Administration.

Staw, B. M. (1984). Organizational behavior. In M. R. Rosenzweig & L. W. Porter (Eds.), *Annual review of psychology* (Vol. 35, pp. 627-666).

Staw, B. M., Bell, N. E., & Clausen, J. A. (1986). The dispositional approach to job attitudes: A lifetime longitudinal test. *Administrative Science Quarterly, 31,* 56-77.

Steers, R. M., & Spencer, D. G. (1977). The role of achievement motivation in job design. *Journal of Applied Psychology, 62,* 472-479.

Stein, M. K., & Wang, M. C. (1988). Teacher development and school improvement: The process of teacher change. *Teaching and Teacher Education, 4*(2), 171-187.

Stoddart, P., Connell, M. L., Stofflett, R., & Peck, D. M. (1991, April). *The reciprocal relationship between content and pedagogy in learning to teach mathematics and science.* Paper presented at the annual meeting of the American Educational Research Association, Chicago.

Terborg, J. R., & Davis, G. A. (1982, February). Evaluation of a new method for assessing change to planned job redesign as applied to Hackman and Oldham's job characteristic model. *Organizational Behavior and Human Performance, 29,* 112-128.

Thomas, J., & Griffin, R. (1983). The social information processing model of task design: A review of literature. *Academy of Management Review, 8,* 672-682.

Toffler, B. L. (1981). Occupational role development: The changing determinants of outcomes for the individual. *Administrative Science Quarterly, 26,* 396-418.

Trist, E. L. (1974). Improving the quality of working life: Sociotechnical case studies. In J. O'Toole (Ed.), *Work and the quality of life.* Cambridge: MIT Press.

Trist, E. L. (1981). *The evolution of sociotechnical systems.* Toronto: Ontario Quality of Working Life Centre.

Turner, J. (1988). *A theory of social interaction.* Stanford, CA: Stanford University Press.

Van Maanen, J., & Katz, R. (1976). Individuals and their careers: Some temporal considerations for work satisfaction. *Personnel Psychology, 29,* 601-616.

Van Maanen, J., & Schein, E. H. (1979). Toward a theory of organizational socialization. In B. M. Staw (Ed.), *Research in organizational behavior* (Vol. 1, pp. 209-264). Greenwich, CT: JAI.

Vance, R. J., & Biddle, T. F. (1985). Task experience and social cues: Interactive effects on attitudinal reactions. *Organization Behavior and Human Decision Processes, 35,* 252-265.

Wall, T. D., Clegg, C. W., & Jackson, P. R. (1978). An evaluation of the job characteristics model. *Journal of Occupational Psychology, 51,* 183-196.

Waller, W. (1932). *The sociology of teaching.* New York: John Wiley.

Walsh, J. T., Taber, T. D., & Beehr, T. (1980). An integrated model of perceived job characteristics. *Organizational Behavior and Human Performance, 25,* 252-267.

White, S. E., & Mitchell, T. E. (1979). Job enrichment versus social cues: A comparison and competitive test. *Journal of Applied Psychology, 64,* 1-9.

Whyte, W. F. (1991). *Social theory for action: How individuals and organizations learn and change.* Newbury Park, CA: Sage.

SIX

Performance Management in Education

STEPHEN M. MITCHELL

The primary goal of schools is to educate students. And the fundamental purpose of education reform is to improve student outcomes. Every element of the educational system has come under scrutiny to identify what can be done to enhance its contribution to improving student outcomes. Educational administration is being changed to emphasize leadership skills. Teachers' roles are being redesigned to emphasize the professional characteristics of teaching. Districts and schools are being restructured. Curriculums are being revised to promote mastery. More accurate and valid assessment methods and tools are being developed. The list goes on. For many educational practitioners, however, the list is composed of add-ons to the current program. Too often, these programs increase educators' workload without making a clear contribution to the fundamental goal of education: improving student's learning. The forest is lost in the trees.

In this chapter, I argue that educational practitioners need to align and focus district-level and individual-level activities toward that

AUTHOR'S NOTE: I would like to thank Sam Bacharach, Bryan Mundell, Scott Bauer, Rose Malanowski, and Peggy Siegel for their helpful comments on earlier drafts of this chapter.

fundamental goal of improved student learning. This requires a methodology that links broad organizational goals to individual performance. One such methodology is performance management.

The goal of performance management is to optimize individual performance to achieve organizational goals. This is done by focusing on three elements:

Results. Performance management helps identify the contribution individual performance makes to the achievement of organizational goals. Too many efforts to improve individual performance do not take organizational goals into account. There is no attempt to ensure that individual performance contributes to achieving organization goals. In other words, there is no attempt to see the individual as part of a larger system (Rumler & Brache, 1990). The key question here is, "What is it that the organization needs for each individual employee to accomplish (individual objectives and instrumental behaviors) to achieve organizational goals?"

Productive Work Environment. Once organization objectives and individual performance objectives are identified, performance management involves ensuring that the work environment facilitates and supports individual performance. Key questions here include, "Does the work environment support individual performance?" and "Do people have the capacity to act?"

Continual Improvement. The final element in performance management is continual improvement. It is a mistake to assume that all is well once performance goals are set. High quality requires continual improvement (Deming, 1986). Key questions include, "Do our controls support continual improvement?" and "Do we promote learning?"

The remainder of this chapter presents some practical ideas on how to carry out performance management. In an effort to promote the development of practical theory (Bacharach & Mitchell, 1981), school systems are used as a referent. I begin by presenting a basic premise underlying performance management in education: that the ability to define, analyze, and redesign work processes in education is necessary to sustain current restructuring efforts targeted on student performance. I then move on to discuss results, considering the development of standards and indicators for school and individual performance. The chapter then examines what is involved in the creation of a productive work environment. The next section discusses how to institutionalize continual improvement. The chapter concludes by showing how effective planning can provide a basis for performance management.

A Premise

Performance management is a means to an end. The focus of performance management in education should be on learning. Learning is a shared responsibility and the chief product of relationships between students and those with whom they interact most closely—their teachers, parents, and peers. Learning also is affected greatly by the larger organizational context in which it occurs. Therefore, the efforts of students, teachers, and parents to focus on the dynamics of learning must be reinforced by the education system in which learning takes place.

Setting rigorous student performance standards and using multiple assessments to evaluate how well students meet those standards are critical elements of improving learning. But adopting higher standards and richer assessments will not result in improved learning—not by themselves. The collective will, activities, and resources of the entire organization also must be aligned toward meeting these ends.

School systems must have the *organizational capacity* to determine how they can work with students to meet higher standards. They must have the organizational capacity to collect, analyze, and use data to improve student and system performance. And they must have the organizational capacity to deploy resources and track progress over time in accomplishing priorities. In other words, the management processes, instructional and noninstructional, that collectively form the education system must be aligned to support learning.

At issue is: What is the best way to ensure that all students (regardless of individual need or talent) and all schools (regardless of wealth) have the chance to succeed? Policymakers and educators need evidence of what organizational structures and processes are most likely to yield success for all students. They also need the opportunity to identify objectively and address the root causes of organizational inefficiencies throughout the system to be able to target their human and financial assets more effectively on learning.

Reinforcing educators to lead their systems—and their ability to make continual improvements over time—is far preferable to the current crisis-driven, ad hoc state of educational decision making.

"The task of educators," contends Darling-Hammond (1992, p. 10), "is to discover and adopt practices that serve students well; the task of policy makers is to create schooling structures and resources that will promote the use and availability of such practices. Genuine accountability requires that practices and policies continually be evaluated and revised in light of how well they achieve these basic goals." Seen in this light, the ability to maintain a clear linkage between organizational goals and individual performance by defining, analyzing, and redesigning work processes in education becomes necessary to sustain current restructuring efforts targeted on student performance. Performance management offers an integrated approach for accomplishing this objective in a systematic manner.

Results

The first element of performance management deals with specifying desired results. Performance management always starts with an objective. There is an abundance of literature on the importance of goal setting. One of the most important insights in this literature is the need to account for the specific context in which goals are established.

The importance of context in setting goals is readily apparent in education reform. Significant attention has been given in recent years to the development of standards and indicators in education (see, e.g., California State Department of Education, 1984; David, 1987; OERI State Accountability Group, 1988). Most of these efforts are commendable; to the degree that they allow educators to specify desired results, they provide a solid foundation for performance management in schools.

The most recent discussions tend to focus on student outcomes. Particular attention is given in these discussions to exit outcomes, that is, the skills and knowledge a student will have on leaving school. One of the fundamental benefits of the attention to exit outcomes is that it focuses school activity on achieving those outcomes. If we know what end results are expected, then we can concentrate on what it will take to produce those results. It is the performances that contribute to achieving those that must be managed. In this context, performance management is offered as the most promising means to assist education organizations in achieving their intended results—continual learning for all students.

Specifying Organizational Results

The typical approach to specifying expected results for organizations involves three steps.

Step 1

The first step is the development of standards of excellence, effectiveness, quality, or high performance. A standard is an area or dimension identified as important to performance.[1]

The quality-planning movement in the private sector (Mitchell, 1990) provides a sound method for beginning the development of standards. An important finding emerging from research on quality control is the importance of developing performance standards that apply to the system (Juran, 1988; Walton, 1986). A key step in quality planning is the identification and modeling of the sources of variability that affect outcome measures. A manager of quality control in a major Canadian steel company begins her training sessions by asking participants to list the sources of variability in the performance of major league hitters. When a hitter performs well or poorly, what are the factors that may vary? A cursory examination of baseball statistics will reveal such factors as time of day, time of year, right-handed versus left-handed pitcher, type of field, number of players in scoring position, and so on.

Educational practitioners are well aware of the sources of variability affecting student outcomes, but do not consistently work with these sources. One of the challenging realities in education is that educators do not all agree on nor are they certain about the linkages between the sources of variability (the recent congressional debate whether to include "opportunity to learn" standards in President Clinton's Goals 2000 Educate America Act reflects this disagreement). This approach requires a clear model of the linkages between the sources of variability. The model should take into account the flow of work, that is, it should consider the interdependence of roles in the organization and the contribution a given role makes to each source of variability (Rumler & Brache, 1990). This requires breaking down the barriers that typically exist between departments in an organization or school.

For example, several schools in North Carolina ("North Carolina's Lead Teacher," 1988) developed school-level accountability models that identified sources of variability in student performance. One school's model included such factors as background conditions, student attitudes, teacher perceptions, instructional arrangements, teacher attitudes, and staff professional development. The model also posited explicit linkages between each of these factors. Each of these factors was seen by this school's staff as an area or dimension identified as important to performance (our working definition of a standard).

There are any number of possible standards. A review of the literature provides many examples that can serve as a good starting point for a school team charged with specifying expected results at the local level. What is important is that the standards chosen reflect the local values and beliefs concerning what is a high-quality educational system and what is a professional performance (David, 1987; Wiggins, 1990).

Step 2

Once standards are developed, the second step is to establish indicators or specific measures for each standard. An educational indicator is a statistic that tells us something about the school or school system. Good indicators suggest whether the school is making progress and warn of potential problems.

There is a benefit to having multiple indicators for each standard. Thus it is advisable to have indicators for inputs, process, and outputs. Some commonly accepted indicators used by schools follow.

Inputs identify the conditions under which the schools operate. Input measures at the district level may include total school-age population, percentage of population that is of school age, urban/suburban/rural, average educational attainment, per capita income, percentage voting, per pupil wealth, preschool participation, percentage disadvantaged, percentage with handicaps, and percentage of students with limited English skills.

Processes are the characteristics or activities of the schools themselves. Process measures may include days/years of instructional time; hours/day of instructional time; time allocated to reading and math, science, social studies, and arts; whether kindergarten is required; graduation requirements; honors and AP course offerings; home and community involvement; number of teachers with advanced degrees; number of in-service programs; and average teacher salaries.

Outputs are the results of educational processes. First, output measures may cover *student performance*. The traditional measure of student performance has been the standardized test. National and state efforts to develop content and outcome standards to define student levels of competence, and the related shift to authentic assessments, promise to redefine our measures of student performance. Typical exit outcomes include number of high school graduates, number of GEDs awarded, and number of students going on to postsecondary schooling or military service. Second, output measures may include *school performance.* School performance indicators assess a school's capacity and performance in improving student achievement. Measures of school performance are typically aggregates of student performance or trend analyses derived from student performance. Third, output measures may also include *customer satisfaction.* The key to total quality is focusing on the customer. Quality should be reflected in improved customer satisfaction. Although it is possible to develop direct measures of customer satisfaction in public schools (e.g., number or percentage of students attending private schools), schools more commonly use subjective indicators such as reactions and opinions of students, staff, and community members. For example, school climate surveys are often used to measure teacher satisfaction, whereas community surveys are used to gauge public confidence.

Good indicators should meet several criteria (Mitchell, 1991b). They should provide meaningful information, reflecting elements identified as important to performance. They should measure elements common to the entire school to make comparisons across classes, students, and so on. They should measure elements that continue from year to year to make comparisons over time. They should provide information that everyone can understand. School or district staff should be able to collect the information without undue effort or cost. They should be valid and reliable statistics. They should enable continual improvement.

An example can help illustrate the relationship between standards and indicators for schools. To develop standards and indicators for a middle school, a school site management council used the school's mission statement (also developed by the school council), to identify five characteristics of a successful middle school. These were student social behavior, high individual student achievement, collaborative environment, positive social setting, and positive physical environment. The council members then went on to identify a preliminary set of indicators for each of these characteristics. Table 6.1 presents the standards and indicators developed by this school council.

Step 3

The final step in specifying expected results is to develop objectives for each indicator. If an indicator identifies the bar you are going to jump over, the objective tells you how high to set the bar.

TABLE 6.1 Middle School Standards and Indicators

Standards	*Indicators*
Student social behavior: Each student should accept responsibility for his or her own behavior. It is the school's responsibility to provide a system for student management that will support and facilitate this goal.	Number of reported incidents of unacceptable behavior Time on task Number of repeat offenses Structured observation report Student contracts Use of in-house suspension Discipline consequences Use of time-out room Number of suspensions Central discipline Needs assessment

High individual student achievement:
 	
We hold high expectations for each student. School programs and activities should ensure each student will achieve his or her maximum potential and enjoy the highest quality of life possible.
	Report card grades
	State and county guidelines for
	    standardized tests
	Regents exams
	Regents Competency Test
	Diagnostic tests
	Retention rates
	Number on honor roll
	Number mainstreamed;
	    number declassified
	Fulfill objectives of IEP
	Teacher tests
	Remedial services
	Extra- and cocurricular activities
	Course: follow up students to high
	    school to track increased difficulty
	    of courses taken
	AP courses
	Guidelines for placement

Collaborative environment: A school community requires confidence and trust between and among the faculty, staff, administration, and parents. Our success with students depends on our collective efforts.	Conference reports Report card conferences Team reports Open house attendance Newsletter Numbers of parents in schools PTA attendance Number of team projects Meeting objectives of school council

TABLE 6.1 *continued*

Standards	Indicators
	Number of assemblies
	Existence of student council
	Number of curriculum committee meetings
	Climate survey
Positive social setting:	Number of and attendance at social events for students
	Number of and attendance at social events for teachers
We believe that the school should be a place where students and staff enjoy working and learning. People should take pride in the school and the part they play in the delivery of educational services to this community.	Number of and attendance at after-school programs
	Increased use of building
	Attendance
	Number of assemblies
	Number of "special days"
	Guidelines for building self-esteem
	Guidance measures
	Student attitudes
Positive physical environment:	Program to maintain attractiveness of building
	Landscaping planned and implemented
The school facilities should be safe, functional, and aesthetically pleasing.	Presence of school sign
	Lack of fence
	Presence of bulletin board displays
	Presence of plants
	Presence of security guards
	Maintenance program exists and is implemented
	Number of incidents of vandalism
	Number of thefts, destruction of property
	Number of police, ambulance calls to school
	Functioning security alarm system

Specific objectives are best developed as part of a needs assessment (Mitchell, 1991b). The information and analysis emerging from a needs assessment supply the data needed to identify areas in need of improvement and to prioritize those areas. In many school systems, identifying and prioritizing objectives are as likely to be based on political pressure or unstable funding sources as rational benchmarks, system goals and objectives, as a needs assessment (Siegel & Byrne, 1994).

Where a needs assessment is performed in schools, it is typically conducted by a school planning team. The team examines the school's current performance using the standards and indicators. The team identifies those measures where improved performance is desirable and then prioritizes those areas. Specific school objectives are then set for each area. For example, each of the schools in the North Carolina project cited above ("North Carolina's Lead Teacher," 1988) developed specific objectives and action plans to address each source of variation in their school accountability model.

Statements of objectives should consist of (a) a specific output for (b) a specific period or time. A fuzzy objective is one that describes inputs or activities; a measurable objective is one that describes specific outputs. There are two basic rules that apply for making fuzzy objectives measurable (Odiorne, 1987). Rule 1: You should always be able to differentiate between inputs, activities, and outputs. Rule 2: Whenever you see an input stated as an objective or an activity stated as an objective, insist that the input- or activity-based objective be rewritten as an output statement. For example, "The school council will conduct a survey of parents" is a poor objective statement. It uses an activity as an objective and has no time frame. A better statement would be "By October 30, 1991, the school council will have received completed surveys from 90% of the parents."

From a practical perspective, one trick in setting objectives is to establish a range of output levels. One of the lessons in the quality movement is to recognize the natural variation in performance (Deming, 1986). It is not realistic to expect people to achieve peak performance at all times. On the other hand, it is also important to recognize the motivational value of stretch goals (Boyett & Conn, 1988). Establishing a range for each objective recognizes variations in performance while providing motivational goals. Setting up a range assures that objectives fall within an acceptable level of performance possible in most circumstances.

You can set up a range by asking three questions (Boyett & Conn, 1988; Odiorne, 1987). First, "What is the most realistic level of results?" This may be seen as a short-term objective. Second, "What is the most optimistic figure you can think of?" This may be seen as a long-term objective and serves as a stretch goal. Third, "What is the most pessimistic figure you can think of?" Performance below this figure warrants corrective action (see the section on continual improvement).[2]

Linking Organizational and Individual Performance

Performance management requires that a clear link be drawn between organization objectives and expectations for individual performance. This necessity arises from the view of organizations as systems and the recognition that organization performance is an aggregate of individual performances. Performance management requires that we be able to identify which behaviors contribute to the organization's goals and objectives (Odiorne, 1987).

Linking organizational and individual performance is a difficult challenge. The challenge can be met by working through the same three steps followed in developing organizational objectives.

Step 1

The first step is the development of standards of high performance for individuals.

Although most personnel texts emphasize the importance of accurate job descriptions and recommend periodic updating of job descriptions to ensure their accuracy, the demands emerging from organizational restructuring have resulted in a fresh look at job descriptions and performance standards. Some recommend doing away with job descriptions altogether (Peters, 1988); others have recommended reducing unwarranted detail and specification in order to promote multiple skills (e.g., Levering, 1989). The common thrust is the effort to align individual performance expectations with the organizational objectives.

In schools, the current effort to reconceptualize what it means to be an effective teacher will have little impact if we cannot link desired teacher behaviors to school results. Berryman and Bailey (1992) note that much of

> the current reform discussion focuses on content. But . . . no matter which content areas are deemed to be basic, *how* content is taught makes all the difference in whether content is *learned*, *retained*, and *appropriately used*. If we want spectacular improvements in learning, we must expand the reform discussion to include pedagogy.

Further,

> current discussions of national tests entertain substantial changes
> in content, in the operations that students are expected to perform
> on content, and in the use of portfolios or projects for assessments.
> But the knowledge and skills needed by teachers to meet these
> changed standards are not widely available in our school systems.
> In some cases, experts are not even clear about the pedagogic and
> curricular approaches needed to generate the desired student com-
> petencies. These new standards need to be complemented with
> standards of best content and best pedagogic practice, and the
> standards must be professional and substantive, not bureaucratic
> or regulatory. (Berryman & Baily, 1992, pp. 113-115)

The National Board of Professional Teaching Standards (1990) has
identified five standards or propositions concerning accomplished
teaching: Teachers (a) are committed to students and their learning; (b)
know the subjects they teach and how to teach those subjects; (c) are
responsible for managing and monitoring student learning; (d) think
systematically about their practices and learn from experience; and (e)
are members of learning communities.

Although the traditional image of the teacher's role emphasizes
instruction, the notion of the teacher as professional requires an elaboration of this image. The new image includes such activities as participating on a school team, action research, and planning—all of which
may be seen as taking away from "time on task." Each school should
identify its standards for teacher performance. A school's standards for
teaching should take into account district and school restructuring and
reform objectives to capture the entire range of a teacher's responsibilities
(Bacharach, Conley, & Shedd, 1986).[3]

Step 2

Once standards are developed, the second step is to establish indicators
for each standard. One or two performance indicators cannot capture the
complexity of teaching. The need for multiple indicators becomes even
more salient considering the changes in the teacher's role.

An example can illustrate the relationship between standards and
indicators for teacher performance. A labor-management committee in
a small urban district was charged with developing a new teacher
evaluation system. The committee began by identifying the key re-

sponsibilities that make up effective teaching. Using these responsibilities, they developed a job description for an effective teacher. The members believed that if every teacher fulfilled these responsibilities, the school would meet its school objectives. The committee then identified several indicators for each responsibility. Their emphasis was on identifying indicators that an administrator could observe during a classroom visit. If an administrator saw an indicator, they would know that the teacher was meeting that responsibility. Table 6.2 presents a sampling of the standards and indicators of effective teaching developed by this committee.

Step 3

The final step is to develop individual performance objectives for each indicator. Individual performance objectives may emerge from two different sources. First, they may emerge from an organizational or department plan developed to achieve organization objectives. This is the most effective way to link individual behavior to organizational objectives (Rumler & Brache, 1990). In a school, school staff may set school-level objectives for the year, and then set individual targets based on what that individual must accomplish for the school to achieve its annual objectives. This layered format provides a foundation for good school-level coordination.

Second, individual performance objectives may emerge from a review of the core competencies or responsibilities in a position. The performance evaluation should identify the employee's strengths and weaknesses relative to the core competencies and responsibilities.[4] Performance objectives should then be set to address any identified weaknesses. As noted above, for teachers, it is important that this type of objective include ties to instruction, that is, that they account for what goes on in the classroom.

Typically, teacher objectives emerge from a professional improvement plan that is rarely tied to school objectives and is often seen as a pro forma annual exercise. In many districts, evaluation is seen as a necessary evil. Teachers consider observations a formality and do not consider feedback from evaluations useful (Corcoran, Walker, & White, 1988). Effective performance management requires follow-up work. Unfortunately, most leaders lack the time or skills for more than the prescribed minimum of supervision (Corcoran et al., 1988). Performance management cannot succeed in such a school system.

The drawbacks of failing to establish a clear linkage between school objectives and individual performance are evident in one district that

(Text continued on page 218)

TABLE 6.2 Sample Teacher Standards and Indicators

Standards	*Indicators*
Carries out an effective instructional program:	
Formulates chapter/unit goals consistent with state and district goals and students' needs and abilities	Specifies goals in terms of students' needs and current readiness Specifies goals in terms of available textbook material
Constructs or adapts knowledge and skill objectives consistent with goals and students' assessed needs and abilities	States objectives in terms of observable learner outcomes Plans different objectives for students at different instructional levels
Makes students aware of objectives	States objectives at the beginning of the lesson Draws connection between learning activities and objectives
Uses a variety of methods to meet objectives	Selects methods that provide for student action and interaction Selects methods appropriate to students' needs and abilities Varies teacher-centered and child-centered techniques
Develops learning activities to meet objectives	Chooses activities that suit students' attention span Uses more than one learning activity in an instructional period Selects activities that suit students' needs, interests, and so on
Paces the presentation according to students' needs and abilities	Rephrases where necessary Reteaches where necessary
Uses appropriate questioning techniques	Asks questions designed to develop all the critical thinking skills Responds to students' questions and comments Respectfully accepts all responses but provides for the correction of those that are errors
Encourages student involvement and active participation	Uses a variety of ways of grouping students Allows students to design activities and materials for use by other students

TABLE 6.2 *continued*

Standards	Indicators
	Provides alternative assignments and activities that suit specific interests and abilities
Uses appropriate instructional aids	Uses supplement to basic texts Evaluates student learning from print, audio or visual media
Provides transitions between objectives/activities	Shows connection between past and present activities Shows connection between activities and objectives
Provides transitions between content area, skills, and so on	States connections between past and current activities Shows connections between skills and knowledge
Provides learning equity	Calls on boys and girls about the same number of times
Adjusts instruction based on evaluation and feedback from students	Rephrases Completely answers questions
Provides follow-up and reinforcement activities	Assigns homework regularly
Uses vocabulary appropriate for students and subject	Matches vocabulary to students' level of development Uses standard grammar and usage
Gives directions that are clear and complete	Determines that students understand directions
Models behavior to be used in activities	Explains the thinking used in completing the example
Effectively organizes and manages the classroom:	
Provides a clean, attractive environment	Provides instructionally relevant and attractive bulletin boards
Arranges classroom materials in an orderly, usable fashion	Arranges furniture according to instructional activity Displays classroom work on bulletin boards

(continued)

TABLE 6.2 *continued*

Standards	Indicators
Formulates and maintains procedures for students' safety and health	Students demonstrate a knowledge of fire safety procedures Identifies and makes referrals of health problems
Designs and uses various procedures for movement of people and materials	Assigns students to seats/tables Ensures that movement between desks and learning centers is smooth and nondisruptive
Maintains effective scheduling	Begins and ends lessons on time Adheres to blocks of instructional time Keeps plan book up to date
Adjusts classroom activities to changes and emergencies	Keeps extra learning activities available for emergencies Continues instructional activities despite hindrances, room changes, and other temporary disruptions Makes a smooth transition from an emergency, for example, fire drill, to the planned activities
Establishes and enforces rules and routines	Maintains daily routine tasks Establishes fair and consistent discipline Informs parents of rules and regulations of school and class/subject
Explicates, models, reinforces acceptable behavior for students	Encourages and acknowledges positive student behavior Provides leadership and guidance in helping students develop appropriate behavior
Demonstrates effective techniques, strategies for eliciting acceptable behavior	Makes corrections with a minimum of disruption of the learning process Employs fair and impartial discipline Refocuses questions to generate positive behavior Provides alternative approaches for the inattentive and disruptive student
Keeps appropriate records	Reviews and updates students' cumulative folders

TABLE 6.2 *continued*

Standards	Indicators
	Records students' attendance daily
	Submits report cards and progress reports accurately and on time
Provides appropriate materials for substitutes	Maintains accurate plan book
	Provides plans that cover the appropriate amount of time
	Provides supplementary materials
Uses appropriate evaluation techniques:	
Makes an assessment of pupil capabilities and handicaps prior to instruction Pretests students	Confers with students' guidance counselors
Uses formal and informal methods to evaluate students' attainment of objectives	Constructs tests in a variety of formats
Provides meaningful assignments and grades them appropriately	Develops assignments that require active involvement of students with subject matter
	Develops assignments that meet requirements of course of study and achievement levels of students
Constructs evaluation instruments that focus on what has been taught and are used in a timely fashion	Correlates criterion-referenced tests with goals and objectives of the course
	Uses test results to improve instruction
Reviews evaluation results with parents and students	Discusses student progress with student and parents
Works cooperatively with the administration and staff	Fulfills assignments
Conducts him- or herself in a professional manner at all times:	
Submits records in accurate and timely fashion	Updates records periodically
Upholds administration regulations and board policy	Enforces all policy mandates
	Reports to class(es) on time

(continued)

TABLE 6.2 *continued*

Standards	Indicators
Fulfills responsibilities to parents and community	Sends written communications to parents regarding students' progress Accommodates cultural needs of parents and community
Participates in self-development activities aimed at achieving excellence	Works toward achieving the goals of Professional Improvement Plan Consults with specialists for advice
Demonstrates concern for students throughout the school	Demonstrates a warm and caring attitude Promotes courtesy and respect
Relates with other staff members in a collegial fashion; participates in collaborative activities	Shares innovative and/or successful ideas with others Works on school/district committees
Provides 180 days of instruction	

drew a distinction between curriculum (dealing with course content) and instruction (dealing with teaching strategies). Suppose this district wanted to evaluate the implementation of a new curriculum. If data indicated that some group of students did not achieve the desired performance, how could the district determine if the cause of poor performance was in the curriculum (content) or in how it was presented (instruction)? By distinguishing between curriculum and instruction, they in essence separated objectives from individual behavior. It would have been better if they had identified specific instructional strategies that were needed to successfully implement the curriculum, that is, if they had linked organizational objectives to individual performance.

Performance management links organizational goals to individual performance. The key question here is, "What is it that the organization needs the individual employee to accomplish (individual objectives and instrumental behaviors) to achieve organization goals?" The question is best answered by setting organizational objectives, and then using these objectives to set individual performance objectives. This section of the chapter has attempted to detail the steps involved in this process.

Productive Work Environment[5]

Once organizational and individual performance objectives are identified, you must ensure that the work environment facilitates and supports individual performance. The second element of performance management requires that the organization maximize each individual's capacity to act (Nadler, Gersten, & Shaw, 1992), thus permitting the organization to use the full potential of its people.

Success in this effort requires creating a productive work environment. Of particular importance is the creation of a work environment in which (a) individual effort results in successful performance and (b) successful performance is rewarded (Newsom, 1990). We will discuss each of these requirements.

The Effort-Performance Linkage

An enhanced capacity means that increased individual effort leads to better performance. The linkage of effort to performance can be improved through two possible strategies: (a) improving the work context and (b) improving the individual's abilities and attitudes. The first removes barriers to action in the workplace, whereas the second removes barriers to action in the individual.

Work Context

Traditionally, there has been a tendency to ignore the effect of work conditions on teaching. People assumed that school work conditions have little effect on the quality of work (Bacharach, Bauer, & Shedd, 1986). Only recently have researchers examined the school as a workplace (Johnson, 1989, 1990; Wilson & Corcoran, 1988).

The research on teachers' stress shows the importance of work conditions on the effort-performance linkage (e.g., Bacharach, Bauer, & Conley, 1986). The stress literature says that conditions in the work environment that constrain the effort-performance linkage serve as stressors. Individual teachers' reactions to these stressors vary. The research suggests that younger teachers or others with high intrinsic motivation will expend significant amounts of energy working around these barriers to performance. Over time, however, the effort required to work around these stressors wears the individual down, leading to burnout or malaise.

Whether a school has a good teaching environment depends on whether teachers can perform. Three elements of the work environment affect teachers' performance: physical conditions, resources, and collegiality (Levering, 1989; Webb & Ashton, 1986). We will consider each in turn.

Physical Conditions. The school's commitment to provide a safe and attractive working environment is a key indicator of whether it is a good place to work (Levering, 1989; Wilson & Corcoran, 1988). In a study of urban schools, Corcoran et al. (1988) found that they could differentiate good and poor buildings based on four factors: facility, space, maintenance, and safety.

Facility refers to the actual physical plant. Recent renovations, modern and practical design, solid construction, and appropriate furnishings characterize a good facility. A good facility is not too expensive to maintain and operate. In contrast, obsolete features, poor design, shoddy construction, and inadequate furnishings characterize a poor facility. A poor facility may use up most of the available budget for operating and maintenance expenses.

Space refers to both the amount and flexibility of the teaching area. Workspace is a critical part of the design of a productive workplace (Becker, 1981). For a teacher, ample and large classrooms, adequate teacher workspace, adequate storage space, team offices, and a renovated faculty lounge characterize space in a good workplace. Not enough classrooms, small classrooms, no offices or teacher workrooms, no storage space, and overcrowding characterize space in a poor workplace. Teachers also require a variety of types of space for special activities (Bacharach, Bauer, & Shedd, 1986). The maintenance of a proper learning environment requires the flexible use of space.

From a teacher's perspective, the *maintenance* and cleanliness of the school are indicators of the school system's attitude toward teachers. In a good workplace, there are few repair problems, an emphasis on cleanliness, enough custodial staff, adequate cleaning supplies, timely repairs, and proven pride in the building. In a poor workplace, there may be broken windows, burned-out lights, major repair problems, shortages of cleaning supplies, custodial staff cutbacks, and a lengthy process for repairs.

Reports of school violence make us very sensitive to the issue of *safety* in schools. A school located in an unsafe neighborhood may generate teacher fears, and incidents of vandalism may make them worse. It is difficult to concentrate on teaching if you are afraid for your physical safety. You can make a workplace safer by closely watching the building, providing adequate security staff, and securing the parking area. Open access to the building, inadequate security staff, or an unsecured parking area can detract from the safety of the working environment.

Resources. A primary part of any job design is providing incumbents with the resources necessary to carry out assigned tasks. Inadequate basic resources drain teachers' energy away from teaching their students. Rather, their effort goes to locating the necessary teaching materials (Bacharach, Bauer, & Shedd, 1986). Resource problems are made worse by increased workloads, usually in the form of increased class sizes, additional paperwork, or excessive noninstructional duties. In a better workplace, teachers have access to the necessary resources and have a reasonable workload. In a poor workplace, the scramble to find missing resources adds to the teacher's workload, and additional duties make it difficult to use the resources that are available. Three resources have an immediate impact on a teacher's ability to perform: time; support staff; and equipment, materials, and supplies (Bacharach, Bauer, & Shedd, 1986).

One of the primary characteristics of an effectively designed job is that the incumbent is given enough *time* to complete the responsibilities associated with the position. Time is especially important in teaching, where day-to-day activities vary and in which problem solving is a major part (Sykes, 1990a). The provision of enough time to perform varied tasks and the discretion to allocate time for task completion are essential to teachers' success. Beyond this, there is a need for enough "slack time" for teachers to participate in development activities and to experiment with new teaching techniques (Wilson & Corcoran, 1988).

Bacharach, Bauer, and Shedd (1986) found that more than 60% of the teachers responding to a national survey experience at least occasional problems with time. The tasks that teachers do not spend enough time on reflect the problems associated with lack of adequate time. Counseling, grading, and planning, in particular, are given less attention than teachers feel they deserve (Bacharach, Bauer, & Shedd, 1986). Teachers report that increased class size prevents them from giving individual students the attention they deserve (Corcoran et al., 1988). Smaller class sizes, then, may contribute to an improved workplace. Beyond that, a change in the priorities and responsibilities in teaching would improve the school as a workplace (Corcoran et al., 1988). For example, teachers would like less paperwork and more time for planning.

In today's schools, even if teachers have enough time for teaching, they often must use that time fulfilling other role responsibilities. This is especially true if their school lacks *support staff.* The social and emotional problems associated with single-parent families, divorce, drug use, teenage pregnancy, and an increasing percentage of minority students have increased the scope of services people expect schools to provide. On a day-to-day basis, it is the teacher who must face these problems and these expectations. Teachers need advice and help from others to fulfill these expectations. In particular, teachers and administrators cite the need for support staff such as counselors, nurses, social workers, security staff, and aides (Corcoran et al., 1988).

Equipment, materials, and supplies represent the most basic tools of teaching. For effective teaching, schools must outfit each classroom with the right quantity and quality of textbooks, workbooks, chalk, erasers, and so on. Although the evidence suggests that these basic tools are not a problem for many teachers (Bacharach, Bauer, & Shedd, 1986), in some schools (particularly those in urban areas), lack of equipment, materials, and supplies is a significant problem (Corcoran et al., 1988). In some schools, administrative procedures that further constrain access to what resources are available make conditions worse.

Collegiality. One of the basic practices of total quality is the use of teams. The use of teams, particularly cross-functional teams, helps to break down barriers between departments. This is in keeping with the view of organizations as systems. The use of teams also helps to create or reinforce a common sense of purpose and promote organizational learning (Nadler et al., 1992; Senge, 1990).

Teaching is a social activity (Sykes, 1990b). If the education process is to be effective, teachers must communicate, learning continuously from each other. They must discuss the idiosyncrasies of particular students, the techniques that work for particular classes, the subject matter mastered already and the subject matter not yet mastered by a particular student or group. Teachers depend on their relationships with each other and other members of the school system. New teachers highly value this interaction (Hart & Murphy, 1990).

In a good workplace, teachers feel free to discuss both personal and staff educational and instructional issues. As professionals, they exercise free speech without fear of retribution and can face those in authority (Levering, 1989). There is an attitude of "we are all in this together." In an autocratic and/or bureaucratic school, teachers are silent or guarded about what they say and whom they say it to. They often hide behind the closed doors of their classrooms.

Collegiality has an important influence on organization cultures and structures; schools are no exception (Barth, 1990; Johnson, 1989). Just as research on organizations in general has emphasized the impact of employee involvement on collegiality (Lawler, 1988), researchers have linked collegiality to teacher participation in decision making (Corcoran et al., 1988). Rosenholtz (1985) states that "teacher involvement in decision making encourages the deliberate evaluation and modification of curriculum and instruction required to enhance the quality of classroom learning." It encourages clear and conscious choices and provides the flexibility necessary to accommodate the varied needs of individual students.

A lot of attention in the education reform movement has been on school-based management as the proper method for providing teacher participation in school decision making. This is true although there is little agreement on what exactly school-based management is or should look like (Mitchell, 1990). More conventional forms of teacher participation (such as teaming or school councils) promote discussion of educational and instructional issues between peers (Wise, 1988). Other structures, such as mentors, peer coaching, and department meetings, can promote collegiality without directly affecting participation in decision making. These more traditional forms deserve consideration because they may meet less opposition from administrators (Corcoran et al., 1988).

Improving the physical conditions of the teaching environment and the resources available to teachers would go a long way toward enhancing teachers' performance. Because good workplaces provide the conditions necessary to fulfill the responsibilities assigned to a position, assuring that schools are good workplaces should enhance educational productivity. What evidence is there to support this belief? Research shows that work conditions affect teacher attendance, level of effort, classroom efficacy, teacher morale, and job satisfaction (Conley, Bacharach, & Bauer, 1989; Corcoran et al., 1988). These researchers found that an adequate physical plant, staff collegiality, participation in decision making, and strong administrative leadership resulted in teachers who were enthusiastic, cooperative, and willing to take responsibility. Such conditions also foster a high level of staff morale. In contrast, a lack of resources, low staff collegiality, poor professional development, little influence in decision making, few rewards, and poor administrative leadership all resulted in higher teacher absenteeism, reduced effort, less effectiveness in the classroom, low staff morale, and reduced job satisfaction.

Individual's Ability and Attitudes

Whereas attention to work context can help remove barriers to action in the workplace, attention to individual ability and attitudes can help remove barriers to action in the individual. The question is which programs or policies can have an impact on individual abilities and attitudes so as to strengthen the linkage between effort and performance.

Three personal characteristics of the individual affect the effort-performance linkage (Newsom, 1990): capability, confidence, and challenge.

Capability. Do individuals have the necessary skill and knowledge to perform? Do they know why the desired performance is important? If an individual lacks the necessary skills and knowledge, or does not see how his or her performance contributes to achieving organization goals, he or she is less likely to put forth the effort necessary for good performance. "The need to produce an outcome or results creates the need for competence, which is the purpose of training" (Odiorne, 1987, p. 109). Furthermore, as change becomes a way of life in organizations, ensuring lifelong learning will become a central part of any successful organization (Nadler et al., 1992; Senge, 1990).

The knowledge and skills needed by teachers to implement many of the proposed reforms in education are not widely available in our school systems. That is why the importance of professional development to the successful implementation of curriculum and other reforms is a recurring theme in proposals for reform. Effective reforms, by their very nature, require significant changes in understanding, attitudes, and behavior to succeed. Reform requires a consistent and continual investment in people's development. Staff development, mentoring, and formative performance evaluations are illustrative of programs that may help to enhance teachers' capabilities.

All curriculum development and other reform efforts should include a staff development component. All teachers who will be affected by the reform should attend, and the staff development component should be sufficient to prepare teachers to implement that particular curriculum or reform. Providing teachers with the knowledge and abilities to implement new curricula and other reforms is a crucial part of supporting and facilitating the work of teachers as professionals.

Recent advances in teacher preparation, training, and professional development highlight the types of skills and abilities teachers require to fulfill their responsibilities as they change over the course of their careers. For example, Hawley (1991) argues that teachers' skill development begins with the development of the capabilities and motivation to learn to teach in preservice teacher preparation. Teachers then develop specific competencies needed to belong to school systems as novice teachers. Career teachers' skill development continues with further education and professional development.

Confidence. Capability is not enough. Are individuals physically, mentally, and emotionally able to perform? Self-confidence gives a professional the ability to become engaged in work; the lack of self-confidence disrupts professional attention and detracts from performance (Csikszentmihalyi, 1990). Although a teacher may know how to teach, if he or she lacks confidence, his or her efforts will be hesitant and less likely to lead to good performance.

Research has shown that the public image and status of teaching have a negative impact on people's decision to enter or remain in teaching (Schlechty, 1984). This contributes to low self-esteem. An unanticipated positive benefit of helping teachers to make legitimate external comparisons emerged from one study (Shedd & Malanowski, 1985). To identify positions outside of education whose responsibilities and demands were similar to teaching, teachers conducted interviews with lawyers, TV news managers, and people in several other occupations. The structured interviews enabled direct comparisons of teaching to other jobs. Those participating in the research gained a renewed respect for and pride in what they actually do as teachers.

Webb and Ashton (1986) argue that the teacher's sense of efficacy is crucial to teacher motivation. Teachers who believe that they have the ability to teach and that their students have the ability to learn are highly motivated. The essence of a sense of efficacy is a perceived linkage between effort and performance: the belief that if a teacher makes the right effort, he or she will get a desired educational outcome.

Supervisory behavior is especially crucial in bolstering teachers' confidence. Goal clarity and helpful performance feedback enhance teachers' instructional success with students. There could be improvement in supervisory interaction with teachers (Clark & Meloy, 1988). Most teachers in a national survey reported that their supervisors do not provide helpful information and suggestions, clarify what is expected of them, discuss instructional problems and techniques, or discuss teachers' individual performance (Bacharach, Bauer, & Shedd, 1986).

Challenge. For an individual to make the effort to perform well, his or her skills should match the challenges he or she faces. Challenges beyond a person's skill level promote anxiety, whereas challenges beneath a person's skill level lead to boredom (Csikszentmihalyi, 1990). Creative use of staff assignments to ensure a match between skills and challenge enhances both capability and confidence. Proper assignments encourage individuals to grow to meet the challenge of the task, without demotivating them by providing them an impossibly difficult task (Krupp, 1983). Research has also shown the importance of challenge in leadership development (McCall, Lombardo, & Morrison, 1988).

The issue of challenge is linked to the setting of individual performance objectives discussed in the earlier section on results. Providing an adequate challenge should be a significant criterion in developing and assessing a teacher's professional improvement plan.

The Performance-Reward Linkage

If managers create a productive work environment, individual effort is likely to result in better performance. Better performance must in turn lead to higher (more valued) rewards for high-performing individuals (Locke, 1976; Vroom, 1964). Two elements deserve consideration for their effect on the linkage between performance and rewards (Newsom, 1990): credibility and consistency.

Credibility

Credibility refers to the ability of the organization or superior to deliver the desired rewards. Failure to deliver promised rewards leads to a lack of trust in the organization or superior (Levering, 1989). This breaks the linkage between performance and rewards, reducing the individual's motivation to act.

One of the unanticipated consequences of organizational downsizing and other restructuring efforts has been a significant decrease in the level of trust (Horton & Reid, 1991). When individuals go to work for an organization, they enter into a psychological contract with the organization. For many individuals, the recent round of organizational restructuring amounted to a violation of the psychological contract. Indeed, several people talk about the set of expectations that are emerging as the basis for the new psychological contract in organizations (Bardwick, 1991; Goman, 1991; Horton & Reid, 1991). The new contract carries with it a different set of performance requirements and associated rewards than the old contract it replaces.

The variety of education reforms are also altering the psychological contract between school staff and the school system. Teachers who began their careers working with middle-class children from intact families find their expectations challenged by disadvantaged children from broken homes. Teachers who want to teach find that the need to take on the additional roles of social worker, disciplinarian, special education teacher, and so on becomes a violation of their psychological contract. Teachers who want to be left alone in their classrooms to teach find the request to serve on a school council an unanticipated responsibility. Thus the impact on the psychological contract of the changes being wrought by education reform may reduce the school's or principal's credibility in the teachers' eyes.

On a more mundane level, the political nature of school systems (Bacharach & Mitchell, 1987; Siegel & Byrne, 1994) can also reduce the school's and principal's credibility. Shifting priorities, unstable funding, fragmented leadership, and other accoutrements of the political side of schools make the ability to deliver on promised rewards a constant challenge. As stated before, the failure to deliver on promises breaks the linkage between performance and rewards.

Consistency

Consistency is present if individuals receive similar rewards for good performance and receive similar (and less valued) rewards for poor performance. Internal comparisons of performance to rewards, that is, comparisons to other individuals in the same organization, are a key part of an individual's perception of consistency (Adams, 1963; Levering, 1989). The failure to achieve a sense of internal equity reduces an individual's motivation to act.[6]

Rules, policies, and procedures try to provide some standards of treatment that can serve as a base for internal equity. The debate between the proponents of the unified salary schedule and proponents of merit pay is of interest here. On the one hand, unified salary schedules based on seniority or education provide consistency, but fail to draw a direct link between performance objectives and rewards. On the other hand, merit increments based on subjective evaluations may help draw a link between performance and rewards, but foster feelings of inequity due to perceived inconsistency (Bacharach, Lipsky, & Shedd, 1984).

One of the most significant difficulties in addressing the issue of consistency is that the essence of consistency (or fairness) is perceptual (Huseman & Hatfield, 1989; Sheppard, Lewicki, & Minton, 1992). There is no single, absolute standard for deciding fairness in any given situation. Sensitivity to the issue, however, can help achieve a balanced sense of consistency.

The arguments for and against merit pay also highlight the fact that consistency is but one element in the larger issue of organizational justice (Sheppard et al., 1992). The first principle of justice requires a judgment of balance. Applying that principle requires one to compare a given action against other similar actions in similar situations. A decision, action, or procedure is also evaluated against a second principle, that of correctness: that quality which makes a decision seem right. Justice matters when actions or decisions by people within organizations potentially benefit or harm the interests of some individuals or groups in a differential manner. Concerns for justice may also be invoked when actions or outcomes violate people's expectations concerning "the way things should happen" or "the way things are supposed to be." Issues of justice emerge strongly in day-to-day decisions, such as who gets what office, who gets which class assignments, and so on. Teachers who feel, as a result of these everyday decisions, that administrators do not treat them fairly will not perceive a linkage between performance and rewards.

For performance management to work, all of the elements of the school system have to be aligned and working in a common direction, that is, they must be consistent. For example, one school system that implemented school-based management added the responsibility of working with the school councils to its principals' responsibilities. So far, so good. But the principals were on a merit pay system that rewarded them for achieving specific school objectives, objectives that were best achieved by working around, rather than through, the school council. The elements of the system were out of alignment.

Credibility and consistency are key to establishing a link between performance and rewards. For performance management to succeed, the available rewards must be valued by the individuals. The rewards may appeal to either intrinsic or extrinsic motivators (Herzberg, 1966). Sergiovanni (1992) argues that the moral aspects of teaching and leadership, which thrive on intrinsic rewards, should take precedence if education reforms are to succeed. Specific management policies can address intrinsic needs such as recognition, achievement, or increased responsibility. Teacher recognition programs try to set up a direct link between performance and intrinsic rewards (in this case, recognition). Research on school improvement programs suggests, however, that although these psychic rewards are important, they are not enough to sustain long-term improvement in performance. Districts must supplement intrinsic rewards with extrinsic rewards (e.g., salary, or pay for performance) for teachers to put forth the maximum effort over an extended period of time (Carnoy & McDonnell, 1989).

Management's task is to find ways to balance the need for intrinsic and extrinsic rewards (Benveniste, 1987). To maintain that intrinsic rewards are a substitute for extrinsic rewards is simply a justification for exploitation. To maintain that extrinsic rewards are interchangeable with intrinsic rewards is to ignore the professional ethos of teachers. The most productive teachers are those who have both their extrinsic and intrinsic needs fulfilled.

A productive work environment facilitates and supports individual performance; it ensures that increased individual effort results in better performance. The linkage of effort to performance can be improved by removing barriers to action in the workplace (improving the work context) and by removing barriers to action in the individual (improving the individual's abilities and attitudes). Thus "the most constructive action for improving productivity is for managers to figure out why people behave the way they do and then to shape their management systems into patterns which will result in people wanting to produce more" (Odiorne, 1987, p. 169).

Continual Improvement

The final element in performance management is continual improvement. It is a mistake to assume that all is well once performance goals are set and a productive work environment has been established. High quality requires continual improvement (Deming, 1986).

Continual improvement requires tracking the key indicators that are associated with organizational and individual performance objectives (see the earlier section on results). The identification of performance indicators and establishing objectives sets the plan; a means of assessing results, and taking action to ensure improved performance in the future, must be added to ensure continual improvement.

One of the challenges to continual improvement stems from the fact that many of the traditional performance indicators (e.g., standardized tests, graduation rates, etc.) only allow for improvement after the fact. A more effective system would recognize the value of making adjustments while an activity is still in progress (Newman, 1975). Recognizing the importance of corrections in process is the key to high quality (Juran, 1988).

There have been some promising developments in the use of predictors in education. Districts are starting to use measures that allow for adjustments while the activity is still in progress. Two illustrations can show the value of this approach. The first example involves at-risk students. For years, the bulk of programs for aiding at-risk students involved actions taken after students were already in danger of dropping out. More recently, research efforts have concentrated on identifying sets of predictors for a child becoming at risk (Orr, 1987; Sartain, 1989). By identifying the characteristics that predict that a child will become at risk, schools can offer programs to lessen the impact of these elements. This reduces the likelihood that the child will become at risk.

Many of the computerized instruction packages offer another example of adjustments while an activity is still in progress. These programs provide teachers with daily or weekly summaries of their students' performance. These ongoing assessments enable teachers to adjust their instruction to assure that students are learning. For example, suppose the feedback showed that only 40% of a class understood iambic pentameter. The teacher could go back over that section of the curriculum to ensure that everyone understood the lesson.

Because continual improvement requires an assessment and corrective action, efforts to implement performance management in schools inevitably result in a discussion of accountability. The "fishbowl" of public education colors the definition of accountability—there is a focus on failure. In particular, there is a tendency to finger-point and look for an individual to blame. One of the basic changes necessary for performance management to succeed is a shift from a focus on failure and blame to a focus on continual improvement. The first question should always be, "How can we improve?" People should not be afraid of identifying deficiencies so that they can be addressed. Accountability must be seen as a normal and positive aspect of school management. The district must link accountability to continual improvement of the school system and the ongoing professional development of school staff.

This does not mean that districts should ignore *summative evaluation* (as noted earlier, it is important to link performance to rewards). For the school, the idea of summative evaluation means the ability to recognize when a program has failed and to take appropriate action. For the individual, any summative evaluation would be related to rewards and sanctions in the performance evaluation program.

For example, the district proposal for school-based management in Boston calls for individual schools to set performance objectives. If the school does not meet its objectives, there is a formative review of the school by the district administration. If necessary, the district sends a district intervention team in to help the school. If the school still fails to meet its objectives, then the district has the authority to replace or reorganize the school staff (Steinberger, 1990).

Performance evaluation remains as the primary mechanism for assessing and developing plans for improving an individual's performance in his or her role. We touched on the strengths and weaknesses of performance evaluations in our earlier discussions of individual performance objectives and the contribution of individual abilities and attitudes in creating a productive work environment.

The Importance of Information

Continual improvement requires that valid and reliable data on performance indicators be available in a timely manner to the proper staff. Access to information and the ability to analyze the information are crucial elements of continual improvement.

As restructuring proceeds in many districts, decentralization of district data will be essential to continual improvement at the school level. Many districts are computerizing their district and school data to allow appropriate staff easy access (Bank & Williams, 1987). However, access to performance data is problematic in some school systems. Fragmented and inflexible databases cannot generate timely information.

Access alone is not enough. The data must be available in such a manner as to facilitate analysis (the staff must also have the necessary skills to perform any data analysis). Analysis to identify needs and causes is a crucial element of continual improvement (Juran, 1988; Walton, 1986). For example, in a given semester, 30% of a high school's students may fail a course. An analysis of the failure rate by teacher and class, however, may reveal that one teacher fails 80% of his students. Improving performance would dictate that a discussion of that teacher's high failure rate is in order.

The level (e.g., district, school, or class) at which the system collects, organizes, and reports data will determine the nature of the information flow. Careful attention should be given to these decisions in designing an information management system to support continual improvement (OERI State Accountability Group, 1988).

Learning Organizations

Continual improvement produces learning organizations. Learning organizations have environments that extract and disseminate learning (Nadler et al., 1992; Senge, 1990). This requires that the organization provides time to reflect. In schools, public demands for performance and immediate results, educators' tendency to adopt a defensive posture ("we are the professionals here"), and the failure to provide adequate forums for learning (largely due to time pressures) combine to produce faulty or incomplete reflection. This, in turn, results in limited or incorrect learning.

Learning organizations also facilitate and support an action orientation, that is, motivation toward risk taking and experiments structured for learning. Without action, alternatives to the existing state are not attempted. In schools, shifting priorities, a traditional tendency to focus on putting programs in place without evaluating their true effectiveness, the existence of a blaming culture, and a sense of powerlessness on the part of many members of the staff all detract from the school's ability to become a learning organization.

One solution is to promote *action research* as a method of dealing with change. It asks school staff and individual teachers to monitor and evaluate the programs and activities they implement in an effort to achieve their school or job objectives. It asks each staff person, as a professional, to systematically reflect on his or her practice to identify what works and why, and what doesn't work and how can it be improved. The goal is to build learning opportunities and to create a process to share successes and deal constructively with mistakes and failure.

Promoting an action research orientation is consistent with two trends in education reform. First, action research at the school level takes advantage of the movement toward school-based management. It provides a framework for truly empowering school councils to become self-managed work teams (Lawler, 1988). Second, action research at the classroom level treats teachers as professionals. In so doing, it acknowledges one of the implicit premises in much of the current management literature: that the ultimate control in any organization is the self-control that an employee brings to bear when he or she has internalized the values, goals, and plans of the organization (Peters, 1988).

Conclusion

Performance management is a methodology for clearly linking broad organizational goals to individual performance. I have argued in this chapter that performance management can help educational practitioners align and focus district-level and individual-level activities in support of student learning.

What does it take to carry out performance management in education? Performance management should be part of a comprehensive district improvement effort. A good strategic plan will identify key variables to integrate district activity and localize the administration of other controls. Several elements of an integrated plan facilitate and support performance management.

First, an integrated plan should provide clear priorities integrating district, school, and individual activity (Rumler & Brache, 1990). Not everything can be done at once. Education has too often been guilty of an "add-on" mentality: adding programs rather than establishing sound criteria for setting priorities. Good plans start with a mission or vision and proceed to identify a limited set of goals for a given year. The operationalization of these goals integrates district, school, and individual activity, identifying the specific contribution each makes in accomplishing the goals.

Second, the use of hard data and analysis to identify issues and opportunities while developing the plan reinforces the importance of standards and indicators. Standards and indicators form the foundation of performance management.

Third, an effective plan provides clearly defined issues or opportunities for improvement. The analysis that goes into plan development should consider what the problem is, where it occurs, when it occurs, to what extent it is a problem, and changes over time. This activity ensures that the planning team will use the appropriate quality indicators in setting performance objectives.

Finally, the use of action plans to operationalize all plans sets up the basis for continual improvement. An action plan forces schools to state specific objectives, list the activities necessary to achieve each objective, identify the person responsible for seeing that each activity gets done, set completion dates for each activity, and identify the success signals or indicators used to evaluate each objective. The action-planning format also can play a significant part in communicating district and school activity to the broader educational community.

Good planning improves quality because it ties goals to specific measures, sets objectives based on those measures, and evaluates progress using those measures. Without these linkages, quality improves haphazardly, if at all. First, without measures, there is no way of documenting whether quality has improved. It is impossible to take advantage of the enthusiasm and public relations value of success without documentation. Second, program efforts lack focus and become scattered without clear goals. There is no way of knowing what programs worked or did not work. Program efforts fade away when someone gets enthusiastic about a replacement. Quality improvement demands a measurable sense of progress.

The success of performance management requires that districts involve teachers in the development of the district and school plans.

The growing trend toward the formation of school teams or councils to develop school plans is a positive step. Districts also must move to integrate individual plans for professional development (emerging from teachers' performance evaluations) with school goals. Most districts rarely make this linkage.

Although district and school administrators can use policy to create an environment that facilitates and supports high performance, they *cannot* determine whether teachers will accept the challenges and opportunities created by the policies. The district's leverage is in creating the conditions that will "allow teachers to reach their potential" (Bacharach, Bauer, & Shedd, 1986). Teachers must choose to respond actively to the workplace created by the district management (DePree, 1989).

Getting teachers to respond is one of the basic tests of school leadership (Bacharach & Mitchell, 1991a). It is crucial that administrators communicate performance objectives to the members of the educational community. For objectives to have an impact, everyone must understand how they relate to the district's mission, how their job contributes to that mission, and how use of the objectives will improve performance (Rumler & Brache, 1990). In short, performance management must become part of the district's vision. District leaders must infuse the principles of performance management into the district culture. They must show how mission, objectives, and behaviors are linked together (Boyett & Conn, 1988; Moses & Whitaker, 1990; Sambs & Schenkat, 1990). The challenge to the leader is to instill performance management into the district through example, organizational design, and the effective use of social processes (Lodahl & Mitchell, 1980). Performance management is institutionalized when the practices, processes, and tools are no longer an add-on program or fad, but are part and parcel of how the company does business each and every day, and when the change efforts continue despite the turnover of key change agents. In short, performance management needs to be made an integral part of the organizational culture (Schein, 1992).

Notes

1. This is an example of a content standard. Content standards are different from performance standards; performance standards are ideal or expected achievements on specific performance indicators. For example, running a 4-minute mile or scoring 800 on an SAT are both performance standards.

2. In some cases, it is possible to use statistical techniques to establish control limits on performance. Objectives can then be set to reduce the distance between the upper and lower control limits, that is, to reduce the variation and/or to raise the absolute level of performance.

3. Although my emphasis here is on teachers, it is important to recognize that the programs and restructuring of schools resulting from the education reform are changing all of the traditional roles in a school system. For example, one of the major changes in the principal's role is the need to become a participative manager. Two additional responsibilities include building team competence and skills, and managing internal and external linkages. One of the key challenges for a district office staff will be to balance their traditional emphasis on control with the new requirement for service. A strategic approach to performance management should take these changes into account.

4. Recent research on effective teaching suggests, however, that individual evaluators using a generic set of indicators may be right for beginning teachers. With more experienced teachers, however, a collaborative approach that poses problems to a group does more to enhance professional development and teacher performance (O'Neill, 1991; Willis, 1991).

5. This section draws heavily on Bacharach and Mitchell (1991a, 1991b).

6. Individuals also rely on external comparisons in evaluating equity. Levering (1989) notes that rewards in a good workplace will be seen as fair if they are similar to comparable organizations and in line with the organization's ability to pay.

References

Adams, J. (1963). Toward an understanding of inequity. *Journal of Abnormal and Social Psychology, 67*, 422-436.

Bacharach, S. B., Bauer, S., & Conley, S. (1986). Organizational analysis of stress: The case of elementary and secondary schools. *Journal of Work and Occupations, 13*(1), 7-32.

Bacharach, S. B., Bauer, S., & Shedd, J. (1986). *The learning workplace: The conditions and resources of teaching.* Ithaca, NY: Organizational Analysis and Practice, Inc.

Bacharach, S. B., Conley, S., & Shedd, J. (1986). Beyond career ladders: Structuring teacher career development systems. *Teachers College Record, 87*, 563-574.

Bacharach, S. B., Lipsky, D., & Shedd, J. (1984). *Paying for better teaching: Merit pay and its alternatives.* Ithaca, NY: Organizational Analysis and Practice, Inc.

Bacharach, S. B., & Mitchell, S. M. (1981). Toward a dialogue in the middle range. *Educational Administration Quarterly, 17*, 1-14.

Bacharach, S. B., & Mitchell, S. M. (1987). Schools as organizations: The generation of practical theory. In P. R. Lawrence & J. W. Lorsch (Eds.),

The handbook of organizational theory (pp. 405-418). Englewood Cliffs, NJ: Prentice Hall.

Bacharach, S. B., & Mitchell, S. M. (1991a). Motivation in organizational contexts. In M. Alkin (Ed.), *Encyclopedia of educational research*. Englewood Cliffs, NJ: Prentice Hall.

Bacharach, S. B., & Mitchell, S. M. (1991b). The school as a workplace: Examining the teachers' work environment. In M. Alkin (Ed.), *Encyclopedia of educational research*. Englewood Cliffs, NJ: Prentice Hall.

Bank, A., & Williams, R. (1987). *Information systems and school improvement.* New York: Teachers College Press.

Bardwick, J. (1991). *Danger in the comfort zone.* New York: AMACOM.

Barth, R. S. (1990). *Improving schools from within: Teachers, parents, and principals can make the difference.* San Francisco: Jossey-Bass.

Becker, F. D. (1981). *Workspace: Creating environments in organizations.* New York: Praeger.

Benveniste, G. (1987). *Professionalizing the organization.* San Francisco: Jossey-Bass.

Berryman, S., & Bailey, T. (1992). *The double helix of education & the economy.* New York: Institute on Education and the Economy.

Boyett, J., & Conn, H. (1988). *Maximum performance management.* Macomb, IL: Glenbridge.

California State Department of Education. (1984). *Performance report for California schools.* Sacramento: Author.

Carnoy, M., & McDonnell, J. (1989). School district restructuring in Santa Fe, New Mexico. *Educational Policy, 4*(1), 49-64.

Clark, D. L., & Meloy, J. M. (1988). Renouncing bureaucracy: A democratic structure for leadership in schools. In T. J. Sergiovanni & J. H. Moore (Eds.), *Schooling for tomorrow: Directing reforms to issues that count.* Boston: Allyn and Bacon.

Conley, S. C., Bacharach, S. B., & Bauer, S. (1989). The school work environment and teacher career dissatisfaction. *Educational Administration Quarterly, 25*(1), 58-81.

Corcoran, T., Walker, L., & White, J. L. (1988). *Working in urban schools.* Washington, DC: Institute for Educational Leadership.

Csikszentmihalyi, M. (1990). *Flow: The psychology of optimal experience.* New York: Harper & Row.

Darling-Hammond, L. (1992). *Standards of practice for learner-centered schools.* New York: NCREST.

David, J. (1987). *Improving education with locally developed indicators* (Report RR-004). New Brunswick, NJ: Center for Policy Research in Education.

Deming, W. E. (1986). *Out of the crisis.* Cambridge: MIT Press.

DePree, M. (1989). *Leadership is an art.* New York: Doubleday.

Goman, C. (1991). *The loyalty factor.* New York: MultiMedia Limited.

Hart, A., & Murphy, M. J. (1990). New teachers react to redesigned teacher work. *American Journal of Education, 98,* 224-250.

Hawley, W. (1991). Toward a "re-visioning" of education for teaching. *Education Week, 10*(34), 36.

Herzberg, F. (1966). *Work and the nature of man.* Cleveland, OH: World.

Horton, T., & Reid, P. (1991). *Beyond the trust gap.* Homewood, IL: Business One Irwin.

Huseman, R., & Hatfield, J. (1989). *Managing the equity factor.* Boston: Houghton Mifflin.

Johnson, S. M. (1989). School work and its reform. In J. Hannaway & R. Crowson (Eds.), *The politics of reforming school administration.* New York: Falmer.

Johnson, S. M. (1990). Redesigning teachers' work. In R. F. Elmore & Associates (Eds.), *Restructuring schools: The next generation of educational reform.* San Francisco: Jossey-Bass.

Juran, J. M. (1988). *Juran on planning for quality.* New York: Free Press.

Krupp, J. A. (1983). How to spark an aging staff: Some suggestions. *Illinois School Research and Development, 20*(1), 38-46.

Lawler, E. (1988). *High involvement management.* San Francisco: Jossey-Bass.

Levering, R. (1989). *A great place to work.* New York: Random House.

Locke, E. A. (1976). The nature and causes of job satisfaction. In M. D. Dunnette (Ed.), *Handbook of industrial and organizational psychology* (pp. 1297-1349). Chicago: Rand McNally.

Lodahl, T., & Mitchell, S. (1980). Drift in the development of innovative organizations. In J. Kimberly & R. Miles (Eds.), *The organizational life cycle* (pp. 184-207). San Francisco: Jossey-Bass.

McCall, G., Lombardo, M., & Morrison, A. (1988). *The lessons of experience.* Lexington, MA: D. C. Heath.

Mitchell, S. (1990). *The principal in a participative environment.* Ithaca, NY: Organizational Analysis and Practice, Inc.

Mitchell, S. (1991a). *Implementing school based management.* Ithaca, NY: Organizational Analysis and Practice, Inc.

Mitchell, S. (1991b). *School based management council handbook.* Ithaca, NY: Organizational Analysis and Practice, Inc.

Moses, M., & Whitaker, K. (1990, September). Ten components of restructuring schools. *The School Administrator,* pp. 32-34.

Nadler, D., Gersten, M., & Shaw, R. (1992). *Organizational architecture.* San Francisco: Jossey-Bass.

National Board for Professional Teaching Standards. (1990). *Toward high and rigorous standards for the teaching profession.*

Newman, W. (1975). *Constructive control.* Englewood Cliffs, NJ: Prentice Hall.

Newsom, W. (1990). Motivate, now! *Personnel Journal, 69*(2), 51-55.

North Carolina's lead teacher/restructured school pilot project: An interim report. (1988, Spring). *Forum.*

Odiorne, G. (1987). *The human side of management.* Lexington, MA: Lexington Books.

OERI State Accountability Group. (1988). *Creating responsible and responsive accountability systems* (PIP 88-808). Washington, DC: U.S. Department of Education.

O'Neill, J. (1991). New era dawns on teaching research. *ASCD Update, 33*(6).

Orr, M. T. (1987). *Keeping students in school.* San Francisco: Jossey-Bass.

Peters, T. (1988). *Thriving on chaos*. New York: Alfred A. Knopf.

Rosenholtz, S. J. (1985). Effective schools: Interpreting the evidence. *American Journal of Education*.

Rumler, G., & Brache, A. (1990). *Improving performance: Managing the white space on the organizational chart*. San Francisco: Jossey-Bass.

Sambs, C., & Schenkat, R. (1990, April). One district learns about restructuring. *Educational Leadership*, pp. 72-75.

Sartain, H. (1989). *Non-achieving students at risk*. Washington, DC: National Education Association.

Schein, E. (1992). *Organizational culture*. San Francisco: Jossey-Bass.

Schlechty, P. (1984). *Restructuring the teaching occupation—A proposal* (NIE-G-84-0004). Washington, DC: National Institute of Education.

Senge, P. M. (1990). *The fifth discipline: Mastering the five practices of the learning organization*. New York: Doubleday.

Sergiovanni, T. (1992). *Moral leadership*. San Francisco: Jossey-Bass.

Shedd, J., & Malanowski, R. (1985). *From the front of the classroom: A study of the work of teachers*. Ithaca, NY: Organizational Analysis and Practice, Inc.

Sheppard, B., Lewicki, R., & Minton, J. (1992). *Organizational justice*. New York: Lexington Books.

Siegel, P., & Byrne, S. (1994). *Using quality to redesign school systems: The cutting edge of common sense*. San Francisco: Jossey-Bass.

Steinberger, E. (1990, September). Teachers unions handling tricky turns on the road to reform. *The School Administrator*, pp. 26-31.

Sykes, G. (1990a). Fostering teacher professionalism in schools. In R. F. Elmore & Associates (Eds.), *Restructuring schools: The next generation of educational reform*. San Francisco: Jossey-Bass.

Sykes, G. (1990b). Inspired teaching: The missing element in effective schools. In S. B. Bacharach (Ed.), *Education reform: Making sense of it all*. Boston: Allyn and Bacon.

Vroom, V. (1964). *Work and motivation*. New York: John Wiley.

Walton, M. (1986). *The Deming management method*. New York: Dodd, Mead.

Webb, R., & Ashton, P. (1986). Teacher motivation and the conditions of teaching: A call for ecological reform. *Journal of Thought*, 21(2), 43-60.

Wiggins, G. (1990, January 24). Standards should mean qualities, not quantities. *Education Week*, p. 36.

Willis, S. (1991). Supervising empowered teachers. *ASCD Update*, 33(6).

Wilson, B. I., & Corcoran, T. B. (1988). *Successful secondary schools: Visions of excellence in American public education*. New York: Falmer.

Wise, A. E. (1988). Professional teaching: A new paradigm for the management of education. In T. J. Sergiovanni & J. H. Moore (Eds.), *Schooling for tomorrow: Directing reforms to issues that count*. Boston: Allyn and Bacon.

SEVEN

The Assessment
of Teaching Based on
Evidence of Student Learning

GARY SYKES
JASON MILLMAN

Should evidence of student learning enter into the evaluation of teachers? This question of great import in the current movement to reform American education represents a central issue in a yet larger debate within our society about the most effective means for directing the work of complex organizations. The debate plays out in a spate of popular books on management and in the more rigorous contributions of scholars studying the social, political, and economic organization of postmodern life. The counterposing lines of thought reflect tensions nascent in the classic works of such administrative theorists as Barnard, Simon, and MacGregor, but with contemporary extensions and refinements:

AUTHORS' NOTE: An earlier version of this chapter was commissioned by the National Board for Professional Teaching Standards (NBPTS). We wish to acknowledge their support but to indicate that the views expressed here are not endorsed by the NBPTS.

- Challenging rational models of organizational decision making are provocative images of organized anarchies, garbage-can decision making, and loose coupling proposed in the work of March, Weick, and others;
- Over against management-by-objectives/results schemes championed by Drucker and his disciples is an insistence on the cultural aspects of organizations evident in the work of Ouchi, Peters, and Waterman, and many others;
- Complicating the exercise of authority within bureaucratic organizations is the increasing presence of professionals representing an alternative source of authority;
- Crosscutting the traditional cultural predicates of modern organization are the new politics of gender and race; and
- In rebuttal to assumptions of centralized planning and social problem solving within public and private sectors alike are arguments for the market and for the privatization of service delivery.

These tensions today interact in complex ways that both shape and are shaped by our central institutions, including the schools. In this chapter, we pull one thread from this tapestry for closer examination. Our interest is in efforts to discipline the work of teaching through systematic attention to the learning outcomes that are teaching's target. Efforts over the years to evaluate teaching for various purposes by measuring student learning represent one central strategy for achieving control in schools. We explore a set of historical cases for their lessons.

This analysis arises in response to one contemporary reform effort in particular. In 1986, a new organization was created in the teaching field, the National Board for Professional Teaching Standards. The mission of this board is to create a system of assessments for the voluntary certification of teachers—to establish, that is, a national, advanced standard of teaching excellence. Among the many thorny issues facing the National Board is this question of the assessment of student learning in the evaluation of teaching. The board represents a strategic case for examining several of the general tensions just sketched. Most evidently, we can query the application of management by results to education as well as the interplay of professional and bureaucratic bases for teaching practice.

What follows, then, is an analysis of precedents for the use of student learning to evaluate teaching, set within the emerging context of National Board certification for teachers. Our aim will be threefold: to interrogate several prominent precedents for their lessons, to note the more general significance of these education cases for organization and management, and to advance principles for the National Board's procedures.

Definitions and Caveats

Before proceeding further, we pause to consider the meaning of "student learning" as used here and to issue a few caveats. By student learning, we mean the words, actions, and work products of students. For us, student learning is broader than subject matter knowledge. It includes other learned aspects such as attitudes, physical and mental skills, ways of acting, and values.

We offer four caveats:

- Think of student learning as a broader concept than acquisition of subject matter knowledge;
- Regard indicators of teacher knowledge and behavior as related to but different from student learning;
- Note that attempts to assess teaching, particularly in light of the emerging, ambitious goals for student learning, are likely to be more subjective than attempts to employ outcome measures in the evaluation of other kinds of work for which standard outcomes are available (e.g., in industrial, clerical, or similar settings); and
- Keep in mind that student-provided data are not limited to test scores but include any means by which students exhibit what they know and believe and how they act.

The fourth caveat admonishes the reader to avoid equating evidence of student learning with any particular method of gathering such evidence. Obeying this last injunction will require imagination and a constant effort not to be bewitched by the familiar specter of standardized, multiple-choice tests. As we discuss below, reforms of student assessment point to the use of student work samples, portfolios, documented performances, group and individual projects, and other means to exhibit what students know and can do.

Organization of This Chapter

In the sections that follow, we review three types of evidence to reach some warranted conclusions about the use of student learning in teacher evaluation: (a) several prominent historical and contemporary precedents; (b) prevailing views held by the public, professionals, and testing experts; and (c) the impact the contemporary reform movement is having on teaching, learning, and assessment. In a final section, we derive some principles in answer to the question, "Should evidence of student learning be a component of the evaluation of teachers for National Board certification, and if so, what form should it take?" Throughout, we will draw connections between this case and the more general issues explored in the book as a whole.

Historical and Contemporary Precedents

We consulted several examples of applying student learning outcomes to teacher evaluation and six instances of test use to document student learning are worth recounting:

In the early 1970s, an experiment in *performance contracting* was launched in which a number of private firms supplied instruction in public schools on a pay-for-results basis;

Also in the 1970s, *teaching performance tests* were created, in part, as an attempt to strengthen the causal link between a teacher's competence and student learning;

In the 1980s, many states and localities instituted *merit pay* or *career ladder plans*, some of which incorporated evidence of student learning in their evaluation schemes;

Evidence of student learning is typically included in a *teacher goal-setting* approach to teacher assessment;

The routine use of student achievement measures for *public accountability* and for the oversight of teaching is examined; and

The experience of the *Prospect School* illustrates an alternative way to look at student learning.

Performance Contracting

In 1969, an apparent educational success story captured national attention. A private firm, Dorsett Educational Systems, operating under an incentive contract, was reported to have doubled and even tripled achievement gains for disadvantaged students in Texarkana, Arkansas. The contract stipulated that the firm would be paid only for increased achievement. Students considered below average academically were placed in a special program where they received instruction from Dorsett staff. The students "graduated" from the program when they had gained one grade level in reading and mathematics achievement. Dorsett received $80 for each student who graduated in 80 hours, the break-even point in terms of per pupil cost. If students improved more quickly than that, Dorsett made a profit; if progress was slower, Dorsett lost money. Representatives from more than 200 school districts visited Texarkana to learn about the program, and by the 1970-1971 school year, over 100 districts had adopted a similar program (Gramlich & Koshel, 1975).

The Texarkana project, however, was badly botched (Bumstead, 1970). Dorsett was discovered to have included items verbatim from the achievement tests on which rewards were based directly in the instructional materials used prior to the exit test.

Meanwhile, the psychometricians cast a dubious eye on this experiment (see, e.g., Lennon, 1971; Schutz, 1971; Stake, 1971). They warned of additional measurement difficulties, a story line dozens of others would repeat in the years to follow in the context of public accountability, the last precedent discussed below.

Texarkana was not the first trial of economic incentives in education. Over 100 years earlier, the English educational system awarded grants to schools based on a combination of student achievement and attendance. The grants provided the funds for teacher salaries. This experiment lasted over 30 years, from 1863 into the 1890s, but was ultimately discontinued because it resulted in low pay and financial insecurity for schoolmasters and limited instruction to the subjects tested (see Coltham, 1972).

In the enthusiasm for the Texarkana "miracle," this earlier experiment was forgotten, and national leaders, including then President Nixon, stressed accountability as a new theme in education. The Office of Economic Opportunity (OEO) quickly picked up on this theme and mounted an experiment to test the merits of performance contracting.

In this large-scale experiment, eight firms were selected to provide reading and mathematics instruction at three sites in the first, second, and third grades as well as in the seventh, eighth, and ninth grades. The hope was that a healthy dose of the profit motive would stimulate a learning breakthrough for disadvantaged kids. In each grade, 100 of the lowest achievers were identified and given at least 1 hour of instruction daily in both subjects, supplied by the firms in specially designed rooms. Control group students also were identified so that pre-post achievement score gains from the two groups could be compared over the course of 1 academic year. The belief was that pay-for-results would focus the instruction, provide motivation to the instructors, and promote use of the most powerful and effective methods available.

Performance contracting bombed. Analysis of achievement data revealed no significant differences between experimental and control groups. No single contractor produced outstanding results, and the outcomes suggested that control group students performed better in content areas not tested, a sign that teaching to the test had narrowed the curricular focus in the experimental group. At one site, some evidence also indicated that pay-for-results not only promoted teaching to the test, it biased the instruction toward those students most likely to increase their scores, rather than to all the students selected for remedial instruction. Further, this innovation produced hostility among the regular teachers, as well as a range of implementation problems such as replacement of experimental group students who dropped out of school or failed to attend regularly. A year after the experiment, only one site signed a performance contract.

The experiment with performance contracting both repeats some familiar findings and raises some fundamental questions about the nature of schools as organizations and of teaching and learning as work. At least since Blau's (1963) study of a state employment agency, sociologists have observed that organizational behavior tends to drift toward compatibility with performance measures used to evaluate workers. This can be both good and bad news—good if the measures are valid indicators of agency objectives, bad if they are incomplete, invalid, or otherwise misleading. Blau's study uncovered behavioral responses that parallel several of the pathologies manifest in the performance contracting experiment: disregard for unmeasured outcomes, avoidance of hard cases, number fudging, and competition among workers that led to hoarding of information. In these respects, then, educational performance contracting repeats the behavioral consequences discovered in studies of other organizations. Theorists (Rowan, 1990; Thompson, 1967) suggest that factors such as technology type and goal diffusion/ambiguity will influence choice of control strategy. In the case of teaching, particularly in light of constructivist theories of learning, the teaching "technology" is uncertain and the goals are both diffuse and ambiguous. Efforts to reduce and constrain outcomes in the manner pursued via performance contracting likely will fail to capture the deeper ideals of educators and so risk misdirecting organizational effort, attention, and learning.

Teaching Performance Tests

Teaching performance tests (see, e.g., Popham 1971) are assessments and attitude scales given to students. The students' responses serve as a measure of the teacher's performance. Teaching performance tests are measures of teaching effectiveness that emphasize student learning rather than the teacher's methods of instruction. Successful teaching is defined once again by what students have learned with respect to carefully defined objectives. The knowledge and skills the students must learn are explicitly stated, and the corresponding student tests match these objectives. Teaching performance tests share a common heritage with performance contracting, namely, the behavioral objectives and criterion-referenced testing movements. Here is how the system works:

> First, teachers are provided with a mini-lesson, written material about a particular subject they will be asked to teach. Frequently, the subject is one with which students are unfamiliar, so that student mastery of the material can be credited to the teacher's efforts rather than to the previous knowledge of the students.
>
> Second, the teachers are given sufficient time to plan their teaching strategy. The teachers are not told how to teach. Their goal is to maximize student learning using whatever methods they feel will work best under the circumstances.
>
> Third, the teachers then instruct groups of students (or colleagues) for a specified time. The length of time given is a function of the scope and complexity of the objectives and the ability of the learners.
>
> Fourth, at the conclusion of the instruction, students are tested with items similar to, but not identical with, those examples made available previously to the instructor. The degree to which the students can answer the questions provides a measure of teaching effectiveness. (Millman, 1981, pp. 152-153)

Packets of mini-lessons, testing materials, and suggestions for teaching were marketed as Teaching Improvement Kits (Popham, Baker, Millman, & McNeil, 1972). However, one motivation for teaching performance tests was to create a psychometrically defensible student-learning indicator of teaching effectiveness. Toward that end, typically the students had no prior knowledge of the mini-lesson subjects (e.g., at the lower elementary school level, scoring a shuffleboard result or selecting the appropriate article before an Italian noun). Because students were expected to score zero on the preinstruction test, the postinstruction test score was taken as a direct reflection of the teacher's contribution to learning.

Teaching performance tests never took hold, for evident reasons. In the effort to create psychometrically sound measurement conditions, the teaching and learning were trivialized and decontextualized. From today's vantage, the ecological validity of such procedures approaches zero. Teachers and students were engaged in short-term, contrived trials unrelated to their actual joint work in classrooms around the school curriculum. These trials robbed teachers of their subject-matter-based expertise (because the content of the lessons was explicitly and intentionally *un*related to the school curriculum), created an unreal motivational context for student learning, and rested conclusions about teaching effectiveness on an extremely thin and inauthentic slice of classroom behavior. Ironically, the experiment failed even on its own terms. A teacher might look good based on the test results for one task but the same teacher might fare far less favorably on another task (Millman, 1973). Hence score reliabilities were poor. Unrealistic teaching tasks were required to control for myriad confounding factors, and an unreasonable number of trials was required to obtain a reliable measure of teacher effectiveness.

The "New" Merit Pay

Yet another context for linking teacher actions to the assessment of student learning is the concept of merit pay, a covering term for a variety of incentive plans used in business, industry, and government. Merit pay designs incorporate a range of variable features including the size of awards, the timing and nature of assessments, the conditions constraining output production, and others. Both the nature of the work involved and its organizational context affect the viability of pay-for-results schemes. Sales work, for example, lends itself readily to merit pay as a useful device for motivating workers. But other kinds of work are less susceptible to productive direction via forms of merit pay. Lion tamers, Albert Shanker once remarked, are not likely to pay closer attention to their work if their productivity is carefully measured and linked to merit pay. Is schoolteaching more like sales work than lion taming? Perhaps design features may accommodate to differences in work and its organization, but the record of such attempts in education provides grounds for skepticism.

Merit pay is an old idea in American education. In 1918, nearly half the school districts sampled in one study reported compensation by merit. Interest waned in the 1930s and 1940s as districts adopted uniform pay schedules, but was rekindled in the late 1950s. During the 1960s, 10% of U.S. districts had merit pay plans, but this number dropped to 5.5% by 1972. By 1978, a survey of 11,500 districts identified only 115 with merit pay plans (Murnane & Cohen, 1986).

However, the reform movement of the 1980s stimulated interest once again, and by 1991, 25 states supported a variety of teacher incentive programs under such rubrics as merit or performance-based pay, career ladders, or mentor teacher programs (Southern Regional Education Board, 1991). Several states, notably South Carolina, Arizona, and Utah, even mandated that student achievement be used to evaluate teachers. Their experience is a potential gold mine of information on how to use evidence of student learning to evaluate teachers. Surely such evidence has been routinely used to allocate pay and advanced positions. The raison d'être for merit pay in industry is to increase productivity, which in education is measured in terms of student learning.

We can appraise this experience two ways. One is to report on the general patterns, trends, and tendencies that surfaced when states or districts attempted to link pay to performance. The other is to search for exemplars that, even if they are rare, point to promising approaches. Each perspective is worth brief attention.

Historically, most merit pay plans have failed, as schools have had difficulty in devising criteria for excellent teaching. Significantly, most plans have not used student learning as a criterion, relying instead on ratings that typically have failed "to show a stable connection between teachers' merits and students' performance" (Cohen & Murnane, 1985, p. 5). In the few districts that have longstanding merit pay plans, features of both the plan and the setting contribute to the longevity. According to one study, common strategic elements include the following:

- Define the scheme as extra pay for extra work, rather than higher salaries for higher performance of the common classroom tasks of teaching.
- Solve the problem of defensible criteria in political rather than scientific terms; make the invention of criteria a collaborative project with teacher representatives, or let teachers define the criteria for themselves, or both.
- Manipulate the merit awards so as to minimize provocation; either keep the amounts negligible, keep the differences between awards small, or pass them out to nearly everyone.

- Keep a low profile on merit pay; make participation voluntary, and do not fuss unduly about who does and does not receive awards (Cohen & Murnane, 1985, p. 7).

These authors go on to note that merit pay appears to survive best in "communities that are economically and socially advantaged, have decent salary schedules, and enjoy good labor-management relations" and where "the criteria of merit include a broad conception of teacher performance that is unconnected to student performance" (p. 20). What is striking in this account is the *avoidance* of using student learning to allocate merit pay, and the recourse to political, not technical, processes to legitimate differential rewards.

Glass (1990), who also studied the use of student achievement to award merit pay, came to similar conclusions as those arrived at by Cohen and Murnane. Glass provides a summary depiction, using an imaginary district as a composite of the districts he actually studied. Here are his points:

Using student achievement data to evaluate teachers

1. is nearly always undertaken at the level of a school (either all or none of the teachers in a school are rewarded equally) rather than at the level of individual teachers because
   (a) no authoritative tests exist in most areas of the secondary school curriculum, nor for most special roles played by elementary school teachers;
   (b) teachers reject the notion that they should compete with their colleagues for raises, privileges, and perquisites;
2. is always combined with other criteria (such as absenteeism or extra work) that prove to be the real discriminators between who is rewarded and who is not;
3. is too susceptible to intentional distortion and manipulation to engender any confidence in the data; moreover, teachers and others believe that no type of test nor any manner of statistical analysis can equate the difficulty of the teacher's task in the wide variety of circumstances in which they work;
4. elevates tests themselves to the level of curriculum goals, obscuring the distinction between learning and performing on tests; and
5. is often a symbolic administrative act undertaken to reassure the lay public that student learning is valued and assiduously sought after (Glass, 1990, p. 239).

As this critical synthesis indicates, the tendency since the 1980s has been to move away from rewarding individuals and move toward school-based awards that in theory support cooperation, not competition, among faculty members. But we might also ask whether any locales use student data to allocate pay. Three cases are worth mentioning.

In Danville, Virginia, promotion on the career ladder is partly based on evidence of student learning, pursuant to school board wishes. Here, however, teachers submit individual plans that specify the learning outcomes they intend to pursue, together with measures of student progress. Committees of teachers and administrators review the plans, assess the information presented, and recommend promotions accordingly (see Brandt, 1990).

In Aiken, South Carolina, the state's Teacher Incentive Program allocates merit pay based on a set of criteria that includes student achievement. The district administers pre-post criterion-referenced tests in over 40 curriculum areas, based on a commercially produced item bank. Student gain scores are combined with in-class performance ratings, the teacher's attendance record, and evidence of professional development to award merit pay. Among these criteria, student achievement counts for 50% of the total score (N. Beard, personal communication).

Kentucky has devised a pilot project that uses student achievement data in conjunction with the state's career ladder plan. This project, described in greater detail in the next section, involves the teachers in negotiating a set of learning results and measurements within a standardized format (see Redfield, 1988a).

In the case of merit pay in education, the predominant response has been to avoid using student learning measures to evaluate teachers. Most plans have not relied on them, instead allocating merit awards for work done outside the classroom. Recent plans that use student achievement data provide awards to entire school faculties, not to individuals. But where merit pay plans have lasted, a key element has been the political processes by which teachers agree to and become involved in the award criteria and procedures.

When teachers are offered choices, they are more likely to perceive the process as being fair and related to their particular teaching situation. The benefits of teacher acceptance and fidelity to the complex circumstances of teaching are offset by a psychometric loss, however. If procedures are not standardized and applied uniformly to all teacher candidates, comparative judgments across candidates will be difficult to render, and bias of various sorts can creep into the assessment.

Contemplating the varieties of government agency, Wilson (1989) writes,

Outcomes—results—may be hard to observe because the organization lacks a method for gathering information about the consequences of its actions . . . ; because the operator lacks a proven means to produce an outcome . . . ; because the outcome results from an unknown combination of operator behavior and other factors . . . ; or because the outcome appears after a long delay. (p. 159)

Under such conditions, the institutionalization of genuine merit pay is likely to be difficult if not impossible. The modifications that ensue attenuate and extenuate in various ways the connection between individual performance, results, and rewards. Such has been the experience in education and more generally with managerial work in public sector organizations (Wilson, 1989, pp. 143-145).

Teacher Goal Setting

The common element of all teacher goal-setting plans is that the teacher negotiates with the evaluator the goals that the teacher will be responsible for meeting and the indicators of whether these goals have been achieved. In some applications, the goals are not directly related to student achievement (e.g., a goal to increase the teacher's knowledge of cooperative learning techniques via workshop attendance, or to increase class participation via student oral reports). Other applications of the teacher goal-setting approach, however, require direct evidence of student achievement.

Iwanicki (1981) refers to five basic steps of "contract plans":

1. The teacher conducts a self-evaluation and identifies areas in need of improvement.
2. The teacher develops a draft performance contract.
3. The teacher and the evaluator discuss and finalize the performance contract.
4. Both teacher and evaluator monitor progress in meeting the goals specified in the contract.
5. The teacher and evaluator discuss which goals have been met and which goals the teacher should pursue. (pp. 213-214)

In pilot plans for Kentucky and Georgia, Redfield (1988a, 1988b) spells out similar steps in much greater detail. Teachers are given a form on which they are to list their student achievement goals, together with methods of documentation. The teachers also rate the educational significance of each goal, the ease of attainment, and the relation between the goal and its documentation. The teachers also categorize each goal as general or specific, academic or nonacademic (a or n). General goals (g) apply to all students in the class; specific goal(s) to a targeted subset of students or even to one individual student. Under one plan, teachers must choose a set of goals that represent each possible combination of the four goal types (g-a, g-n, s-a, and s-n).

Under teacher-selected goal approaches, teachers are encouraged to pick goals that they planned to pursue anyway. That feature, plus the emphasis on a cooperative process that uses constructive feedback, results in a favorable reception by participants. Limiting factors are the amount of training teachers need to state appropriate goals and establish satisfactory documentary evidence, and lack of uniformity in the goals and documentation methods chosen by the teachers, which threatens the fairness of the system.

Iwanicki (1981) expresses the strengths and weaknesses of teacher-selected goal approaches:

Strengths
> Promotes professional growth through correcting weaknesses and enhancing strengths.
> Fosters a positive working relationship between the teacher and the evaluator.
> Focuses on the unique professional growth needs of each teacher.
> Clarifies performance expectations and sets explicit criteria for evaluation.
> Integrates individual performance objectives with the goals and objectives of the school organization.

Weaknesses
> Cannot be used to rank teachers.
> Places too much emphasis on the attainment of measurable objectives.
> Is not realistic in terms of the time and in-service resources available in most school settings.
> Requires too much paperwork.
> Forces evaluators to make decisions about teacher performance in areas in which they are not qualified. (p. 226)

The teacher-selected goals approach shares with successful career ladder plans the feature of teacher choice. This feature allows teachers to focus on goals and methods best suited to their particular situations. Each teacher identifies areas of needed improvement. A faculty development component in the system fosters professional growth.

However, the approach, which allows greater teacher choice as it is typically implemented, fails to meet the dual criteria of feasibility and fairness. The amount of training and preparation required to equip all candidates equitably for carrying out this phase of the evaluation competently and meaningfully is significant. The diversity of goals and indicators across candidates generates little assurance that the evaluation system will identify candidates whose students have learned the most.

Goal-based approaches to personnel development and evaluation have a history in a number of fields (see Locke & Latham, 1984). The emphasis in such procedures is developmental rather than evaluative. However, as we indicate below, it appears prudent to combine aspects of teacher goal setting with student assessment to reap the benefits of teacher involvement and acceptance. In light of the fundamental conditions facing teachers—variability of student input, uncertain technology, and instability and ambiguity of goals—the effort to impose uniform, corporate goals linked to standardized measures of output does not match well with the experienced realities of the work and so cannot gain widespread legitimacy among the workers. The future use of student assessment to judge teaching, we speculate, will have to accommodate variability and even idiosyncrasy. Goal-setting contracts represent one vehicle for such accommodation.

Student Testing for School Accountability

Large-scale student testing programs have a long history of use in the majority of states and in many large city school districts. The Regents Examinations in New York State, for example, date back to 1865. By contrast, the use of testing program results as a measure of school, district, state, and national quality has a shorter history. The public's increasing demand for educational accountability over the past quarter century has sent legislatures and state and national education departments scurrying to find student achievement-based indexes by which to gauge education's health. The obviously ill-advised use of the Scholastic Aptitude Test (SAT) results as an indicator of educational quality exemplifies this craving. The National Assessment of Educational Progress (NAEP) in this country and the Assessment of Performance Unit (APU) in Britain constitute serious nationwide efforts to chart educational quality over time. But the bulk of the accountability movement has taken and continues to take place at the state and school district levels. Although school superintendents and principals are most often under the gun, the state and local accountability movement produces a trickle-down effect on teachers.

On the positive side, these mandated testing programs arguably serve useful purposes in directing teacher efforts unambiguously to officially sanctioned learning outcomes. Many teachers may appreciate the resulting clarity.

From a systemwide vantage point, the negative effects of tests used for school accountability "stem partly from the nature of American tests and partly from the ways in which the tests have been used for educational decision making" (Darling-Hammond, 1991, p. 220). Shepard (1991) offers six negative effects of high-stakes standardized testing at the state and district levels:

- When political pressure and media attention attach high stakes to test results, scores can become inflated, thus giving a false impression of student achievement.
- High-stakes tests narrow the curriculum.
- High-stakes testing misdirects instruction even for the basic skills.
- The kind of drill-and-practice instruction that tests reinforce is based on outmoded learning theory.
- Because of the pressure to achieve high test scores, more hard-to-teach children are rejected by the system.
- The dictates of externally mandated tests reduce both the professional knowledge and the status of teachers. (pp. 233-234)

One recent study points out the negative aspect of student testing for school accountability from the vantage point of the individual teacher. Based on a qualitative study of the role of external testing in a sample of Arizona elementary schools, Smith (1991) concludes:

- The publication of test scores produces feelings of shame, embarrassment, guilt, and anger in teachers and the determination to do what is necessary to avoid such feelings in the future.
- Beliefs about the invalidity of the test and the necessity to raise scores set up feelings of dissonance and alienation.
- Beliefs about the emotional impact of testing on young children generate feelings of anxiety and guilt among teachers.
- Testing programs reduce the time available for instruction. Time required for the tests, the time teachers elect (or principals require) to prepare pupils to take the tests, and the time spent in recovering from the tests amounted to about a 100-hour bite out of instructional time.

- The focus on material that the test covers results in a narrowing of the possible curriculum and a reduction of teachers' ability to adapt, create, or diverge. The received curriculum is increasingly viewed as not amenable to criticism or revision.
- Because multiple-choice testing leads to multiple-choice teaching, the methods that teachers have in their arsenal become reduced, and teaching work is deskilled. (pp. 9-10)

In the context of organizational control in other public sector agencies, theorists have highlighted some of the same difficulties (see, e.g., Lipsky, 1980; Wilson, 1989). They point to the danger of goal displacement, as workers turn their attention to what is measured and away from what is valued. The drive in organizations to increase managerial and policy control through tighter specification and measurement of objectives produces unintended problems. March (1978) writes,

> Every introduction of precision into managerial evaluation and the incentives associated with evaluation involves a trade-off between the gains in outcomes attributable to closer articulation between action and performance on an index and the losses in outcomes attributable to misplaced precision in measurement and to the concentration of managerial effort on irrelevant ways of beating the index. (p. 241)

The accountability-oriented use of student learning data points to a significant tension in organization between managerial imperatives for control and worker desires for autonomy and for a humane work environment. Since the time and motion studies of Frederick Taylor led to the close monitoring of factory work and its output, industrial workers have resisted tight controls and scholars have debated the value of technocratic approaches to worker motivation and learning. And in bureaucratic organizations employing professionals, similar tensions are manifest in the dual forms of authority that are present. No less than for other semiprofessional workers, tight controls threaten to "deskill" and "deprofessionalize" teaching by substituting routinized procedures for the cultivation of professional skill, knowledge, and discretion. At least within the regimen of high stakes, standardized testing for basic skills achievement, various observers have described such deskilling processes in teaching (see Apple, 1987; Carlson, 1992). Among the multiple outcomes at stake in teacher evaluation practices, then, are control over work conceptions and process and long-term influences on occupational formation.

Concern about high-stakes educational testing also has led to efforts to identify ethical and unethical methods of preparing students to take tests (see Haladyna, Nolen, & Haas, 1991; Mehrens & Kaminski, 1989; Popham, 1991). After reviewing the growing concerns about *test pollution*, a term describing unethical teaching methods that boost students' scores without promoting real learning, Haladyna et al. judge that "until there is serious reform in the way schools prepare students to take standardized achievement tests, test results will continue to misrepresent American public education and its accomplishments" (p. 6).

In the climate thus created, many educators are leery of tests and can be expected to react with suspicion and hostility to crude efforts to equate good teaching with high student scores. Moreover, some evidence (see Darling-Hammond & Wise, 1985) suggests that the most professionally oriented teachers are the most critical of current testing practices.

We have chosen to highlight commentary that casts a critical eye on testing for accountability and organizational control, although such purposes clearly are legitimate. When high-stakes student testing is used to evaluate teaching, the record is troubling. Attaching rewards and sanctions of various kinds to test scores often influences the actions of administrators, teachers, and students in negative ways. The curriculum is narrowed, teaching can become deskilled, and instructional time is devoted to test preparation activities, some of which are unethical. As a result, there is a chilling effect on adventuresome teaching, and the climate for teaching and learning can be adversely affected. Based on research, it is difficult to gauge how widespread and penetrating these problems are, but we believe there is ample reason to heed the warnings and the available evidence.[1]

Eliminating the influence an assessment component exerts on the actions of administrators, teachers, and students is not possible; increasing the positive effects may be possible. For example, substituting alternative assessments congruent with the goals of the new reforms directly addresses concerns about the harmful effects of inappropriate assessment. Curricula and instruction need not be narrowed in ways that dilute the educative process. And involving teachers in the development, administration, and scoring of performance assessments can contribute positively to their professional development.

Prospect School

A final precedent worth reviewing serves as a provocative challenge to such mainstream practices as assessment for accountability or merit pay. Within the United States, a counter-cultural tradition in assessment goes back to the Deweyan wing of the Progressive movement (Cremin, 1961) and represents a lively alternative to conventional testing. Progressive educators have long argued that assessment should support teaching and learning rather than be oriented to external record keeping and standardized testing. This tradition holds that teachers' formal and informal methods of observing and documenting children's development are central to good teaching. Over the years, many teachers, particularly at the elementary school level, have employed a variety of sensitive methods for recording and studying children's development as a result.

One well-documented instance of this tradition is the Prospect School in North Bennington, Vermont. Founded in 1965 by Patricia Carini, Prospect was a private, nonprofit school that closed in 1990. It served approximately 60 children aged $4\frac{1}{2}$ to 14 who were assigned to multiage groups that allowed them to remain for up to 3 years with the same teacher and classmates. Over the life of this school, Carini and her colleagues pioneered a range of practices for observing and documenting the growth of children, which included sharing their work through publications and summer workshops that were widely attended by educators from around the country. In 1979, Prospect also founded an archive of children's work that documented their growth over extended periods of time, in some cases up to 10 years.

The assessment methods developed at Prospect School relied on the close, daily observation of individual children; the cumulative collection of children's work, accomplished individually and collectively; interviews with children to explore their emerging ideas; and the practice of formal, integrative appraisals of individual students that came to be known as the "descriptive review of the child" (Carroll & Carini, 1991):

> The Descriptive Review was developed at Prospect to give teachers and other educators the opportunity to gain a deeper, collective understanding of children and childhood by focusing on a teacher's description of a particular child. The purpose of the review is not to change the child, not to explain certain behaviors, not to "fix up" perceived problems, but to help the presenting teacher become more attuned to the child's strengths and possi-

bilities as a person and a learner. Any specific concerns about the child are discussed within that broader understanding. (p. 42)

This approach to assessment is suggestive on a number of points. First, assessment is woven into the progressive philosophy of a school that encourages teachers to build on the natural interests of individual children toward organized bodies of knowledge that constitute a formal education. This approach defines learning as the active construction of knowledge by the learner and emphasizes that learning is a personal and idiosyncratic process that unfolds in often unpredictable ways. Because learning and development are unique, the teachers must study the children closely to better understand the course of development for each child. Furthermore, development is considered broadly to include physical, emotional, and social as well as intellectual factors. Descriptive reviews encourage teachers to supply holistic narratives that give a fuller portrait of children's development than traditional methods.

Unlike the other precedents we have reviewed, Prospect School emphasized student assessment oriented to the improvement of teaching and learning. The Prospect Archive also suggests certain cautions. Drawing a trajectory of children's development from the evidence of their work can be problematic. David Carroll (personal communication, December, 1991), a former staff member at Prospect, relates the story of Iris, a student whose work is included in the archive. Iris's early work suggested that she lived in a world of her own. Her writing, for example, would often begin with sentence fragments in the middle of complex ideas. By age 10, however, she produced a remarkably lovely and coherent poem, an indication of a major developmental advance. As children struggle with ideas and as their work becomes more complex, it may appear sloppy and disjointed. Arrayed in an extended developmental sequence, however, the work typically reveals extraordinary continuity, constituting a record of the child's mind in action, evolving over time. Thin samples of children's work can be deceiving, for they fail to reveal this continuity in development and the often sensitive work teachers do over time with children. Further, children must have opportunities to make choices and express their own preferences for projects if they are to explore and reveal their understandings. The Prospect School supplied such opportunities in richer abundance than many schools.

The Prospect Archive contains powerful evidence of the uneven and individual trajectories children make in the process of learning. The archive contains assessment of student learning that is holistic, takes place in a developmental context of some duration, and is grounded in a range of student work that reveals evolving mental qualities. Without these rich, in-depth qualitative portrayals, evidence of student learning may be too easily misinterpreted.

The Prospect School supplies an alternative image for the assessment of student learning and for its purposes in schools. Assessment practices at this school challenged the predominance of standardized testing for external accountability and the administrative uses of such tests. At Prospect, student assessment relied on the painstaking accumulation and review of qualitative data by teachers for the improvement of instruction. Such practices bear philosophical affinity with one stream of management advice in business and industry, propounded most notably by Deming. The primary points of agreement include an emphasis on quality improvement through engagement in learning, inquiry, and innovation by all members of the work organization, where the collection of outcome data is part of an organization-wide drive to improve (for a detailed application of Deming's 14 points to education, see Forester, 1991). The Prospect example, then, is a strategic case reminding that evidence of student learning may be used to evaluate teaching for a variety of purposes under a range of organizational assumptions about the leadership and management of professional work.

Views of the Public,
Professionals, and Testing Experts

The prevailing views regarding student learning as a measure of teacher effectiveness should be carefully heeded in creating a teacher assessment system that is acceptable to all parties.

The Public and the Profession

Discrepancies between appraisals by the public and the teaching profession about the value of evidence of student learning for determining the effectiveness of teachers are widespread, longstanding, and deep seated. Consider this conversation between a parent who is active in school affairs and a veteran teacher with high professional standards:

PARENT: My kids have sure had some good teachers and some rotten ones over the years. I'm really concerned about establishing some kind of a standard here.

TEACHER: What do you think makes a teacher good?

PARENT: What seems to make the difference is having a teacher who's both demanding and interesting, who stimulates the kids and gets them excited about what they're doing, but doesn't put up with goofing around. They have to believe the teacher is fair. I think kids really *want* to learn, but the teacher makes all the difference. It's up to the teacher to capitalize on that natural inclination.

TEACHER: I couldn't agree more. After all, I'm a parent, and I want my kids to develop their abilities. Most teachers really want kids to learn—as much as you and your kids do. We have the same goal. But parents need to be realistic, too. You have to keep in mind, there are some things that can really be a handicap, like having a kid with behavioral problems in class. And how do you standardize the results for teachers of different subjects?

PARENT: You've got a point there.

TEACHER: I think teachers need to be held accountable for results. But it's a big mistake to judge them on the basis of how well the kids do on a single test. That completely ignores a lot of things that are happening in the classroom.

PARENT: Well, take my job, for example. I'm a marketing analyst. There are a multitude of things that affect my company's sales—the state of the economy, our advertising budget, trends, even people's moods. But the bottom line is: my job is to boost sales. If we can't sell our product, I'm not doing my job. It's as simple as that, and I think that's also true for teachers. Their job is to get kids to learn. That's what we're paying them for, and it's the cutting edge of excellence.

TEACHER: Your analogy is a good one, but in one sense, it doesn't fit. Teaching is not a business; it's harder to tabulate the results. There's so much more for kids to learn than the four Rs, though they're absolutely essential. Kids also learn character development, citizenship, self-worth, and the ability to analyze, to visualize, and use their minds. Now, how do you measure those things? I'm not opposed to being judged on my ability to motivate my students—

PARENT: Then we're in agreement.

TEACHER: In theory, yes. But hear me out. Years of experience in this profession have really made me cynical about using tests to measure my worth as a teacher. I've seen testing abused so many times. Talk to any of the other really seasoned folks around here; you'll hear the same story. Testing tends to focus on a narrow range of achievements. It reduces the whole process of learning—and your kids' minds, while we're at it—to a few simplistic numbers. That doesn't really reflect anybody's abilities.

PARENT: Yes, I can see your point.

TEACHER: When teachers really teach to the test, the kids don't learn in progressive ways they can build on later. If what you want is for me to run them through that kind of a drill, I can do it; anybody can do it. That's my whole point. It makes my job less challenging, not more so. I want your kids to grow up to be creative participants in their own future.

PARENT: But there has to be *some* basis, some way of deciding who's a good teacher and who's not. Otherwise, my kids' education is just a gamble. I want to know they're in good hands.

TEACHER: So do I.

The concept of good teaching is at stake here. We can judge teachers in terms of their own performances, over which they exert a relatively high level of control, or we can judge teachers in terms of their effects on students, over whom they have little control. This dual referent—self and other, performance and result, output and outcome—complicates the assessment of teaching practice and raises basic questions about how to combine and weigh the two sources of evidence.

In one of his insightful essays, sociologist Robert Merton (1976) comments that

> laymen tend to appraise professional performance in terms of outcome: whether it succeeds or fails to solve the problem. Professionals tend to judge performance in terms of what is accomplished in relation to what, under the circumstances, could be accomplished. (p. 29)

Merton argues that this fundamental difference in perspective not only makes quality judgments difficult but produces inevitable conflict between laypersons who care mostly about results and professionals who confront uncertainty in the face of circumstances they imperfectly control. Between outright rejection and a full-scale embrace of evidence on student learning, there may be a middle ground best suited to the difficult task of assessing good teaching. We suggest a possible middle ground later in this chapter.

The Testing Experts

Psychometricians generally oppose use of student learning as a measure of teacher effectiveness except under the most controlled conditions. Discussions of the difficulty of interpreting such data or changes in student achievement levels abound (e.g., Berk, 1988, 1990; Cooper, 1974; Glasman & Biniaminov, 1981; Goldstein, 1983; Haertel, 1986; Linn, 1981; Medley, Coker, & Soar, 1984; Millman, 1973, 1981, 1986; Soar, Medley, & Coker, 1983; Soar & Soar, 1975). These discussions are not nit-picking quarrels advanced against a backdrop of standards of 100% accuracy. Indeed, testing experts have shown great tolerance for far-from-perfect measures as long as the errors of measurement are more or less random. The chorus of howls in this case is against procedures that are deemed unfair, and student learning-based measures of teacher effectiveness are deemed unfair. Depending on the details of implementation, the student learning indicators are likely to favor teachers in more affluent communities who teach advanced courses to a stable student body and handicap others who work with less able, more mobile youth from impoverished environments. These claims of bias and unequal treatment are valid and are not to be taken lightly.

Berk (1988) discusses dozens of variables related to student achievement that are beyond the teacher's control and hence contribute to the unfairness of using student achievement to evaluate teaching. Three of his categories and some examples of variables he lists are:

Student characteristics
    Intelligence or academic aptitude
    Academic aspiration
    Self-concept
    Locus of control (i.e., the extent to which the student believes
        outcomes are attributed to self-action or to external factors)
    Economic level
    Parental educational level
    Age
    Attendance

School characteristics
 Class size
 Number of books in the library per student
 Age of the building
 Size of school site
 Size of school enrollment
 Size of staff
 Turnover of staff
 Expenditures
 Quality of instructional materials and equipment
 Schoolwide learning climate
 Instructional support (e.g., aides, resource teachers, team teaching)
Pretest-posttest design characteristics
 History (i.e., gain may be due to events outside the school setting)
 Maturation (i.e., changes in students over the year are expected as they grow older)
 Statistical regression (i.e., tendency for extreme scores, on retesting, to regress toward the mean even if no instruction took place)
 Mortality (i.e., students present in the class at the end of the year may differ from those present at the start of the year)
 Small class size (i.e., fluctuations causing unreliable measures can be expected with low numbers of students)
 Variations in test administration
 Teaching to the test
 Coaching on test-taking skills

Medley et al. (1984) summarize the situation this way:

> Both the validity and the reliability of such evaluation procedures are far too low to be useful. The basic difficulty arises from the multiplicity of factors not under the teacher's control that affect pupil achievement, the operation of which prevents the most competent teachers from obtaining the highest scores and the least competent from obtaining the lowest scores. . . . The consequence is that the poorer teachers often do as well [as] or better than the better teachers. (p. 40)

Test experts could be expected to offer the following retorts to those who, on reading the above, might be inclined to dismiss the objections to student learning measures and say, "Nothing's perfect." First, although any one factor listed above may not be that important in determining student learning, as a collection they add so much noise to the system that any true teacher effect is no longer detectable. Second, sophisticated implementation designs and esoteric statistical analyses can reduce the effect of these invalidating factors, but they cannot control them satisfactorily. Third, the distortions are far worse in measuring an individual teacher's effectiveness than in measuring a school's or a district's effectiveness. Fourth, the distortions are far worse in a context of high-stakes evaluation than in an assessment used for teacher improvement. Last, these difficulties are present in any student learning-based system of teacher evaluation, regardless of the instrumentation used to measure learning. Substituting in-fashion student assessment measures (e.g., authentic assessments, portfolio entries, performance indicators, or cooperative learning projects) for standardized multiple-choice tests does *not* address the test experts' concern that the above variables, rather than teacher effectiveness, are responsible for student achievement.

Use of new assessment measures does address the criticism that multiple-choice measures of learning do not measure the most important outcomes of teaching. Overcoming this serious and legitimate concern does not fix the basic problem of accounting for factors that are beyond the teacher's control. The new assessment measures do not fix the fundamental problem that from the test expert's point of view, student learning measures of teacher effectiveness are so flawed as to prevent valid and unbiased estimates of teaching competence.

Implications

The dismaying reality that emerges is that the public, teachers, and test experts have different opinions with respect to teacher evaluation based on student achievement. The implication of this lack of consensus is that no single treatment of student achievement as a component of a teacher assessment system will find favor with all groups. These diverse opinions must all be heeded, however, in developing a student learning component that is publicly acceptable, professionally respected, and as fair as possible.

The Reform Context

American education appears to be both stubbornly resistant to change and in an ongoing state of reform. The context for any particular innovation, including board certification, includes both stable elements and emerging trends and events. We have highlighted one important continuity, the tension between public, professional, and testing experts' ideas about a student learning criterion of good teaching. No faction, we suspect, will persuade the others. Because the governance of American education features a longstanding but unstable mix of democratic, bureaucratic, market, and professional controls (see Darling-Hammond, 1989; McDonnell, 1989), this conflict is likely to persist.

However, some things have changed, even since the National Board's founding in 1986. The prospects for using evidence of student learning to assess teaching must be gauged against the backdrop of several emerging trends, and we draw attention to three that are associated respectively with learning, teaching, and assessment.

New Goals for Learning

The most significant current development concerns the setting of learning goals for American education. Whether the venue is the national goals panel convened by the president, various state-initiated efforts to develop new curriculum frameworks, professional association task forces that articulate goals (e.g., for mathematics or science education), or local school board decisions, a consensus is beginning to emerge around an ambitious, academically rigorous set of learning goals. The older agenda of basic skills has been eclipsed, and not just for the academically advantaged student. Vanguard thinking in cognitive psychology now stresses that the old formula of teaching basic before advanced skills is a serious misconception (see Resnick, 1987, pp. 44ff.). Rather, basic and so-called higher order skills cannot—and should not—be separated conceptually, or in curriculum and instruction. Furthermore, skills associated with the traditional three "Rs," and with the new fourth "R," reasoning, are best taught in the context of the academic disciplines, where students acquire substantive knowledge as they engage in problem-solving tasks that motivate them to learn.

This emerging consensus on setting ambitious learning goals for all students is consistent with the view of a number of influential policy analysts who advocate greater coherence and instructional guidance among public and professional goal-setting bodies at the national, state, and local levels (see Cohen & Spillane, 1992; Smith & O'Day, 1990; and the volume edited by Fuhrman, 1993). One aspect of policy coherence is the systematic alignment of instruments that shape instruction:

curriculum frameworks, goal statements, student testing, staff development, and teacher education (see Sykes & Plastrik, 1993).

New Conceptions of Teaching

Concurrent with the renewed emphasis on ambitious learning goals is a growing awareness that teaching to these goals will require innovation and risk taking. The drive to create "break the mold" schools captures this sentiment, as does the effort in many states to develop more sophisticated instruments to evaluate teachers. The heyday of general teaching prescriptions to cure learning ills is over. Most experts now regard generic competencies (e.g., time use or classroom management) as a helpful but limited basis for excellent teaching (see Shulman, 1986).

Instead, two current aphorisms for research on teaching are that "the subject matters" and "the context counts." The first statement draws attention to the importance of teachers' subject matter knowledge and their strategies for engaging students' interest with rich representations of subject matter. The second aphorism notes the situational complexity of teaching—the effects of setting and milieu, time, and the individual and group characteristics of students. It appears, then, that excellent teachers adapt to particular features of context and situations.

The Shifting Face of Student Assessment

The third trend worth noting is the ferment over student assessment. There is growing unhappiness not only with the particular tests in use but with the psychometric paradigm that defines standards and procedures for test development. Technical experts are beginning to raise fundamental questions about the nature of validity (see Cronbach, 1987; Shepard, 1993); the model of intelligence underlying conventional testing (see Wolf, Bixby, Glenn, & Gardner, 1991); and the unfortunate results of excessive testing (see Shepard, 1989; Smith, 1991). As a result, interest in alternative forms of assessment is growing, and the search is under way for new approaches. But no new paradigm has yet emerged. Meanwhile, another group of experts is questioning innovative approaches on the basis of traditional conceptions of validity, reliability, and fairness (Faggen & Melican, 1991; Frechtling, 1991; Fremer, 1991; Linn, Baker, & Dunbar, 1991; Mehrens, 1991; Millman, 1991; Sanders, 1976; Williams, Phillips, & Yen, 1991).

It is unclear where this trend in student assessment procedures will lead. The experiments with innovative assessment now under way may run up against insurmountable difficulties associated with costs, logistics, legal challenges, or other factors. Yet these assessments may demonstrate convincingly that students are behaving in ways that are consonant with the emerging goals of education. Social and political demand for new assessments could profoundly alter instructional practices, the goals of education, and assessment procedures. A new term, authentic achievement and assessment, has entered the vocabulary of reform that expresses this hope. Here is one author's description:

> What *is* a true test? . . . First, authentic assessments replicate the challenges and standards of performance that typically face writers, business people, scientists, community leaders, designers, or historians. These include writing essays and reports, conducting individual and group research, designing proposals and mock-ups, assembling portfolios, and so on. Second, legitimate assessments are responsive to individual students and to school contexts. . . . If we wish to design an authentic test, we must first decide what are the actual performances that we want students to be good at. (Wiggins, 1989a, pp. 703-705)

In the future, we anticipate that student testing must approximate these conditions, and already some states (e.g., Vermont, Connecticut, and California) are beginning to pioneer assessment exercises that are more authentic (see also Archbald & Newmann, 1988; Wiggins, 1989a, 1989b).

Some Conclusions and Implications

This brief analysis leads to several observations on the teaching and learning that assessment, including procedures developed by the National Board, ought to promote.

First, the emerging aims of education emphasize more ambitious learning than the older regimen of basic skills. Student competency in basic skills will no longer be the standard for judging teaching effectiveness.

Second, conceptions of learning anchored in generic teaching prescriptions are changing to accommodate greater complexity. Assessment criteria based on simple models of teaching will not gain professional credibility. Because no one teaching style is uniformly optimal, no one performance measure is uniformly applicable. The belief that the subject matters and the context counts increases the difficulty of judging a teacher's behavior. As a result, the desire for other sources of evidence for teaching effectiveness, such as student learning, may intensify in the future.

Third, interest is growing in authentic assessments of student learning that emphasize tasks and projects; that test for problem solving, in-depth understanding, and transfer of knowledge; and that motivate and engage students in intrinsically worthwhile activity. Traditional forms of assessment likely will be replaced by authentic measures if student learning is used to assess teachers.

A Student Learning Component for the National Board

This report began with the question, "Should evidence of student learning be a component of the evaluation of teachers for National Board certification, and if so, what form should it take?" We conclude by directly addressing this question with reference to certification.

We begin by presenting a case for developing such a component, while reminding the reader of significant problems that have arisen during previous efforts to use student learning as an indicator of teacher excellence. We then offer a series of questions and recommended answers that constitute general principles for a student learning component.

The Case for a Student Learning Component

The strongest argument for including a student learning component in the National Board's certification assessment system is that it will enhance the credibility of the system in the eyes of many publics. As the imaginary parent put it, "[The teacher's] job is to get kids to learn."

The longevity and strength of numerous efforts to hold schools and teachers accountable for results attests to the public's insistence on getting that evidence. More often than not, the vital signs of school health are expressed in student-derived data such as test scores, percentage of students scoring below standards, and dropout rates. The impact on students is thus key information for the public.

The National Board's work goes beyond certifying teachers; it promulgates educational standards. A second argument in favor of including a student learning component in the certification process is that doing so calls attention to the standards that the National Board values. With a careful choice of learning goals included in this component of the assessment system, the National Board has an opportunity to reinforce the importance of its standards and, in turn, to influence others who train teacher candidates or otherwise affect educational practice.

A third argument is that all methods of teacher assessment have their limitations. The validity of new assessment approaches is yet to be proven. Assessment is best served, this argument goes, by a "union of insufficiencies" (Shulman, 1988), that is, by combining multiple methods with offsetting weaknesses. A student learning component can contribute positively to this union.

Fourth, any effort to include a student learning component in the National Board's system can be enhanced by the lessons learned from previous attempts (see our descriptions above), the changes in testing methodology under way, and the unique context in which National Board certification takes place. The methods of the past that emphasized gains on norm-referenced, multiple-choice tests *need not and should not* be the model the National Board follows.

While making a case for including a student learning component in teacher certification, we are mindful of the limitations of doing so. These limitations have been spelled out above. They include the test experts' admonitions that the process cannot be done fairly, the experience of many groups that student learning measures can be corrupted and then abandoned, and the observations of educators that externally imposed testing requirements can have negative consequences. Although many states have considered adopting such measures and a few have tried pilot versions, at this time none has a system of evaluating individual teachers that uses evidence of student learning (Lynn Klem, personal communication), although Oregon is developing such an approach. This fact alone suggests proceeding with caution.

Design Principles

The design we propose for the use of student learning measures in evaluating teachers for National Board certification can be described by answering four questions. The answers, however, are not stark dichotomies. Possible answers reveal differences among competing interests. More often than not, our guidance strives for a compromise that minimizes the drawbacks and accentuates the advantages of using student-derived evidence.

What evidence should be obtained from students?

The heart of the evidence should support the claim that students have learned as a result of the teacher's efforts. Measurement of some skills requires longitudinal data so that growth can be appraised. The evidence must be consonant with the new goals for learning, such as the standards the National Board's committees produce. In general, the new goals and standards involve higher order thinking skills. Therefore, assessing the students' basic skills is not enough. Furthermore, the student learning evidence must be tailored to each candidate's teaching assignment.

Although measures of their subject matter learning are central, students can give other reliable and valid evidence of their teachers' effectiveness. We suggest three additional types of evidence be obtained from students.

First, all teachers are expected to foster growth in selected student characteristics and values, for example, self-esteem, appreciation of and interest in learning, tolerance of the views of others, and respect for the rights of others. These measures need to be tailored to the teacher candidate's school and classroom setting so the candidate can best have an opportunity to achieve success. For example, questions measuring self-esteem need to focus on the students' appreciation of their own ability and worthiness with respect to the work and interactions in the classroom.

Second, National Board-certified teachers should be perceived as having characteristics, such as being fair, valued by the profession. Although the fairest teachers are not necessarily the most able, we believe there is a threshold that successful candidates should exceed.

Third, students can be excellent reporters of what goes on in the classroom. In particular, they can verify that certain aspects of the student learning component of the assessment have not been compromised. For example, they can report on the evidence-collecting process itself: preparation and coaching, typicality of assignments, and instrument administration.

These three sources of evidence beyond student learning of subject matter require instrumentation that is age specific. Furthermore, data on student characteristics and values should be collected at two widely spaced intervals during the school year so change can be assessed. Data on perceptions about teacher fairness and assessment procedures can be collected once at the end of the school year.

What methods of data collection should be included?

The guiding principle is that the procedures used to collect evidence should be educative for students and candidates alike, as well as being based on the best contemporary standards of learning (Shepard, 1989).

Although this principle does not rule out all multiple-choice tests, it suggests that student learning be measured in ways closer to the instructional process. The so-called new assessments and authentic assessments described earlier in this report provide one promising direction.

Evidence could come from diverse sources including oral discussions, homework assignments, and student worksheets; student products, projects, and presentations, some of which might be collaboratively produced; student journals and lab notebooks; and others. Although each student may have a portfolio of documents, we suggest the teacher candidate prepare a separate collection as evidence of student learning.

How much standardization should be built into
the process of selecting learning goals and of collecting,
assessing, and submitting the student-provided evidence?

In this key question, the word *standardization* does not refer to standardized tests or to standards of performance in the sense of level or goal. Rather, standardization refers to control, and the question could have been worded: "How much control should the National Board exert versus how much choice should the candidate have over the specifics of the assessment?"

The prostandardization advocates argue that valid inferences about teacher competence absolutely require standardized conditions. If each candidate is allowed to submit evidence on different goals, using different instrumentation, used in different ways, and reported without restrictions on procedures, then it becomes nearly impossible to evaluate the strength of the evidence fairly and validly. The fact that candidates teach in very different contexts (see Berk's list above) is troublesome and not unlike the problem faced by judges of diving competitions who must rate dives of very different difficulties against a common standard.

The advocates of candidate choice, on the other hand, point out that the very range of teaching contexts argues for treating candidates differently and allowing room for negotiation. They also note that the merit pay systems that have lasted and the contract plans that have been positively received allow teachers ample choices.

A judgment call is required. Which is the lesser of two evils? At one end of the spectrum is a standardized assessment that approximates the principles of valid teacher evaluation but runs the risk of provoking teacher resistance and reducing instruction to a bland common denominator. At the other end is a teacher-choice assessment that will be acceptable to teachers and closer to the realities of individual classrooms but runs the risk of adding invalid information to the decision process.

We favor a position of teacher choice within rather tight constraints. Without such restrictions, we expect the documentation will become "mere displays, an 'exercise in amassing paper,' and a waste of time both for the teachers who prepare them and for the persons who review them" (Bird, 1990, pp. 254-255).

In some situations, the constraints might take the form of a menu of choices. Candidates could be asked, for example, to choose 3 learning goals out of a list of 10, or four sources of documentation out of a list of seven. In other situations, the constraints might take the form of rules. Candidates could be asked, for example, to select at random from their class lists the students whose work is to be documented.

All areas of the assessment should be subject to some degree of standardization. These could include, but are not limited to choice of learning goals; types of evidence; data collection procedures (including the administration of instruments, selection of students for in-depth monitoring, and frequency of obtaining documentary information); verification procedures (including attestations from superiors); and scoring procedures.

*How much weight should the student-based
evidence carry in the total assessment?*

We believe that student learning indicators of teacher effectiveness are advisable on nonpsychometric grounds. They send messages to the public, teachers, and others, but they add little to the validity of the assessment. Therefore, we suggest this component of the assessment receive very low weight, and recommend three tactics to de-emphasize it.

First, the standards of acceptable performance should be modest; in keeping with the shaky validity of the indicators, attempts to discriminate among higher scoring candidates should be minimized. Most candidates for National Board certification will meet this low level; thus the student learning component will not be a powerful gate-keeper. Although the student learning indicators may not be valid grounds for making distinctions along the scale of teacher competence, candidates who cannot exceed the modest standards and who score at the bottom of the scale can reasonably be assumed unworthy of National Board certification.

Second, information on the student learning component should be combined with other assessment information in a compensatory way.

That is, should a candidate fail this portion of the evaluation, it should still be possible to obtain National Board certification if the candidate's performance on other components *compensates* for the low performance on the student learning component.

The main alternative of this approach is to require a minimum performance level on the student learning component as a requirement for National Board certification. Under this alternative, low performance on this one component is sufficient grounds to deny certification. The main drawback to this alternative is that it places more weight on the individual components of the certification system than the favored compensatory scheme.

Third, the use of student learning indicators should be combined with other, more valid assessment options. Under such a scheme, the weight the student learning component receives is supported by two or more sources of evidence.

A reasonable companion assessment strategy is to ask candidates, perhaps during an interview in an assessment center, to reflect on the student learning data. The candidates might discuss their rationale for designing and implementing the learning activities, interpret the meaning of the students' performance, note extenuating circumstances, and offer suggestions for using the student performance data to improve instruction in either this class or next year's class. Additional linkages between the teacher's portfolio documenting student performance and assessment center exercises have been suggested by King (1991, p. 34).

Although we suggest that the student learning component be de-emphasized by using these three tactics, its presence will nevertheless send an important message: The overall evaluation of teaching excellence requires attention to the outcomes of learning and development.

In summary, we have proposed principles that we believe are politically viable and psychometrically tolerable, a classically "satisficing" compromise under political conditions where optimization of any single set of preferences is constrained.

Appendix

One Way to Implement
the Proposed Design

How might the design proposed in the last section of this report look in practice? We attempt here to specify some details that will add concreteness to the general design we have offered above. The plan is intended to portray only one possible way the implementation might proceed, rather than to spell out the necessary form the implementation should take. The details are complex, perhaps cumbersome and inefficient, but they do illustrate that promoting both psychometric adequacy and public acceptability does not come easily.

We use as our example an applicant for certification in the area of adolescent and young adult mathematics. The details of implementation will differ, in some instances markedly, for candidates seeking certification in other disciplines, and for teachers of younger students.

Application Materials

Elements of the design begin with the information sent to the prospective applicant, which describes the certification process and contains application materials. This information tells prospective applicants what kinds of information will be sought from their students, the choices they will have during the evaluation process, and other aspects of the student learning component of the evaluation.

The application form solicits three types of information: (a) classroom teaching assignments (grade level and subject matter taught); (b) the ability level of the students in each class (somewhat below national average—typical student in the class is at the 40th percentile or below on national standardized tests; about at the national average; somewhat above national average—typical student in the class is at the 60th percentile or above on national standardized tests); and (c) the full name of the applicant's principal and subject matter supervisor and whether they are National Board certified as well as the full name of other teachers in the applicant's school who are known by the applicant to be National Board certified.

After Acceptance as a Candidate

Once the applicant has been accepted for candidacy, the certifying agency (a) sends the candidate further information about the evaluation process; (b) indicates who (principal, supervisor, National Board-certified colleague) will act as board liaison; (c) asks the candidate to select from a menu two or more nonacademic goals, three of seven short-term academic goals, and two of five long-term academic goals; and (d) solicits nominations of two "wild-card" goals.

The further information covers the scheduling of data collection instruments, the role of the National Board liaison, and the process of selecting students whose work during the year will be placed in the candidate's documentation file. The information sent to candidates also includes a description of student learning goals, guidelines for creating unique wild-card goals, and, finally, a statement of ethical and professional practices to be followed in preparing students to meet the goals.

The National Board liaison is expected to administer and retain completed instruments in the candidate's file, attest to the accuracy of the candidate's characterization of each classroom's average ability level, verify that any student samples conform to the selection criteria, and mail the documentation file to National Board offices.

The complete menu of choices offered to the candidate consists of academic goals appropriate for the grades and mathematics subjects identified in the candidate's initial application. Five nonacademic goals (e.g., foster appropriate student-student interactions in cooperative learning settings; have a positive attitude toward mathematics) are offered. The candidate must select at least one such goal for each mathematics class, with the restriction that two or more different nonacademic goals will be assessed overall. Five different academic goals must be selected and two academic, wild-card goals nominated, with the restriction that every mathematics class will be assessed with respect to at least one goal and no class will have as many as three goals, unless all classes have at least two goals.

The goals are divided into short- and long-term goals. Short-term goals apply to student learning expected after 6 weeks or less of instruction, whereas long-term goals apply to learning expected after a semester or longer period of instruction. For example, a short-term goal might be that students will improve their ability to estimate the answer to a problem requiring basic arithmetic operations and to judge whether their answer is reasonable. An example of a long-term goal might be that students can demonstrate their understanding of and the relationships among the concepts of symmetry, congruence, similarity, and proportionality by applying the concepts to problems in a wide variety of contexts.

In addition to a statement of each academic goal on the menu, candidates receive both a brief description of the goal, including an explanation of what is specifically included and excluded from it, and a related assessment exercise.

Guidelines are furnished describing the required characteristics of wild-card goals and the evidence that can be used to document that the goal has been reached. Examples of acceptable wild-card goals and documentation procedures are also included. The guidelines require one short-term and one long-term wild-card goal, and that progress on the long-term goal be measured at least four times during the year on five to seven students selected according to a procedure spelled out in the guidelines.

After receipt of the candidate's nomination of wild-card (and other) goals, the National Board notifies the candidate whether the wild-card goals and documentation plans are acceptable and, if not, what modifications are required. The candidate also receives a copy of an instrument containing two scales: teacher perceived fairness and appropriateness of instructional practices in preparation for the assessment.

Collection of Baseline Data

The National Board liaison administers to each of the candidate's mathematics classes a very short questionnaire addressing the one or two nonacademic goals the teacher has selected and one exercise addressing each of the academic goals (typically one or two) selected from the menu for that classroom. The exercise is "authentic" or at least open ended. Although several different exercises may be administered to class members to assess baseline knowledge related to a menu-selected academic goal, each student completes only one exercise. The initial assessment lasts no longer than a class period.

The National Board liaison reads a script aloud during administration of the baseline exercises. The script informs students that the mathematics question may be hard and not something they have studied, but they should give the best answer they can. Students are asked to place their names on all answer documents. The National Board liaison is expected to share the instrumentation and results with the teacher, but the liaison is responsible for keeping all student responses in the candidate's documentation file.

The teacher is responsible for collecting any baseline documentation related to the two wild-card goals. Documentation procedures agreed on between the National Board and the teacher at the time the teacher nominated the wild-card goals are used. Again, student names are to appear with the student responses.

Collection of Postinstruction Data

The National Board liaison again administers the questionnaire and a different version of the achievement instruments used prior to instruction. Also administered at this time is a separate questionnaire measuring the perceived fairness of the teacher and the appropriateness of the teacher's instructional practices related to the assessment. The students are asked to answer the separate questionnaire anonymously.

The teacher collects data relating to the wild-card goals according to the schedule and procedures agreed to by the National Board.

Sending Data to the National Board

The teacher pairs the baseline and postinstruction data related to the wild-card goals and excludes information for any student not present at one time or another. Data are kept separate by class. The data collected from the five to seven students during the year are kept separate as well. The teacher gives these data to the National Board liaison for placement in the documentation file.

The National Board liaison follows the same procedure for the data from the tests and questionnaires the liaison has administered. That is, the data are organized as described above and placed in the candidate's documentation file, which the liaison sends to the National Board together with the attestations and verification statements.

National Board Processing

The teaching practices scale is scored first. The scale is intended primarily to inform the candidate of what is considered to corrupt the process, rather than to function as an operational screen. Hence the reason the scale is sent to the candidate early in the process, even before the collection of baseline data. Should student responses fail to exceed a threshold of acceptability, investigation of the situation should take place to insure that the assessment has not been compromised.

All responses to exercises related to academic goals are scored holistically according to the guidelines established for each exercise. The perceived fairness scales are scored objectively. This may be true for the nonacademic goals as well.

The perceived fairness scale is scored 0, 1, or 2. A score of 2 indicates the student responses exceed a minimum threshold. Approximately 90% of the candidates are expected to receive this maximum score. That is, above a minimum threshold, there is no discrimination among candidates on the basis of their perceived fairness.

For the other scales, the unit of analysis is the classroom. Each mathematics class supplies data on a nonacademic goal and on typically one or two academic goals. The teacher's score (for each measure) is the classroom's mean rating on the postinstruction measure, adjusted to reflect the ability level of the class and the classroom's mean score on the corresponding baseline measure.

In deriving the overall score for each candidate, performance of students on the academic goals counts 80% and performance on the nonacademic goals and the perceived fairness scale counts 20%.

Then What?

Candidates visit an assessment center, where they answer questions about the student data. They discuss their reasons and rationale for selecting and designing the wild-card goals and documentation, interpret the meaning of the student performance, note extenuating circumstances, and offer suggestions for how the results could be used to improve their instruction.

The interview responses are scored, and this score is combined with the aggregated score based on student-derived responses. The resulting score then assumes a modest weight in calculating the total score used for the certification decision.

Note

1. An additional concern is that test-based comparisons among schools and teachers are inherently unfair because the scores are affected by many factors over which educators have no control.

References

Apple, M. (1987). The de-skilling of teaching. In F. Bolin & J. Falk (Eds.), *Teacher renewal: Professional issues, personal choices* (pp. 59-75). New York: Teachers College Press.

Archbald, D., & Newmann, F. (1988). *Beyond standardized testing: Assessing authentic academic achievement in the secondary school.* Reston, VA: National Association of Secondary School Principals.

Berk, R. A. (1988). Fifty reasons why student achievement gain does not mean teacher effectiveness. *Journal of Personnel Evaluation in Education, 1,* 345-363.

Berk, R. A. (1990). Limitations of using student achievement data for career-ladder promotions and merit-pay decisions. In J. V. Mitchell, Jr., S. L. Wise, & B. S. Plake (Eds.), *Assessment of teaching* (pp. 261-306). Hillsdale, NJ: Lawrence Erlbaum.

Bird, T. (1990). The schoolteacher's portfolio: An essay on possibilities. In J. Millman & L. Darling-Hammond (Eds.), *The new handbook of teacher evaluation* (pp. 241-256). Newbury Park, CA: Sage.

Blau, D. (1963). *The dynamics of bureaucracy* (Rev. ed.). Chicago: University of Chicago Press.

Brandt, R. M. (1990). *Incentive pay and career ladders for today's teachers.* Albany: State University of New York Press.

Bumstead, R. (1970). Performance contracting. *Educate, 3*(5), 15-26.

Carlson, D. (1992). *Teachers and crisis: Urban school reform and teachers' work culture.* New York: Routledge.

Carroll, D., & Carini, P. (1991). Tapping teachers' knowledge. In V. Perrone (Ed.), *Expanding student assessment* (pp. 40-46). Alexandria, VA: Association for Supervision and Curriculum Development.

Cohen, D. K., & Murnane, R. J. (1985). The merits of merit pay. *Public Interest, 80,* 3-30.

Cohen, D. K., & Spillane, J. (1992). Policy and practice: The relations between governance and instruction. In G. Grant (Ed.), *Review of research in education* (Vol. 18, pp. 3-49). Washington, DC: American Educational Research Association.

Coltham, J. B. (1972). Educational accountability: An English experiment and its outcome. *School Review, 81*(1), 15-34.

Cooper, J. M. (1974, April). *Pupil growth measures and teacher evaluation: Pressing for practical applications.* Paper presented at the annual meeting of the American Educational Research Association, Chicago.

Cremin, L. (1961). *The transformation of the school.* New York: Pantheon.

Cronbach, L. J. (1987). Five perspectives on test validation. In H. Wainer & H. Braun (Eds.), *Test validity* (pp. 3-17). Hillsdale, NJ: Lawrence Erlbaum.

Darling-Hammond, L. (1989). Accountability for professional practice. *Teachers College Record, 91*(1), 59-80.

Darling-Hammond, L. (1991). The implications of testing policy for quality and equality. *Phi Delta Kappan, 73*(3), 220-225.

Darling-Hammond, L., & Wise, A. (1985). Beyond standardization: State standards and school improvement. *Elementary School Journal, 85*(3), 315-336.

Faggen, J., & Melican, G. (1991, April). *More than multiple-choice: Research and statistical concerns for constructed response tests.* Paper presented at the annual meetings of the American Educational Research Association and the National Council on Measurement in Education, Chicago.

Forester, A. (1991, October). *An examination of parallels between Deming's model for transforming industry and current trends in education.* Paper presented at the National Learning Foundation's TQE/TQM seminar, Washington, DC.

Frechtling, J. A. (1991). Performance assessment: Moonstruck or the real thing. *Educational Measurement: Issues and Practice, 10*(4), 23-25.

Fremer, J. (1991, April). *Performance testing and standardized testing: What are their proper places?* Paper presented at the annual meeting of the National Council on Measurement in Education, Chicago.

Fuhrman, S. (Ed.). (1993). *Designing coherent education policy.* San Francisco: Jossey-Bass.

Glasman, N. S., & Biniaminov, I. (1981). Input-output analyses of schools. *Review of Educational Research, 51*, 509-539.

Glass, G. V. (1990). Using student test scores to evaluate teachers. In J. Millman & L. Darling-Hammond (Eds.), *The new handbook of teacher evaluation* (pp. 229-240). Newbury Park, CA: Sage.

Goldstein, H. (1983). Measuring changes in educational attainment over time: Problems and possibilities. *Journal of Educational Measurement, 20*, 369-377.

Gramlich, E. M., & Koshel, P. P. (1975). *Educational performance contracting.* Washington, DC: Brookings Institution.

Haertel, E. (1986). The valid use of student performance measures for teacher evaluation. *Educational Evaluation and Policy Analysis, 8*(1), 45-60.

Haladyna, T. M., Nolan, S. B., & Haas, N. S. (1991). Raising standardized achievement test scores and the origins of test score pollution. *Educational Researcher, 20*(5), 2-7.

Iwanicki, E. F. (1981). Contract plans: A professional growth-oriented approach to evaluating teacher performance. In J. Millman (Ed.), *Handbook of teacher evaluation* (pp. 203-228). Beverly Hills, CA: Sage.

King, B. (1991). Thinking about linking portfolios with assessment center exercises: Examples from the Teacher Assessment Project. *Teacher Education Quarterly, 18*(3), 31-48.

Lennon, R. T. (1971, April). *Accountability and performance contracting.* Paper presented at the annual meeting of the American Educational Research Association, New York City.

Linn, R. L. (1981). Measuring pretest-posttest performance changes. In R. A. Berk (Ed.), *Educational evaluation methodology: The state of the art* (pp. 84-109). Baltimore: Johns Hopkins University Press.

Linn, R. L., Baker, E. L., & Dunbar, S. B. (1991). Complex, performance-based assessment: Expectations and validation criteria. *Educational Researcher, 20*(8), 15-21.

Lipsky, M. (1980). *Street-level bureaucracy: Dilemmas of the individual in public services.* New York: Russell Sage.

Locke, E. A., & Latham, G. N. (1984). *Goal setting: A motivational technique that works!* Englewood Cliffs, NJ: Prentice Hall.

March, J. (1978). American public school administration: A short analysis. *School Review, 86*(2), 217-250.

McDonnell, L. M. (1989). *The dilemma of teacher policy* (JRE-03). Santa Monica, CA: RAND.

Medley, D. M., Coker, H., & Soar, R. S. (1984). *Measurement-based evaluation of teacher performance: An empirical approach.* New York: Longman.

Mehrens, W. A. (1991, April). *Using performance assessment for accountability purposes: Some problems.* Paper presented at the annual meeting of the American Educational Research Association, Chicago.

Mehrens, W. A., & Kaminski, J. (1989). Methods for improving standardized test scores: Fruitful, fruitless, or fraudulent. *Educational Measurement: Issues and Practice, 8*(1), 14-22.

Merton, R. (1976). *Sociological ambivalence and other essays.* New York: Free Press.

Millman, J. (1973, April). *Psychometric characteristics of performance tests of teaching effectiveness.* Paper presented at the annual meeting of the American Educational Research Association, New Orleans, LA.

Millman, J. (1981). Student achievement as a measure of teacher competence. In J. Millman (Ed.), *Handbook of teacher evaluation* (pp. 146-166). Beverly Hills, CA: Sage.

Millman, J. (1986, April). *Some questions about using student performance as a measure of teacher effectiveness.* Paper presented at the annual meeting of the American Educational Research Association, San Francisco.

Millman, J. (1991). Teacher licensing and the new assessment methodologies. *Applied Educational Measurement, 4*, 368-370.

Murnane, R. J., & Cohen, D. K. (1986). Merit pay and the evaluation problem: Why some merit pay plans fail and a few survive. *Harvard Educational Review, 56*(1), 1-17.

Popham, W. J. (1971). Performance tests of teaching proficiency: Rationale, development, and validation. *American Educational Research Journal, 8*(1), 105-117.

Popham, W. J. (1991). Appropriateness of teachers' test-preparation practices. *Educational Measurement: Issues and Practice, 10*(4), 12-15.

Popham, W. J., Baker, E., Millman, J., & McNeil, J. D. (1972). *Teaching improvement kit* (7 different books). Los Angeles: Instructional Appraisal Services.

Redfield, D. L. (1988a, April). *Expected student achievement and the evaluation of teaching.* Paper presented at the annual meeting of the American Educational Research Association, New Orleans, LA.

Redfield, D. L. (1988b). *Guide: Teacher productivity appraisal process.* Unpublished paper prepared for the Georgia Department of Education.

Resnick, L. (1987). *Education and learning to think.* Washington, DC: National Academy Press.

Rowan, B. (1990). Applying conceptions of teaching to organizational reform. In R. F. Elmore & Associates (Eds.), *Restructuring schools: The next generation of educational reform* (pp. 31-58). San Francisco: Jossey-Bass.

Sanders, J. R. (1976, April). *Measurement problems and issues related to applied performance testing.* Paper presented at the annual meeting of the American Educational Research Association, San Francisco.

Schutz, R. E. (1971). Measurement aspects of performance contracting. *Measurement in Education, 2*(3), 1-4.

Shepard, L. A. (1989). Why we need better assessments. *Educational Leadership, 46*(7), 4-9.

Shepard, L. A. (1991). Will national tests improve student learning? *Phi Delta Kappan, 73*(3), 232-238.

Shepard, L. A. (1993). Evaluating test validity. In L. Darling-Hammond (Ed.), *Review of research in education* (Vol. 19, pp. 405-450). Washington, DC: American Educational Research Association.

Shulman, L. (1986). Paradigms and research programs in the study of teaching: A contemporary perspective. In M. C. Wittrock (Ed.), *Handbook of research on teaching* (3rd ed., pp. 3-36). New York: Macmillan.

Shulman, L. (1988). A union of insufficiencies: Strategies for teacher assessment in a period of educational reform. *Educational Leadership, 46*(3), 36-41.

Smith, M. L. (1991). Put to the test: The effects of external testing on teachers. *Educational Researcher, 20*(5), 8-11.

Smith, M. S., & O'Day, J. (1990). Systemic school reform. In S. Fuhrman & B. Malen (Eds.), *The politics of curriculum and testing. The 1990 Politics of Education Association yearbook* (pp. 233-265). London: Taylor & Francis.

Soar, R. S., Medley, D. M., & Coker, H. (1983). Teacher evaluation: A critique of currently used methods. *Phi Delta Kappan, 64*(2), 239-246.

Soar, R. S., & Soar, R. M. (1975). *Problems in using pupil outcomes for teacher evaluation.* Washington, DC: National Education Association.

Southern Regional Education Board. (1991). Linking performance to rewards for teachers, principals, and schools. In *The 1990 SREB career ladder clearinghouse report.* Atlanta, GA: Author.

Stake, R. E. (1971). Testing hazards in performance contracting. *Phi Delta Kappan, 52*(10), 583-588.

Sykes, G., & Plastrik, P. (1993). *Standard setting as educational reform* (Trends and Issues Paper No. 8). Washington, DC: ERIC Clearinghouse on Teacher Education.

Thompson, J. D. (1967). *Organizations in action.* New York: McGraw-Hill.

Wiggins, G. (1989a). A true test: Toward more authentic and equitable assessment. *Phi Delta Kappan, 70*(9), 703-713.

Wiggins, G. (1989b). Teaching to the (authentic) test. *Educational Leadership, 46*(7), 41-49.

Williams, P. L., Phillips, G. W., & Yen, W. M. (1991, April). *Measurement issues in high stakes performance assessment.* Paper presented at the annual meeting of the American Educational Research Association, Chicago.

Wilson, J. Q. (1989). *Bureaucracy: What government agencies do and why they do it.* New York: Basic Books.

Wolf, D., Bixby, J., Glenn, J., & Gardner, H. (1991). To use their minds well: Investigating new forms of student assessment. In G. Grant (Ed.), *Review of research in education* (Vol. 17, pp. 31-74). Washington, DC: American Educational Research Association.

Striking a Balance

BOUNDARY SPANNING AND ENVIRONMENTAL MANAGEMENT IN SCHOOLS

ELLEN B. GOLDRING

Recent reform efforts and calls for school restructuring are changing the nature of the relationships between principals and their constituencies as the external boundaries of schools change. Principals must measure accountability, recruit students and teachers, include parents in decision making, and mobilize resources. All of these changes link schools with their environments, ultimately increasing the impact of the external environment on the management and control of the internal functioning of schools.

This chapter is based on the assumption that principals must pay increased attention to managing their schools' external environments and consequently must define their roles as boundary spanners. Reform and restructuring efforts destroy old boundaries and define new ones. Only those schools with sufficient adaptive capacity will flourish

AUTHOR'S NOTE: I acknowledge the insightful comments from the editors on an earlier version of this chapter and the assistance of Anna Sullivan.

283

in these new environmental realities. Environmental impacts on schools have grown so great that it is imperative for principals to understand environmental management strategies.

The environment of an organization refers to "all elements existing outside the boundary of the organization that have the potential to affect all or part of the organization" (Daft, 1983, p. 42). The general organizational behavior literature also reflects the increasing effect on the importance of the environment on all types of organization. Much of this literature has moved from a closed-systems perspective to an open-systems perspective. The open-systems view of organizations emphasizes the interrelationships between organizations and their environments, stressing that this interchange is essential for organizations to be viable (Buckley, 1967). The open-systems model stresses the organization's adaptation to a changing environment and its ability to deal with the variables in the environment not directly controlled by organizational members (Aldrich, 1979). This relationship between an organization such as a school and its external environment determines an organization's goals (Parsons, 1956a).

The open-systems view does not suggest that organizations do not have boundaries but rather suggests that the boundaries are permeable. These boundaries serve as the barriers between personnel and activities under the responsibility and control of the organization and those outside these domains. Boundaries "establish demarcation lines for the domains of tasks and people which an organization stakes out for itself" (Corwin & Wagenaar, 1976, p. 472). The boundary also indicates the borders of the organization's discretion regarding its activities (Pfeffer & Salancik, 1978). For example, school principals encounter limits in the extent of the changes they can advocate, depending on the community surrounding the school.

Organizational boundaries of schools perform many important functions. They create limits for the types of transactions between elements both within and outside the organization, namely those elements constituting the organization's external environment (Katz & Kahn, 1978). Put more succinctly, boundaries have a filtering function: They screen inputs and outputs because organizations cannot deal with all elements from the environment. Boundaries also help organizations homogenize inputs. For example, elite schools have certain admissions requirements to homogenize the student body (Kast & Rosenzweig, 1985). Boundaries also serve as mechanisms to secure a certain amount of organizational independence from the environment. "Complex systems are open systems and consequently, mindful of the need to adapt to changing environmental conditions. On the other hand, complex organizations have need for determinateness, for internal rationality and efficiency" (Miles, 1980, p. 251). In essence, boundaries contribute to organizational rationality (Scott, 1981). They help insulate schools as organizations from their environments so that a balance is reached between the constantly changing external environment and the need for stability and rationality in the school's internal functioning.

It is important to note that organizations differ in the permeability of their boundaries (Katz & Kahn, 1978). Permeability is defined as "the extent to which marginal outsiders participate in or influence organizational activities" (Corwin & Wagenaar, 1976, p. 472). The main function of boundary spanners and environmental managers is to manage the permeability of the boundaries. Certain types of organizations, however, have less leeway in managing this permeability. Schools have very permeable boundaries. For instance, parents as outsiders have considerable influence on school activities. Principals cannot insist that parents stay out of the school, although they may require specific procedures during their visit (a boundary-spanning strategy).

The boundary-spanning function in organizations is essential to manage organization-environment relations. Although boundary spanning is carried out by many people in the organization simultaneously, it is important to focus on the boundary spanning of leaders, including principals, who typically set policy and manage many of the crucial relationships vis-à-vis the environment. In this age of reform and restructuring, it is imperative to examine questions about boundary spanning in school organizations. It is surprising that the notion of environmental management and boundary spanning is relatively scant in the educational administration literature. Goldring (1986, 1990a) has examined principals' relationships with parents from an environmental perspective; others have referred to boundary spanning when examining parent-teacher relationships (Corwin & Wagenaar, 1976) and communication networks among principals (Licata & Hack, 1980). Most research on the environment, however, focuses on superintendents and the district level, rather than on principals and the school site/local level (Wills & Peterson, 1992). This chapter presents the concepts of boundary spanning from the context of organizational theory in the hope that they may become part of the repertoire of educational leaders generally and principals specifically.

The guiding premise throughout this chapter is that although leaders are constrained in their actions regarding the environment, they have considerable latitude for making choices. In fact, organizations have the power to manipulate and control their environments (Child, 1972). The ultimate tension between schools as organizations and their environments, and the challenge to their leaders, is ensuring a balance that affords the school both the necessary resources and relationships that require a certain level of environmental dependence while achieving enough independence to adapt and ensure change. For instance, schools that receive grant money for a special project from a local business do not want the business to begin to intervene regarding the way in which the teachers implement the program in the classroom.

Given this tension, a resource dependency perspective, based on two premises, is adapted throughout this chapter (Pfeffer & Salancik, 1978). The first premise holds that an organization's dependence on the environment for survival creates constraints on the organization. That is, schools that operate under strict controls from the central office have less opportunities for ingenuity. The second holds that leaders attempt to manage these dependencies by adapting to environmental demands while retaining autonomy over internal organizational activities. In other words, principals adhere to central office policies while asserting independence in their schools. Balancing these tensions becomes the underlying motivation behind boundary-spanning activities.

The population ecology approach describes another prevalent theoretical view of organization-environment relations (Hannan & Freeman, 1977), emphasizing the environmental role in selecting populations of organizations for survival over time. Although many writers (Pfeffer, 1981; Scott, 1981) highlight differences (i.e., level of analysis and time frame) between these two perspectives, others (Ulrich & Barney, 1984) suggest that the two can be integrated. It is not the purpose of this chapter to review the perspectives on organization-environment relations, yet it suggests that these perspectives intertwine.

The framework for this chapter considers boundary spanning at two levels. The organizational, or macro level, conceptualizes the boundary spanner as acting as a representative of the school as organization. "In this view, the boundary relations of an organization are simply the set of external ties its members maintain" (Shrum, 1990, p. 497). At this level, the primary function is designing and positioning the school to ensure the proper balance between autonomy and dependence. The second, or micro level, refers to specific boundary-spanning power tactics. Boundary-spanning incumbents such as principals use these tactics to maneuver the school in the environment as they balance autonomy and dependency.

The framework for examining these functions at the two distinct levels of analysis includes four interrelated parts. At the macro level are (a) the environmental map of an organization and (b) environmental management strategies. At the micro level are (a) environmental perceptions and (b) boundary-spanning power tactics acquired through environmental contingencies. A final section discusses interrelationships between these components.

The Environmental Map of an Organization

The concept of an organization's environment is broad and complex. Boundary spanners require a basic understanding of the elements and functions in the organization's environment. This is called an *environmental map*. Organizational environments, or environmental maps, have been described and classified in many ways. A review of the literature reveals three basic categories that constitute an environmental map: (a) external elements, (b) external attributes, and (c) uncertainty and dependency (Bourgeois, 1980).

External Elements

A basic analysis of the elements in an organization's environment requires a distinction between the general and the specific environments (Miles, 1980). The general environment consists of those elements that are potentially relevant for the organization. The organization does not deal with these elements every day but does need to be aware of them and interact with them occasionally. For example, in a school district, the general environment might include employers and the armed forces. These elements are interested in the schools' output (the students) but not on a continuous, daily basis. As Thompson (1967) suggests, "The environment beyond the task environment may constitute a field into which an organization may enter at some point in the future" (p. 28).

In comparison, the specific or immediate environment (Gross, 1968) comprises those elements that have immediate, direct relevance for the organization and therefore interact continuously with it. Environmental constituencies for schools include unions, regulatory agencies, educational associations, social service agencies, and even, at the individual school level, the central office. The parents of the students from a particular school are part of the specific environment of the school. It is unlikely that a day would pass in which no individual parent would come in contact with the school organization. Even though this contact may be comprised of parents as individuals, the net result is a continuous flow of individual parents interacting with the school. By the nature of the distinction between the general and specific environments, boundary spanners are more attuned to, and interact more frequently with the specific environment.

Generally, the organization is bound to its specific environment in two major ways (Katz & Kahn, 1978). First, it uses the environment to dispose of its products, by-products, and wastes (Perrow, 1970). In profit-oriented business, this is achieved through marketing and advertising, thus encouraging the public to purchase the product. This becomes more and more the case as parents choose schools. In essence, the schools must work to legitimize their goals in terms of their importance and significance for the environment, namely the parents (Parsons, 1956b). Second, the organization uses its environment for the procurement of resources and input materials. This is evident as school leaders are encouraged to become more entrepreneurial by applying for grants or seeking out resources to continue programs.

Attendant to the disposal of products and the procurement of resources is also an exchange process between the organization and its specific environment (Thompson, 1967). The organization must offer the environment desirable products to get the necessary resources for survival. For instance, the school must produce acceptable outcomes to win taxpayer support. This exchange relationship depends on domain consensus. "Domain consensus defines a set of expectations both for members of an organization and for others with whom they interact about what the organization will and will not do" (Thompson, 1967, p. 28). Thus an exchange relationship can result if the school and the taxpayers facilitate some type of common understanding about what the school should accomplish. The role of environmental management is crucial to achieving this balance.

External Attributes

To strike the appropriate balance, a boundary spanner must know how to analyze the abundance of symbols, information, and elements permeating the organizations' boundaries from its environment. Organizational theorists and researchers have identified numerous aspects of the environment that have a bearing on environmental management.

Important attributes of an organization's environment center around four dimensions: volatility (stable-dynamic), capacity (abundant-scarce), clustering (structured-anarchy), and complexity (simple-complex) (see Jurkovich, 1974; Katz & Kahn, 1978; Robbins, 1990; Thompson, 1967). Taken together, these dimensions indicate the level of environmental uncertainty and dependency.

Volatility refers to the extent to which elements in the environment are stable or dynamic. In stable environments, there is little change, and change that does occur is slow and predictable. Dynamic environments change rapidly in abrupt, unpredictable ways (Hoy & Miskel, 1987). For example, Israeli principals indicate that they face turbulent environments. A major source of the instability is the thousands of Russian immigrants moving to the country. One of the impacts of this mass immigration is the changing enrollment patterns of many schools. Some principals are beginning to market their schools to capitalize on this new influx, whereas others cannot accept all those who have moved into their neighborhoods.

Capacity refers to the extent to which resources are available from the environment to sustain organizational activities. Hoy and Miskel (1987) suggest that when student enrollments decline, principals may be reluctant to transfer students to other programs in the district. It is clear that when resources are scarce, competition both between members in the organization and between organizations within the same environment increases. This is often the case when social service agencies compete with educational institutions for part of the national budget. Capacity also indicates whether there is room for expansion and growth in relation to environmental concerns. Organizations situated in resource-rich environments can expand with relative security (Robbins, 1990).

Clustering indicates the extent to which the elements in the environment are organized and structured, rather than being randomly distributed in a disorderly fashion. Emery and Trist (1965) identify three levels of clustering in their organizational typology: randomized, clustered, and reactive. Randomized environments are relatively unorganized with little coordination between constituents or elements in the environment. Hence the total impact of the environment on the organization is small. Clustered environments are more organized in their response to organizations. There is a sense that elements are coordinated and coupled. Reactive environments are composed of elements that are linked to one another, react in tandem, and consequently can have a strong impact on the focal organization. School-social service linkages present an example of environments that display increasingly reactive characteristics. Social service agencies, welfare agencies, and health services, all external to the school, coordinate with schools to attend to children's needs at school.

Complexity indicates whether environmental elements are homogeneous or heterogeneous. Simple environments are homogeneous, whereas complex environments include elements that are heterogeneous. For example, if parents come from similar socioeconomic and ethnic backgrounds, then the environment is simple. If parents represent different social-class groups, then the environment is heterogeneous and complex.

The four dimensions, taken together, create numerous types of environments which with school leaders must contend. At one extreme are stable, organized, homogeneous, and resource-abundant environments. These are the easiest to work in, whereas a shift in any one dimension creates complexity for the boundary spanner.

Environmental Uncertainty and Dependency

The attributes discussed previously indicate levels of uncertainty and dependency for the organization. Thompson (1967) proclaims that "coping with uncertainty [is] the essence of the administrative process" (p. 159). Uncertainty is defined as the "lack of information of future events, so that alternatives of present decisions and their outcomes are unpredictable" (Miles, 1980, p. 198). Others define it as "the difference between the amount of information required to perform the task and the amount of information already possessed by the organization" (Galbraith, 1973, p. 5). Under conditions of relative certainty, managers function more efficiently. That is, they work in environments that are stable, organized, homogeneous, and resource-abundant. It is possible for them to collect the necessary information to make decisions as well as to predict the outcomes of these decisions.

Uncertainty poses obstacles for administrators in their attempts to achieve internal calm. Under conditions of uncertainty, it is difficult for the administrator to judge decision alternatives, predict cause-effect relationships, and decide among outcome preferences. Consequently, uncertainty requires the boundary spanner to expend resources and energy to remove, confront, or control sources of uncertainty. For example, Goldring (1986), in her study of principals' relationships with parents, found that suburban elementary school principals tend to engage more with parents in heterogeneous communities than in homogeneous communities. In heterogeneous parental communities, principals engaged with parents because these parents were a source of uncertainty for them. They did not know how the diverse group of parents would respond to school initiatives.

Milliken (1987) maintains that three types of perceived environmental uncertainty have a bearing on boundary spanners' functioning: state, effect, and response. State uncertainty is the inability to understand how elements in the environment are changing. In other words, when it is difficult for managers to predict how components in the environment will act or change, they most likely face state uncertainty. State uncertainty is most apt to occur in volatile, random, heterogeneous, or scarce environments. Principals of schools that are experiencing rapid changes in demographic composition and shrinking economic budgets face state uncertainty if they are unable to predict how these simultaneous impacts will affect the schools.

Effect uncertainty is the inability to know how environmental change will have an impact on the organization. It is not enough to know or perceive that an environment is changing, the question is to what extent will that change affect the manager's particular organization. Managers may not experience uncertainty about the state of the environment, but they may face uncertainty regarding the implications of the state of the environment for organizational functioning. During state budget negotiations, school leaders may be aware that change is inevitable, yet have no specific information on how this will impact their individual schools.

Response uncertainty confronts administrators when they perceive the need to react or decide among strategies in response to environmental threats, changes, and impacts. This occurs when the organization's available alternative response options and the response's value and utility are both unclear. School leaders may not know which options to select in developing new curricular guidelines when several options for such changes are being discussed, even though they know that the changes are necessary.

When examining boundary spanners' strategies, it is important to focus on the three types of uncertainty. For example, an environment may be changing, albeit in an organized, clustered manner. Consequently, managers may not sense state uncertainty, because the nature of the environment can be predicted, but effect and response uncertainty may be encountered. Managers may not know (for lack of information or lack of past experience) how the change will affect the organization. As a result, there is difficulty in judging which alternative modes of action are best. For example, initiatives to join schools and social service agencies introduce unprecedented challenges in coordinating areas such as employment counseling, housing assistance, health, and nutritional needs (Crowson & Boyd, 1992). For principals, these changes introduce uncertainty in knowing which services to provide and how to implement the programs once the selection occurs.

The surge of mandates from state levels also provides examples of the different types of uncertainty. Schools face state uncertainty as legislatures debate educational reforms. School systems do not know the outcomes of these deliberations, nor do they know how the changes will affect their particular school systems, creating effect uncertainty. Response uncertainty follows, as educators at all levels of the hierarchy are expected to respond to new state mandates.

The dimensions or properties of the environment not only affect the degree of uncertainty but also influence organizational dependence, or the extent to which the focal organization depends on environmental elements or constituencies. It is quite clear that the scarcity dimension affects organizational dependence (Scott, 1981). As organizations are situated in environments with abundant resources, they are less dependent because they have alternative sources for acquiring resources (Aldrich, 1979; Pfeffer & Salancik, 1978). For example, principals may build coalitions with community constituents to achieve certain goals, such as passage of a proposal for funding a building. In the process, they relinquish some of their decision-making autonomy and become dependent on the community-school coalition to obtain the needed resources (Goldring & Rallis, 1993).

The degree of clustering also affects organizational dependency. If the actions of environmental elements are highly organized and coordinated, organizational dependency increases (Scott, 1981). In highly clustered environments, organizations are left with few viable alternatives (i.e., in resource mobilization) because all elements are highly connected to one another.

It is important to note that the dimensions of the environment do not necessarily affect the degree of uncertainty and the degree of dependence in similar ways. For instance, schools situated in environments with scarce resources face both uncertainty and dependency. In contrast, schools in highly clustered environments face less uncertainty but are highly dependent. Principals working with groups of parents who coordinate with one another know that they ultimately interact with one larger coalition of parents. Yet because this parent group encompasses a large representation of all parents, principals are dependent on this group. The covariance of uncertainty and dependency makes the boundary spanner's role even more complex.

Summary

This section defined an organization's boundaries and characterized its environment in terms of the elements that comprise that environment and the dimensions or properties of these elements that have an impact on the organization. Together these elements and properties define an environmental map that affects organizations and

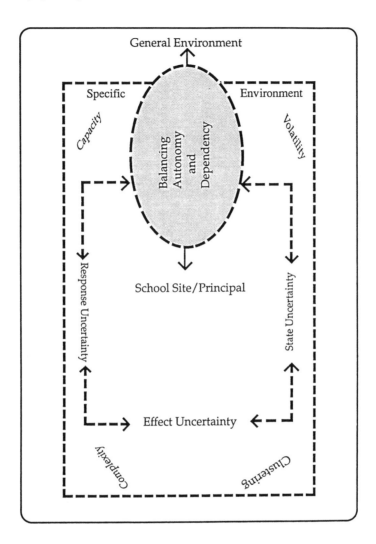

FIGURE 8.1. The Environmental Map of an Organization

their leaders as representatives of those organizations by creating degrees of uncertainty and dependence.

As illustrated in Figure 8.1, the organization's specific environment functions within the general environment. This is marked by the environmental attributes of volatility, capacity, clustering, and complexity. Although all four simultaneously affect the general and the specific environments, each attribute carries varying degrees of influence that can fluctuate at any time. As a result, their combined influence independently shapes the levels of environmental uncertainty and dependence experienced by the organization, creating tension between the macro and micro levels within the organization.

Environmental Management Strategies

Organizational leaders employ various strategies to respond to their environments. Strategies are long-term courses of action, which usually imply the allocation of resources to reach certain goals (Chandler, 1962). Environmental management strategies interconnect with ongoing, routine boundary tactics and require broad-based planning and action. These strategies are tools that aid organizational leaders in adapting to their environments and in modifying themselves to thrive in a given environment. They can be grouped into three broad categories: (a) strategies aimed at reducing the dependencies between organizations and their environment (independent strategies), (b) strategies aimed at environmental adaptation to promote organization-environment relations (cooperative strategies, organizational design), and (c) strategies aimed at changing the environment to maintain the organization (strategic maneuvering, socialization).

Strategies Aimed at Reducing Dependencies

Independent strategies aim at reducing environmental influence on the focal organization. "The independent strategies are means by which the organization can reduce the uncertainty and/or dependency which may threaten its existence by drawing on its own resources and ingenuity" (Galbraith, 1977, p. 204). Independent boundary-spanning strategies are directed at responding to the environment through organizational self-control to increase its own independence and autonomy in relation to its environment. In schools, this is exemplified when principals move to control proactively as many environmental elements as possible rather than reacting to environmental pressures.

Four independent strategies are most prevalent: competition, public relations, voluntary response, and buffering. One is a competitive response: When an organization faces uncertainty regarding environmental support, one response is to compete for that support by seeking alternatives. Competition reduces organizational dependency by providing alternative means of acquiring resources. In this strategy, internal processes are strengthened to provide the best alternative to the environment and gain maximum support, thus reducing dependencies on any one source in the environment. School leaders who are attuned to alternative sources of funding, such as special grant programs, demonstrate a competitive response. Further, schools that compete for special status in district reform plans are gaining independence from their environment. For example, in Detroit, "empowered" schools are given greater flexibility over their budgets and programs because they are freed from many district rules and regulations (Bradley, 1992).

Highly related to the competitive response, and often a connected aspect, is the public relations response. Organizational leaders apply public relations strategies to control and manage their environments by trying to influence the environment's perceptions of and knowledge about the organization. This is crucial in attracting support and resources but also necessary to maintain clients and personnel. By promoting a positive image and acquiring numerous alternatives for resources and support, the individual as organizational boundary spanner reduces environmental dependencies. Organizations vary in the amount of public relations expenditures, but Thompson (1967) suggests that this strategy reduces environmental dependency by gaining prestige at a relatively low cost.

In some educational systems, principals must spend more time and energy on public relations. Various constituencies continually scrutinize and judge the school's internal operations, even though they may not have adequate information. Through strategies such as information dissemination and advertising, effective principals proactively create an image for the school by providing information to shape these judgments.

To successfully engage in public relations, leaders collect information. Principals are exposed to large amounts and types of information. They must filter this information and decide who gets what information. Hence they serve as both filters and facilitators (Aldrich & Herker, 1977). Some information is stored for later use, some is immediately passed on to other units for processing, and other information is acted on autonomously by the boundary spanner.

Boundary spanners collect information by constantly scanning their environments (Daft, Sormunen, & Parks, 1988). Environmental scanning is essential to collect the necessary information to influence strategic policy making and planning. Daft et al. (1988) report that managers tend to use personal modes for scanning as environmental uncertainty increases. Under conditions of uncertainty, when environments are rapidly changing and unstable, it is difficult to obtain clear, hard data. They also found that high-performing firms, defined by profitability, use scanning more frequently when uncertainty is high than do low-performing firms. In a recent study of strategies used by superintendents to implement school improvement plans in response to state mandates, Wills and Peterson (1992) found that the large majority of superintendents in the study prefer external and personal sources of information when responding to state reform mandates.

The central role of information as an independent strategy can be seen when examining the impact of national reports calling for educational reform. Entities in the schools' environments, including state and federal governments, the public at large, businesses, and parents, began to pay closer attention to schools when these reports focused attention on the numerous problems facing schools. In response to this external attention, those school leaders indicating progress toward school improvement will be more independent from external involvement and pressures than will those that either do not report their efforts or do not engage in such efforts. In fact, in some states, like California, if a school does not indicate improvement over a given number of years, the school becomes a "ward" of the state.

A third independent boundary-spanning strategy is the voluntary response, which occurs when the organization responds to elements of a task environment more than is necessary or generally expected. Voluntary responses can result in independence because "the organization may avoid the stricter, more rigid standards set by outsiders . . . and outside intervention may reduce the organization's ability to act in the future" (Galbraith, 1977, p. 206). Voluntary responses often arise out of a sense of social responsibility. Examples of such strategies are when schools maintain the hiring of all school aides from within the community or when parent volunteers are "employed" to coordinate press releases for the local newspaper (Goldring & Rallis, 1993). This increases the satisfaction of the environment with the organization and increases organization-environment interdependencies. This strategy can counterbalance dissatisfactions in other areas (i.e., criticisms of low achievement in neighborhood schools) or can be used at a later date when resources and support are scarce. In addition, the voluntary response often functions as a strategy to establish groups or constituencies in the environment that depend on the organization. For example, mothers who work in neighborhood schools are totally dependent on the school for their employment and livelihood.

In many cases, the boundary spanner's preferred strategy is to reduce environmental influence as much as possible, that is, "to seal off core technologies from environmental influences" (Thompson, 1967, p.

19). This strategy is termed *buffering*. For instance, principals usually achieve this by creating formal procedures to respond to parental requests. Hollister (1979) found that schools with high parental demands adopted rationalistic, bureaucratic controls to deflect these demands. Formal controls, rules, and regulations often serve as buffers.

Buffering includes principals' insistence that local agencies, businesses, or other groups (including parents) contact them first before approaching teachers. One example is the principal who refused to allow a parent group raising money for playground equipment to ask teachers to coordinate magazine sales by the children. "While it may have been for a good cause, I saw a source of major conflict in the arrangement, so I just made the choice not to allow the group to approach the teachers. I felt I could deal with their initial annoyance easier than I would be able to handle all the problems that could arise later" (Goldring & Rallis, 1993, p. 119).

Obviously, buffering strategies can entail cost because the source of the vulnerability (i.e., the parents) is not removed and no attempt is made to control the source to reduce uncertainty in the long run. Negative consequences prove both swift and intense, as one principal discovered when his planning team proposed eliminating the school's honors classes. Although he thought he had sufficiently managed environmental influence by discussing the proposal with key groups, an active protest group nearly succeeded in blocking the measure (Goldring & Rallis, 1993).

Independent boundary-spanning strategies aim at responding to the environment through organizational self-control. That is, the organization's leader acts to increase its own independence and status in relation to its environment. Insufficient independent strategies, such as poor public relations or inadequate buffering, can often result in a vocal opposition group, such as the parents of special education students, successfully blocking a proposed innovation. This type of situation indicates a high level of dependency between the school and the environment.

Strategies Aimed at Environmental Adaptation

Through adaptive strategies, boundary spanners attempt to increase cooperation and joint action between the focal organization and the environment. These strategies generally require that the focal organization relinquish some autonomy to adjust to the environment.

Implicit cooperation, the least planned and least difficult environmental management strategy aimed at adaptation, occurs when a focal organization acts in tandem with elements in its environment without explicitly trying to coordinate behaviors. When organizations and other elements in the environment are coordinated, and the coordination is not planned, this strategy emerges. For example, when there are few schools in a district, implicit cooperation may occur when responding to environmental elements, such as budget reductions. This contrasts with explicit cooperation that occurs when smaller schools are regionalized with several others in adjacent small communities to formalize their relationships.

Contracting is another cooperative strategy. When the leader of the focal organization negotiates directly with elements in the environment to reach an explicit agreement, then a contract of cooperation occurs. Usually, contracting occurs after a lengthy exchange of information and communication. "The parties negotiate only those issues that are important to the task environment and which cannot be managed through independent actions or implicit cooperation. The issues are generally around uncertainty of future actions where the signaling and cuing of implicit cooperation do not provide enough information for coordination" (Galbraith, 1977, p. 213). Contracts allow boundary spanners to coordinate the organization's future activities with environmental elements to reduce uncertainty in a changing environment (Scott, 1981).

Contracting usually results in loss of autonomy and a great investment in time and energy for the focal organization. It also allows elements in the environment to have influence in the decision-making processes of the focal organization. Consequently, it is a strategy used when uncertainty and dependency are major issues facing the focal organization. An example of contracting is when a school system arranges with specific agencies to provide services such as those to students with special needs. Generally, this implies joint planning and decision making about the level of instruction, curricula, and graduation requirements for these students. The organization of private practice teachers provides a recent example of contracting. These teachers are forming private, group practices where they market services to schools to facilitate specific projects and educational programs (see "The AAEPP umbrella," 1992).

Co-optation occurs when the focal organization absorbs elements from the environment to reduce threats. "The strategy of cooptation involves exchanging some degree of control and privacy of information for some commitment of continued support from the external organization" (Pfeffer, 1972, p. 222). Through co-optation, organizational leaders establish links with environmental elements on which the organization is highly dependent. The cost of co-optation to the focal organization is great because elements from the environment gain control and influence concerning the organization's internal functioning. Co-opted elements carry more influence than do those elements involved in a contracting relationship with organizations because co-optation allows influence in a wide range of activities and topics, whereas contracting is usually confined to specific domains. Consequently, it seems that boundary spanners would engage in co-optation when other boundary strategies are not sufficient. When the focal organization faces high dependency and uncertainty in regard to an external group, and other boundary mechanisms are unavailable, then co-optation seems a viable option.

Co-optation also benefits the focal organization as it allows organizational leaders more control over the environmental element than if it were completely outside the organizations' realm of norms and authority. In fact, the co-opted element often begins to identify with the focal organization and therefore becomes less of an adversary. Further, having taken part in the decision-making processes of the focal organization, the co-opted element may show commitment to the policies that were formed. For example, principals generally co-opt parents through dominating the PTA and using it as a support group for their own decisions (Gracey, 1972; Vidich & Bensman, 1960; Wolcott, 1973).

Coalition building is another form of cooperation used by boundary spanners. In this case, the leader joins elements from the focal organization and the environment for a common purpose. Each unit retains its independence, and the focal organization retains some control over the means used to achieve the common goals with their environmental partners (Corwin, 1965). The coalescing arrangement is one of mutual action and commitment to joint decision making, not one of exchange (Thompson, 1967). Because the organizational leader will not act without consulting representatives of the coalition partner from the environment, this strategy affords the partner considerable inclusion in the focal organization processes.

Principals use coalition forming, aimed at complete cooperation between the school and the parents, when the principal and parents work together to achieve common goals. In this case, principals view parents as important allies due to similar aims and interests and seek to involve them. This can be contrasted to the principal who co-opts the PTA. In the former, the principal and PTA work on common agendas in a collaborative atmosphere. In the latter, the principal tries to maneuver the PTA to support the school's agenda. The productivity of the coalition stems from the members sharing a common perspective on particular issues (Scott, 1981). Hence, including representatives from parent or community groups on school decision-making teams, for example, can be either coalescing or co-optation.

A much more complex strategy used by boundary spanners for adapting to external environments occurs through organizational design (Kotter, 1979). "Organizational design is the process of grouping activities, roles, or positions in the organization to coordinate effectively the interdependencies that exist" (Pfeffer & Salancik, 1978, p. 25). With organizational design strategies, the boundary spanner strives to restructure the organization to adapt to the environment. "In a direct way, the organization's design must facilitate the management of its external dependencies; in an indirect way, the design must at least permit necessary strategic flexibility as a tool in managing these dependencies" (Longest, 1981, p. 65). Altering design features allows organizations to survive in particular environmental circumstances, particularly when other strategies (i.e., co-optation, coalition, or buffering) prove too costly.

Restructured schools, or schools engaging in major change efforts, often redesign their organizations as they respond to external environments, especially when environmental demands for such efforts are widespread. Many of these demands result from mandated reforms that shift focus to the local school, its organization, and its delivery of services to the child (Murphy, 1991). Decentralization or school-based management provides examples of organizational redesign meeting environmental demands—demands requiring more broad-based, widespread input into decision making.

Research studies document the congruence between an organization's design structure and its external environment (Burns & Stalker, 1961; Crozier, 1964; Lawrence & Lorsch, 1967). Organizations facing relatively stable environments resemble mechanistic structures, characterized by rigid task definitions, formalization of authority, vertical communication patterns, and centralized control mechanisms. In contrast, organizations in rapidly changing, dynamic environments resemble organic structures. Flexible task definitions, low formalization of authority, lateral communication patterns, and diverse control mechanisms characterize these.

Restructuring presses many schools into a more organic mode. Mandated programs from the state level now require schools to address the needs of specific populations, such as the gifted and at-risk youth. The details of how to implement such programs are often left up to the district and individual schools. Schools must redesign internal processes, curricula, teaching assignments, and collaboration to implement these new programs originating from the school's environment. Many of these processes aim to redesign the work of teachers to move away from a hierarchical definition of their tasks. When embarking on these restructuring efforts, principals should recognize that the internal design of the organization must fit the external environment.

Strategies Aimed at Redefining Environments

The strategies presented thus far are directed at managing relationships with the environment. Under certain circumstances, however, it is either too costly or too difficult to manage such relationships; instead, boundary spanners employ a strategy to try to change environments or redefine domains. Strategic maneuvering is used to influence the nature of the environment in which an organization is situated. These strategies endeavor to afford the organization more autonomy and less dependence on the present task environment (Galbraith, 1977).

Strategic maneuvering can be exemplified by observing the hospital industry (Longest, 1981). Community hospitals facing nonsupportive environments began diversifying into other community health care services, such as outpatient services. In schools, strategic maneuvering is often achieved by defining new missions, such as changing into a magnet school. This strategy allows the school to begin attracting a totally new type of student body.

Principals have crucial roles in defining the school's domain and ensuring smooth environmental interactions. As they use their knowledge of and connections with the environment, principals not only provide valuable insights on program offerings but help establish coordinating ties with the schools' new constituencies resulting from these efforts (Goldring & Rallis, 1993). Principals also are key in maintaining the legitimacy of the "new" structure. Keeping the organization visible and informing constituents about the organization enhances environmental ties. For example, strategic maneuvering can be seen when a school's participation in national school improvement measures, such as the Coalition of Essential Schools (Sizer, 1984), allows it to realign and widen its support system (Goldring & Rallis, 1993).

Strategic maneuvering often demands that principals use an entrepreneurial approach to achieve their plans. Seeking external funding from a foundation or a corporation requires that they communicate the schools' newly defined mission both to the immediate funding sources and to the community constituents who can influence the sources' funding decision.

Boundary spanners use an additional environmental change strategy when they attempt to socialize elements of the environment into accepting the norms, values, and operating procedures of the focal organization. This is similar to co-optation, but no formal role is given to the elements representing the environment. Principals engage in socialization as they attempt channeling and molding parental involvement into acceptable, manageable styles by creating congruence between the school's resources and parental expectations. Through socialization, principals encourage parents to accept the school's goals and methods as they "de-educate the public about the school's capabilities and re-educate it about what it can reasonably expect from the school" (Morris, Crowson, Porter-Gehrie, & Hurwitz, 1984, p. 116). Socialization is crucial when engaging in strategic maneuvering, as constituencies should be socialized to accept the changes impacting them.

Summary

This section presented three broad environmental management strategy dimensions. The first includes strategies used by organizations to protect their independence vis-à-vis their environments. The second dimension indicates the extent to which the organization adapts to the external environment, and the third suggests strategies used by organizations to change their environments.

Within the first dimension, independent strategies focus on increasing the organization's autonomy through competition, public relations, and voluntary response. At one extreme of this dimension is buffering, which seeks to isolate aspects of the focal organization from the environment.

In the second dimension, the organizational leader attempts to selectively increase environmental dependency. This is marked by strategies such as implicit cooperation, contracting, and co-optation that allow the organization to retain some element of control over the adaptive process. At the other extreme is organizational design, characterized by the extent to which the focal organization will change its structures and processes due to environmental contingencies.

The third dimension refers to boundary spanners' strategies that aspire to change the environment itself. Strategic maneuvering attempts to alter organizational domains, thus withdrawing the organization from the influence of the present environment or widening the base of support. Another strategy includes socializing environmental elements to persuade those elements to accept the various aspects of the focal organization.

Surveying all the strategies together, it is clear that they may be categorized as either reducing or increasing organization-environment interactions. Some appear to be more costly, difficult, and complex than others. Consequently, when the aim is increasing the organization-environment relationship, organizational design may be a proper strategy only after public relations or voluntary response strategies have been unsuccessful. Correspondingly, when the goal is reducing this relationship, strategic maneuvering may be best employed after independent and buffering strategies indicate that the focal organization remains lacking in independence from the task environment.

Clearly, organizations do not always use a single strategy. The ultimate challenge to leaders is achieving an ongoing balance between independence and dependence: independence for change and autonomy, dependence for support and resources. The organization-environment interchange is reciprocal; "organizations not only adapt and change in response to their environments, they also act upon and change their environments" (Trice & Beyer, 1993, p. 301).

Boundary Spanning and Environmental Perceptions

The previous sections of this chapter presented the role of the boundary spanner as negotiating the relationships between organization and environmental dependency and autonomy. This section presents an additional aspect of this role. The organization-environment relationship, facilitated by the boundary spanner, is affected by how individuals perceive the environment, rather than by the objective state of an environment. "The environment which members of an organization respond to and act upon is the environment they perceive" (Trice & Beyer, 1993, p. 303).

Daft and Weick (1984) suggest that organizations in general, and boundary spanners in particular, must interpret their environments. Boundary spanners must formulate the organization's interpretation of the environment and design an appropriate response. In other words, only through perception or interpretation can environments become "known" to organizations. Thus most researchers study perceived environmental uncertainty because they claim that what is important is whether managers perceive that the environment is volatile, complex, stable, or simple (Duncan, 1972; Lawrence & Lorsch, 1967). Consequently, although environmental management remains essentially an organizational function, it is affected by the boundary-spanner incumbent, the individual who filters environmental perceptions and interpretations back to the organization.

This does not mean that boundary spanning and environmental perceptions are influenced by a single person or organizational function. Boundary-spanning roles are highly cross-functional (Hambrick, 1981). Some boundary roles, such as collecting information, may be carried out by many people in an organization, whereas others, such as domain identification, may be carried out only by individuals in specific organizational functions. For example, although both principals and teachers gather information from parents, only principals may engage in resource mobilization. In some organizations, boundary roles are concentrated in the hands of specific people; in other organizations, boundary roles cut across many functions. In every case, individuals are called on to interpret, decipher, and understand their environments.

Daft and Weick (1984) suggest that to understand boundary spanners' interpretations of their environments, it is important to examine the extent to which they assume that the external environment is analyzable. If an organization views its environment as concrete with determinant and measurable processes and events, then boundary spanners will most likely see their environments as analyzable. In contrast, if environments are assumed to be subjective, difficult to capture, and changing, then they will be interpreted as unanalyzable. It follows that boundary spanners who perceive their environments as unanalyzable face uncertainty. Wills and Peterson (1992) found that superintendents' perceptions of environmental uncertainty shaped their strategies for implementing reform legislation. Superintendents in unanalyzable environments, that is, working in districts with irregular reports and feedback from the environment as well as limited information, "appeared to have managed the uncertainty by synchronizing their own strategic behavior to the unpredictable nature of their environment" (p. 258).

It is generally suggested that organizational members construct or invent their environments according to their perceptions, and in this sense they create their environments (Robbins, 1990). This is referred to as the enacted environment (Weick, 1969). The power to control, manipulate, and act as boundary spanner often relates to the perceptions and evaluations of environmental characteristics (Child, 1972). Consequently, organizational members perceive and define their environments differently. For instance, a principal perceiving the environment as hostile and disapproving may react defensively, whereas another principal in the same environment may view the criticisms as a source of help in promoting an agenda for change.

Summary

Environmental perceptions, from the individual and the organizational perspective, carry enormous ramifications for the organizations' success because these perceptions and their interpretation enable organizations to respond to the environment. Thus boundary spanners serve as the vital link between the organization and the environment as they filter environmental perceptions and interpretations.

In addition, boundary spanning, occurring on a variety of organizational levels, is often defined by the organizational structure. Some boundary-spanning roles may be concentrated in the hands of a few, select individuals, or the roles may cut across multiple organizational levels. As a result, environmental management strategies derive directly from the boundary spanners' perceptions and evaluations of the environment. Ultimately, these perceptual frameworks form the basis for future action as well as perceived ability to act by the organizational leaders.

Boundary-Spanning Power
Tactics and Environmental Contingencies

As stated previously, a major organizational goal is controlling uncertainties, many of which surface from the environment. Individuals attribute power to boundary role incumbents according to their relationships with external forces and ability to handle environmental contingencies, such as uncertainty (Hickson, Hinings, Lee, Schneck, & Pennings, 1971). Key sources of organizational power derive from such contingencies (Astley & Sachdeva, 1984; Pfeffer & Salancik, 1978). Sources of power dependent on relations with the external environment include resource control, decision premises control, and institutional relationships.

Resource control provides a central source of power for the boundary-spanning incumbent. Resource control does not always refer to a tangible resource, such as money or raw materials. To serve as a basis for power, a resource can be expert knowledge or skills essential for organizational functioning. Such knowledge or skill is concentrated in short supply among few people and is nonsubstitutable and irreplaceable (Mintzberg, 1983). The human resource represents one critical asset for organizations, specifically, the knowledge and expertise of its members. Knowledge vis-à-vis the environment is important because it increases the likelihood that a person or subunit controls or reduces uncertainty on behalf of another person or subunit (Crozier, 1964; Pondy, 1977). Because boundary spanners function at the apex of the organization facing environmental uncertainties, their expertise affords them power from this aspect of their role.

For example, principals often become intermediaries between parents and the central office when conflicts occur. In this situation, "principals often try to buffer the parental demands from central office by containing the complaints and handling them at the school level" (Goldring, 1990b, p. 57). When principals handle these types of complaints successfully they gain power; they control for their superiors at central office uncertainties caused by parental complaints.

Access to information represents another important resource (Mintzberg, 1983). By controlling the flow of information into the organization, a boundary spanner assumes the role of "gatekeeper." A gatekeeper enjoys access to external information channeled into the organization. The person strategically located to control information as it flows in and out of an organization makes crucial decisions as to what information to send to whom, or how much information should be given to whom, thus allowing attention to be focused where the boundary spanner has directed it through the manipulation of the information flow. Bacharach and Lawler (1980) indicate the importance of information flow as it allows opportunity for developing informal networks that are crucial sources of power. By controlling information, boundary spanners protect the organization from stress and other external interferences. For example, principals report using information from their district superintendents about forthcoming state mandates to prepare their schools before the mandate passes (Goldring & Rallis, 1993).

Schools and other organizations ultimately obtain most tangible resources from the environment. Resources seen as the most critical or the most scarce afford the greatest power (Miles, 1980). Consequently, persons who acquire the most crucial resources, and especially those difficult to secure, acquire the most power within organizations. For example, in a school system where "effective" teachers are hard to find, principals successful in luring this scarce resource to the school may be viewed as having power.

Principals must obtain the necessary resources to sustain changes resulting from strategic maneuvering. As the entrepreneur representing the school, the principal acquires these resources by using dual knowledge of the school and its environment to capitalize on strengths and appropriately communicate those strengths to constituents. In the process, the successful principal accrues significant amounts of power.

An additional source of power related to the notion of controlling resources is control of decision-making premises. It is possible for the boundary spanner to wield power because of the ability to affect the decision-making process (Pfeffer, 1981). Specifically, power can be acquired by "confining the scope of decisionmaking to relatively 'safe issues' " (Bachrach & Baratz, 1962, p. 948). Hence, when one person confines the decisions of another person to limited areas, the person making the decision faces less uncertainty and the person who has confined the decision acquires power.

This type of control of information and decision-making premises is a function of network centrality. By controlling decisions and information within an organization, the boundary spanner gains network centrality. "To the extent that actors are located at tightly coupled interconnected nodes in the network, they gain power because their immersion in multiple interdependencies makes them functionally indispensable" (Astley & Sachdeva, 1984, p. 106). Principals have access to multiple sources and types of information and control decision-making premises. As a result, they hold centrality and can functionally facilitate work by those not directly connected to their network.

The boundary spanner centrally located in the network gains legitimacy in the eyes of organizational members and external elements due to the ability to fulfill the linking person role (Litwak & Meyer, 1966). The linking person role allows boundary spanners to mediate between a wider base of persons in the organization as well as between the organization and the environment, thus allowing them to represent a wider circle of organizational interests. Together, knowledge of the organization and environment and the use of this knowledge to link organization and environment increase the boundary spanner's base of power.

Boundary spanners also gain power from external environments irrespective of their ability to contribute to internal operations. They often gain power from their connections and supporters in their environments (Scott, 1981). This has been referred to as the institutional perspective (Meyer & Rowan, 1978). By virtue of their standing in social environments, organizations receive legitimacy, power, and authority. Boundary spanners who are highly valued by institutions in the organization's environment or who develop important relationships with these institutions, especially those that are important constituencies for the focal organization, gain power based on legitimacy. Legitimacy, in turn, is gained by accepting the institutional environment's norms. Principals who are highly regarded by a local university educational administration department, for example, bring legitimacy to their schools because of their connections with the university. These relationships facilitate principals' efforts when they engage in internal change. They gain status and legitimacy in the eyes of their teachers and parent clientele due to their standing in the university community.

Summary

Boundary spanners link organizations with the environment through these sources of power. Centrally located within the organization, they procure and control resources from the environment to facilitate the internal operations of the organization. Acknowledging and developing these power sources are essential tools when planning and implementing environmental management strategies.

Environmental Management:
Balancing Autonomy and Dependency

This chapter began by claiming that a new context of schooling, often associated with reform efforts and calls for restructuring, is altering the external boundaries of schools. As schools attempt to include more diverse voices in policy decisions, meet the needs of all student bodies, and respond to external mandates and demands, leaders must not only attend to the internal functioning of their schools but must also assume an environmental management role.

Environmental management implies taking an active role in engaging with the environment. Rather than reacting to environmental changes and pressures, the leader initiates and plans strategies to help the organization reach an equilibrium with the environment. To reach this equilibrium, leaders serve as the catalyst for change within the environmental context.

The tensions facing leaders, as organizations interact with their environments, are rooted in the need for organizations to be autonomous and independent from excessive demands yet simultaneously

Achieving a Balance		
	Independence	Dependence
Macro Level Environmental Management Strategies	Examples Include Competition, Public Relations	Examples Include Contracting, Coalescing, Redesigning
Micro Level Boundary-Spanning Power Tactics	Examples Include Resource Control	Examples Include Institutional Legitimacy

FIGURE 8.2. Organization-Environment Balance at the Macro and Micro Levels

develop ongoing interrelationships to ensure continued support, such as resources and legitimacy. Hence environmental management aims at meeting both goals, as presented in Figure 8.2.

At the macro level, leaders as organizational agents engage in environmental management strategies that simultaneously afford independence and dependence. Independence is sought through such strategies as public relations and competition. Principals emphasize public relations with parents as a mechanism to keep them informed, which allows the school to progress with implementations of new programs. As one principal commented, "Anytime you have a successful contact, the parents spread the word. They'll shoot down wild rumors" (Goldring, 1990b, p. 60).

Independence, which may eventually lead to support, is also achieved through strategic maneuvering and socialization, strategies geared toward changing the environment. For example, socializing the community to the norms and goals of the schools ultimately provides the school with a wide basis of support. Thus principals may rely on native-language speakers to draw all parents within the school or establish a parent library in the school so parents can become familiar with topics relevant to their children's education (Goldring & Rallis, 1993).

Boundary spanners, acting on behalf of the organization, cultivate dependence by redesigning internal functions, coalescing, and contracting. As environmental managers, principals are increasingly aware of the importance of external coalitions and external resources. For example, the impressive changes implemented in East Harlem, New York's District Four, have reaped much publicity. An extremely impoverished district, it embarked on a program of school choice to establish alternative schools and meet the special needs of the community. As one reviews accounts of the implementation process, the strong links or dependencies between schools and external constituencies abound (Kirp, 1992). For instance, "while every other district in the city was pleading poverty, East Harlem usually found the money to do what it wanted" through federal grants and other partnerships. Principals of alternative schools formed coalitions to meet mutual goals, such as recruiting unique, excellent teachers by word of mouth.

At the micro level, organizational members engaging with the environment balance dependency with autonomy as they foster and negotiate power. Power is gained by acquiring and using crucial resources, thus leading to greater independence. As principals become more entrepreneurial in their roles and go outside the bureaucracy for critical resources, including financial support and expert personnel, they gain independence from their environment, in this case the system hierarchy.

Power afforded boundary-spanning organizational members due to external relationships—institutional power—may lead to increased dependencies between organizations and their environment. For instance, schools that are part of national change projects, such as the Coalition for Essential Schools (Sizer, 1984) and Accelerated Schools (Levin, 1987), gain a certain level of status from being associated with these programs. As the schools come to rely on this legitimacy, however, dependency may develop. In exchange for this dependency, the school receives support and assistance. External constituencies may be more willing to accept these changes due to the institutional relationships.

Reform and restructuring efforts are destroying the old boundaries between principals, their schools, and the environment. Increasingly, that environment is more volatile, with intensifying impact on the management and control of the schools' internal functioning. As a result, principals find their role expanding beyond that of traditional instructional leader to one that includes acquiring resources and measuring accountability. They also function as the crucial link between their school and myriad external constituencies that include parents, businesses, and governmental agencies, among others.

Principals who assume the boundary-spanning role must guide their schools using environmental management strategies to create an appropriate balance between the schools' dependence and independence relative to the environment. The principal controls and manipulates many of the forces that affect the school. Only through such active management will schools be able to adapt sufficiently to survive, much less thrive, in the emerging dynamic environments.

The principal's role as boundary spanner constitutes an entirely new framework for operating, one that proves both challenging and stimulating. In such environments, positioning and strategizing assume the same significance as the moves in a game of chess. Much like a chess master, the principal must exhibit the courage to take risks and seize opportunities that benefit the school today, while using the vision to leap ahead in positioning the school to take advantage of future challenges.

References

The AAEPP umbrella: Enterprising educators. (1992, Summer). *Private Practice Educator, 2*(1), 1.

Aldrich, H., & Herker, D. (1977). Boundary spanning roles and organizational structure. *Academy of Management Review, 2,* 217-230.

Aldrich, H. E. (1979). *Organizations and environments.* Englewood Cliffs, NJ: Prentice Hall.

Astley, W. G., & Sachdeva, P. S. (1984). Structural sources of intraorganizational power: A theoretical synthesis. *Academy of Management Review, 9*(1), 104-113.

Bacharach, S. B., & Lawler, E. J. (1980). *Power and politics in organizations.* San Francisco: Jossey-Bass.

Bachrach, P., & Baratz, M. S. (1962). Two faces of power. *American Political Science Review, 56,* 948-952.

Bourgeois, L. J., III. (1980). Strategy and environment: A conceptual integration. *Academy of Management Review, 5*(7), 25-40.

Bradley, A. (1992, October 7). Contract accord in Detroit ends 27-day teacher strike. *Education Week, 12*(5), 13.

Buckley, W. (1967). *Sociology and modern systems theory.* Englewood Cliffs, NJ: Prentice Hall.

Burns, T., & Stalker, G. (1961). *The management of innovation.* London: Tavistock.

Chandler, A. D. (1962). *Strategy and structure.* Cambridge: MIT Press.

Child, J. (1972). Organizational structure, environment, and performance: The role of strategic choice. *Sociology, 63*(1), 2-22.

Corwin, R. G. (1965). *A sociology of education.* New York: Appleton Century Crofts.

Corwin, R. G., & Wagenaar, T. C. (1976). Boundary interaction between service organizations and their publics: A study of teacher-parent relationships. *Social Forces, 55,* 471-492.

Crowson, R. I., & Boyd, W. L. (1992). *Coordinated services for children: Designing arks for storms and seas unknown*. Philadelphia, PA: Temple University, National Center for Education in the Inner Cities.

Crozier, M. (1964). *The bureaucratic phenomenon*. Chicago: University of Chicago Press.

Daft, R. L. (1983). *Organizational theory and design*. St. Paul, MN: West.

Daft, R. L., Sormunen, J., & Parks, D. (1988). Chief executive scanning, environmental characteristics, and company performances: An empirical study. *Strategic Management Journal, 9*, 123-139.

Daft, R. L., & Weick, K. E. (1984). Toward a model of organizations as interpretation systems. *Academy of Management Review, 9*(2), 284-295.

Duncan, R. B. (1972). Characteristics of organizational environments and perceived environmental uncertainty. *Administrative Science Quarterly, 17*(3), 313-327.

Emery, F. E., & Trist, E. L. (1965). The causal texture of organizational environments. *Human Relations, 18*, 21-32.

Galbraith, J. (1973). *Designing complex organizations*. Reading, MA: Addison-Wesley.

Galbraith, J. (1977). *Organization design*. Reading, MA: Addison-Wesley.

Goldring, E. B. (1986). The school community: Its effects on principal's perceptions of parents. *Educational Administration Quarterly, 22*, 115-132.

Goldring, E. B. (1990a). The district context and principals' sentiments towards parents. *Urban Education, 24*, 391-403.

Goldring, E. B. (1990b). Elementary school principals as boundary spanners: Their engagement with parents. *Journal of Educational Administration, 28*(1), 53-62.

Goldring, E. B., & Rallis, S. F. (1993). *Principals of dynamic schools: Taking charge of change*. Newbury Park, CA: Corwin.

Gracey, H. L. (1972). *Curriculum or craftsmanship*. Chicago: University of Chicago Press.

Gross, B. M. (1968). *Organizations and their managing*. New York: Free Press.

Hambrick, D. C. (1981). Specialization of environmental scanning activities among upper level executives. *Journal of Management Studies, 18*, 299-320.

Hannan, M. T., & Freeman, J. H. (1977). The population ecology of organization. *American Journal of Sociology, 82*, 929-964.

Hickson, D. J., Hinings, C. R., Lee, C. A., Schneck, R. E., & Pennings, J. M. (1971). A strategic contingencies theory of intraorganizational power. *Administrative Science Quarterly, 16*, 216-227.

Hollister, C. D. (1979). School bureaucratization as a response to parents' demands. *Urban Education, 14*, 221-235.

Hoy, W. K., & Miskel, C. G. (1987). *Educational administration: Theory, research and practice*. New York: McGraw-Hill.

Jurkovich, R. (1974). A core typology of organizational environments. *Administrative Science Quarterly, 19*, 380-394.

Kast, F. E., & Rosenzweig, J. F. (1985). *Organization and management: A systems and contingency approach.* New York: McGraw-Hill.

Katz, D., & Kahn, R. L. (1978). *Social psychology of organizations.* New York: John Wiley.

Kirp, D. L. (1992). What school choice really means. *Atlantic Monthly, 270,* 119-132.

Kotter, J. P. (1979). *Power in management.* New York: ANACOM.

Lawrence, P. R., & Lorsch, J. W. (1967). *Organizations and environment.* Cambridge, MA: Harvard University, Graduate School of Business Administration.

Levin, H. M. (1987, March). Accelerated schools for disadvantaged students. *Educational Leadership, 44*(6), 19-21.

Licata, J. W., & Hack, W. G. (1980). School administrator grapevine structure. *Educational Administration Quarterly, 16*(3), 82-99.

Litwak, E., & Meyer, H. J. (1966). A balance theory of coordination between bureaucratic organizations and community primary groups. *Administrative Science Quarterly, 2,* 31-58.

Longest, B. B., Jr. (1981, Spring). An external dependence perspective of organizational strategy and structure: The community hospital case. *Hospital and Health Services Administration,* pp. 50-69.

Meyer, J. W., & Rowan, B. (1978). The structure of educational organizations. In M. W. Meyer & Associates, *Environments and organizations* (pp. 78-109). San Francisco: Jossey-Bass.

Miles, R. H. (1980). *Macro organizational behavior.* Glenview, IL: Scott, Foresman.

Milliken, F. J. (1987). Three types of perceived uncertainty about the environment: State, effect, and response uncertainty. *Academy of Management Review, 12,* 133-143.

Mintzberg, H. (1983). *Power in and around organizations.* Englewood Cliffs, NJ: Prentice Hall.

Morris, V. C., Crowson, R. L., Porter-Gehrie, C., & Hurwitz, E., Jr. (1984). *Principals in actions: The reality of managing schools.* Columbus, OH: Charles E. Merrill.

Murphy, J. (1991). *Restructuring schools: Capturing and assessing the phenomena.* New York: Teachers College Press.

Parsons, T. (1956a). Suggestions for a sociological approach to the theory of organizations. *Administrative Science Quarterly, 1,* 63-85.

Parsons, T. (1956b). Suggestions for a sociological approach to the theory of organizations II. *Administrative Science Quarterly, 1,* 225-239.

Perrow, C. (1970). *Organizational analysis: A sociological view.* Belmont, CA: Wadsworth.

Pfeffer, J. (1972). Size and composition of corporate boards of directors: The organization and its environment. *Administrative Science Quarterly, 17,* 218-228.

Pfeffer, J. (1981). *Power in organizations.* Marshfield, MA: Pitman.

Pfeffer, J., & Salancik, G. (1978). *The external control of organizations.* New York: Harper & Row.

Pondy, L. E. (1977). The other hand clapping: An information processing approach to organizational power. In T. H. Hammer & S. B. Bacharach (Eds.), *Reward systems and power distribution* (pp. 56-91). Ithaca, NY: Cornell University Press.

Robbins, S. (1990). *Organization theory: Design, structure and applications.* Englewood Cliffs, NJ: Prentice Hall.

Scott, W. R. (1981). *Organizations, rational, natural and open systems.* Englewood Cliffs, NJ: Prentice Hall.

Shrum, W. C. (1990). Status incongruence among boundary spanners: Structure, exchange and conflict. *American Sociological Review, 5,* 496-511.

Sizer, T. R. (1984). *Horace's compromise: The dilemma of the American high school.* Boston: Houghton Mifflin.

Thompson, J. D. (1967). *Organizations in action.* New York: McGraw-Hill.

Trice, H. M., & Beyer, J. M. (1993). *The cultures of work organizations.* Englewood Cliffs, NJ: Prentice Hall.

Ulrich, D., & Barney, J. B. (1984). Perspectives in organizations: Resource, dependence, efficiency, and population. *Academy of Management Review, 9*(3), 471-481.

Vidich, A., & Bensman, J. (1960). *Small town in mass society.* New York: Doubleday.

Weick, K. E. (1969). *The social psychology of organizing.* Reading, MA: Addison-Wesley.

Wills, F. G., & Peterson, K. D. (1992). External pressures for reform and strategy formation at the district level: Superintendents' interpretations of state demands. *Educational Evaluation and Policy Analysis, 14*(3), 241-260.

Wolcott, H. F. (1973). *The man in the principal's office.* New York: Holt, Rinehart & Winston.

NINE

Research on School Leadership

THE STATE OF THE ART

LEE G. BOLMAN
RAFAEL HELLER

Consider this trenchant critique of the state of the art in school leadership from a practitioner who is willing to tell it like it is:

> In its present state, school administration is not the live product of clear, far-sighted vision, and keen insight; it is the sluggish resultant of tradition, habit, routine, prejudice, and inertia, slightly modified by occasional and local outbursts of spasmodic, semi-intelligent, progressive activity. In school administration, there is little thinking and leading, but much feeling and following, with faces turned more often to the rear than to the front.

AUTHORS' NOTE: This research was funded in part by a grant from the Office of Educational Research and Improvement of the U.S. Department of Education to the National Center for Educational Leadership (NCEL). We are grateful to our colleagues at NCEL, including Terry Deal, Susan Moore Johnson, Dan Lortie, Joseph Murphy, and Carol Weiss.

315

What is most troubling about this critique is not that it is so harsh, but that it was offered *in 1910* by Frank Spaulding, then superintendent of schools in Newton, Massachusetts (the Spaulding quote is cited in Callahan, 1962, p. 190). What is to be said of a field in which the same critique in the same words is about as timely in 1995 as it was in 1910? That theme threads through this chapter.

It is not that we have learned nothing about managing or leading in the past 80 years; indeed, most of the literature on those topics has appeared since then. Nor is it the case that the job of school adminis-trators has remained unchanged over the past eight decades. The list of challenges facing principals and superintendents keeps growing, and even the most talented are hard-pressed to do it all: manage the budget, tighten the curriculum, rally community support, negotiate with the teachers' union, come up with a new vision for the school, defuse racial tensions, evaluate teachers' performance, respond to calls for drug counseling and sex education, share ideas with other leaders, restructure the decision-making process, supervise instruction, trans-form the organization, take moral responsibility for student achieve-ment, and more. Meanwhile, many key aspects of administrative roles have become increasingly ambiguous or contested. Who should make which decisions? How should teachers participate in leadership? What about parents? Or students? What kind of training should administra-tors receive in order to handle such challenges?

Why Practitioners See Research as Inadequate

Research on school leadership might help principals, superinten-dents, and other practitioners in several ways. It could help them to better understand the challenges that they face and the options that are available to them. It could assist them in assessing the advantages and disadvantages of alternative approaches to their work and help them differentiate best and worst practice. It could help them to understand the skills and capacities that are most crucial to their effectiveness.

Those of us who study school leadership generally hope to provide such services. But research can serve as a form of coaching only if the athletes listen to their coaches. School practitioners sometimes listen, but less often value what they hear. They cite mentors and on-the-job learning, not research or university training as their primary sources of learning about how to do their work (Lortie, 1993). This is particu-larly surprising in a field where scholars and practitioners are overlapping populations. The revolving door between the universities, research foundations, and the public schools spins quickly. Even though principals become professors who become authors, a significant gap between research and practice continues to haunt the field.

For a variety of reasons, the fruits of scholarship reach practicing school leaders with great difficulty if at all. Partly, this reflects the enormous difficulty of doing social research that contributes genuinely to practice. Argyris (1980) and Lawler, Mohrman, Mohrman, Ledford, and Cummings (1985) have argued forcefully that social scientists have often distanced themselves from problems of practice because those issues are so challenging and recalcitrant in the face of traditional views of "rigorous" research.

In the field of school leadership, as in other areas of social inquiry, researchers have been torn by conflicting impulses: to contribute to practice, on the one and, to become more respectable in the eyes of their academic colleagues on the other. Scholars, particularly young ones, often feel pressured to produce research that conforms to traditional notions of rigor and that also has a reasonable chance of being produced in time for a tenure review. All this tends to produce simple, short-term research in a field replete with complex, long-term problems.

Critics have repeatedly suggested that research on school leadership has contributed little to research or practice. Bridges (1982) wrote, "There is no compelling evidence to suggest that a major theoretical issue or practical problem relating to school administrators has been resolved by those laboring in the intellectual vineyards since 1967." Immegart (1988) offered a similarly glum assessment of the research on educational leadership:

> Of over 1000 manuscripts submitted [to *Educational Administration Quarterly* during the 6 years that Immegart was editor], only a small percentage were empirical efforts directed toward leadership and leader behavior. Such efforts were typically of poor quality and were repetitive, not ground-breaking in nature. (p. 267)

How the field got where it is, and where it might go from here are the topics of this chapter. We begin with a historical tour of research on school leadership, to put the current state of the field in context. We then turn to questions of method, and examine a set of methodological and philosophical conflicts that have helped to produce the field's state of cacophony. Then we turn to substantive issues: the evolution of our ideas and our knowledge about school leadership.

A Short History of Research
on School Leadership

Wherever we begin a history of research on school leadership, the choice is arbitrary. The idea of the leader is older than recorded history. In nearly every culture, the earliest literature includes sagas of heroic figures who led their people to physical or spiritual victory over enemies without or within. Those ancient images are still with us and continue to inform our images of leadership, even though the archetype of the leader as a hero on horseback who single-handedly destroys the community's demons is increasingly problematic for the challenges of the late 20th century. We limit our focus to developments in roughly the past 100 years, for several reasons. First, there was so little research on leadership in schools or any other organization before then. Organizations were a much less prominent part of the social landscape, and the idea of systematic empirical research on social phenomena is primarily a development in the past 100 years. Moreover, both society and the schools have changed so dramatically in the past 100 years that developments prior to that time deal with a very different world.

A number of authors have published extensive accounts of the origins and development of scholarship on school leadership and educational administration (e.g., Callahan, 1962; Campbell, Fleming, Newell, & Bennion, 1987; Cuban, 1988; Culbertson, 1988; Griffiths, 1988; Tyack, 1974; Tyack & Hansot, 1982). We will not attempt here to recapitulate all that they have said. Our basic aim is to provide a conceptual overview of where the field has been.

A number of authors have tried to characterize eras in the evolution of thinking about management or school leadership (Button, 1966; Murphy, 1992; Sergiovanni, Burlingame, Coombs, & Thurston, 1987; Tyack & Hansot, 1982). Three examples are given in Table 9.1, one from within school leadership and two from outside. Culbertson (1988) describes the philosophical and methodological development of research on school leadership since 1875. Barley and Kunda (1992) focus on the evolution of managerial ideology since 1870, and Perrow (1986) does the same for organization theory. All three cover approximately the same time frame, and though they differ on specifics, they use essentially the same time intervals, thus providing a useful context for examining the history of research on school leadership.

One important difference is worth noting. Culbertson and Perrow both write of a gradual evolution from the old to the new. Barley and

TABLE 9.1 Intellectual Eras in Ideas of Leadership

Intellectual Eras in Educational Administration (Culbertson, 1988)	*Succession in Managerial Ideologies (Barley & Kunda, 1991)*	*Eras in Organization Theory (adapted from Perrow, 1986)*
"Speculative period" (1875-1900)	Industrial betterment (1870-1900)	Social Darwinism (late 19th century)
"Positivistic period" (1901-1925)	Scientific management (1900-1923)	Scientific management (1900 to mid-1930s)
Pragmatic, positivistic period (1925 to 1950s)	Welfare capitalism/human relations (1923-1955)	Human relations (mid-1930s to 1960s)
Logical positivistic period (1950s to 1970s)	Systems rationalism (1955-1980)	Contingency and institutional theories (1960s to 1980s?)
Postpositivistic, phenomenological, critical (1970s to present)	Organizational culture (1980 to present)	Power theory (1980s to ?)

Kunda (1992) argue differently. They maintain that managerial ideology in the past 100 or so years has oscillated between phases emphasizing rational and normative rhetorics. They link this periodicity to "long-wave" periods of economic expansion and contraction. Barley and Kunda's distinction between rational and normative is similar to distinctions that have also appeared in recent literature on school administration. Cuban (1988) and Sergiovanni (1992) both distinguish between technical-rational and moral-spiritual elements in the roles of school administrators.

In the Beginning

Serious attention to *school* leadership began only after school administration differentiated itself as an area of professional practice distinct from teaching. The idea of the "principal" initially took the form of the principal teacher, who was needed to provide rudimentary management functions in the 17th and 18th centuries as the one-room school-house began to give way to larger, multiclassroom schools (Cuban, 1988). Similarly, the role of the school superintendent arose in the 19th century as school boards in larger districts found themselves increasingly unable to oversee a growing number of individual school buildings. As the industrial revolution and the growth of individual enterprises began to concentrate more people in cities in the late 19th and early 20th centuries, many urban school districts grew rapidly. Such growth led inevitably to greater institutional complexity and increasing problems of control and coordination. As school leaders tried to cope with those new challenges, it was not surprising that they turned to the private sector for help. Business was a valued and powerful segment of the society. Then as now, it was the primary engine of new ideas and technologies for managing institutional complexity. The models that were imported from the private sector profoundly shaped the nature of educational institutions as we know them today.

Industrial Betterment Versus Social Darwinism

In the private sector, an extraordinary management revolution occurred in the late 19th and early 20th centuries. It began with the development of the great railway companies, whose managers faced unprecedented challenges. "No other business enterprise had ever required the coordination and control of so many different types of units carrying out so great a variety of tasks that required such close scheduling. None handled so many different types of goods or required the recording of so many different financial accounts" (Chandler, 1977, p. 94).

There were almost no relevant models, so the managers of the day resorted to intuition and seat-of-the-pants improvisation to develop new management systems. These experiments often worked, but created many problems in their wake. Perrow (1986) emphasizes that this era brought to the fore a major tension between traditional American ideology and the requirements of the new industries:

> On the one hand, democracy stressed liberty and equality for all. On the other hand, large masses of workers and nonsalaried personnel had to submit to apparently arbitrary authority, backed up by local and national police forces and legal power. Their right to combine into organizations of their own was severely limited or simply prohibited. (p. 53)

This tension spawned an ideological debate. Emphasizing one side of the debate, Barley and Kunda (1992) label the era from 1870 to 1900 the era of "industrial betterment." This movement was spawned by reformers and enlightened managers who focused on improving employees' living and working conditions. Cornelius Vanderbilt built YMCAs along the railroad lines, Andrew Carnegie built libraries, and George Pullman built residential communities for his employees, all in the name of improving workers' quality of life. Perrow (1986) emphasizes the other side of the coin:

> From about 1880 to 1910 the United States underwent the most rapid economic expansion of any industrialized country for a comparable period of time. The rapid expansion was accompanied by ruthless treatment of workers; the United States lagged far behind Britain in social reforms and unionization. Perhaps for this reason, the doctrine of Social Darwinism—the theory of survival of the fittest applied to social life rather than to animals—found more ready reception here than in Britain. Successes and riches were regarded both as signs of progress for the nation and as the reward for those who had proved themselves in the struggle for survival. . . . All agreed that successes entitled a man to command; failure indicated the lack of the requisite personal qualities. (p. 54)

Both industrial betterment and Social Darwinism were moral stances: Both focused on questions of rights and benefits in an evolving industrial society. School administrators of the era, following the intellectual lead of Horace Mann, were similarly concerned about moral issues, particularly the role of education as "the great equalizer" that would help America to defend against "the domination of capital and the servility of labor" (Mann, cited in Ravitch, 1990, p. 80). Culbertson (1988) characterizes the period from 1875 to 1900 as a speculative period in the study of school administrators. The social sciences were just beginning to differentiate themselves from philosophy, so it was natural for the "Queen of Sciences" to be taken as the appropriate knowledge base for educational administration. The assumption was that study of the conceptual and moral principles of such thinkers as Plato, Aristotle, Kant, and Hegel would give school administrators the depth of intellect and character necessary for their work. Such an intellectual diet contained very few specifics about managing schools, but it did offer food for thought on larger questions of human meaning and purpose that rarely surfaced in the educational administration curriculum for much of the 20th century.

Scientific Management

A major transition occurred around the turn of the century. The modern industrial corporation came into its own when new techniques of mass distribution (pioneered by firms like Montgomery Ward and Sears Roebuck) were integrated with techniques of mass production. For the first time, firms in such industries as chemicals (E. I. du Pont), food (H. J. Heinz), and tobacco (American Tobacco Company) were able to mass-produce and mass-market on a national basis. These new firms were able to achieve unprecedented levels of efficiency, which allowed them to produce and sell at a cost well below their more traditional competitors. The lesson was driven home in one industry after another: efficiency or death. The stage was set for the emergence of a new set of players.

Inspired by the productivity of great inventors like Bell and Edison, Frederick Taylor (1911) and a number of his contemporaries developed an approach that they labeled "scientific management." They sought to demonstrate that scientific techniques of systematic observation and experimentation could produce dramatic gains in efficiency and productivity. Taylor's famous account of how he converted Schmidt the pig iron handler into a much more efficient "high-priced man" has been justly criticized for encouraging management to manipulate and objectify workers. But his basic point was very persuasive at the time: Schmidt became a lot more efficient (his productivity was up 400%, which made his bosses happy) and earned more money (his pay increased 60%, which made him happy).

Many of the methods now thought of as the rusty old approaches to running large organizations developed in that era: time-and-motion studies, standardized work incentives, top-down planning, control, evaluation, routinized and divided labor, strict time schedules, and so on. The new methods of organizing required more sophisticated and professional managers, people responsible for monitoring production and finding ways to make the enterprise more productive. The economic successes of the new techniques swept aside much of the opposition, and America fell in love with the prospering industries. The Fords, Carnegies, Morgans, and Taylors became national heroes.

The first two decades of the 20th century were also a period of incredible growth in public school enrollments as a result of immigration (at a rate of about a million new Americans every year), urbanization, and the spread of compulsory education. Rapid change and increasing scale entailed more complex institutional forms, and school districts adopted the dominant model of the time: the command-and-control bureaucracy. The new bureaucracies needed a larger and more differentiated group of administrators, and a zealous group of experts swept into the new superintendencies and professorships, preaching the values of scientific management. A cohort of "educational engineers" like John Franklin Bobbitt of the University of Chicago, Elwood Cubberly of Stanford, and George Strayer of Columbia came on the scene. As Callahan (1962) described them:

> To a man they were able, energetic, and practical, and to an amazing degree they represented in their interests and actions the dominant tendencies in American life in the first decades of the twentieth century. They not only manifested a great interest in and admiration for businessmen and industrialists, but they resembled these men in their behavior. They were active in introducing and using business and industrial procedures and terminology in education, and they centered their attention almost exclusively upon the financial, organizational and mechanical problems. Their attainment of positions of great leadership in education was due in part to the fact that the kind of ability and orientation they had was precisely the kind that was sought after in an efficiency-conscious, business society. [They] played a leading role in shaping the new "profession" of educational administration and, through it, the American schools. (pp. 180-181)

This new group came to the fore in an era when the big issues of education were perceived as costs and accountability rather than teaching and curriculum. The methods that were beginning to put a car in every garage now promised to bring efficiency to every school. A panoply of new approaches to regulation and record keeping began to pervade the growing school districts, including standardized tests, Carnegie units, bells and routine schedules, tracked curricula, and multipurpose buildings.

During this period, school administrators themselves conducted research as a way of life (Callahan, 1962). In their quest for productivity, they used surveys, teacher rating scales, cost-benefit analyses, and other problem-solving techniques derived from industry. In particular, they imported the idea that science required measurement. Even among the most enthusiastic advocates of scientific management were many educators who recognized that the problems of measurement were considerably different and more challenging in a school than a steel mill. But faith in the methods was so high that educators decided to measure what was measurable—such things as per pupil expenditures, class size, or classroom use. Measurement of the last led to a number of serious efforts to use school plant more efficiently by scheduling longer days, longer school years, and instruction on weekends. In an era when the watchword was efficiency rather than "close to the customer," using classrooms on Saturdays seemed to make a lot of sense. Although such improvements were conclusively demonstrated to increase "efficiency," none turned out to be durable.

By current standards, the approach seems naively mechanistic, but the principals and superintendents of that time saw research in a way that many experts might now see as exemplary: They used research directly to inform their work. Such extraordinary faith is also a reminder that the inherent complexity and uncertainty of education have rendered it continually vulnerable to a succession of new faiths, each one professing to take us to the promised land. Educational administration has historically been a derivative field: much more an importer than an exporter of ideas. But something often gets lost in the translation. Then and now, educators often imported specific techniques shorn of a full understanding of the context in which they were produced and the rationale on which they were built.

Today's scholars might envy the personal power of Cubberly, Strayer, and other members of an "educational trust" (Tyack & Hansot, 1982) that wielded enormous influence over appointments to key superintendencies and principalships. Their ideology was explicitly antipolitical, with an emphasis on merit and management by the fittest, but this select group held the reins of a massive "old boy network," which influenced entry into and success in the profession for many years. The "Placement Barons" of Stanford, Columbia, and other university departments of education groomed and supported a huge cadre of loyal practitioners, nearly all white Protestant men of appropriate character and background.

The Human Relations Era

Despite Taylor's (1911) argument that scientific management benefited workers as much as management, it generated substantial resistance from labor unions and other observers who feared the substantial potential for abuse and exploitation in such a unilateral version of "science." Employees, said the critics, are not simply cogs in the industrial machines but human beings who deserve to be treated as such. They should not have to slave away at repetitive tasks, their every movement watched and their every mistake punished.

The limits of the scientific management movement were widely recognized in the private sector by the early 1920s (Perrow, 1986), but that recognition came much later in education. Well into the 1930s, basic texts for school principals still focused heavily on questions of efficiency and plant management (Callahan, 1962). Criticism of the "cult of efficiency" (Callahan, 1962) came from a number of places, some of which proved important to educational leadership. John Dewey and others in the Progressive movement advocated democratic leadership as part of a broader philosophy of education. Mary Parker Follett early in the century and the classic boys' club studies in the 1930s (Lewin, Lippitt, & White, 1939) stressed the importance of common interest and consensual decision making in organizations. The Hawthorne studies (Mayo, 1933; Roethlisberger & Dickson, 1949) demonstrated the importance of informal aspects of work, such as interpersonal relationships and group norms, that came to fall under the heading of human relations. Mayo (1933) observed incisively that "the enthusiasm of the efficiency engineer is excellent," but that it leads him "to solve the many human difficulties involved in cooperation by [organizing] without any reference whatever to workers themselves. This procedure inevitably blocks communication and blocks his own admirable purposes" (p. 76).

A second major conceptual development of this period was the publication in 1938 of Chester Barnard's *Functions of the Executive,* at the time the most comprehensive effort in English to develop a theory of organizations. (Max Weber's powerful theory of bureaucracy predated Barnard, but few Americans read it until it was translated into English after World War II.) Barnard argued that organizations were essentially cooperative systems, held together ultimately by the shared goals of the participants in the enterprise. He also wrote one of the first discussions of the managerial decision-making process and discussed some of the positive functions that groups can serve in organizations.

The work of Mayo, Roethlisberger, Barnard, and some of their contemporaries lay the foundation for an effort to develop a rigorous science of management and organizations that burgeoned after World War II. The underpinnings of the effort were developments in the previous half century in the social sciences, particularly psychology and sociology. Both of those disciplines had labored to carve out independent identities in the late 19th century. Psychology, literally, is the science of mind, and early psychologists attempted to study mind largely through reflection and introspection. But to justify its independence from philosophy the field began to emphasize its scientific characteristics.

Contemporary psychological thought is heavily determined by the fact that psychology gained its independence from philosophy only in the last half of the nineteenth century. The right to independence, the justification for separate status, was the psychologist's ability to employ experimentation and measurement. These two marks of "science" served as marks of respectability among psychologists. "If you can't manipulate it experimentally, or at least measure it, you shouldn't talk about it" became the psychologist's creed. (Cartwright, 1959, p. 10)

Sociology, a phrase coined by Comte in the mid-19th century, took a slightly different route to arrive at a similar place. American sociologists, badly needing some coherent sense of what they were about, leapt on Darwinism in the late 19th century with the eagerness of a lion pouncing on a gazelle. Through careful empirical observation, Darwin had built a grand theoretical synthesis of astonishing power and parsimony. Surely the same basic approach could be applied to the study of society. Might it not be that individuals within a society prosper or wither in terms of their fitness for their environment? Such were the origins of the very powerful intellectual current that became known as Social Darwinism—the view that individuals in a society, like species in the natural world, vary in their "fitness" and therefore in the life outcomes they are likely to achieve. This basic idea that differences in individual outcomes stem from differences in their native endowment has been under attack for decades, yet exerts great influence over our thinking about leadership, organization, and education.

Despite the many differences that developed between different social science disciplines, by the mid-20th century most practicing social scientists had arrived at a similar understanding of their basic task: to understand social behavior through systematic empirical investigation, development of hypotheses and theories to account for what is observed, and subsequent testing of those hypotheses through further research. It had enabled natural scientists to understand the laws of nature. Would it not also lead social scientists to the laws of individual and social behavior? W. K. Estes (1959), a proponent of statistical models of human behavior, confessed to a "frank preference for carrying over the methods and goals of physical science into psychology and maintaining a common language in so far as it is possible to do so" (p. 383). Scientists in various disciplines differed in their predilection for induction as opposed to deduction, or for laboratory as opposed to field work, but the underlying view was similar across the social sciences: The job at hand is to develop laws of social behavior through observation and experiment.

At midcentury, a convergence of forces brought this new view of social science into the field of educational administration (Murphy, 1992). The marriage of schools and scientific management was at a practical and conceptual dead end. Many in the educational administration professoriat were former administrators who taught whatever they had learned from their personal experience, but such atheoretic, seat-of-the-pants knowledge seemed to be going nowhere. Two things came together: pressures from the outside for the field of education administration to become more professional, coupled with the availability of the growing body of theory and method from the social sciences. To the question, "Where do we go from here?" came a new version of an old answer: become scientific.

The Theory Movement

The proponents of what became the theory movement believed that research on educational administration was in trouble because it was atheoretical, nonrigorous, noncumulative, and too focused on solving local problems instead of building general principles. Although the approach of the theory movement has since come under heavy attack and has sometimes been caricatured, it was built on a coherent and nontrivial set of assumptions. First was a realist view of the social world. Like other social scientists of the time, the proponents of the theory movement in educational administration assumed that the social world had enough stability and lawfulness across place and time that it was possible and, indeed, the purpose of science, to develop and test hypotheses and theories about how it works.

A theory, according to this view, is a set of generic concepts, or variables, related to one another by a set of explicit propositions. A theory can be tested only by developing operational definitions of its concepts so that they can be measured empirically.[1] Wherever possible, the operational definitions of concepts should produce quantitative data, so that mathematical and statistical techniques can be applied. The job of social science was to make the world clearer, more understandable, and therefore, more manageable. The scientists' most important contribution to practice was to develop good theories and teach those theories to practitioners. To do more than that would go beyond their expertise. As social *scientists*, they could develop a better understanding of how the world works, but had no basis for making claims about how it *ought* to work. Practitioners ultimately had to decide what values and purposes they would pursue in their work.

The new approach was intrinsically more abstract than prior traditions in the field. In earlier decades, people often asked questions like, "How can we make School X more efficient?" Such questions encouraged broad consideration of anything that might influence efficiency in School X. They gave little assurance that what was learned about School X would be helpful anywhere else. The new scholars focused on more generic questions, such as "How does a principal's relative emphasis on task versus people influence school efficiency?" Answers to that question might be helpful to someone taking up a principal's role in any of a range of different schools *if* the finding was robust and the new principal knew how to apply it.

For a variety of reasons—trends in schools, research on school administration, and trends in outside disciplines—there was continual evolution of theories about educational administration from the 1950s to the 1980s. One important trend in school administration was the rapid consolidation of smaller school districts into larger ones (Strang, 1987). The efficiency theorists had set this trend in motion earlier in the century, but its initial impact was mostly limited to urban districts. Beginning in the 1930s, this process spread rapidly into suburban and rural areas.

> Over 100,000 school districts were eliminated between 1940 and 1980. The average number of districts per state declined eightfold from 2,437 to 318, while the number of pupils per district increased from 216 to 2,646. In the 1940s most districts consisted of informal community arrangements with little organizational structure. By 1980 most districts were bureaucratically organized, relatively insulated from the communities they served, and oriented toward the larger professional definition of educational administration. (Strang, 1987, p. 352)

As school districts grew more complex, so did the theories used to understand them. By the 1970s, many of the one-dimensional models had evolved into contingency theories that emphasized contextual differences in schools and the need for different leadership styles to respond to different situations. Fairly complicated diagrams often accompanied the theories, showing the match and mismatch of types of administrators to types of organizations. Questionnaires and observation protocols to determine principal styles and school profiles came along as well. Despite a flurry of interest among scholars, the new ideas often seemed to have little impact on what practitioners did.

All of this does not mean that the theory movement had no impact. Because it came to dominate the thinking of the professoriat that trained the nation's school administrators, it has had enormous influence on the way that we think and talk about school administration and school leadership. It defined many of the terms that both scholars and practitioners use to describe schools as organizations. It dictated the nature of the training offered to aspiring principals. It launched journals, conferences, university programs, and professional associations. The scholars of the theory movement provided intellectual underpinnings for the design of today's complex, bureaucratic school systems. In a narrow sense, the theory movement never delivered the promised goods: It never provided very much explicit guidance that practitioners could use in their day-to-day practice. But it did influence the worldviews that they brought with them: how they understood their work and the context in which they performed it.

. . . To the Present

In 1974, Thomas Greenfield addressed an international convention of scholars of educational administration and helped to usher in the current tumultuous era of research in educational administration (Greenfield, 1975). More than one observer has characterized Greenfield's speech as a major turning point, perhaps the death knell of the theory movement (Griffiths, 1988; Walker, 1984). Greenfield challenged the idea that either leadership or research on leadership could be value free. He argued that every theory hinges on biases and assumptions of one sort or another. By reifying the school bureaucracy and insisting on rationalistic management, said Greenfield, the movement denied that administrators make moral choices. It encouraged them to act as cogs within a machine, removing them from responsibility for the consequences of their actions. It tried to sanitize the difficult, human, willful nature of decision making, as though it were simply a matter of pulling strings and levers.

Greenfield's was not the only shock wave of the 1970s. Another one was generated by a group of theorists, many of them colleagues at Stanford University, who offered an unsettling new perspective on school organization. John Meyer, Brian Rowan, and their colleagues at Stanford wrote a series of articles with such provocative titles as

"Formal Structure as Myth and Ceremony" (Meyer & Rowan, 1977, 1978; Meyer, Scott, & Deal, 1981), arguing that much of the supposed rationality of school organization was mythical and that school organization was dominated not by functional but by cultural imperatives: Schools were managed so as to align with myths in the larger society. Cohen and March (1974) described universities as "organized anarchies" in which the "garbage can" was the best metaphor for how decisions came about. Weick (1976) made similar points in arguing that educational organizations were "loosely coupled" systems and explicitly linked his thesis to an argument about epistemology:

> The guiding principle is a reversal of the common assertion, "I'll believe it when I see it" and presumes an epistemology that asserts, "I'll see it when I believe it." Organizations as loosely coupled systems may not have been seen before because nobody believed in them or could afford to believe in them. It is conceivable that preoccupation with rationalized, tidy, efficient, coordinated structures has blinded many practitioners as well as researchers to some of the attractive and unexpected properties of less rationalized and less tightly related clusters of events. (pp. 2-3)

Gradually, since 1974, interpretive, value-driven approaches and methodologies have built strong bases of support and scholarship. Just as the pioneers of the theory movement reflected the social science zeitgeist of the 1950s, the new theorists reflected an emerging intellectual movement of the 1970s and 1980s. Similar criticisms had already exploded in other fields; it was inevitable that this discipline would also be compelled to grapple with the questions facing the rest of the social sciences, the humanities, and even the physical sciences.

The new critique reflected elements of two different lines of attack that had been developing in the social sciences over a number of years. One came from a direction that we will label *qualitative/pragmatic*. The qualitative critique argued that the complexity and subtleties of the world of educational administration are entirely lost by any research strategy that focuses on quantitative measurement of a narrow spectrum of variables. Proponents of ethnography and other qualitative methods (Van Maanen, 1979) argue that an insistence on quantitative measurement produces simplistic caricatures that lose much of what is important in schools. The pragmatic side of the attack came from scholars who questioned both the utility and the validity of purely descriptive approaches to educational administration. Argyris (1980) and Lawler et al. (1985) argued that any form of social science research is an intervention into the phenomena under study, and that so-called rigorous research unintentionally creates conditions that are unnatural or anomalous. In consequence, the results of such research are neither valid nor of use to practitioners.

In the 1970s, the qualitative/pragmatic tradition helped spawn what became the most powerful empirical trend in educational administration in the past two decades—the effective schools movement. This began as a reaction to the argument from sociologists like Coleman and Jencks, who claimed that schooling was much less important than demographic variables in determining student outcomes. That argument was based on empirical research of just the kind that the theory movement encouraged: large-scale, quantitative research using variables drawn from sociological theory.

Ron Edmonds, a pioneer of the effective schools movement, began not with social science theory but with a simple but powerful practical observation: Even though many schools serving the urban poor were doing badly, there were some schools serving the same populations that were remarkably effective. Edmonds's basic idea was straightforward: Study the unusual schools to find out what makes them effective. The lessons from those unusually effective schools can then be used to assist other schools. One of the factors consistently associated with school effectiveness turned out to be strong administrative leadership.

The second major strand of the attack on the theory movement is from a direction that we will label *constructivist/critical*. Constructivists (Berger & Luckmann, 1966) insist that the world of human affairs, unlike the natural world, is not an objective world that waits passively to be understood but a socially constructed one that is inevitably shaped by the values and assumptions that we bring to it. This implies that the theories that social scientists develop can alter the very world that the theories seek to explain and that changing the theories could change the world. How can theories capture the underlying lawfulness of social behavior if there is no enduring lawfulness to capture? Critical theorists launched a frontal attack on the idea of objective theory, arguing that theory, like other forms of discourse, inevitably reflects the values and biases of the person(s) who constructed the argument. Because those values and biases are often implicit and hidden, critical analysis needs to deconstruct the text to reveal what its author(s) sought to obscure.

The current cacophony in educational administration, as in the social sciences in general, results from the conflicting shouts of at least four different camps, which are represented in Table 9.2. Different

TABLE 9.2 Views of the Terrain of Educational Administration

Teleology: View of the Purpose of Inquiry	Epistemology: View of Social Reality	
	Objective-Lawful	Constructivist-Anarchic
Conceptual-analytic	Logical positivism (theory movement)	Critical theory
Prescriptive-pragmatic	Social engineering (scientific management)	Qualitative/pragmatic (effective schools movement)

NOTE: Both dimensions are, of course, continua rather than dichotomies. We hope that the table justifies itself in the degree to which its expository value outweighs the inevitable oversimplification.

perspectives are arrayed in Table 9.2 along two different dimensions: a teleological dimension that deals with the purpose of social inquiry and an epistemological one that deals with perspectives on the nature of the social world. On the teleological dimension, we group together the strange bedfellows of logical positivism and critical theory because both emphasize the development of ideas that produce better and deeper analysis and description of the phenomena at hand. Although it is true that critical theory is much more explicitly value laden where the theory movement sought to be value free, both tend not to develop arguments about what ought to happen:

> Because the Postmodern tradition avoids committing itself to a political/moral metanarrative of its own, it often discloses and rejects the shortcomings of other views without positing clear alternatives to them. Instead, it relies on an implicitly normative vocabulary of liberation, empowerment, and issue-specific critique that is much clearer in specifying what it is against than what it is for and why. (Burbules & Rice, 1991, p. 397)

Scientific management and the effective schools movement, on the other hand, are grouped together because of their shared reformist and pragmatic impulse: Both explicitly have (or had) an explicit intention of using research as a basis for pragmatic prescriptions.

Epistemologically, the past several decades have seen a gradual shift in the social sciences away from a realist view, which sees the social world as very much like the natural one: subject to immutable natural laws that science seeks to uncover and explicate. The alternative constructivist-anarchic perspective sees the social and natural worlds as fundamentally different from one another because the social world is socially constructed and is continually in the process of being reconstructed. (The distinction here is similar to the objective-subjective dimension used by Burrell and Morgan, 1979, in their conceptual taxonomy of organization theory.) Because social science is itself a process of social construction, it is part of and it influences the very thing that it is supposed to study. Thus any science of human behavior is a science of the artificial. It attempts to understand and explain the worlds that humans and human cultures have chosen to create. In the social sciences, there is no ultimate distinction between valid prediction and self-fulfilling prophecy.

Realist perspectives assume an objective reality independent of human theories—laws of social behavior exist and wait patiently for us to find them. In their most extreme form, constructive-anarchic perspectives imply the opposite: Reality is simply a product of our theories. Truth is a figment of our imagination. In their more extreme forms, both views oversimplify and mislead. Neither humans nor the worlds that they create are infinitely malleable, and some stubborn realities resist our most determined efforts to change them. But the great variety in cultures and institutions makes it clear that humans can come to believe an astonishing variety of different ideas about the nature and purposes of the human enterprise.

This "paradigm diversity," as Griffiths (1988) politely terms it, makes for a hectic, often angry, some would say "postmodern," arena. In the pages of *Educational Administration Quarterly, Phi Delta Kappan,* and other journals in the field, we find articles on disparate topics, written in very different styles, one on top of the other. Although allegedly addressing the same topics, scholars with conflicting attitudes toward research speak different languages and rarely communicate with those who speak other dialects. Some scholars relish epistemological debate, whereas others roll their eyes at the mere mention of philosophy. For some, a discussion of educational administration quite naturally invokes Wittgenstein, Habermas, and Foucault and obliges a review of antifoundationalism or a critique of the Aristotelian ideal of the Philosopher King (e.g., Hodgkinson, 1991). For another group, it is much more likely to invoke Sergiovanni, Bennis, Senge, or Bolman and Deal. For still a third group, including many dissertation writers, discussion focuses on such issues as "What causes stress for Illinois school administrators?" or "Managing the allocation and distribution of Chapter 1 funds in two urban school districts."

What implications does this theoretical chaos hold for the ability of researchers to positively influence what goes on in schools? If it is difficult to assess the influence of the theory movement, it is all the more difficult to ascertain the influence of the current splintered state of the field, beyond the obvious and obligatory call for more dialogue among those who hold different perspectives.

Some scholars doubt that the recent evolution of research will prove valuable, or that the relentless self-questioning will pay off. Has research on school leadership justified an oppressive status quo? Has it emphasized technical performance at the expense of concern for the culture of schools? Has it ignored women and minorities, reserving leadership for white men? Does it pander to corporate America? Does empirical study reify various unsavory aspects of schooling such as hierarchy, teacher-centered instruction, or the avoidance of moral responsibility? Should we simply admit that our theories, concepts, and research methods have failed?

Sometimes, it all sounds like the academic equivalent of a midlife crisis: "What have I done? Have I accomplished anything? Can I change at this age, and do I really want to?" But some do take comfort in the struggle and in the give and take of critique and countercritique. Pluralism need not entail polarization, and there have been a number of calls for complementary scholarship, for a cease-fire in the war of dualities (Bolman & Deal, 1984; Sergiovanni, 1984). The human impulse to seek comfort and certainty in the face of turbulence and complexity may explain part of our propensity to choose up sides, to choose one faith or another. Theoretical pluralism sounds easy enough, but the spirit of inclusion and compromise has not always characterized writings on educational leadership. Mostly, one theory preys on another, the writer citing friendly research the way a wolf calls the pack to the slaughter. With a glance through an article's title and bibliography, anyone familiar with the field can guess the author's thesis.

Too often, we ignore or dismiss those who see the world differently, rather than engaging one another in the kind of debate that we need to move the field forward. Quantitative, interpretivist, neo-Marxist—whatever the perspective—scholars tend either to condemn other views wholesale or to ignore those views and press on as if no critique existed. This sort of effort at conceptual cleansing serves no one's interests. Scholars have confused practitioners too many times with incomplete or one-sided ideas.

Of the four traditions described in Table 9.2, those at the realist end of the spectrum (social engineering and logical positivism) have receded, for the moment at least, into the background. Neither is dead, but neither is likely to be a dominant voice in research on school leadership for the remainder of the decade. The other two traditions, critical theory and qualitative/pragmatic approaches, are very much alive. The dialogue and debate between those two traditions is likely to dominate the intellectual and research agendas around school leadership for the foreseeable future. Apple (1993) provided a succinct summary of the kind of contribution that critical theory and related strands have been making and will continue to make in coming years:

> Because of the recent influence of postmodern and poststructuralist theories, critical educational studies have widened the concerns that tended to provide the organizing principles behind earlier critical work. There is now (thank goodness) a greater recognition of the multiplicity and complexity of relations of power—race, gender, class, and sexuality; the list could be continued. Challenges are also being made to our usually accepted definitions of rationality, science, and ways of knowing, especially by the multiple positions associated with feminism. . . . "Reality," it seems, is constructed by real people with real interests. There is no single privileged way of coming to grips with the "real." All forms of knowing are ultimately implicated in relations of power. (p. 33)

Depending on one's perspective, it can be said that the greatest strength of critical and postmodern approaches is that they refuse to accept the taken-for-granted and in so doing lay the basis for transformation. The counterargument from many pragmatists is that they are naively millennial: of no practical use to anyone who wants to make schools better because of an insistence that to change anything requires changing everything. Carlson (1987) provides one of many examples of the reasoning that attracts such a critique:

> The organization of schools is powerfully constrained by the role they serve in reproducing the structured inequalities and ideologies of domination typical of advanced capitalist society. Reproductive work necessitates a great deal of top-down control, including the bureaucratic subordination of teachers. The paradox of reform under existing conditions is that the system cannot create the conditions most suitable to the pursuit of excellence by teachers and students without giving teachers and students much more control over the schooling process; and there is no assurance that teachers and students will then use their newfound power, or define excellence, in ways that are consistent with corporate and state interests. . . . A democratic Left must insist that while the

system may be humanized somewhat under existing political and economic conditions, strong pressures will exist to reassert top-down bureaucratic control and disempower teachers (along with students) within the schooling process. We will need to move beyond the priorities and social organizational forms of U.S. industrial capitalism in order to implement more basic changes. (p. 306)

The envisioning of social forms that will transcend "advanced capitalism" is no doubt interesting and important work, particularly for academics who are free to think long term and big picture and for whom the poor are more an abstraction than a daily face-to-face reality. Meanwhile, practicing teachers and administrators worry about what to do today and tomorrow to improve the life prospects of the particular children for whom they are responsible. Those leaders rarely expect that the postcapitalist transformation of society will arrive in time to help this year's students. To the argument of many critical theorists that reform is not enough, the qualitative-pragmatist responds, "Perhaps, but what other hope is there for helping real children in real time?"

The dialogue between these two very important streams of thinking will continue and, perhaps, gradually converge in the remaining years of this decade. In the remaining sections of this chapter, we discuss the recent evolution of ideas about and research on leadership.

The Idea of Leadership

Almost everyone believes that the idea of leadership is important, yet the concept has often been shrouded in controversy and confusion. In English, the words *lead* and *leader* are very old, but *leadership* is surprisingly young: The first recorded use was in an early 19th-century reference to leadership in the British House of Commons. Historically, the word leadership had not been particularly necessary because the idea had not been separated from concepts of strength, direction, and domination. The image of the leader was a strong, usually male, heroic figure who knew what needed to be done and directed others to do it. This image was serviceable during the many centuries in which most systems were small and simple, and most cultures accepted autocratic governance as the natural order of things. But the past two centuries have witnessed a dramatic set of changes in institutions and societies; those changes require rethinking traditional views of leaders and leadership. Table 9.3 sets out a set of hypotheses about the directions of these changes.

TABLE 9.3 Trends in Human Institutions

Dimension of Change	Changes in Systems	Changes in Conceptions of Leadership
Structural-technological	From local and simple to global and complex	From autocrat to analyst and social architect
Human	From focus on material needs (e.g., food and shelter) to psychic needs (e.g., lifestyle)	From good father to catalyst and servant
Political	From centralized and authoritarian to decentralized and democratic	From great warrior to negotiator and advocate
Cultural	From monocultural and univocal to multicultural and multivocal	From hero as destroyer of demons to hero as creator of possibilities

SOURCE: Adapted from Bolman and Deal (1993).

These changes are farther along in wealthier, more developed nations and have barely begun in some of the poorest. In some places (such as North America, Japan, and much of Western Europe), they are virtually accepted as facts of life. Other places are undergoing major transition, typically accompanied by controversy, conflict, even violence.

As systems change, so must our understanding of leadership. Many scholars and practitioners alike still hold traditional conceptions of leadership that are increasingly disconnected from the complex realities of modern systems. The third column in Table 9.3 sets out a set of hypotheses about the way that our ideas about leadership are evolving and will continue to evolve. Embedded in all these changes are two fundamental shifts in how we think about leadership.

Leadership by and for the Few to Leadership by and for the Many

This is a change from the idea that leadership is reserved for a few people in high places, or for those fortunate enough to belong to the right social class, ethnic group, or gender. The causes of this shift are both functional and ideological. Functionally, the forms of leadership that worked for machine bureaucracies are maladaptive for the complex new institutional forms of the late 20th century. Ideologically, this shift is necessary to rescue leadership from the view that it is identical to power and, by extension, to oppression.

In the study of school leadership, this shift requires that we end the common practice of treating school administration and school leadership as synonyms. One of the most important strands in recent reform efforts has been the spread of efforts to empower teachers and share decision making. Recent research makes it clear that such reforms are much easier to espouse than to enact. Weiss, Cambone, and Wyeth (1991) and Murphy, Evertson, and Radnofsky (1991) argue that shared leadership can produce real benefits for students only as teachers become more capable at group interaction, focus on substantial change rather than tinkering, and are given the time, resources, and trust necessary to take risks and assume new responsibilities. Although the success of shared decision making is still unproven, Sarason's (1982) exhortation to trust those who work most closely with students to know best what those particular students need has made its way into the folk wisdom of the profession, repeated by practitioner, union representative, and researcher alike.

Leadership as Relationship and Mutual Influence

Leadership is often seen as a one-way process: Leaders lead and followers follow. In reality, leadership is fundamentally a complex relationship between leaders and their constituents. Despite its many contributions, the effective schools tradition has sometimes added to the confusion by emphasizing strong leadership from principals and de-emphasizing collegiality and collaboration (Barth, 1990; Sykes & Elmore, 1988). Even sophisticated current models of school leadership accept the "one-way" assumption. Ames and Maehr (1989) and Bossert, Dwyer, Rowan, and Lee (1982) present one-way causal models. They depict principals' instructional leadership as a consequence of factors *external* to the school, but solely as an independent variable with respect to *internal* school variables. Such an assumption misleads both research and practice. Cronin (1984) captures this issue well:

> The study of leadership needs inevitably to be linked or merged with the study of followership. We cannot really study leaders in isolation from followers, constituents or group members. The leader is very much a product of the group, and very much

shaped by its aspirations, values and human resources. The more we learn about leadership, the more the leader-follower linkage is understood and reaffirmed. A two-way engagement or two-way interaction is constantly going on. When it ceases, leaders become lost, out of touch, imperial, or worse. (pp. 24-25).

Experienced school administrators feel and know all too well that leaders are not independent actors and that their relationships with those they lead is not static. It is a two-way street: Leaders both shape and are shaped by their constituents. Leaders often promote a new idea or initiative only *after* large numbers of their constituents already favor it (Cleveland, 1985). Leaders respond to what is going on around them. Their actions generate responses from others that, in turn, affect the leaders' capacity for further influence (Hart, 1993; Murphy, 1988). Leadership never occurs in a vacuum. It requires an organic relationship between leaders and followers.

This issue of the relationship between leader and context is also at the heart of a seemingly simple question that has generated enormous controversy in recent years: Do leaders make a difference? Historically, the commonsense view has always been that leaders make an enormous difference. The revisionist view that began to gain substantial credence in the 1970s is that leadership is essentially a post hoc, attributional phenomenon (Meindl & Ehrlich, 1987). In this view, school administrators received credit or blame for whatever happens on their watch, even though they may have had little to do with the outcomes:

> The [leader] is a bit like the driver of a skidding automobile. The marginal judgments he makes, his skill, and his luck will probably make some difference to the life prospects of his riders. As a result, his responsibilities are heavy. But whether he is convicted of manslaughter, or receives a medal for heroism is largely outside his control. (Cohen & March, 1974, p. 203)

A classic study of the impact of CEOs on firm successes (Lieberson & O'Connor, 1972) argued that, in fact, leaders made only a small difference in outcomes. Thomas (1988) argued persuasively, however, that Lieberson and O'Connor had neglected to make an important distinction: the impact of leadership on variance within and between organizations. Thomas's point, applied to school leadership, is this: Much of the variance in school performance is due to environmental variables (one of the most important being differences in student demographics). If we do not control for the great differences between schools, we will probably find that leadership counts for no more than 10% of the variance in outcomes. But if we use each school as its own control, we may find that leadership accounts for 60% to 70% of the remaining variance (Thomas, 1988).

Traditional notions of the solitary and heroic leader have led us to focus too much on identifying the characteristics of superheroes. The hope has been that if we know what they are like, we can reform education by finding or making more of them. There *are* heroic leaders, and they are worth studying, but not at the expense of understanding leadership as service:

> The servant-leader *is* servant first. It begins with the natural feeling that one wants to serve, to serve *first*. Then conscious choice inspires one to aspire to lead. The servant-first is sharply different from the person who is *leader* first, perhaps because of the need to assuage an unusual power drive or to acquire material possessions. The difference manifests itself in the care taken by the servant-first to make sure that other people's highest priority needs are being served. The best test, and difficult to administer, is: do those served grow as persons; do they, *while being served*, become healthier, wiser, freer, more autonomous, more likely themselves to become servants. (Greenleaf, 1973, p. 7)

A pressing problem in educational administration as elsewhere is that our organizations, institutions, and societies are changing very fast while our ideas about leadership lag. Those ideas change slowly because they are deeply rooted in cultural values and beliefs that are remarkably stable over years and even decades. This makes for a dangerous but exciting time. Figuring out the kinds of leadership that schools will need is a big challenge, and figuring out how they will get that leadership is even harder.

Trends in Research on School Leadership

For several decades, research on school leadership suffered under narrow interpretation and stolid execution of the tenets of positivist social science. Much of the research has focused on narrow problems with a narrow range of variables. Much has been either atheoretic or based on concepts uncritically borrowed from other fields. Studies of school leadership have often relied on static lists of administrative behaviors rather than on dynamic and integrated notions of what leadership is. That is, certain activities of administrators are judged to be "leadership behaviors" and these actions, in turn, are assumed to promote improvement in school climate and instruction. Relatively few investigators have examined the degree to which the same leader behaviors may be positive in one setting but neutral or negative in another (Murphy, Weil, & McGreal, 1986). If leadership is a relationship, then the "fit" (Duke, 1986) or the "congruence" (Lotto, 1983) between the actions of leaders and the perceptions of others must be considered. We need better understanding of how any given set of leader behaviors is affected by such variables as timing, constituents' meaning making, and conditions in the school and the community (Cohen, March, & Olsen, 1972; Duke, 1986; Marshall & Weinstein, 1984; Pitner & Ogawa, 1981).

Most studies of administrative leadership have ignored both the environmental and organizational context of work in schools (Firestone & Wilson, 1985; Greenfield, 1982; Pink, 1984; Sirotnik, 1985). Those researchers who have examined environmental influences on administrative leadership have primarily used socioeconomic status to represent context (Andrews, Soder, & Jacoby, 1986; Hallinger & Murphy, 1985; Miller & Sayre, 1986; Miller & Yelton, 1987). Although the scope of this research is limited, it does suggest that the context of leaders' work has considerable consequence for what they do. For example, in their study of effective elementary schools of varying social composition, Hallinger and Murphy (1985, 1987) found that effective principals in low-SES communities tended to exhibit a highly directive leadership style, whereas their counterparts in high-SES communities tended to orchestrate more from the background. Johnson (1992) and Johnson and Verre (1993) found that the success of new superintendents depended heavily on how well their agendas and strategies fit the context in which they found themselves. Hart (1993) argues that the entry of new principals is appropriately viewed as a process of organizational socialization that determines whether the new administrator will become "an integrated and respected member of the social system whose leadership has received the affirmation of the school as a whole" (Hart, 1993, p. 299). Such findings suggest that if we are to understand leadership in schools, we must study what leaders do in a variety of settings.

Research has also tended to underestimate the kind and number of leadership activities that school administrators typically perform. By focusing on behaviors that are directly observable and closely linked to prescribed curriculum and instruction, researchers tend to miss or undervalue the leadership component of such managerial tasks as assigning students to class (Monk, 1984) or budgeting funds, as well as the symbolic and cultural activities of leadership (Firestone & Wilson, 1985; Pitner & Ogawa, 1981; Sergiovanni, 1982, 1984; Wimpelberg, 1986).

Most who review research about school leadership judge it to be too abstract and detached from practice, or too narrow and disengaged from person and context, and therefore, of little use to those in schools. One of most notable exceptions in the past two decades has been the effective schools research (Brookover, Bready, Flood, Schweitzer, & Wisenbaker, 1987; Edmonds, 1979; Levine & Lezotte, 1990), which has had direct effects on practice. In a series of studies, researchers repeatedly concluded that building leadership was a central factor in school functioning. A review of the effective schools research literature (Levine & Lezotte, 1990) found more than 15 studies in which the leadership of the building principal was one of the most important correlates of school effectiveness. Effective school leaders, according to Levine and Lezotte's (1990) review, were individuals who (a) were aggressive in selecting and replacing teachers, (b) were mavericks who protected their building from outside interference, (c) spent time in classrooms working on instructional issues, (d) supported teachers, (e) found resources, and (f) spent much of their time working on school improvement issues.

But there are many unanswered questions about the effective schools research. Successful schools have been identified solely on the basis of test scores. Subsequent research linking leadership to student performance has used achievement in reading and mathematics almost exclusively as the dependent variable (Chubb, 1988; Murnane, 1981; Persell, Cookson, & Lyons, 1982; Rowan, Bossert, & Dwyer, 1983). However, the validity of test scores as a measure of learning has been widely questioned (Madaus, 1987; Murnane, 1981).

However, to the extent that schools have multiple goals, those that are not tested are generally overlooked in assessing the effects of administrative leadership (Murphy, Hallinger, & Mesa, 1985; Porter, 1983; Rowan et al., 1983). Even in those cases where researchers have considered multiple goals, they have usually treated them one at a time, without considering interactions among outcomes (Bossert et al., 1982; Purkey & Smith, 1983). This limited use of outcome measures severely limits our confidence in conclusions about the effects of school leadership.

Moreover, the correlational nature of most of the effective schools research has not permitted us to examine how much the principal's behavior is cause rather than effect. That is, favorable circumstances may produce positive leadership behaviors as much or more as positive behaviors produce favorable circumstances. For example, a new principal who enters a school with a highly motivated faculty and a supportive parent group may find it much easier to be seen as a strong, instructional leader than a counterpart who encounters an embittered faculty and a bitterly divided community. Roberts (1985) provides an intriguing case study of a school administrator who was viewed as highly effective and charismatic in one situation, yet plodding and ineffective in another. Such longitudinal study of the same leader in multiple situations is extremely rare, yet is critical to gaining a better understanding of the degree to which leader behavior is cause or consequence.

Research Directions

It should come as no surprise that the 1980s "management revolution" in American industry has had substantial influence on research and policy initiatives in educational leadership. Management techniques from the private sector have been used as models for school administration since the scientific management era.

Influenced by such important writers as Peters and Waterman (1982) and Bennis and Nanus (1985), the literature on school leadership now abounds with calls for the devolution of decision-making authority, for the encouragement of risk taking and entrepreneurial behavior, for collegiality among teachers, for flexibility to solve problems locally and to change with the times. Although not always sensitive to the ways that particular ideas do or do not translate from business to education, writers have been enormously successful in promoting those models to school policymakers, administrators, and teachers. What we need now is much more careful research to examine the meaning of these ideas in the context of education. This research needs to be mindful of both the pragmatist's question (e.g., Will total quality management improve schools?) and the critical theorist's question (e.g., Is total quality management simply an updated way to legitimize hierarchy and control?).

Vision, Passion, and Moral Leadership

It was "the vision thing," as much as anything else, that doomed George Bush's efforts to get reelected in 1992, and Bush never seemed to understand what it was or why people cared so much about it.

Before the early 1980s, vision and leadership were almost never found in the same article or conversation; in the past few years, they have increasingly become virtual synonyms. It has become a truism that good school leadership requires a well-articulated purpose, a direction in which to lead. But, as scholars in both management and education have cautioned, vision does not by itself propel an organization forward. A vision must fit its audience, and the leadership process must rally people together, to create and sustain a momentum. Vaill (1982), in a study of "high-performing systems" across a variety of sectors, identified "passion" as one of the characteristics almost invariably found in the leaders of unusually successful groups. Clifford and Cavenagh (1985) found the same thing for corporate CEOs (their phrase was "commitment to the point of obsession"). Levine and Lezotte (1990) report that unusually effective schools usually have leaders who care deeply and passionately about children and about making the school a better place for them. Yet we know very little about where passion and commitment come from or how they are sustained. We know that such characteristics are problematic—Blumberg and Greenfield (1986) found that weariness rather than passion was the most common shared feeling among veteran principals.

Similarly, we have little understanding of vision and its origins. Johnson (1992) found that all of the new superintendents in her sample reported that vision was very important and that they had one, but they differed greatly in their ideas about what a vision is and where it comes from. Some brought a fully formed vision with them to their new district; others hoped to generate a vision through a collaborative process in their districts. Bolam, McMahon, Pocklington, and Weindling (1992) found that heads of British elementary schools all claimed to have a vision, but that the visions "lacked detail and tended to simply reflect the general aims of primary education" (p. 22).

Finally, an increasing number of authors emphasize that vision and commitment must be rooted in values, in "moral leadership" (Blumberg & Greenfield, 1986; Bolman & Deal, 1992a; Sergiovanni, 1992). In an era of turbulence and conflict, when agreement about values has become more and more elusive and the traditional sources of faith and moral instruction have lost much of their hold, we are increasingly asking managers to provide moral direction and to become, in effect, spiritual leaders (Bolman & Deal, 1993; Vaill, 1989). So far, this is a trend that is heavily represented in popular works on leadership, but has attracted very little research.

The passionate, visionary leader long ago became a stereotyped image, a composite of assumptions about the sort of person who can rouse constituents successfully to action. A hypothetical great commander sits enthroned in the back of the American mind, part Hercules, part General Patton, part JFK. The leader as charismatic; as male, stubborn, solitary, confident, well-muscled, decisive, and ruthless—these expectations often dictate who gets to lead as well as the support or rejection that leaders receive. No doubt, such images are misleading and cause us to expect too much from leaders and too little from their constituents. But we need more research on the processes by which vision develops, takes hold, and is sustained or lost in schools.

Leader as Versatile Diagnostician

The turbulence of the 1960s, the impact of teacher unionism, desegregation, the escalation of poverty and violence in the cities, the rising populations of linguistic minorities, the demands for a more capable workforce, the spread of AIDS, growing dissatisfaction with public education, and a host of other sources of turbulence and uncertainty all suggest that school leaders need to develop skills and solve problems that they might never before have had to contemplate.

One of those capacities is the ability to know what is going on: to listen, learn, and diagnose the situation at hand. Every school brings its own evolving pattern of relationships, attitudes, expectations, habits, beliefs, politics, and culture. Few doubt that effective leadership requires an appropriate fit between leader and context, but there have been few investigations (such as Blumberg & Greenfield, 1986; Johnson, 1992) on how leaders actually go about reading the situation in which they find themselves or on the subtle mutual shaping that occurs between leaders and their constituents.

Just as contexts vary, so do leaders. A growing body of evidence (Bennis & Nanus, 1985; Gardner, 1990; Vaill, 1982) suggests that effective leaders come in a great variety of shapes, sizes, and hues. They do not necessarily possess great charisma nor stubbornness nor the Y chromosome. They may lead by persuasion, example, coaxing, inspiring, rewarding, and so on. The infinitely complex dynamics of leadership and organizational behavior complicate efforts to predict the sort of person who will best serve a particular school. A number of observers have argued that the increasing complexity of modern institutions puts a greater premium on leaders' possession of a repertoire of styles and strategies. Bolman and Deal (1991), for example, argue that the ability to "reframe"—to reconceptualize the same situation using multiple perspectives—is a central capacity for leaders in the late 20th century. Some research has appeared in support of this claim (Bensimon,

1989, 1990; Bolman & Deal, 1992b; Heimovics, Herman, & Coughlin, in press; Wimpelberg, 1987), but much more is needed.

Leader as Politician

Although there is little systematic evidence on the point, it is widely believed by both practitioners and scholars that the job of school administrators has become much more political since the late 1960s. The myth, at least, is that leaders once worked with a much more homogenous, trusting, and loyal group of constituents. Now they need the political skills of a Tip O'Neill. The job security of principals in the Chicago public schools used to depend on their ability to keep their nose clean and attract sponsorship in the central office. Since the recent decentralization of governance, job security depends on the ability to get reelected by a local school council every 4 years (Lortie, 1993).

Principals today must negotiate intense rivalries within the school; they must mediate between the school and the community; they must secure adequate funding; they must respond to harsh criticism and calls for reform. Only the most politically savvy can hope to navigate the current flood of tough issues: sex education, campus safety, religion in the classroom, bias in the curriculum, allocation of scarce resources, and so on. But only recently has there been much investigation of the political dimension of the school leader's job. Levine and Lezotte (1990), for example, in their review of the literature on effective schools, list political skills such as buffering the school from outside interference and acquisition of resources as characteristics of the principals in those schools.

At the same time, the importance of political issues seems to vary significantly across contexts. Bolman and Deal (1992b) found that political issues were significantly more prominent for principals in the United States than in Singapore. In a similar vein, Blumberg and Greenfield (1986) reported that "sensitivity to power dynamics" was an important characteristic of effective principals in their American sample, but Bolam et al. (1992) did not find it to be salient for heads of British primary schools. Johnson and Verre (1993) found that political issues were much more prominent for superintendents in some U.S. school districts than in others.

We urgently need more research on how the political dimension of the principal's job is changing and on how principals are coping with those changes. More cross-national research might help us to understand why American school leaders are, apparently, haunted by politics more than their colleagues in some other nations.

Management and Leadership

The same emerging consensus that calls for more vision also tells us that American schools, like other organizations, have for too long been overmanaged and underled. As the reasoning goes, the educational system totters on the brink of disaster because school leaders have put too much effort into managing bus schedules and too little into transforming their schools. No doubt, one can be a manager without being a leader, and there are many managers who could not "lead a squad of seven-year-olds to the ice cream counter" (Gardner, 1990, p. 2). The fact that managers are *expected* to lead may make it more likely that they will. But many teachers will vehemently attest that if anyone in their school is providing leadership, "it sure isn't the principal" (Johnson, 1990).

On the other hand, Gardner (1990) wisely argues against contrasting leadership and management too sharply because of the risk that leaders "end up looking like a cross between Napoleon and the Pied Piper, and managers like unimaginative clods" (p. 3). He suggests several dimensions for distinguishing leadership from management. Leaders think longer term and look beyond their unit to the larger world. They reach and influence constituents beyond their immediate jurisdictions. They emphasize vision and renewal. They have the political skills to cope with the challenging requirements of multiple constituencies (Gardner, 1990, p. 4).

It may well be true that preparation programs for school administrators have put too little emphasis on leadership and that much more needs to be done in this area. Bolman and Deal (1992b) found that the qualities associated with effective management were different from those associated with effective leadership. In particular, they found that good managers emphasized reason, analysis, and structure, whereas gifted leaders emphasized symbols, culture, and politics. But there is a risk of going from one extreme to another: It is entirely plausible that schools have been both undermanaged and underled. The truth is, we know very little about the mix of managerial and leadership capacities and activities that are associated with effectiveness in a variety of different contexts.

Equity and Leadership

Most principals and well over 90% of school superintendents are white males. As of 1988, women constituted 70% of all U.S. teachers, but only 25% of all principals (Choy, Medrich, & Henke, 1992), which is particularly striking given that the second population is drawn almost exclusively from the ranks of the first. Minorities and persons of color represented about 13% of both teachers and principals (Choy et al., 1992), an increase over recent years, but still well below their representation in the population at large. White males are particularly likely to hold principals' jobs in secondary schools, larger schools, and schools in the suburbs. Women principals are more likely to be found in smaller schools, elementary schools, and urban schools. African Americans and other persons of color with principalships are found almost entirely in urban schools with predominately minority student populations. In short, white males tend to get the jobs that carry the greatest prestige, women get jobs with less prestige, and African Americans tend to get the hardest jobs.

There is no evidence that this distribution reflects differences in leadership effectiveness. The available evidence suggests that if anything, women principals are more effective than men, although no one knows whether this reflects women's overall greater talent for school leadership or simply that males can be ordinary but women must be extraordinary to attain a principalship. There is a dearth of research on African American or Hispanic principals, so we have little systematic evidence about their experience and what they bring to school leadership. Shakeshaft (1987) pulls together major themes in the research on women as leaders. She outlines five characteristics of women administrators: they place central importance on their relationships with members of the school community; their daily work focuses on teaching and learning; their administrative style emphasizes cooperation and community; they experience sexism frequently; and they draw a thin line between their work and their private lives. This profile is notably different from traditional images of the male administrator: personal power, management removed from instruction, top-down authority, and technical expertise. It does, though, correspond to many of the more recent images of effective school leadership.

As in other fields, theorists have begun to "deconstruct" the assumptions that guide our thinking about leadership. Past scholarship, some say, has reflected both androcentric and Western biases that lend subtle support to the status quo, rationalizing current inequalities (Tetenbaum & Mulkeen, 1988; Yeakey, Johnston, & Adkison, 1986). Although professional opportunities for both women and persons of color have increased in recent years, there is still much to be done. Research and policy have focused primarily on two barriers to equity: recruitment processes and on-site discrimination. Federal laws enacted in the 1960s and 1970s prohibit discriminatory hiring practices, but those laws have been nearly impossible to enforce (Shakeshaft, 1987).

Most school districts lack formal guidelines for promotion, making it very difficult to distinguish between normal and unfair practices. Conventional wisdom holds that connections to "old boy networks" matter far more than do credentials and abilities.

Despite the extraordinary demographic shifts occurring in the United States and despite the evidence of inequitable access to leadership roles, only a few researchers have chosen to focus on the central questions: What helps and hinders access? When people do get in, what helps and hinders acceptance, survival, and success?

Leadership Occurs in an Organizational and Institutional Context

Research on school leadership is often disconnected from research on school organization. Bossert (1988) correctly notes that "a classical model of bureaucratic organization underlies much of the thinking about school effectiveness," and calls for a "multi-level" view of principals' leadership that emphasizes the leader's role in shaping instructional organization and school climate. Similarly, Bolman and Deal (1984, 1991) argue that organizational research and administrative practice are seriously impaired because scholars and practitioners focus on only one or two of four pivotal dimensions of organizations: structure, people, politics, and symbols.

Schools have been and continue to be relatively weak and vulnerable institutions, heavily controlled by larger social and institutional forces. Yet we continue to blame the professionals—administrators and teachers—for most of the real and imagined defects of American education. By the same token, we continue to hope vainly that a new era of better trained leaders, equipped with the latest concepts, techniques and visions, will be able to transform schools. In this area, particularly, there is an urgent need for a rapprochement between critical and pragmatic perspectives. Critical theorists have correctly argued that school leadership cannot be decontextualized and cannot be understood without examining the larger frameworks in which it takes place, but ideology often leads to misunderstanding of both the causes and the solutions for the bureaucratic "sclerosis" that often affects schools. Blaming hierarchy on "advanced capitalist societies" completely misses the fact that it is precisely the most advanced capitalists who are now moving rapidly away from old organizational forms:

> As they grow, firms may become bureaucratic, inflexible and wasteful. Employees, believing themselves to be mere cogs, are

less accountable and harder to motivate. But such "diseconomies" were usually a footnote. They seemed more than outweighed by the benefits of bigness. The triumphs of mass production early in the century had given birth to most of the giant firms which came to tower over their industries. That bigger was better was rarely disputed. Until recently, it was true. The great surprise of the past decade has been that the changes which were supposed to make bigger even better have had the opposite effect. As the advantages of corporate gigantism diminish, its long-ignored costs are becoming painfully evident. Many large firms are scrambling to reduce these, scrapping layers of middle managers, cutting overheads, and reorganizing themselves into "federations" of autonomous business units—that is, they are trying to become more like their smaller rivals. ("The Fall of Big Business," 1993, p. 13. ©1993 The Economist Newspaper Group, Inc. Reprinted with permission. Further reproduction prohibited.)

The same diseconomies have long been evident in schools, as in other public bureaucracies, but a variety of factors have made change less probable. Paradoxically, the most significant barrier to genuine change is our persistent impulse to reform American education. Reform has repeatedly taken the form of top-down efforts to alter existing practices through the imposition of new policies. The result is centralizing efforts to reduce discretion at the service level, which the professionals invariably seek to resist (often for very good reasons). The policymakers get increasingly frustrated with educators, and educators become more and more weary of successive waves of reforms that have little or no impact. We clearly need a systems view. If the current actors are to attain such a view, they will need to study the dynamics of both leadership and organization at every level from the classroom to the Congress. No doubt, it is an extraordinarily ambitious and daunting task (though one in which we can get assistance from scholars in many other disciplines). Yet unless we develop our understanding of these larger system dynamics, all our other efforts will do no more than contribute a few more atomized and disjointed scraps of knowledge.

Conclusion

Frank Spaulding's complaint in 1910 that school leadership was the "sluggish resultant of tradition, habit, routine, prejudice, and inertia" sounds all too familiar and current. That eerie parallel serves to remind us that a sense of history and a respect for the complexity of systems are at the heart of the enormous undertaking ahead of us as we seek to learn more about school leadership.

Research on school leadership is essentially a product of this century, and the field has evolved primarily by following the lead of other fields, particularly management and the social sciences. Early in the century, under external pressures for efficiency, the field embraced much of the intellectual agenda of scientific management, which led it down a path of narrow, atheoretical empiricism. This agenda helped provide both form and content for educational practice, but reached a conceptual dead end by midcentury. It was supplanted by a positivistic view of social research that was borrowed from the social sciences, particularly psychology and sociology, and expressed in the theory movement. This movement produced a stronger connection to other disciplines, thus reducing the intellectual isolation of the field and helping it gain a modicum of respect from colleagues in other university departments. On the down side, it also led to a growing gulf between theory and practice.

Beginning in the 1970s, the field entered an era of turmoil. The theory movement came under attack from at least two directions. Qualitative/pragmatic theorists argued that research had lost touch with practice by relying on an unduly rigid model of science. Constructivist/critical researchers attacked the theory movement's pretensions to science, arguing that it was both epistemologically naive and politically reactionary.

All this occurred in the context of a dramatic set of shifts in education and society. Institutions in every sector, including education, have been changing dramatically, but conceptions of leadership have lagged behind the rapid pace of social and economic change. We find ourselves in a period that is as exciting as it is confusing, as energizing as it is fractionated. An essential function of leadership is to help human groups cope with the two great barriers to shared purpose and collective action—uncertainty and conflict. When uncertainty and conflict increase, leadership becomes both more necessary and more difficult, but obsolete views of the leader as hero lead us to expect superhuman performance from those whom we cast in leadership roles. That is why big city school boards regularly fire superintendents after 2 or 3 years in office. It is also why Americans elect presidents with high hopes that they will lead us out of the wilderness and conclude a few months later that they are failing. In such a time, we need intellectual leadership in the academy to help create the conditions for better leadership in the schools. We hope that readers will join in that important work.

Note

1. Pure operationalists insist that the meaning of a concept is neither more nor less than the operation used to measure it, and that all else is "surplus meaning," but that view has never held great sway in the field of educational administration.

References

Ames, R., & Maehr, M. (1989, March). *A research agenda for the Center for Research and Development on School Leadership.* Paper presented at the annual meeting of the American Educational Research Association, San Francisco.

Andrews, R., Soder, R., & Jacoby, D. (1986, April). *Principal roles, other in-school variables, and academic achievement by ethnicity and SES.* Paper presented at the annual meeting of the American Educational Research Association, San Francisco.

Ames, R., & Maehr, M. (1989, March). *A research agenda for the Center for Research and Development on School Leadership.* Paper presented at the annual meeting of the American Educational Research Association, San Francisco.

Apple, M. W. (1993). Identity, politics and schooling. *Educational Researcher, 22,* 33-34.

Argyris, C. (1980). *Inner contradictions of rigorous research.* New York: Academic Press.

Barley, S. R., & Kunda, G. (1992). Design and devotion: Surges of rational and normative ideologies in managerial discourse. *Administrative Science Quarterly, 37,* 363-399.

Barnard, C. I. (1938). *Functions of the executive.* Cambridge, MA: Harvard University Press.

Barth, R. (1990). *Improving schools from within.* San Francisco: Jossey-Bass.

Bennis, W., & Nanus, B. (1985). *Leaders: Strategies for taking charge.* New York: Harper.

Bensimon, E. M. (1989). The meaning of "good presidential leadership": A frame analysis. *Review of Higher Education, 12,* 107-123.

Bensimon, E. M. (1990). Viewing the presidency: Perceptual congruence between presidents and leaders on their campuses. *Leadership Quarterly, 1,* 71-90.

Berger, P. L., & Luckmann, T. (1966). *The social construction of reality.* Garden City, NY: Doubleday.

Blumberg, A., & Greenfield, W. (1986). *The effective principal: Perspectives on school leadership.* Newton, MA: Allyn and Bacon.

Bolam, R., McMahon, A., Pocklington, K., & Weindling, D. (1992, April). *Teachers' and headteachers' perceptions of effective management in British primary schools*. Paper presented at the annual meeting of the American Educational Research Association, San Francisco.

Bolman, L. G., & Deal, T. E. (1984). *Modern approaches to understanding and managing organizations*. San Francisco: Jossey-Bass.

Bolman, L. G., & Deal, T. E. (1991). *Reframing organizations: Artistry, choice and leadership*. San Francisco: Jossey-Bass.

Bolman, L. G., & Deal, T. E. (1992a). Images of leadership. *American School Board Journal, 179*(4), 36-39.

Bolman, L. G., & Deal, T. E. (1992b). Leading and managing: Effects of context, culture and gender. *Education Administration Quarterly, 28*, 314-329.

Bolman, L. G., & Deal, T. E. (1993). *Changing world, changing leadership*. Unpublished manuscript, Harvard Graduate School of Education.

Bossert, S. T. (1988). School effects. In N. J. Boyan (Ed.), *Handbook of research on educational administration*. New York: Longman.

Bossert, S. T., Dwyer, D. C., Rowan, B., & Lee, G. (1982). The instructional management role of the principal. *Educational Administration Quarterly, 18*(3), 34-64.

Bridges, E. M. (1982). Research on the school administrator: The state of the art, 1967-1980. *Educational Administration Quarterly, 18*(3), 12-33.

Brookover, W., Bready, C., Flood, P., Schweitzer, J., & Wisenbaker, J. (1987). *School social systems and student achievement: Schools can make a difference*. New York: Praeger.

Burbules, N. C., & Rice, S. (1991). Dialogue across differences: Continuing the conversation. *Harvard Educational Review, 61*, 393-416.

Burrell, G., & Morgan, G. (1979). *Sociological paradigms and organizational analysis*. London: Heinemann.

Button, H. W. (1966). Doctrines of administration: A brief history. *Educational Administration Quarterly, 2*, 216-224.

Callahan, R. E. (1962). *Education and the cult of efficiency*. Chicago: University of Chicago Press.

Campbell, R. F., Fleming, T. L., Newell, L. J., & Bennion, J. W. (1987). *A history of thought and practice in educational administration*. New York: Teachers College Press.

Carlson, D. (1987). Teachers as political actors: From reproductive theory to the crisis of schooling. *Harvard Educational Review, 57*, 283-307.

Cartwright, D. (1959). Lewinian theory as a contemporary systematic framework. In S. Koch (Ed.), *Psychology: A study of a science* (Vol. 2). New York: McGraw-Hill.

Chandler, A. D., Jr. (1977). *The visible hand: The managerial revolution in American business*. Cambridge, MA: Harvard University Press.

Choy, S. P., Medrich, E. A., & Henke, R. R. (1992). *Schools and staffing in the United States: A statistical profile, 1987-88*. Washington, DC: National Center for Educational Statistics.

Chubb, J. E. (1988). Why the current wave of school reform will fail. *Public Interest, 90*, 28-49.

Cleveland, H. (1985). *The knowledge executive: Leadership in an information society.* New York: Dutton.

Clifford, D. K., & Cavanagh, R. E. (1985). *The winning performance.* New York: Bantam.

Cohen, M. D., & March, J. G. (1974). *Leadership and ambiguity: The American college president.* New York: McGraw-Hill.

Cohen, M. D., March, J. G., & Olsen, J. P. (1972). A garbage can model of organizational choice. *Administrative Science Quarterly, 17*(1), 1-26.

Cronin, T. E. (1984). Thinking and learning about leadership. *Presidential Studies Quarterly,* pp. 22-34.

Cuban, L. (1988). *The managerial imperative and the practice of leadership in schools.* Albany: State University of New York Press.

Culbertson, J. A. (1988). A century's quest for a knowledge base. In N. J. Boyan (Ed.), *Handbook of research on educational administration.* New York: Longman.

Duke, D. L. (1986). The aesthetics of leadership. *Educational Administration Quarterly, 22*(1), 7-27.

Edmonds, R. (1979). Some schools work and more can. *Social Policy, 9,* 32-43.

Estes, W. G. (1959). The statistical approach to learning theory. In S. Koch (Ed.), *Psychology: A study of a science* (Vol. 2). New York: McGraw-Hill.

The fall of big business. (1993, April 17). *The Economist,* p. 13.

Firestone, W. A., & Wilson, B. L. (1985). Using bureaucratic and cultural linkages to improve instruction: The principal's contribution. *Educational Administration Quarterly, 21*(2), 7-30.

Gardner, J. W. (1990). *On leadership.* New York: Free Press.

Greenfield, T. B. (1975). Theory about organization: A new perspective and its implications for schools. In R. F. Campbell & R. T. Gregg (Eds.), *Administrative behavior in education.* London: Athlone.

Greenfield, W. D. (1982, October). *Research on public school principals: A review and recommendations.* Paper prepared for the National Conference on the Principal, convened by the National Institute of Education.

Greenleaf, R. K. (1973). *The servant as leader.* Newton, MA: Greenleaf Center.

Griffiths, D. E. (1988). Administrative theory. In N. J. Boyan (Ed.), *Handbook of research on educational administration.* New York: Longman.

Hallinger, P., & Murphy, J. (1985). Instructional leadership and school socioeconomic status: A preliminary investigation. *Administrator's Notebook, 33*(5), 1-4.

Hallinger, P., & Murphy, J. (1987). Instructional leadership in the school context. In W. Greenfield (Ed.), *Instructional leadership: Problems, issues and controversies.* Boston: Allyn and Bacon.

Hart, A. W. (1993). *Principal succession: Establishing leadership in schools.* Albany: State University of New York Press.

Heimovics, R., Herman, R., & Coughlin, C. J. (in press). Executive leadership and resource dependence in nonprofit organizations: A frame analysis. *Public Administration Review.*

Hodgkinson, C. (1991). *Educational leadership*. Albany: State University of New York Press.

Immegart, G. L. (1988). Leadership and leadership behavior. In N. J. Boyan (Ed.), *Handbook of research on educational administration*. New York: Longman.

Johnson, S. M. (1990). *Teachers at work*. New York: Basic Books.

Johnson, S. M. (1992). Vision in the superintendency. *Executive Educator*.

Johnson, S. M., & Verre, J. (1993, April). *New superintendents and school reform*. Paper presented at the annual meeting of the American Educational Research Association, Atlanta, GA.

Lawler, E. E., Mohrman, A. M., Mohrman, S. A., Ledford, G. E., & Cummings, T. G. (1985). *Doing research that is useful for theory and practice*. San Francisco: Jossey-Bass.

Levine, D. U., & Lezotte, L. W. (1990). *Unusually effective schools*. Madison, WI: National Center for Effective Schools Research and Development.

Lewin, K., Lippitt, R., & White, R. (1939). Patterns of aggressive behavior in experimentally-created social climates. *Journal of Social Psychology, 10*, 271-299.

Lieberson, S., & O'Connor, J. F. (1972). Leadership and organizational performance: A study of large corporations. *American Sociological Review, 37*, 117-130.

Lortie, D. (1993, April). *Chicago principals under school reform*. Presentation at the annual meeting of the American Educational Research Association, Atlanta, GA.

Lotto, L. S. (1983). Revisiting the role of organizational effectiveness in educational evaluation. *Educational Evaluation and Policy Analysis, 5*(3), 367-378.

Madaus, G. (1987). *Testing and the curriculum: From compliant servant to dictatorial master*. Unpublished manuscript, Boston College, Chestnut Hill, MA.

Marshall, H. H., & Weinstein, R. S. (1984). Classroom factors affecting students' self evaluations: An interactional model. *Review of Educational Research, 54*, 301-325.

Mayo, E. (1933). *The human problems of an industrial civilization*. New York: Macmillan.

Meindl, J. R., & Ehrlich, B. (1987). The romance of leadership and the evaluation of organizational performance. *Academy of Management Journal, 30*, 91-109.

Meyer, J., & Rowan, B. (1977). Institutionalized organizations: Formal structure as myth and ceremony. *American Journal of Sociology, 30*, 431-450.

Meyer, J., & Rowan, B. (1978). The structure of educational organizations. In M. W. Meyer & Associates, *Environment and organizations* (pp. 78-109). San Francisco: Jossey-Bass.

Meyer, J., Scott, W. R., & Deal, T. E. (1981). Institutional and technical sources of organizational structure: Explaining the structure of educational organizations. In H. Steen (Ed.), *Organization and human services: Cross disciplinary perspectives*. Philadelphia, PA: Temple University Press.

Miller, S. K., & Sayre, K. A. (1986, April). *Case studies of affluent effective schools.* Paper presented at the annual meeting of the American Educational Research Association, Washington, DC.

Miller, S. K., & Yelton, B. (1987, April). *Correlates of achievement in affluent effective schools.* Paper presented at the annual meeting of the American Educational Research Association, Washington, DC.

Monk, D. H. (1984, April). *Assigning elementary pupils to their teachers: The principal's role.* Paper presented at the annual meeting of the American Educational Research Association, New Orleans, LA.

Murnane, R. J. (1981). Interpreting the evidence on school effectiveness. *Teachers College Record, 83*(1), 19-35.

Murphy, J. (1992). *The landscape of leadership preparation: Reframing the education of school administrators.* Newbury Park, CA: Corwin.

Murphy, J., Evertson, C. M., & Radnofsky, M. L. (1991). *Restructuring schools: Fourteen elementary and secondary teachers' perspectives on reform* (Occasional Paper No. 8). Cambridge, MA: Harvard Graduate School of Education, National Center for Educational Leadership.

Murphy, J., Hallinger, P., & Mesa, R. P. (1985). School effectiveness: Checking progress and assumptions and developing a role for state and federal government. *Teachers College Record, 86*(4), 615-641.

Murphy, J., Weil, M., & McGreal, T. (1986). The basic practice model of instruction. *Elementary School Journal, 87*(1), 83-95.

Murphy, J. T. (1988, May). The unheroic side of leadership: Notes from the swamp. *Phi Delta Kappan, 69,* 654-659.

Perrow, C. (1986). *Complex organizations: A critical essay.* New York: Random House.

Persell, C. H., Cookson, P. W., & Lyons, H. (1982, October). *Effective principals: What do we know from various educational literatures?* Paper prepared for the National Conference on the Principalship, convened by the National Institute of Education.

Peters, T. J., & Waterman, R. H. (1982). *In search of excellence.* New York: Harper & Row.

Pink, W. (1984). Creating effective schools. *Educational Forum, 49*(1), 91-107.

Pitner, N. J., & Ogawa, R. T. (1981). Organizational leadership: The case of the school superintendent. *Educational Administration Quarterly, 17*(2), 45-65.

Porter, A. C. (1983, January-February). The role of testing in effective schools. *American Education,* pp. 25-28.

Purkey, S. D., & Smith, M. S. (1983). Effective schools: A review. *Elementary School Journal, 83*(4), 427-452.

Ravitch, D. (1990). *The American reader: Words that moved a nation.* New York: HarperCollins.

Roberts, N. (1985). Transforming leadership: A process of collective action. *Human Relations, 38,* 1023-1046.

Roethlisberger, F. J., & Dickson, W. J. (1949). *Management and the worker.* Cambridge, MA: Harvard University Press.

Rowan, B., Bossert, S. T., & Dwyer, D. C. (1983, April). Research on effective schools: A cautionary note. *Educational Researcher*, pp. 24-31.

Sarason, S. (1982). *The culture of the school and the problem of change* (2nd ed.). Boston: Allyn and Bacon.

Sergiovanni, T. J. (1982). Leadership and excellence in schooling. *Educational Leadership, 39*(5), 330-336.

Sergiovanni, T. J. (1984). Leadership and excellence in schooling. *Educational Leadership, 41*(5), 4-13.

Sergiovanni, T. J. (1992). *The moral dimension in school leadership.* San Francisco: Jossey-Bass.

Sergiovanni, T. J., Burlingame, M., Coombs, F. D., & Thurston, P. W. (1987). *Educational governance and administration* (2nd ed.). Englewood Cliffs, NJ: Prentice Hall.

Shakeshaft, C. (1987). *Women in educational administration.* Newbury Park, CA: Sage.

Sirotnik, K. A. (1985). School effectiveness: A bandwagon in search of a tune. *Educational Administration Quarterly, 21*(2), 135-140.

Strang, D. (1987). The administrative transformation of American education: School district consolidation, 1938-1980. *Administrative Science Quarterly, 32*, 352-356.

Sykes, G., & Elmore, R. F. (1988). Making schools manageable: Policy and administration for tomorrow's schools. In W. L. Boyd & C. T. Kerchner (Eds.), *Politics of Education Association yearbook* (pp. 77-94). Philadelphia, PA: Falmer.

Taylor, F. W. (1911). *The principles of scientific management.* New York: Harper & Row.

Tetenbaum, T., & Mulkeen, W. (1988). Counteracting androcentrism: Putting women into the curriculum in educational administration. In F. Wendell & M. Bryant (Eds.), *New directions for administrative preparation.* UCEA monograph.

Thomas, A. B. (1988). Does leadership make a difference to organizational performance? *Administrative Science Quarterly, 33*, 388-400.

Tyack, D. (1974). *The one best system: The history of American urban education.* Cambridge, MA: Harvard University Press.

Tyack, D. B., & Hansot, E. (1982). *Managers of virtue: Public school leadership in America.* New York: Basic Books.

Vaill, P. B. (1982, Autumn). The purposing of high performance systems. *Organizational Dynamics*, pp. 23-39.

Vaill, P. B. (1989). *Managing as a performing art.* San Francisco: Jossey-Bass.

Van Maanen, J. (1979). The fact of fiction in organization ethnography. *Administrative Science Quarterly, 24*, 539-550.

Walker, W. G. (1984). Administrative narcissism and the tyranny of isolation: Its decline and fall, 1954-1984. *Educational Administration Quarterly, 20*, 6-23.

Weick, K. E. (1976). Educational organizations as loosely-coupled systems. *Administrative Science Quarterly, 21*, 1-19.

Weiss, C. H., Cambone, J., & Wyeth, A. (1991). *Trouble in paradise: Teacher conflicts in shared decision making* (Occasional Paper No. 8). Cambridge, MA: Harvard Graduate School of Education, National Center for Educational Leadership.

Wimpelberg, R. K. (1987). Managerial images and school effectiveness. *Administrators' Notebook, 32,* 1-4.

Yeakey, C. C., Johnston, G. S., & Adkison, J. A. (1986). In pursuit of equity: A review of research on minorities and women in educational administration. *Educational Administration Quarterly, 22,* 110-149.

TEN

Administrator Succession in School Organizations

RODNEY T. OGAWA

People generally agree, the doubts of some academics and social critics notwithstanding, that individuals who hold high-level positions are crucial to the success and improvement of organizations. Executives direct their companies' fortunes; coaches orchestrate their teams' victories.

This abiding belief in the importance of people in positions of leadership is also evident in discussions about the current wave of educational reform. Although many reforms are aimed at empowering teachers and parents, analysts agree that the leadership of principals and superintendents is essential to their successful implementation (Murphy, 1991). In schools, principals can undermine reform, but they can also catalyze and nurture it. In districts, superintendents can block the adoption and implementation of reform, but they can also sow the seeds of reform and provide resources to sustain it.

An important corollary to the belief that administrators can make a difference is the belief that one way to improve an organization is to replace its top-level administrator. Major corporations with financial losses replace their chief executive officers; athletic teams with losing records or dwindling ticket receipts fire their coaches. Similarly, boards of education replace superintendents when, among other reasons, they seek to improve the performance of their districts. Under such circum-

359

stances, the hiring of a new superintendent can mark a board's intention to institute significant change (Carlson, 1961). The increased frequency with which boards are replacing superintendents is evidenced by the well-documented decline of the average tenure of superintendents.

In this period of intensive reform efforts aimed at enhancing the performance of public schools, it is likely that school districts are and will be replacing superintendents to spur the development and implementation of reform. Further, with the delegation of decision-making authority and, thus, accountability to the school level through such reform strategies as school-based management, districts may well begin to replace principals with the frequency that they now replace superintendents.

But what impact does the replacement of administrators actually have on organizations and their performance? Can the replacement of administrators facilitate the successful implementation of reforms? Over the past three decades, a body of research has been amassed on the subject of the replacement, or succession, of administrators. Although most of that research was conducted in noneducational settings, scholars have paid increasing attention to administrator succession in school organizations. The purpose of this chapter is to review the research on administrator succession and to consider the implications of its findings for educational policy and practice and for future research.

Defining Administrator Succession

Administrator succession has been defined as the process of replacing key officials in organizations (Grusky, 1961). In the case of school organizations, it involves the replacement of individuals in the top office of each functional level of districts' organizational hierarchies, namely, superintendents at the district level and principals at the school level. As such, the concept of administrator succession seems deceptively straightforward. On closer examination, however, the concept is shrouded in ambiguity.

This ambiguity takes three forms. The first concerns the many issues other than succession itself that pertain to the replacement of administrators (Miklos, 1989). Administrator succession is a complex matter. It has many facets, several of which have been the focus of research. For example, the process by which administrators are selected—including the impact of candidates' sex, race, or ethnicity—is relevant to understanding the replacement of administrators. Similarly, the process by which administrators are socialized to new roles and new organizations is a potentially important dimension of administrator succession. These and other matters are obviously relevant to understanding administrator succession. However, in an effort to provide conceptual clarity, this chapter will be confined to reviewing studies that focus on succession itself.

The second form of ambiguity surrounding the concept of administrator succession concerns the age-old problem of drawing a conceptual distinction between administration and leadership. Many authors (Barnard, 1938; Bennis & Nanus, 1985; Katz & Kahn, 1978; Selznick, 1957) argue that leadership exceeds the influence that results simply from holding an administrative office. Nevertheless, the term *administrator* has been used almost interchangeably with the term *leader* in the succession literature. To avoid the tricky conceptual ground that lies between these twins separated at birth, the term *administrator* will be employed exclusively in this chapter. This choice was made because the vast majority of studies of both administrator succession and leader succession have examined the replacement of individuals in administrative positions. Thus, although it may be debatable whether these are studies of leader succession, they clearly are studies of administrator succession.

The third form of ambiguity concerns the aims of research on administrator succession. Studies of succession generally have one of two purposes (Pfeffer & Davis-Blake, 1986). One is to examine administrator succession, per se. Examples of this type of research are found in studies of the effects of organizational size on the frequency of administrator succession (Gordon & Becker, 1964; Grusky, 1961; Kriesberg, 1962) and in studies of the symbolic meanings attached by organizational members to succession events (Gephart, 1978).

Another purpose of research on administrator succession is to assess and explain the impact of administrators on the performance of organizations (Gordon & Rosen, 1981; Miskel & Cosgrove, 1985). Studies of this type do not study succession, itself. Rather, they employ succession as an opportunity to observe the effects of naturally occurring variation in administrative factors on organizational performance while holding organizational and environmental factors more or less constant (Hart & Ogawa, 1987; Lieberson & O'Connor, 1972; Ogawa & Hart, 1985; Salancik & Pfeffer, 1977; Weiner & Mahoney, 1979). This type of research should be distinguished from research that assesses the impact of succession, per se, on organizational performance. Admittedly, a fine conceptual line separates the two types of research, but the difference in intent is significant.

This chapter will be confined to reviewing research on administrator succession for its own sake.[1]

Literature Review

Research on administrator succession, even as it has been framed for the purposes of this review, is quite varied. This variety occurs along at least three dimensions. First, studies of administrator succession adopt various research designs and employ a range of procedures for collecting and analyzing data. They include case studies, correlational studies, actuarial studies, and laboratory and field experiments (Gordon & Rosen, 1981). Second, studies focus on a wide variety of factors associated with administrator succession, including antecedents to succession, aspects of succession itself, and outcomes of succession. Third, studies examine various relationships among different succession factors. Some studies assess the direct effect of succession on organizational outcomes, including performance or change; some determine the impact of antecedents, such as the size of organizations, on aspects of succession, such as frequency; others estimate the influence of aspects of succession, such as the successor's management style, on subordinates' responses to succession; still others attempt to gauge the relative and interactive relationships of some combination of antecedents, aspects of succession, subordinates' responses, and organizational outcomes.

Due to this methodological and empirical variety, a framework for organizing the findings of research on administrator succession necessarily must be broad in nature. Indeed, previous reviews have employed very general frameworks composed of broad categories. For example, Gordon and Rosen (1981) categorized studies according to the types of research designs that they employed. Miskel and Cosgrove (1985) organized their review of research on administrator succession in educational settings according to temporal categories adapted from the model of succession dynamics developed by Gordon and Rosen (1981) in their earlier review.

The review reported in this chapter is loosely organized around five categories of factors associated with administrator succession: organizational outcomes, organizational members' responses to succession, successor/organization fit, conditions of the succession process, and antecedents to succession. The review unfolds in five steps, moving backward from organizational outcomes through the four other sets of factors. The purpose of this backward tracking is to produce a map that traces the relationships among succession factors that may link succession to organizational outcomes. The map reveals which of those linkages have been verified, even equivocally, by past research and which remain to be examined by future research. Many of the studies cited in this review examine the relationships between more than two types of succession factors. However, the structure of this chapter necessitates the treatment of one type of factor and its relationship to one other type of factor in each section. Thus the findings of a given study may be scattered across the five sections of the review. The threat that this may pose to the integrity of any given study I hope will be mitigated by the empirical map that emerges from the review of research.

Effect of Succession on Organizational Outcomes

As previously discussed, it is widely believed that because administrators affect organizational outcomes, the replacement of administrators also will affect organizational outcomes. Thus a major thrust of research on administrator succession has been to verify the existence of the links between succession and two organizational outcomes: performance and change.

Organizational Performance

Several studies have examined the relationship between administrator succession and organizational performance. A few of these studies have been conducted in production organizations and school organizations, but the majority have focused on athletic teams. This may be due to the apparent clarity of measuring performance through win-loss records and the fairly high turnover rate of coaches.

Two early case studies of production organizations resulted in contradictory findings. Gouldner (1954) examined the succession of a manager in a gypsum mine. He found that although the manager had been replaced to enhance productivity, the succession resulted in lower productivity. Guest (1962) studied administrator succession in an automobile plant. Unlike Gouldner, Guest found that the succession seemed to enhance productivity.

Studies of school organizations do not provide a clearer picture of the relationship between administrator succession and organizational performance. Miskel and Owens (1983) studied the succession of school principals. They found that succession exerted no statistically significant effect on perceived organizational effectiveness. Rowan and Denk

(1984) also studied the succession of principals in elementary schools. Their findings were mixed. Whereas succession negatively affected the performance of students from higher socioeconomic backgrounds on a standardized achievement test, it positively affected the performance of students from lower socioeconomic backgrounds on the same test.

The findings of research on the impact of replacing coaches of athletic teams are also mixed. Eitzen and Yetman (1972) found that coaching changes had no significant effect on teams' performance. Ten years later, Brown (1982) concluded that changing coaches produced either no effect or, worse, a negative effect on team performance. Pfeffer and Davis-Blake (1986) replicated the earlier finding that succession exerted no effect on team performance. Allen, Panian, and Lotz (1979) conducted what arguably is the most detailed analysis of the relationship of the succession of coaches and team performance. Consistent with the findings of other studies that succession exerted no effect on performance, they reported that teams' prior performance accounted for far more of the variance in subsequent performance than did succession.

Thus research does not consistently support the assumption that the replacement of administrators significantly affects organizational performance. Even in studies of athletic teams, where coaches safely may be assumed to exert greater control over factors associated with team performance than administrators exert over factors associated with school or district performance, the findings indicate little or no effect. However, research, including some of the studies cited in this section, identifies factors that mediate the relationship between administrator succession and organizational performance. These factors are suggestive of the conditions under which administrator succession exerts no effect, a positive effect, or a negative effect on organizational performance.

Organizational Change

Another organizational outcome that has been linked to administrator succession is change. Although some scholars view change as a factor that affects the relationship between succession and organizational performance (Salancik & Pfeffer, 1977), a handful of studies have focused on organizational change, itself, as a product of succession. All of the studies that have expressly examined the relationship of administrator succession and organizational change have been conducted in school organizations. The results are mixed, apparently confounded by administrative level.

The findings of research on school principals are mixed. Two studies did not uncover an association between the succession of principals and indicators of change at the school level. Keith (1975) found that the succession of principals was not associated with rates of the diffusion of innovation in schools. Similarly, Miskel and Owens (1983) reported that the replacement of principals did not produce changes in structural linkages in schools. However, Hoy and Aho (1973) and Ganz and Hoy (1977) reported that teachers perceived successor principals to be change agents.

Research provides consistent evidence that the succession of superintendents is associated with organizational change at the district level. Carlson (1961) found that successor superintendents can, under certain conditions, produce changes in their new districts, a finding corroborated later by Reynolds (1966). Firestone (1990) documented that the two superintendents whose successions he studied initiated systematic but very different changes in their respective districts.

Thus research suggests that level in the administrative hierarchy of school districts can affect the relationship between administrative succession and organizational change. On the one hand, evidence clearly points to an association between the succession of superintendents, who sit atop the administrative hierarchy of districts, and organizational change. On the other, evidence concerning the relationship between the succession of principals, who operate as midlevel administrators, and change at the school level is at best equivocal. One study points directly to the mediating effects of administrative level. In Knedlik's (1968) study of the succession of principals and superintendents, the succession of superintendents produced organizational change, but the succession of principals did not. Other studies identify different factors that mediate the relationship of administrator succession and organizational change. These will be discussed in the sections of this chapter that follow.

Organization Members' Responses to Succession

Because individuals comprise organizations, it is plausible that the responses of organization members to administrator succession may mediate the effects of succession on organizational outcomes. Research indicates that subordinates' responses to administrator succession do vary and that members' responses may correspond with, if not necessarily affect, organizational performance. Although one study (Miskel & Owens, 1983) found that the succession of school principals did not significantly affect teachers' satisfaction or students' attitudes, several studies have exposed the negative and positive responses that organization members can have to succession. However, research provides little evidence of the impact that organization members' responses to succession have on organizational outcomes.

Negative Responses to Succession

Several studies reveal the dysfunctional effects that administrator succession can have on organizations. Administrator succession can disrupt organizational lines of communication, power relationships, decision-making processes, and the equilibrium of operations (Miskel & Cosgrove, 1985). Brown (1982) attributes the findings of some studies that the replacement of coaches negatively affects the performance of athletic teams to the disruptive effects of succession.

Two related types of organization members' responses to succession seem to be associated with diminished organizational performance. One is a general sense of disruption. Brown (1982) attributed findings that succession had a negative or no effect on athletic team performance to the disruption that accompanies the replacement of managers. Rosen (1969) employed a different term in drawing a similar conclusion about the effect of succession on the performance of production organizations. He suggested that succession upsets organizational "equilibrium" and thus negatively affects performance.

A second negative response to succession identified by research is conflict and tension. Five studies, one conducted in an elementary school, revealed this response among organization members. Studies of a maintenance team in a telephone company (Jackson, 1953), a mining crew (Gouldner, 1954), a laboratory experiment (Daum, 1975) and a psychiatric care unit (Oskarsson & Klein, 1982) all found that administrator succession resulted in subordinates experiencing stress and tension that resulted in unproductive behaviors. Ogawa's (1991) study of the succession of an elementary school principal echoed the results of these studies conducted in noneducational settings. He found that after a brief period during which teachers responded positively to the successor, most teachers grew insecure and mistrustful and retreated to the sanctuary of their classrooms.

Positive Responses to Succession

The picture painted by research of organization members' responses to administrator succession is not entirely bleak. Other studies have found instances in which organization members responded positively to administrator succession. Guest (1962), whose study seems forever linked with Gouldner's (1954) because the results of the two studies stand in such stark contrast, found that workers in an auto plant responded positively to the successor. A laboratory experiment (Goldman & Fraas, 1964) and a study of factory work groups (Rosen, 1969) revealed that under one particular circumstance, which will be discussed in the next section of this review, subordinates responded positively to the successor. Kunz and Hoy's (1976) study of school principals identified the same factor as producing a positive response of teachers toward successor principals.

In tracking backward from organizational performance to identify factors that may mediate the influence of administrator succession on performance, the findings of research suggest that the response of organization members to succession may be one link. Studies provide fairly clear evidence that organization members' responses to succession vary from experiencing the disruptiveness of conflict and stress to reacting positively to succession.

Impact of Subordinates'
Responses on Organizational Outcomes

Although research provides substantial evidence that organization members' responses to administrator succession can vary widely, it sheds little light on the relationship of these responses to organizational outcomes. Research provides little direct evidence of the impact of subordinates' responses to administrator succession on organizational performance. Brown (1982) speculated that the negative relationship between succession and the performance of athletic teams that was revealed by his research resulted from the disruption experienced by team members. Similarly, Rosen (1969) attributed downturns in performance associated with succession to a loss of organizational equilibrium. Both Gouldner (1954) and Guest (1962), whose studies of production organizations are cited above, linked subordinates' responses to succession to subsequent organizational performance. Gouldner found that subordinates' negative responses resulted in poorer performance; Guest concluded that subordinates' positive responses resulted in improved performance.

Research provides even less information about the relationship of subordinates' responses to succession to organizational change. One study, a comparative case study (Firestone, 1990) of two school districts undergoing successions of superintendents, examined the reaction of subordinates to successors' attempts to introduce organizational change. Although both successors initially met resistance from subordinates, they ultimately produced different types of changes. The differences were attributed to different dynamics within the two district organizations and to different circumstances in the districts' external environments.

Impact of Successor/Organization
Fit on the Response of Organization Members

The existence of evidence that organization members' responses to administrator succession vary and that there may be a link between these responses and organizational performance points to an obvious question: What accounts for differences in responses to succession? Research suggests that part of the answer lies in the relationship between successors and their organizations. Essentially, when there is a poor fit between successor and organization, organizational members tend to respond negatively; when the fit is good, organizational members tend to respond positively. More specifically, when successors fit their new organizations, disruption is minimized; when successors fail to adhere to organizational norms, conflict and tension rise; when successors behave in ways that reveal their concern and expertise, subordinates respond favorably.

Successors' Adherence to Organizational Norms

Several studies link the responses of subordinates to the fit between successors and organizations. They indicate that subordinates' responses may be based on the extent to which successors adhere to organizational norms. Two studies reveal that successors to administrative positions by and large adopt the norms and expectations of the organizational settings into which they move. Merei (1958) conducted an experiment using groups of nursery school children. He found that when an acknowledged leader was added to a group with established norms, the group absorbed the new leader, and the new leader adopted the group's norms. Lieberman (1956) similarly found in his study of production teams that new supervisors over time met the role expectations set by superordinates, peers, and subordinates.

Another set of studies describes the responses of subordinates to successors who fail to adopt organizational norms. Gouldner (1954) found that gypsum plant workers, who had come to believe that the plant should operate with the leniency to which they had grown accustomed under their former supervisor, experienced stress and tension when the successor enforced existing, formal rules. Similarly, Daum's (1975) laboratory experiment revealed that subordinates responded with anxiety when they perceived successors to be different from the group, and Oskarsson and Klein (1982) revealed that members of psychiatric care units became apprehensive when they discovered the existence of philosophical differences between themselves and new supervisors. Ogawa's (1991) study of the succession of a school principal showed that teachers grew insecure when they began to question the successor's commitment to the school, in part, because he was perceived to share little socially or economically with the school and, thus, with many members of its faculty. Jackson (1953) conducted a field experiment and found that telephone maintenance workers became disturbed when supervisors, who previously had remained with work teams for prolonged periods, were frequently rotated across teams. Although Jackson attributed the workers' distress to their attachment to the predecessor supervisor, Gordon and Rosen (1981) suggested that workers were troubled by their perception that a legitimate reason for the succession had not existed. That is, the succession itself violated a norm regarding what constituted an appropriate reason for replacing a supervisor. Jackson's attribution of attachment to the previous supervisor also begs the question of the impact that frequency of succession may have on subordinates' responses.

Two studies, one of the succession of a school principal, reveal the importance of the fit between administrator and organization from a different perspective. Gephart's (1978) study departed from conventional approaches to examining succession in two ways. First, he studied what happened before rather than after a succession occurred. Second, he studied himself being replaced as the president of a graduate student organization. Gephart revealed that members of the organization participated in rituals aimed at degrading his status as the incumbent president for not adhering to organizational norms and reinforced the norms by including them among the criteria for selecting a successor. Fauske and Ogawa (1987) studied the succession of an elementary school principal, in part, to extend Gephart's effort to develop a grounded theory of administrator succession. They concluded that teachers employed norms of their profession rather than norms of the school to criticize the incumbent principal and to set expectations for the successor. Although these studies examined presuccession events, they reinforce the importance of the fit between successors and, for that matter, predecessors and group norms in shaping organizational members' responses to administrator succession.

The findings of a single study suggest that the assessment of successor/organization fit may not always be as simple and direct a matter as earlier research would seem to indicate. Firestone's (1990) study of the succession of two school superintendents revealed that teachers

resisted the efforts of their new superintendents to implement districtwide changes. In other words, teachers countered successors' attempts to deviate from established district norms. However, in each
district, members of the board of education and an administrator who
oversaw the change program mediated the conflict between the superintendent and staff.

Although Firestone (1990) did not explicitly examine how board
members, administrators, and teachers assessed the fit between the
new superintendents and existing district norms, the finding that
various individuals and groups had different responses to superintendents' efforts to initiate change may be revealing. It suggests that different
stakeholders may make different assessments of successor/organization
fit and, thus, respond differently to administrator succession. Furthermore, it questions an implicit assumption that has guided succession
research: that organizations' responses to succession are framed by a
unity of norms and values. The presence of differing responses to
administrator succession across various groups of stakeholders suggests that organizations' overall responses to succession may reflect
the results of political contests between contending coalitions.

Influence of Successor Behavior on Subordinates' Responses to Succession

Research also suggests that two types of successors' behaviors are
associated with subordinates' responses to successors: showing concern for subordinates and exhibiting expertise. Both types of behavior
are related to the fit between successors and their organizations. By
exhibiting the former, successors integrate themselves into the human
system of organizations. By exhibiting the latter, they reveal their
ability to contribute to the completion of tasks and, ultimately, to the
attainment of organizational goals. Many readers probably recognize
that both showing concern for subordinates and exhibiting expertise
are behaviors that traditionally have been associated with leadership
(Yukl, 1989). This is no coincidence. As noted earlier, administration
and leadership are overlapping concepts. Thus descriptions of behaviors associated with one are often associated with the other.

Showing Concern. Two studies link subordinates' negative responses
to the failure of successors to show concern for subordinates. Daum's
(1975) laboratory experiment found that subordinates responded with
anxiety when successors were viewed as unfeeling and critical. In a
study of the succession of a principal, Ogawa (1991) discovered that

teachers initially responded positively to the successor's personable ways. However, most teachers drastically changed their assessment when they perceived the principal to be uncaring and insincere.

Studies also show that subordinates respond positively when successors show concern for subordinates. Guest (1962) revealed that the new supervisor in his case study of an automobile plant used informal contacts to learn about subordinates' needs. This, in part, explained subordinates' positive response to the successor. Rosen (1969) similarly found that factory work teams responded favorably to administrative successors who were pleasant in personal interactions. Rosen observed that this pleasantness was one means by which organizational equilibrium was restored after successions in administrative positions.

Expertise. Although research provides some evidence that subordinates respond favorably to successors who show concern, it provides even stronger evidence that subordinates respond positively to successors who exhibit behaviors that reveal expertise relevant to the operation of the organization. Both Guest (1962) and Rosen (1969), whose studies documented that subordinates respond positively when successors show consideration, document that it may be even more important for successors to demonstrate technical and administrative skills to gain the acceptance of subordinates. Three other studies, one conducted in schools, reinforce this point. Goldman and Fraas's (1964) laboratory experiment revealed that followers were more prone to accepting leaders who had established their ability to contribute to the completion of the group's task. Pfeffer and Davis-Blake (1986) supported the findings of previous research that the replacement of coaches did not affect the subsequent performance of athletic teams, when prior performance was controlled. However, when coaches' previous win-loss records were taken into account, succession significantly influenced subsequent team performance. That is, successful coaches tended to have a positive impact on their new teams' performance, whereas unsuccessful coaches tended to have a negative impact. In a study of principal succession, Kunz and Hoy (1976) found that task-related behaviors were more influential than behaviors showing consideration in gaining teachers' acceptance of successor principals.

To summarize, research on administrator succession reveals that organizational disruption and subordinates' responses to successors and thus to the succession are affected by the fit that exists between successors and organizations. There is fairly consistent evidence that successors tend to adopt the norms of their organizations and that such adjustments may contribute to their being received positively by subordinates. However, the bulk of the evidence is drawn from negative cases where successors failed to adhere to organizational norms and incurred the disapproval of subordinates. In addition, one study indicates that different individuals and groups may vary in their assessments of successor/organization fit, suggesting that organizations' overall responses to successors may be the product of political contests between contending coalitions. There is also significant evidence that successors gain the approval of subordinates by acting in ways that show their concern for subordinates and exhibit task-relevant expertise.

Conditions of the Succession Process

The possibility that certain behaviors of successors may affect how organization participants respond to succession raises yet another empirical question: What produces or is, at least, associated with those behaviors? Given the micro and macro traditions of social science, the answer to this question is likely to be sought in two sources: the successors themselves and the conditions under which successions occur. Although research is mute on the first source, it identifies two conditions of the succession process that appear to be associated with the tendency of successors to conform with organizational norms and to behave in ways that reveal task-related competence and concern for subordinates. Those conditions are the frequency of succession and the source of the successor.

Frequency of Succession

There is evidence, however scant, that the frequency with which organizations undergo administrative succession may both directly affect subordinates' responses to succession and affect the tendency for successors to exhibit behaviors that may be linked to subordinates' responses. Jackson (1953) conducted a field experiment and found that telephone maintenance workers became disturbed when supervisors, who previously had remained with work teams for prolonged periods, were frequently rotated across teams. As noted earlier, Jackson attributed the workers' distress to their attachment to the predecessor supervisor. However, subordinates' negative responses might also have been the product of the destabilizing effects of the high frequency of successions. Helmich (1974) found that when successions occurred frequently in the manufacturing plants he studied, successors tended to take an authoritarian and task-oriented approach to administration.

In light of research findings that subordinates tend to respond positively to successors who show concern for them, Helmich's finding suggests one possible factor accounting for subordinates' negative response to frequent succession.

Source of Successor

Research also suggests that the source of successors to administrative positions may directly affect both organizational performance and change as well as successors' behaviors. Successors may be drawn from two sources: inside the organization and outside the organization.

Research on the impact of the source of successors on organizational performance is scant. Allen et al. (1979) studied the effects of replacing coaches on athletic teams' performance. They found that teams that hired successors from the outside performed worse than teams that promoted from within. Birnbaum's (1971) study of the succession of college and university presidents offers indirect corroborating evidence. Birnbaum found that when colleges and universities hired presidents, they tended not to promote insiders but to recruit outsiders from similar institutions. The rationale for employing this strategy is that successors who have been socialized as administrators in similar institutions are more likely to fit their new institutions, much like insiders, and thus are less likely to be disruptive.

Other researchers have viewed the change sometimes introduced by administrative succession as being positive rather than disruptive. Several studies of administrative succession in school organizations reported that outsiders tended to initiate more change than insiders (Carlson, 1961; Ganz & Hoy, 1977; Hoy & Aho, 1973; Knedlik, 1968). One study offers a qualification to this apparently general finding. Reynolds (1966) found that although outsiders initially made more changes than insiders, insiders increased the amount of change they implemented over the first few years of their tenures.

Evidence, although limited to the findings of a single study, suggests that the source of successors may affect their tendency to exhibit a type of behavior that is associated with positive responses of subordinates to succession. Ganz and Hoy (1977) studied the succession of secondary school principals. They found that outsiders tended to be less authoritarian and expressed greater emotional attachment than insiders. As previously noted, some research suggests that subordinates respond positively to successors who show concern for the personal well-being of subordinates.

To summarize, although relevant findings are scarce, some research identifies two conditions of succession that may be associated with the impact of succession on organizational performance and change and with behaviors on the part of successors that affect subordinates' responses to succession. Frequent successions may evoke negative responses from subordinates and may contribute to successors' adopting a task-oriented approach to their new positions. Successors recruited from the outside may negatively affect their new organizations' performance. However, they also may introduce more change and express greater emotional attachment for subordinates.

Antecedents to Administrator Succession

We now come to the end of the empirical trail that has led backward from organizational outcomes that have been associated with administrator succession through three types of factors that may mediate that relationship: the responses of organizational participants, factors that may affect participants' responses, and conditions of the succession process. The final stop concerns factors that are exogenous to succession itself, but might affect the conditions of succession that may be associated with organization participants' responses to succession. Studies provide some evidence that three antecedents to administrator succession—organization size, organization performance, and environmental conditions—affect the frequency of succession or the source of successor or both. In addition, one of the antecedents—environmental conditions—may affect the nature of organizational changes initiated by successors.

Organization Size

Research provides mixed evidence on the relationship of the size of organizations to the frequency of administrator succession. Both Grusky's (1961) and Kriesberg's (1962) studies found that the size of corporations in their samples was positively associated with the frequency of administrator succession. However, Gordon and Becker (1964) revealed that the relationship of organization size and rate of succession was much less clear. Holding age of executive, compensation rates and other factors constant, they found no clear relationship between size of organization and succession rate. Although no research has explicitly examined the relationship between school or district size and frequency of administrator succession, one study provides indirect evidence. Berger's (1983) study of superintendent succession revealed that per pupil expenditure, which tends to covary with district size, was positively related to the frequency with which superintendents were replaced.

Organization Performance

Research also provides mixed evidence concerning the relationship of organization performance to frequency of succession and source of successor. Grusky (1963) took the initial step in identifying another organizational antecedent of the frequency of administrator succession: performance. He found that the prior records of athletic teams were negatively associated with the rates at which coaches were replaced. That is, teams that won more replaced coaches less often. However, Gamson and Scotch (1964) countered that replacing coaches was "ritual scapegoating" and that teams' records did not cause the frequency with which coaches were replaced nor did the frequency of replacement cause teams' records. Allen et al. (1979) extended Grusky's and Gamson and Scotch's work by examining the succession of managers of major league baseball teams. They concluded that, indeed, team performance was negatively related to frequency of succession.

Organization performance may also be associated with the tendency of organizations to hire from the outside when replacing administrators. Carlson (1961) found that school districts tended to hire outsider superintendents when districts' performance was unsatisfactory.

Environmental Conditions

Research on the succession of school superintendents provides some indication that the actions of individuals and organizations in school districts' external environments can affect at least two aspects of administrator succession: the selection of successors and the nature of organizational change initiated by successors.

Two studies indicate that the sentiments of local electorates can influence the choice of successors. Freeborn (1967) and Iannaconne and Lutz (1970) concluded that the selection of an outsider to fill the position of superintendent was more likely following the defeat of incumbent school board members.

A single study demonstrates that the policy environments in which school districts operate can influence the direction of organizational change initiated by administrative successors. Firestone's (1990) case studies of the succession of two superintendents found that state educational policies shaped both superintendents' initiatives to enhance the professionalism of their districts' teachers.

Thus research provides limited evidence concerning the relationship of antecedents to succession that are associated with frequency of succession or source of successors or both. It appears that the size of organizations, including school districts, may be positively associated with frequency of administrator succession, although the evidence is equivocal. There is clearer evidence that organizations' previous performance is negatively related to succession rates. With regard to source of successors, research on the succession of district superintendents tentatively suggests that districts tend to hire outsiders when district performance is deemed unsatisfactory, particularly when incumbent boards of education are defeated. Finally, a single study demonstrates that the policy environments in which districts operate can influence the nature of organizational change initiated by administrative successors.

Summary and Conclusions: Mapping the Empirical Terrain

A map of the overall empirical terrain of administrator succession summarizes and combines the reviews of research on specific succession factors (see Figure 10.1). The map traces linkages that connect factors and that may, together, connect succession to organizational outcomes. Thus the map provides an initial step toward explaining the inconsistency of research findings on the influence of succession on organizational outcomes. The map reveals which linkages have been verified, even equivocally, by past research and which remain to be examined by future research.

Summary

The map begins with antecedents to administrative succession (the first set of mediating factors). Research indicates that antecedents to succession, namely, organization size, organization performance, and environmental factors, can affect conditions of succession (the second set of mediating factors) and that the last of these antecedents might be linked to organizational change. Some evidence suggests that organization size is positively associated with the frequency of succession (Berger, 1983; Grusky, 1961; Kriesberg, 1962). Although one study offers a dissenting voice (Gamson & Scotch, 1964), evidence also indicates that organization performance is negatively associated with frequency of succession (Allen et al., 1979; Grusky, 1963). Organization performance also has been documented to affect the source of the

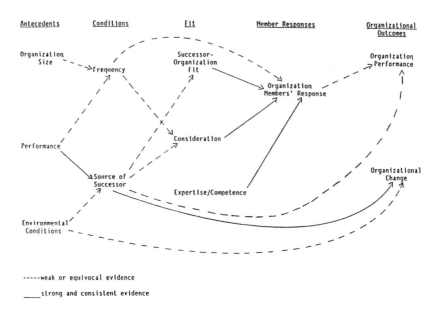

FIGURE 10.1. Empirical Map of Research Findings on Administrator Succession

successor. Research, all of which was conducted in school districts, consistently indicates that poor performance is associated with the selection of successors from the outside (Carlson, 1961), particularly when incumbent school boards are defeated (Freeborn, 1967; Iannaconne & Lutz, 1970). One study (Firestone, 1990) suggests that the policies set by legislative bodies in organizations' environments may influence the nature of organizational changes that successors initiate.

Research reveals that two conditions of succession—frequency of succession and source of successor—may affect successor/organization fit (the third set of mediating factors), affect subordinates' responses to succession (the fourth set of mediating factors), and directly influence organizational outcomes. Research on the effects of frequency of succession are sparse. One study (Helmich, 1974) indicates that frequent successions contribute to successors' adopting an authoritarian and task-oriented management style. Another study (Jackson, 1953) suggests that subordinates respond negatively to frequent successions. Research has not examined the relationship between frequency of succession and either successor/organization fit or the tendency for successors to exhibit task-relevant expertise.

The weight of the evidence on the impact of the source of successors is more abundant but uneven. A single study (Ganz & Hoy, 1977) reveals that outsider successors are less likely than insiders to be authoritarian and more likely to show emotional attachment. Another study (Birnbaum, 1971) provides indirect evidence that outsider successors fit their new organizations less well than do insider successors. A third study (Allen et al., 1979) suggests that organizations perform less well under outsiders. Several studies (Carlson, 1961; Ganz & Hoy, 1977; Hoy & Aho, 1973; Knedlik, 1968) consistently indicate that outsiders tend to introduce more change to organizations. One study (Reynolds, 1966) offers an important qualification: Over time, insiders slowly increase the number of changes that they introduce. There is no empirical evidence on the relationship between source of successor and the tendency for successors to possess task-relevant expertise.

A fair amount of research documents the relationship between successor/organization fit, including two specific types of behavior that contribute to this fit, and the responses of organization members to administrator succession. Two early studies (Lieberman, 1956; Merei, 1958) illustrate the tendency of successors to adopt the norms of their new groups or organizations. Several studies (Daum, 1975; Gouldner, 1954; Ogawa, 1991; Oskarsson & Klein, 1982) reveal the tendency of subordinates to respond negatively to successors who fail to adhere to organizational norms. Moreover, two studies (Fauske & Ogawa, 1987; Gephart, 1978) indicate that organization members invoke group norms to criticize predecessors and to select or set expectations for successors. However, one study (Firestone, 1990) suggests that different groups may assess successor/organization fit differently and, thus, that overall organizational responses to succession may be the product of political contests between coalitions.

Research also consistently documents that subordinates respond favorably to successors who show them consideration and exhibit task-relevant expertise. Two studies (Daum, 1975; Ogawa, 1991) suggest that subordinates react negatively to administrative successors who fail to show concern; three other studies (Guest, 1962; Kunz & Hoy, 1976; Rosen, 1969) suggest that subordinates react positively to successors who show concern. Several studies (Goldman & Fraas, 1964; Guest, 1962; Kunz & Hoy, 1976; Rosen, 1969) document the favorable response of subordinates to successors who exhibit their ability to contribute to task accomplishment and goal attainment. In addition, three of those studies (Guest, 1962; Kunz & Hoy, 1976; Rosen, 1969) indicate that subordinates are positively swayed more by successors' expertise than their show of consideration. These findings are reinforced by the findings of a study (Pfeffer & Davis-Blake, 1986) that indicates that successors' competence is directly and positively linked to organizational performance.

Finally, there is little direct evidence concerning what is arguably the most important link in the empirical chain—the one that connects organization members' responses to succession and two organizational outcomes: change and performance. There is a bit more evidence on the impact of succession on organizational performance than on the impact of succession on organizational change. Two studies (Brown, 1982; Rosen, 1969) interpret the negative effects of succession on performance as resulting from the disruption and loss of equilibrium experienced by organization members. A comparison of the findings of two often-cited studies further suggests that subordinates' responses to succession can affect organizational performance. Gouldner (1954) found that workers' negative responses contributed to a loss of productivity; Guest (1962) found that workers' positive responses contributed to an increase of productivity.

A single comparative case study of two school districts (Firestone, 1990) focuses on the relationship of subordinates' responses to succession and the implementation of organizational change. That study explains that subordinates initially resisted the attempts of both successors to institute change. However, the two successors ultimately produced different types of change due to both different political dynamics in the two districts and different circumstances in the districts' external environments.

Conclusions

What can be concluded from this review of research on administrator succession? The first and most general answer is that little is really known about administrator succession, its effects on organizations, and the factors that may color those effects. This is due to several limitations of the research that has been conducted on the subject. One limitation of the research is that there is little of it. There are relatively few studies of administrator succession in general and even fewer studies of administrator succession in school organizations in particular. A second limitation is that many of the studies are single or comparative case studies or cross-sectional, correlational studies. Both types of research can be revealing; neither provides conclusive evidence that any particular factor associated with succession causes another factor, let alone that succession affects organizational outcomes. A third limitation is that studies of administrator succession have not taken a comprehensive view of the subject. All of the studies reviewed here focused on one or a small handful of factors associated with succession; none has examined the relationships among a broad set of factors. Taken together, these limitations make it difficult, if not impossible, to draw conclusions about administrator succession with any degree of confidence.

Despite the limitations of the research base on administrator succession, the literature review seems to warrant a few conclusions, albeit tentative ones. The empirical map produced by this literature review sheds a diffuse light on some factors that may affect the overall relationship between administrator succession and organizational outcomes. It also reveals specific relationships that are relatively well documented as well as those that remain in complete empirical darkness.

A General Pattern. The empirical map reveals a set of relationships among succession factors that may explain the persistence of problems that plague some school organizations. It appears that both large organizations and those that perform poorly tend to replace administrators relatively frequently. Moreover, organizations that perform poorly tend to select administrator successors from the outside. This combination may have dire consequences, for several reasons. First, high frequency of succession is linked with the tendency of successors to take an authoritarian administrative style, a style that tends to produce negative responses from subordinates. Although outsider successors are more likely to show consideration (a behavior that may endear successors to subordinates), they also are less likely to fit the existing norms of their new organizations and are more likely to institute changes. There is consistent and fairly strong evidence that organization members respond negatively to successors who do not adhere to existing norms. Although research has not clearly documented the link between organization members' responses to succession and organizational performance, this series of factors may begin to explain why poorly performing organizations tend to continue to perform poorly and why organizations tend to perform poorly under administrator successors from the outside.

Well-Documented Relationships. The empirical map reveals a set of relationships that are relatively well documented by research. At the core of these relationships is the response of organization members, especially subordinates, to administrator succession. Strong evidence links subordinates' responses to two factors. First, the extent to which successors adhere to organizational norms is positively related to subordinates' responses to the successor. That is, successors who adhere to norms are well received; successors who do not are not. Second, two types of behavior are also positively related to subordinates' responses to successors. Successors who show consideration for subordinates tend to be accepted by subordinates. Similarly, successors who demonstrate task-relevant expertise, or competence, tend to be accepted by subordinates. In fact, successors' competence may be more important than consideration in gaining subordinates' acceptance. The importance of successors' competence is underscored by the positive relationship that one study (Pfeffer & Davis-Blake, 1986) uncovered between successors' competence and organizational performance.

Gaps in the Research. The empirical map also exposes several gaps in the research on administrator succession. That is, some links between types of factors associated with succession have yet to be examined by research. Beginning with antecedents to succession, research has not plumbed the relationship between size of organizations and source of successors. Moving to the conditions of succession, there is no research on the relationship of frequency of succession to successor/organization fit or the competence of successors. Nor are there studies on the relationship of source of successor to the tendency for successors to exhibit task-relevant expertise. In terms of organization members' responses to succession, research provides little direct evidence on the relationship between that set of factors and organizational outcomes, including both performance and change.

Finally, although research has treated organizational performance and change as separate outcomes of administrator succession, it has not examined their possible relationship. This review of research reveals that organizations may operate under a questionable assumption: that change improves performance. Research indicates that organizations tend to replace administrators with outsiders to improve sagging performance and that outsiders tend to introduce organizational change. However, research also indicates that organizations perform less well with outsider successors than with insider successors, calling into question the assumption that change improves performance. That is a question that has escaped the attention of researchers.

Implications Derived From the Literature Review

The inconclusive and spotty nature of research on administrator succession makes it difficult if not risky to draw clear-cut implications for policymakers and practitioners. However, these same qualities make it relatively easy to derive implications for future research.

Implications for Policy and Practice

The findings of research on the relationship of factors associated with administrator succession for the most part remain inconclusive. However, tentative implications can be drawn for both school boards and administrative successors.

School Boards

The research on administrator succession raises several issues that school districts' boards of education would be wise to ponder when considering both the general problem of replacing administrators to enhance district and school performance and the more specific strategy of replacing administrators to encourage the adoption and implementation of reform.

The findings of research have several implications for how boards of education approach the general problem of replacing administrators. The first concerns large districts. Research suggests that large districts may be prone to frequently replacing administrators. This is a highly questionable strategy; when administrators are frequently replaced, organizational performance is negatively affected. Moreover, successors in organizations that frequently replace administrators tend not to behave in ways that express consideration for subordinates, evoking negative responses from subordinates and, thus, jeopardizing organizational performance.

Second, school districts often replace administrators when district or school performance is deemed unsatisfactory. However, research suggests that this strategy may backfire; several studies indicate that school boards, in seeking to improve the lagging performance of their districts or schools, are likely to select outsiders to replace incumbents. This may not have the intended effects, because outsiders may not conform to existing organizational norms and, thus, cause disruption and conflict, resulting in deteriorated rather than improved performance.

Third, many school districts routinely rotate principals. This apparently is done because it is believed that by rotating principals, both principals and schools will not become stagnant. There is no evidence in the research on administrative succession to support this practice. In fact, as noted above, some evidence suggests that highly frequent succession negatively affects organizational performance and is related to the tendency of successors to engage in behaviors that evoke negative responses from subordinates.

Finally, the findings of research on administrator succession reinforce the importance of two criteria in selecting and appointing administrators. Research reveals that successors who manifest two skills can evoke positive responses from subordinates. The important skills are (a) showing consideration for subordinates and (b) demonstrating task-related expertise, or competence. Of the two, research indicates that expertise is more important. In addition, it may be particularly important to document the consideration of in-house candidates for administrative posts, because one study indicates that insiders may be more authoritarian and less likely to show emotional attachment to subordinates.

Research on administrator succession also has implications for school districts that contemplate replacing administrators with the specific intention of effecting reform. Research reveals that the appointment of outsider successors to pursue reform may involve a trade-off. On the one hand, outsider successors are more prone to introduce change, suggesting that superintendents who are hired from outside the district or principals who are new to a school are more likely to aggressively pursue reform efforts. On the other hand, outsiders are also less likely to conform to existing norms and, thus, are more likely to be met by negative responses from subordinates. Thus boards of education and top-level district administrators must carefully assess local conditions and weigh the urgency of pursuing reform against the need to maintain positive staff relations.

Research also indicates that the positive effects of change introduced by successors may not be immediately realized. In fact, changes instituted by the successor may initially have a negative impact. Three specific findings shed light on why this may be so: (a) Successors can upset organizational equilibrium, which can negatively affect performance; (b) subordinates who initially resist changes introduced by successors may later accept them; and (c) the overall response of organizations to successors may be the result of political contests between coalitions, because different groups' reactions to successors vary. This set of findings suggests that school boards should make explicit, sustained commitments to reform and to the administrators to whom they entrust its implementation. This would provide successors with the time to overcome resistance to reform and establish a new organizational equilibrium. The board's commitment would also provide successors with a valuable resource on which they could rely in swaying the political interests of coalitions in their districts or schools.

Boards should also provide successors with resources, financial and otherwise, to fuel reform. These resources would provide successors with both the means to implement reform and resources to ply their influence in shaping successful political coalitions.

Administrative Successors

Research also has several implications for individuals who find themselves as successors in administrative positions in school districts and schools. First, administrative successors, particularly those who are given a mandate to improve organizational performance, must be realistic about the difficulty and complexity of turning around an organization. Research does not provide clear evidence that successors can quickly or substantially have an impact on organizational performance. In fact, research indicates that organizations that have performed poorly in the past are likely to continue to do so, even after the introduction of a new administrator.

Second, successors, even those who hope to change their organizations, must be aware of the importance of conforming to existing norms. Research indicates that successors who are perceived as not fitting in tend to be dismissed by subordinates, thus losing the chance to affect their organizations. Outsider successors should be especially conscious of the need to comply with the norms of their new organizations, because research suggests that outsiders are prone to deviating from existing norms and, thus, run the risk of alienating other organization members.

Third, successors should keep in mind that research indicates that subordinates tend to respond favorably to successors who exhibit consideration and task-relevant expertise, with an emphasis on the latter. Insider successors should pay particular attention to showing consideration, because one study suggests that insiders may be prone to exhibiting authoritarian behaviors, which can alienate subordinates.

Implications for Research

As noted earlier, research on administrator succession leaves a number of specific questions unanswered and suffers from more general limitations. These unanswered questions and limitations suggest future directions for research. At least four implications for designing future studies of administrator succession can be drawn from the findings of this literature review.

The Need for Research

First, research simply should be conducted. As already noted, few studies of administrator succession have been undertaken in schools and school districts. The impending, wholesale replacement of school administrators offers both a rationale and opportunity to study succession.

Unanswered Questions

Second, this review of research revealed several specific questions that remain unanswered and, thus, might guide future studies. These questions concern the following relationships between factors associated with administrator succession: size of organization and source of successor; frequency of succession and successor/organization fit; frequency of succession and the tendency of successors to exhibit task-relevant expertise; source of successor and the tendency of successors to exhibit task-relevant expertise; organization members' responses to succession and organizational outcomes, including change and performance; and organizational change and organizational performance.

Complex Conceptualizations

Third, research should reflect more complex and comprehensive conceptualizations of administrator succession. Most studies of succession have focused on unidirectional relationships among a small number of succession factors. More adequate conceptualizations might include multiple succession factors, interactive effects among factors, or alternative theoretical perspectives.

Multiple Succession Factors. The empirical map derived from this literature review suggests that numerous factors may be associated with succession and its outcomes. Thus research should employ more comprehensive models of succession to assess the relative impact of several factors in mediating the effect of administrator succession on organizational outcomes.

Interactive Effects. Although Figure 10.1 may represent a reasonable starting point for the development of more complex models of administrative succession, it does not incorporate a potentially important element: the possible interactive effects among succession factors. For example, studies have documented that administrative successors initiate organizational change. However, no attention has been given to the possibility that organizations may change, precipitating the removal and replacement of incumbent administrators. Other plausible interactive effects may exist between factors that research has treated and, thus, Figure 10.1 depicts as having unidirectional relationships.

Alternative Theoretical Perspectives. Researchers who study administrative succession might adopt theoretical perspectives other than those that have directed previous research. For example, several studies indicate that organization members' responses to administrative successors can be colored by the members' assessment of the fit between successors' actions and organizational norms. This research implicitly assumes that organizations are characterized by a unity of norms and values. However, several scholars have argued convincingly that organizations, including schools and school districts, are political systems (Bacharach & Lawler, 1980; Pfeffer, 1981). From this political view, organizations are composed of shifting coalitions, and organizational goals and structures reflect the results of political contests among coalitions. Similarly, existing research focuses primarily on intraorganizational succession factors, such as size, frequency of succession, organizational norms, and organization members' responses. This ignores the widely accepted view that organizations are open systems and, thus, are strongly affected by forces in their external environments.

Sophisticated Research Designs

Fourth, researchers should move toward employing more sophisticated designs in their studies of administrative succession. Most existing studies use single case study and cross-sectional correlational designs. Although studies employing these designs can be revealing, they cannot unravel the complex relations among the numerous factors assumed to be associated with and produced by administrator succession. To examine more complex models of administrator succession, researchers could employ two general approaches. On the one hand, researchers could embark on a series of comparative case studies. Cases could be selected to provide variation on factors included in Figure 10.1. For example, case studies could be conducted in large and small districts or schools, in high-performing and low-performing districts or schools, and so on. On the other hand, researchers could employ various methods of statistical analysis, such as path analysis, to test causal models that incorporate the factors identified in Figure 10.1. For such quantitative examinations of administrator succession to be feasible, a number of difficult issues would first have to be addressed. For example, researchers would have to develop adequate measures for many of the factors associated with succession, such as successor/organization fit. Researchers would also have to collect data in several phases because the relations of many factors would occur over time. Thus, as already recommended by others (Gorden & Rosen, 1981; Miskel & Cosgrove, 1985), researchers must employ longitudinal designs to capture the temporal relations among succession factors.

Note

1. Studies that employ administrator succession to assess the influence of administrators on organizational performance are often treated as studies of the influence of leadership. As noted in the text, the distinction between leadership and administration is ambiguous, and leadership is the topic of the chapter by Bolman and Heller found in Chapter 9.

References

Allen, M., Panian, S., & Lotz, R. (1979). Managerial succession and organizational performance: A recalcitrant problem revisited. *Administrative Science Quarterly, 24,* 167-180.

Bacharach, S. B., & Lawler, E. J. (1980). *Power and politics in organizations.* San Francisco: Jossey-Bass.

Barnard, C. I. (1938). *Functions of the executive.* Cambridge, MA: Harvard University Press.

Bennis, W., & Nanus, B. (1985). *Leaders: The strategies for taking charge.* New York: Harper & Row.

Berger, M. A. (1983, April). *Predicting succession under conditions of enrollment decline.* Paper presented at the annual meeting of the American Educational Research Association, Montreal, Quebec, Canada.

Birnbaum, R. (1971). Presidential succession: An inter-institutional analysis. *Educational Record,* pp. 133-145.

Brown, M. C. (1982). Administrative succession and organizational performance: The succession effect. *Administrative Science Quarterly, 27,* 1-16.

Carlson, R. O. (1961). Succession and performance among school superintendents. *Administrative Science Quarterly, 6,* 210-227.

Daum, J. (1975). Internal promotion—A psychological asset or debit. *Organizational Behavior and Human Performance, 13,* 404-473.

Eitzen, D. S., & Yetman, N. (1972). Managerial change, longevity, and organizational effectiveness. *Administrative Science Quarterly, 17,* 110-116.

Fauske, J. R., & Ogawa, R. T. (1987). Detachment, fear, and expectation: A faculty's response to the impending succession of its principal. *Educational Administration Quarterly, 23,* 23-44.

Firestone, W. A. (1990). Succession and bureaucracy: Gouldner revisited. *Educational Administration Quarterly, 26,* 345-375.

Freeborn, R. M. (1967). School board change and the succession pattern of superintendents. *Dissertation Abstracts International, 28,* 424A.

Gamson, W. A., & Scotch, N. A. (1964). Scapegoating in baseball. *American Journal of Sociology, 70,* 69-72.

Ganz, H. J., & Hoy, W. K. (1977). Patterns of succession of elementary principals and organizational change. *Planning and Changing, 8,* 185-196.

Gephart, R. (1978). Status degradation and organization succession. *Administrative Science Quarterly, 23,* 553-581.

Goldman, M., & Fraas, L. (1964). The effects of leadership selection on group performance. *Sociometry, 28,* 82-88.

Gordon, G., & Becker, S. (1964). Organization size and managerial succession: A reexamination. *American Journal of Sociology, 70,* 215-222.

Gordon, G. E., & Rosen, N. (1981). Critical factors in leader succession. *Organizational Behavior and Human Performance, 27,* 227-254.

Gouldner, A. (1954). *Patterns of industrial bureaucracy.* Glencoe, IL: Free Press.

Grusky, O. (1961). Corporate size, bureaucratization and managerial succession. *American Journal of Sociology, 67,* 261-269.

Grusky, O. (1963). Managerial succession and organization effectiveness. *American Journal of Sociology, 69,* 21-31, 72-76.

Guest, R. H. (1962). Managerial succession in complex organizations. *American Journal of Sociology, 68,* 47-54.

Hart, A. W., & Ogawa, R. T. (1987). The influence of superintendents on the academic achievement of school districts. *Journal of Educational Administration, 25,* 72-84.

Helmich, D. L. (1974). Executive succession in the corporate organization: A current integration. *Academy of Management Review, 2,* 252-266.

Hoy, W. K., & Aho, F. (1973). Patterns of succession of high school principals and organizational change. *Planning and Changing, 4,* 82-88.

Iannaconne, L., & Lutz, F. W. (1970). *Politics, power and policy: The governing of local school districts.* Columbus, OH: Charles E. Merrill.

Jackson, J. M. (1953). The effect of changing the leadership of small work groups. *Human Relations, 6,* 25-44.

Katz, D., & Kahn, R. L. (1978). *The social psychology of organizations* (2nd ed.). New York: John Wiley.

Keith, P. M. (1975). Administrative and faculty turnover and diffusion of an educational innovation. *Urban Education, 10,* 297-304.

Knedlik, S. M. (1968). The effect of administrative succession pattern upon educational innovation in selected secondary schools. *Dissertation Abstracts International, 28,* 4415A.

Kriesberg, L. (1962). Careers, organization size, and succession. *American Journal of Sociology, 68,* 355-359.

Kunz, D., & Hoy, W. K. (1976). Leader behavior of principals and the professional zone of acceptance of teachers. *Educational Administration Quarterly, 12,* 49-64.

Lieberman, S. (1956). The effects of changes in roles on the attitudes of role occupants. *Human Relations, 9,* 385-402.

Lieberson, S., & O'Connor, J. (1972). Leadership and organizational performance: A study of large corporations. *American Sociological Review, 37,* 117-130.

Merei, F. (1958). Group leadership and institutionalization. In E. Maccoby, T. Newcomb, & E. Hartley (Eds.), *Readings in social psychology* (3rd ed., pp. 522-532). New York: Holt, Rinehart & Winston.

Miklos, E. (1989). Administrator selection, career patterns, succession, and socialization. In N. J. Boyan (Ed.), *Handbook of research on educational administration* (pp. 53-76). New York: Longman.

Miskel, C., & Cosgrove, D. (1985). Leader succession in school settings. *Review of Educational Research, 55,* 87-105.

Miskel, C. G., & Owens, M. (1983, April). *Principal succession and changes in school coupling and effectiveness.* Paper presented at the annual meeting of the American Educational Research Association, Montreal, Quebec, Canada.

Murphy, J. (1991). *Restructuring schools: Capturing and assessing the phenomena.* New York: Teachers College Press.

Ogawa, R. T. (1991). Enchantment, disenchantment, and accommodation: How a faculty made sense of the succession of its principal. *Educational Administration Quarterly, 27,* 30-60.

Ogawa, R. T., & Hart, A. W. (1985). The effect of principals on the instructional performance of schools. *Journal of Educational Administration, 23,* 59-72.

Oskarsson, H., & Klein, R. H. (1982). Leadership change and organizational regression. *International Journal of Group Psychotherapy, 32,* 145-162.

Pfeffer, J. (1981). *Power in organizations.* Marshfield, MA: Pitman.

Pfeffer, J., & Davis-Blake, A. (1986). Administrative succession and organizational performance: How administrator experience mediates the succession effect. *Academy of Management Journal, 29,* 72-83.

Reynolds, J. A. (1966). Innovation related to administrative tenure, succession and orientation: A study of the adoption of new perspectives by school systems. *Dissertation Abstracts International, 26,* 2946A.

Rosen, N. (1969). *Leadership change and work-group dynamics.* Ithaca, NY: Cornell University Press.

Rowan, B., & Denk, C. (1984). Management succession, school socioeconomic context, and basic skills attainment. *American Educational Research Journal, 21,* 517-537.

Salancik, G. R., & Pfeffer, J. (1977). Constraints on administrative discretion. *Urban Affairs Quarterly, 12,* 475-496.

Selznick, P. (1957). *Leadership in administration.* Berkeley: University of California Press.

Weiner, N., & Mahoney, T. A. (1979). A model of corporate performance as a function of environmental, organizational and leadership influences. *Academy of Management Journal, 24,* 453-470.

Yukl, G. A. (1989). *Leadership in organizations* (2nd ed.). Englewood Cliffs, NJ: Prentice Hall.

The Implicit
Action Beneath
Explicit Organizing Models

SAMUEL B. BACHARACH
BRYAN MUNDELL

The ten chapters in this book exhibit the diversity of possibilities by which general theories of organizational behavior can be applied to a specific empirical setting—school organizations. Some of the chapters are descriptive, aiming to use the language of organizational behavior to describe schools as they really exist; some of the chapters are prescriptive, aiming to show how schools could and ought to look like; some are both prescriptive and descriptive.

Each of the four chapters in Part I presents a different answer to the question of what must be organized in schools to make them better organizations. Rowan suggests that it is structure. Kerchner and Caufman argue that it is decision making. Rait suggests that it is the organization's capacity to learn. Deal claims that it is a school's culture.

The first three chapters in Part II focus on what must be organized in schools to improve the role of the teachers who work in them. Hart makes a fundamental argument, arguing that what needs to be reorganized is the actual work of the teacher. Mitchell argues that it is goals and resources. Sykes and Millman suggest that it is evaluation methods. In the next three chapters, the focus shifts to what must be organized in schools to improve the role of the administrators. Goldring suggests that the role of administrator needs to be organized around managing the boundary between the school and the environment. Bolman and Heller suggest that it be organized to provide better leadership. Ogawa uses research findings to describe how the process of fitting a specific individual to the role of administrator of a specific school can be more effectively organized.

Whether about organizing on an organizational level or a role level, each of the chapters in this book is concerned with the actions taken by certain actors and the effects of those actions on other actors in the school. In other words, beneath all these perspectives aimed at solving the problems of our educational system, there are hidden agendas of action implying how actors on different levels will affect each other. In that context, this conclusion is organized around two dimensions—the first dimension corresponding to the answer to the question of *who initiates action in school organizations* and the second dimension corresponding to the answer to the question of *how action is initiated within school organizations.*

These dynamics are either explicit or implicit in the preceding chapters and can be made more apparent by a discussion of the perspective adopted by each author. In other words, each author either explicitly or implicitly analyzes the decisions or actions in terms of three components: initiating actors, actions, and the object of action. The relationships between these components are summarized in Table 11.1.

Note that because Rowan's essay is an explicit comparison of two general organizational models, we have categorized each of his models separately. Table 11.1 is divided according to each author's answer to the question of who initiates action in school organizations—external forces, the school organization itself, managers, or teachers. A quick comparison between Table 11.1 and the table of contents reveals some commonalities, but also some significant differences between the level of analysis at which the chapters are generally focused and the authors' assumptions about who initiates the actions that occur in school organizations.

At the organizational level of analysis (Part I of this book), the Deal essay is based on the assumption that school organizations are self-sustaining cultures beyond the control of individual members. Thus his chapter is placed in the top category of Table 11.1, wherein action is initiated by external actors and/or the organization itself. Although Kerchner and Caufman's essay was placed in the first (organizational) part of this book, it is structured around a typology that covers all types

TABLE 11.1 Action Perspective of Each Chapter

Author	Initiating Actor	Object of Action	Action
Ogawa	School board	Managers	Succession process
Sykes and Millman	Society	Teachers	Testing students for learning
Deal	Organization	Organization	Creating cultural meaning for members
Goldring	Managers	Environment	Organization-environment mediation
Rowan_mechanistic	Managers	Teachers	Command control bureaucracy
Mitchell	Managers	Teachers	Improving the work environment
Bolman and Heller	Managers	Teachers	Situation-contingent leadership service
Rait	Teachers	Organization	Double-loop learning
Rowan_organic	Teachers	Organization	Participative management
Hart	Teachers	Organization	Work redesign
Kerchner and Caufman	All levels	All levels	Decision framing

of decision-making actors—external interests, the organization itself, managers, and teachers—and so is placed at the bottom of Table 11.1 as a separate category.

Although Rait's model and Rowan's two models are also all at the organizational level of analysis (Part I of this book), they can be differentiated according to who the actors are: The mechanistic model described by Rowan is based on the assumption that managers act on teachers, and the organic model described by Rowan as well as the model of organizational learning proposed by Rait are based on the assumption that teachers (and to a lesser extent, managers) act to create and develop a learning organization.

Of the six essays in Part II, only Hart's focuses primarily on the actions taken by teachers. Mitchell focuses on actions that managers can take to improve the work environment of teachers to improve their performance. Sykes and Millman focus on whether and under what conditions it is worthwhile for us as a society to control teachers by assessing them according to measures of their students' achievement.

Of the three chapters in Part II that focus on the role of school administrator, both the Bolman and Heller essay and the Goldring essay focus on managers as key actors. Thus they are placed in the same category in Table 11.1. On the other hand, the Ogawa essay is focused on managers as objects of organizational action, rather than as key actors—instead, Ogawa discusses how organizations can understand the process and outcomes of management succession as determined by the organizational context.

The second dimension of our typology corresponds to the answer that our contributors offer to the question of how action is initiated within school organizations. In line with Bolman and Heller's (Chapter 9) suggestion that leaders be politicians, diagnosticians, and visionaries, we offer three types of means by which individual decisions and actions can be organized within the school organization: *democratic or political processes, rational or technical decisions,* and *cultural or normative forces.*

Democratic or political processes are the first type of means by which some actors initiate or organize the actions of others in school organizations. An actor's ability to effectively use political tactics to get something from the democratic process depends on the extent of other actors' dependence on the first actor for something. Managing that dependence so that there is a balance between access to resources and operational autonomy (i.e., *in*dependence) is the focus of Goldring's analysis (Chapter 8) of the role of boundary spanners in school organizations. She describes how boundary spanners mediate between the operational needs of the organization and the political demands coming from groups in the environment that provide the organization with needed resources.

Kerchner and Caufman's discussion (Chapter 2) of schools as decision-making arenas covers not only school actions defending themselves from groups in the environment but the external groups' attempts to influence school policies through political action. Their typology describes external groups (bomb-throwers, pressure groups, and the public good) as well as internal groups fighting for their vested interests (e.g., teachers' unions during strikes).

Alternatively, actors can initiate or organize actions within school organizations by rational or technical processes. These require the assumption of rational behavior by members of school organizations. Rowan's mechanistic model of organizational structure (Chapter 1) is the purest example in this book, with teachers rigidly controlled by managers through the use of rules imposed by managers who are higher up in the hierarchical chain of command. Mitchell (Chapter 6) also describes how managers control the behavior of teachers for rational purposes.

However, for Mitchell, effective managers motivate teachers to higher levels of performance indirectly, by setting clear goals, linking individual behaviors to desired incentives, and improving the work context so as to facilitate the desired behaviors. Sykes and Millman's program (Chapter 7) is built on the assumption that it is worthwhile to control teachers even more indirectly than in Mitchell's. Instead of performance management, Sykes and Millman suggest evaluating teachers by the effect that they have had on their students.

Rait assumes a different order of rational control in school organizations. Rait's suggestion (Chapter 3) is that all members of school organizations need to continually reflect on their actions to continuously adjust their organizational behavior and create a "learning organization." His assumption is that school organizations will be more rationally managed if the technical workers (i.e., the teachers) have more say in how they are managed.

The third type of organization of action described as occurring in school organizations is cultural or normative. Deal's essay (Chapter 4) is the one that corresponds most closely to this type; he suggests that instead of trying to make schools more rational, we might be better off paying attention to making them seem more meaningful (i.e., sacred, understandable, important) to all those who work in them. However, Deal does not fully explain the link between more meaningful schools and better organized ones.

Rowan's organic model of school organizations (Chapter 1) provides a clue as to how normative controls might indirectly result in more organized schools. He suggests that the professional model of schools, characterized by collaborative and network forms of decision making and teacher participation, tends to result in better decisions, higher teacher morale, and the formation of a sense of community in schools. Such a model tends to replace formal hierarchical authority with strong cultural and professional norms based around shared values. In such a system, deviants are socially sanctioned into compliance by their peers, rather than being disciplined by managers.

The power of cultural or professional norms to affect individual behavior is also apparent in Ogawa's (Chapter 10) analysis of the management succession process in school organizations. Research shows that the fit between a new school manager and his or her school organization depends largely on the extent to which that person complies with the norms already existing in that organization. The norms also restrict the range of behaviors and strategies available for use by the new administrator.

On the surface, it might seem that Hart's study (Chapter 5) of an innovative computer-enhanced teaching method would fit under the category of rational or technical means of control, rather than cultural or professional means of control. However, her emphasis is on the social context of instructional technology and the difficulties involved in the redesign of the job of teaching. She points out that many of these difficulties come in the form of tension and pressure on teachers caused by changing expectations about behaviors that are appropriate for both teachers and students. Instead of lecturers, teachers become problem posers, skeptics, and questioners. Instead of passive recipients of lectures, students are forced to become active learners, developing rules and techniques to use the computer to solve problems. In essence, the culture of schooling is turned on its head; teachers and students reverse roles.

The variety of different perspectives presented in this book can be understood better by combining the two dimensions discussed above, as shown in Figure 11.1. For each chapter, the horizontal axis places the essays according to their general answers to the question of who initiates action in school organizations, and the vertical axis places them according to their answers to the question of how action in schools are organized. Specifically, on the horizontal axis, we place the level of the most important actor and the object of the action, and on the vertical axis, we present the general model of control as well as the specific action mechanism proposed.

We began this book by using "organizing" as the key integrating device to bring this book together. We seem to be concluding it with a somewhat belabored effort to analyze and classify the actions implied in each of the essays. At this point, the reader may, with some justification, maintain that we have forgotten our original intent. But have we? In a recent essay (Bacharach & Mundell, 1993), we argued that school systems, like any organizational system, are composites of action. In that essay, in the Weberian tradition, we maintained that organizations must be understood as systems in which actors try to control and direct not only their own actions but also the actions of others. Indeed, we argued that most organizational life is a struggle over means-ends rationality—that is, over what we labeled "the logic of action."

The construct of the logic of action is an expansion of the Weberian notion of "social action." Logics of action are constructs to designate forms of coherence among objectives (goals), which then become criteria that can be used to evaluate individual decisions and procedures and organizational practices (means). Rather than each ambiguous

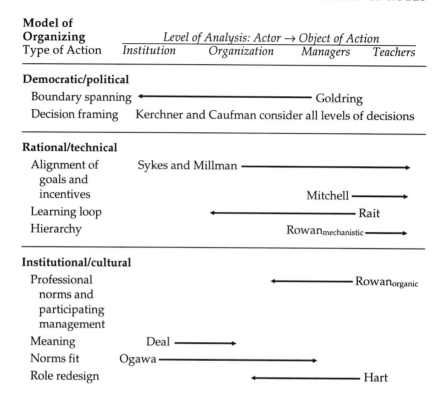

FIGURE 11.1. Models of Organizing Behavior in Schools

NOTE: The chapter by Bolman and Heller is not present in this figure because they present all three models of organizing, claiming that leaders must simultaneously be politicians, diagnosticians, and visionaries.

means and goals being separately subject to negotiation, means and goals are all interlinked in a network of underlying logic. In essence, a logic of action may be seen as the implicit (that is, often unstated) relationship between means and goals that is assumed by actors in organizations (Bacharach & Mundell, 1993).

In the final analysis, each of these essays has shed light on a different logic of action used to organize behavior in schools. Deal implies that it is a cultural logic of action. Kerchner and Caufman imply that the logic of action is determined by the locus of decision making. Bolman and Heller maintain that leadership is the key to understanding the logic of action in a school. Sykes and Millman argue that the evaluation system will affect the logic of action. No matter what type of logic of action that these authors implicitly suggest for the organizing of schools, each essay is testimony to a reality that in each different effort to organize, there is a different micropolitical conflict. In each effort to organize, there is a collision of different actors with different means-end rationalities. Because of this, the selection of goals, means, and the cognitive logic that links them can easily become the source of political activity within organizations. Indeed, politics may be reduced to the debate, negotiation, and conflict over the logic of action that manifests itself as the decision rules that link goals and means for individual members of the organization (Bacharach & Mundell, 1993).

The point of this effort to map out the implicit logics of action embedded in these various perspectives on organizing schools is to illustrate that perhaps the real obstacle to effectively organizing behavior in schools is our failure to understand that like society as a whole, schools are arenas of institutionalized conflict between parties with diverse logics of action. Indeed, each strategy that we propose to change schools will, like the pebble thrown into the pond, bring political ripples to the surface. This is not to be cynical of our own efforts in this book; it is simply to warn the reader that without an understanding of political dynamics, we will achieve theory but we will never achieve praxis.

Reference

Bacharach, S. B., & Mundell, B. (1993). Organizational politics in schools: Micro, macro, and logics of action. *Educational Administration Quarterly, 29*, 423-452.

Name Index